Congratulations

You have just purchased a book that was developed by hospitality industry experts.

Keep this book — you will use it throughout your career.

SUPERVISION in the HOSPITALITY INDUSTRY

Educational Institute Books

MAINTENANCE AND ENGINEERING FOR LODGING AND FOODSERVICE FACILITIES
Frank D. Borsenik

CONVENTION MANAGEMENT & SERVICE
Frank W. Berkman/David C. Dorf/Leonard R. Oakes

HOSPITALITY FOR SALE
C. DeWitt Coffman

UNIFORM SYSTEM OF ACCOUNTS AND EXPENSE DICTIONARY FOR SMALL HOTELS AND MOTELS
Revised Edition

RESORT DEVELOPMENT AND MANAGEMENT
Chuck Y. Gee

BASIC FINANCIAL ACCOUNTING FOR THE HOSPITALITY INDUSTRY
Clifford T. Fay, Jr./Raymond S. Schmidgall/Stanley B. Tarr

PLANNING AND CONTROL FOR FOOD AND BEVERAGE OPERATIONS
Jack D. Ninemeier

STRATEGIC MARKETING PLANNING IN THE HOSPITALITY INDUSTRY: A BOOK OF READINGS
Edited by Robert L. Blomstrom

TRAINING FOR THE HOSPITALITY INDUSTRY
Lewis C. Forrest, Jr.

UNDERSTANDING HOTEL/MOTEL LAW
Jack P. Jefferies

SUPERVISION IN THE HOSPITALITY INDUSTRY
John P. Daschler/Jack D. Ninemeier

SANITATION MANAGEMENT: STRATEGIES FOR SUCCESS
Ronald F. Cichy

ENERGY MANAGEMENT
Robert E. Aulbach

PRINCIPLES OF FOOD AND BEVERAGE OPERATIONS
Jack D. Ninemeier

MANAGING FRONT OFFICE OPERATIONS
Charles E. Steadmon

STRATEGIC HOTEL/MOTEL MARKETING
David A. Troy

MANAGING SERVICE IN FOOD AND BEVERAGE OPERATIONS
Anthony M. Rey/Ferdinand Wieland

THE LODGING AND FOOD SERVICE INDUSTRY
Gerald W. Lattin

SUPERVISION in the HOSPITALITY INDUSTRY

John P. Daschler
Jack D. Ninemeier, Ph.D.

Disclaimer

The authors, John P. Daschler and Jack D. Ninemeier, are solely responsible for the contents of this publication. All views expressed herein are solely those of the authors and do not necessarily reflect the views of the Educational Institute of the American Hotel & Motel Association (the Institute) or the American Hotel & Motel Association (AH&MA). Nothing contained in this publication shall constitute an endorsement by the Institute or AH&MA of any information, opinion, procedure, or product mentioned, and the Institute and AH&MA disclaim any liability with respect to the use of any such information, procedure, or product, or reliance thereon.

Neither AH&MA nor the Institute make or recommend industry standards. Nothing in this publication shall be construed as a recommendation by the Institute or AH&MA to be adopted by, or binding upon, any member of the hospitality industry.

1407 South Harrison Road
East Lansing, Michigan 48823

The Educational Institute of the American Hotel & Motel Association is a nonprofit educational foundation.

Accredited by the Accrediting Commission of the National Home Study Council.

Printed in the United States of America
10 9 8 7 6 5 4 3 89 88 87 86 85

Library of Congress Cataloging in Publication Data

Daschler, John P.
Supervision in the hospitality industry.
Includes index.
1. Hotel management. 2. Motel management.
3. Food service management. I. Ninemeier, Jack D.
II. Title.

TX911.3.M27D37 1984 647'.94'068 83-20722

ISBN 0-86612-016-5

Editors: Marj Harless
Liz Arasim

Contents

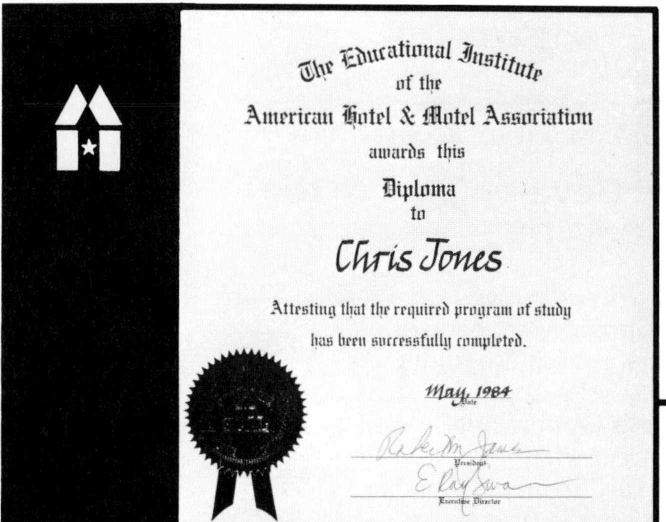
The Educational Institute
of the
American Hotel & Motel Association
awards this
Diploma
to
Chris Jones
Attesting that the required program of study
has been successfully completed.
May, 1984
Date
President
Executive Director

This text, used in conjunction with the corresponding student manual, is one in a series of courses available through the Educational Institute of the American Hotel & Motel Association leading to completion of a certification program. To date, nearly 400,000 courses have been taken by 235,000 students interested in furthering their knowledge of the hospitality industry. For information regarding the available programs, please contact:

The Educational Institute of AH&MA
Stephen S. Nisbet Building
1407 South Harrison Road
East Lansing, Michigan 48823
(517) 353-5500

Preface

The hospitality industry is labor-intensive; many staff members at all organizational levels are needed to produce the products and services offered to guests by a lodging and food service operation. The majority of these employees are entry-level personnel. Their work is directed by supervisors who, in many cases, were nonsupervisory employees in their earlier positions. These first-level managers are critical to the success of any hospitality operation. They not only implement policies and procedures developed by upper levels of management, but they represent employees to those in higher levels of the organization.

Supervision in the Hospitality Industry is the first book to detail principles of supervision as they apply specifically to hospitality operations. It is true that basic supervisory principles are applicable to any industry. However, the ways in which they are applied should correspond to the nature of the particular industry and its employees.

We hope that professionals who are working in the industry every day will find much useful information in this book. To the extent that their ability to supervise effectively is enhanced, this book will be successful.

Likewise, we hope that students, as they read the text, will place themselves in a role requiring supervisory skills, regardless of the job title. Through such identification, we believe that students will learn the techniques of supervision and will be better able to cope with challenges facing them.

The authors are indebted to five professionals with many years of hospitality experience who helped shape this book by freely providing both technical assistance and general information. We wish to publicly thank Clayne W. Dice, CHA, Hilton Inns, Orlando, Florida; James E. Hart, Mississippi Management, Inc., Jackson, Mississippi; Michael B.

Mallott, Holiday Inn University, Olive Branch, Mississippi; Paul H. Shelton, CHA, Mid-Florida Technical Institute, Orlando, Florida; and Bruce Stone, Westin Hotel, Chicago, Illinois.

The authors have come in contact with hoteliers in many parts of the world. *Supervision in the Hospitality Industry* reflects many of their ideas. We wish to thank them collectively for their contributions and want them to know that this book really was written by the industry, for the industry. All of these professionals are really "silent authors" in this endeavor.

The authors would like to thank George R. Conrade, the Educational Institute's Director of Educational Programs, who provided us with many creative ideas and helped with the research, writing, and critiquing of earlier drafts of the manuscript.

Part I: Background Information

You are beginning the study of a fascinating subject: how to get work done by directing people. You probably know that the hospitality industry is labor-intensive; it requires many people to perform a variety of tasks—and someone, of course, must supervise them.

It is probably not possible to be a "good" manager or executive at any organizational level unless one can lead others in the attainment of organizational goals. Whether you have already begun your hospitality career, or whether you are aspiring to such a career, your "people" skills are likely to have a dramatic impact upon your success in climbing the organizational ladder.

How, then, do we start learning about principles of directing people? Chapter 1 introduces the topic by explaining the activity of management, and where the task of supervising fits into the process.

Given this background, Chapter 2 focuses our attention directly on the supervisor; we will review the "who, what, how, and when" of the job. As a result of reading Chapter 2, you will learn that the job is complex and often difficult. Many of the technical skills which make one an effective employee will be of lessened assistance in improving one's supervisory abilities, since human and conceptual skills become more important to the supervisor.

Chapter 3 provides information about leadership techniques. It tells us about different leadership styles, what their potential impact upon employees might be, and, just as important, *when* they should be used. You will learn that the old saying "it all depends" can often be used to guide the supervisor's actions. Analysis of the exact situation is an important first step in assessing the appropriate leadership approach.

Chapter 4 explains the role of the supervisor in improving work. You should know that the employee's ability is not the only factor that affects work performance. The working environment, including the tools and equipment available, also has an important impact upon both the amount and quality of work that is performed. The supervisor, then, must be very concerned about the management of these nonhuman resources.

We will conclude our introduction to the study of supervision by looking at the process of change. The supervisor must serve as a change agent, working to facilitate or discourage it as the situation warrants. Recognition of the natural reaction to change—resistance—must be followed by the application of techniques to overcome it. We will study basic principles that influence the effectiveness of change. You will be a better supervisor as they are incorporated into the strategies which you use to influence employees.

1 Management: An Overview of the Process

PAGE ONE

Supervision at the Brandywine Room

When Stacey Francis reported to work, she found the memo in her time card rack. Ray George, the food and beverage director, wanted to see her in his office. Stacey was nervous but hopeful; she knew what the meeting was about.

It had all started about three years ago. She was a student majoring in hospitality management at the local community college. She needed a job and thought she could dovetail her financial needs with a little practical experience. The Brandywine Room was the only dining room in the Midtown Hotel (there was also a coffee shop). It seemed they were always looking for help. She had no trouble landing a job as a day-shift food server. What started as a part-time position had since turned into a career. Stacey had graduated from the two-year community college program and had recently enrolled at the university several miles away taking night classes in food and beverage management.

About two months ago she learned that the dining room manager was retiring. If she could get the promotion, she thought it would be an excellent opportunity to put into action many of the principles and practices she was learning in school. There had been many times when she thought, "If I were the supervisor, I would sure do things differently." Now—maybe—she would have her chance!

She knew that two other staff members were also being considered for the position. They were probably as qualified as she was for the job and she wondered not only about how Mr. George would decide among the three but also, what the verdict would be. As she walked back to the food and beverage office she knew that the two-month wait was over.

She was going to find out whether she got the job. She knew she could do it. She had lots of good ideas and felt very qualified and competent for the position. But—the big question was—did Mr. George agree?

She reached the door to the office, paused for only a second, took a deep breath, put a smile on her face, and walked in.

An effective supervisor in the hospitality industry is one who, first, knows and understands basic principles of management and, second, applies them to managing all the resources of the lodging and/or food service operation. While this book focuses on the supervisor's activities in managing people, it should be understood that human resources are but one of the many assets of the organization which must be managed. Consider also that the property has available, and must put to the wisest possible use, money, time, procedures, products, services, equipment, and energy as it attempts to attain its goals.

Perhaps one thing which has set civilized people apart from their primitive ancestors is the need to cooperate with others as life—and business—evolves. Naturally, we want to attain goals with a minimum expenditure of time, money, and other resources; the process of management makes it possible.

Supervisors Are Managers

The management process is important at all levels of the organization. We might think, for example, that top management is responsible for attaining organizational goals. However, activities of middle- and lower-level managers—as well as subordinate employees themselves—are critical to the success of organizational goals. The process of management is essentially the same in any type of business (including hospitality operations) and at all levels in an organization—although the goals and the environment within which managers must work are, of course, different.

In the hospitality industry the term **supervisor** has come to mean a manager at a lower organizational level who supervises entry-level or other employees who themselves do not have supervisory responsibilities. Thus, a "head cook" who supervises cooks and assistant cooks (who do not supervise others) and housekeeping floor supervisors who are responsible for work done by room attendants serve as examples.

Supervisors are critical to the success of the organization; they represent middle- and top-level management to the majority of employees within the property. Conversely, they also represent the subordinate employees to higher management levels. In this role, then, they serve as **linking pins**.

While supervisors must have or be familiar with many technical skills, many of their efforts focus on dealing with people—both above and below them in the organization. It can be seen, then, that supervisors must be very knowledgeable—about technical aspects of the work and about basic principles of managing the organization's resources; they must know how to supervise employees. These two responsibilities—applying basic principles of management and supervising staff members—are common to all supervisors in all hospitality operations. Since the effective supervision of employees is part of the general process of management, it is important to understand what management is, how it works, and how its basic principles can be used to direct the work that must be performed.

Definition of Management

Simply stated, management is the process of using what you have, to do what you want to do. What the manager *has* is resources; what the manager wants to *do* is attain organizational objectives.[1] Resources are the assets of lodging and food service operations. There are seven basic categories of resources to be managed:

1. People
2. Money
3. Time
4. Work procedures and methods
5. Energy
6. Materials (food and beverage products, room linens, etc.)
7. Equipment

All resources are in limited supply; no manager has all the resources that he/she would like to have. Therefore, the job of the manager becomes, in part, one of determining how best to use the limited resources which are available to attain organizational goals. In the context of supervision the manager might ask—and react to—such questions as:

- How can we recruit and select the best applicants?
- What are the best training activities that we can offer?
- What can we do to reduce turnover and keep our employees on the job?
- How can we increase motivation and morale levels in order to make employees productive and happy so that both organizational and personal goals can be attained?

While the list of questions can go on, the point is: Managers maximize the use of limited resources by practicing basic management principles.

The second part of our management definition involves attaining goals. Goals tell what the hospitality operation wishes to accomplish; they indicate why the business exists. Goals of hospitality operations relate to:

1. Profit levels (for commercial operations) or maximum cost levels (for institutional operations)

2. Maintenance or growth of financial strength during changing social and economic conditions

3. Defining and attaining quality standards for all products and services offered

4. Guest, employee, and management concerns

5. Professional obligations

6. Societal concerns (for example, the property's role in the community)

While general goals and specific objectives vary among properties, it is important that managers at all levels know what they are trying to do. Once they have defined these concerns, policies and strategies to attain them can be developed.

Evolution of the Management Process

It is obvious that early Greek, Egyptian, and Roman civilizations could not have developed without considerable expertise in managing the structures of political bureaucracies which ran them. Other examples of effective early management practices include the Roman Catholic Church and military organizations and campaigns which were used to conquer entire nations. But management generated little interest as a process or study; it was merely accepted as a fact of life.

It is ironic that, while there historically has been a pressing need for principles and policies to help managers become more effective, the actual development of theories and models of management occurred relatively recently. In fact, only since World War II has there been a continuing and concentrated focus and study on the management process. For many centuries the conduct of business was held in low esteem by scientists, philosophers, and writers—all of whom were more preoccupied with the study of other disciplines. Even economists (who, in comparison with other management professionals, practice a more "exact" science) were often more concerned with political, economic, and related nonmanagerial aspects of business.

Another factor important in the delay of the study of management is that many areas of social science, such as sociology and psychology, have only recently focused on, respectively, group and personal behavior in business organizations. Further, some still argue that management cannot be discussed in terms of principles—it is an *art*—not a *science*. While these concerns were raised in the past, business people themselves discouraged the review and development of basic management principles. Some believed there was no need: you either do or do not know how to manage. Others were certain that procedures which worked in the past would be adequate for the future.

The development of management principles has been influenced since the 1930s by several management thinkers and by several social and political forces. World War II and later defense programs stressed optimal production at minimal cost—application of sound management practices was necessary to accomplish this. Also, as business enterprises became larger and more complex, there was a need to carefully consider how business "works." Today, in an era of heavy competition, the need to obtain a competitive edge is critical. Consumer demands for value have coupled with rising prices for products and materials which businesses must purchase, making the knowledge and practice of management principles absolutely essential to success.

The study of management as we know it today actually began in the late 1800s by Frederick W. Taylor, who is called the founder of modern scientific management.[2] While it is true that elements of many of his ideas are found in earlier writings, he was among the first to carefully consider and build upon earlier findings in an attempt to establish a body of management information. Taylor's principles were designed for broad application, but they were developed from observation of shop-level management—not general organizational management. His concerns arose, in part, from the need to increase productivity; since labor was in short supply, efforts to increase worker efficiency were important. Special concerns included procedures to conduct time studies and the development of performance standards and pay rates. He also studied factors affecting work quality, worker morale, and related job-improvement concerns. His contributions yielded the development of a true science of management principles. Likewise, he suggested procedures for selecting workers and identified the needs for scientific education and development of workers. Taylor also studied the need for maintaining a friendly, cooperative environment for managers and workers.

During the same period, Henry Gantt experimented with wage incentive and employee motivation techniques. He also developed the Gantt chart which is still in use today for scheduling production, employees, and/or equipment; see Exhibit 1.1 for an example. Likewise, Frank and Lillian Gilbreth looked at worker fatigue, ways to improve work, and the need to promote the welfare of individual workers.

The work of these management scientists focused upon increasing worker productivity and upon the needs of the individual employee. Another branch of management theory deals with organization and the need to manage complex organizations. Henri Fayol is regarded as the founder of management behavior because he attempted to blend sound management practices into usable systems.[3] He broke the management process into functions (see the discussion later in this chapter), studied the abilities of successful managers, and developed the following basic

Exhibit 1.1 Typical Application of Gantt Chart

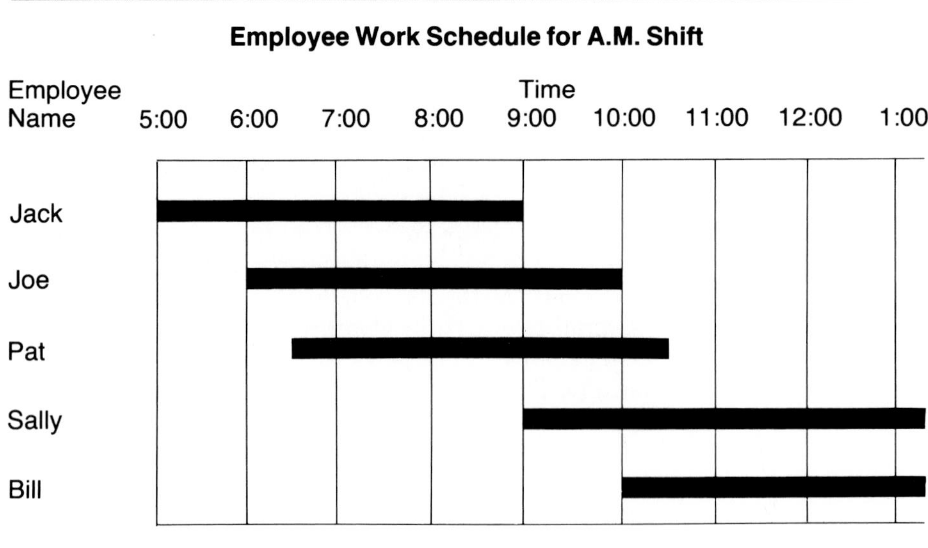

concepts and principles of management, many of which are commonly applied today:

1. *Division of labor*—employees should specialize in specific work tasks.

2. *Concept of authority*—managers must be able to give orders.

3. *Discipline*—employees must respect rules and policies that govern the organization.

4. *Unity of command*—each employee should have only one boss.

5. *Unity of direction*—only one plan should be developed to attain each specific objective.

6. *Common good*—the interests of specific employees or employee groups cannot be more important than the interests of the organization.

7. *Compensation*—fair wage and salary administration plans must be used.

8. *Centralization*—many management processes should be centralized.

9. *Organizational hierarchy*—the line of authority should run from top management down to the lowest organizational levels.

10. *Matching*—people should be placed in the positions most suitable for them.

11. *Staff stability*—high employee turnover rates lead to inefficiency.

12. *Employee initiative*—employees should be given some freedom to develop and implement plans that affect them.

13. *Team spirit*—when employees work together as a team, there will be a sense of unity that will be beneficial to the organization.

Fayol's writings were in German. They were not translated into English until the 1930s (more than five years after his death). Extensive discussions of his research are found in most basic management textbooks. You will see many of his ideas incorporated into later chapters of this book.

In the late 1930s Chester Barnard formulated theories dealing with the need for an organization to mesh its goals with those of the employees.[4] Without this balance, he thought, organizational success was not possible. These and related behavioral concepts were also incorporated into the human relations movement in the 1930s. Elton Mayo is famous for his Hawthorne experiments at Western Electric which yielded several findings—one of which was that productivity is likely to increase when special attention is given to workers by management.[5] He also concluded that individuals were motivated by emotional needs rather than by personal economic needs.

Mayo developed many procedures which he thought should influence one's style of management. Attention began to focus on people—management skills rather than technical skills. Principles of group dynamics were developed. There were, however, limitations to the usefulness of these theories; improved working conditions and human relations skills of management staff did not yield the dramatic productivity increases that were expected.

Later (in the 1960s), behavioral scientists such as Maslow and McGregor offered theories of human behavior which were said to apply to people at work. Maslow suggested that a series of human needs provides internally directed reasons (motives) for change within most individuals/employees.[6] He reasoned that, if a supervisor were able to understand the employees and their key levels of concern, then the supervisor would have a good start in planning activities which would motivate the employees. In other words, each individual is motivated by an inner drive to satisfy some need; if the supervisor can identify this need and can help the employee satisfy the need on the job, both the employee and the organization will benefit.

What are the five basic needs that Maslow identified? They are illustrated and defined in Exhibit 1.2 as basic physical needs, safety needs, social needs, ego (esteem) needs, and self-realization needs. In Maslow's view a person must reach a level of satisfaction with a lower-level need before he/she will become interested in attaining higher-level needs. When a lower-level need becomes satisfied to a minimum degree set by

Exhibit 1.2 Maslow's Hierarchy of Needs: How to Meet Them on the Job

Self-Realization Needs — those for personal development and achievement; the desire to do one's best. Met on the job through participative management techniques that permit input to goal-setting, decision-making, etc., and through opportunities to learn and advance within the organization.

Ego (Esteem) Needs — those of feeling good about oneself, being respected by others. Met on the job by use of reward systems, successful completion of challenging work, and recognition programs.

Social Needs — those for companionship, a feeling of belonging, and affiliation. Met on the job by joining groups, forming friendships, and getting along with co-workers.

Safety Needs — those of self-protection, avoiding risk, pain, and harm. Met on the job by safe working conditions and equipment, job security programs, and insurance programs.

Basic Physical Needs — those for food, clothing, shelter, and survival. Met on the job by good working conditions, acceptable pay, adequate rest periods, etc.

the person, he/she will become concerned about satisfying the next higher need. While no need may ever be completely satisfied, the need that is most unfulfilled is the strongest motivation. At any moment one or more needs can be active while others are dormant.

At about the same time, McGregor advanced theories of leadership styles and made predictions about techniques that might be utilized for different types of employees.[7] His now famous Theory X and Theory Y leadership models provide ideas about how supervisors may feel about employees; these beliefs, then, are likely to influence the approaches to leadership which will be used to manage employees. According to McGregor, a traditional view of many managers (Theory X) is that most employees do not like work and, therefore, must be forced—and constantly supervised—in order to get work done. Theory X contends that employees try to avoid work and attempt to avoid responsibility; they lack ambition and must often be threatened to provide a "fair day's work for a fair day's pay."

In contrast, a more modern view—Theory Y, supported by the research of many experts—is that the average employee likes work and can exercise self-control and effort to attain work-related goals. Managers who hold the modern view believe that employees desire responsibility and can do much more to help the organization attain goals than has been traditionally acknowledged.

We will learn more about leadership styles—and how to apply them in helping employees work more effectively—in later chapters. However, you should remember that the supervisor who believes employees do not like to work, and who really does not respect them, is likely to use an entirely different set of leadership approaches than the supervisor who believes employees can enjoy work—and respects them for it. Likewise, these differing leadership styles will produce differing results. There are times when, and employees with whom, one or the other leadership approach may be most effective. Also, there are other approaches to leadership which we will discuss. The point being made here is that the supervisory task is complex, and employees and work situations differ. The effective supervisor, then, is one who is able to apply techniques gained from a wide background of knowledge and experience—such as will be gained from this book—to the resolution of ever-changing problems.

An Integration of Approaches

Classical approaches to management looked at the work environment and the people within it. Behavioral models focused on the individual alone and/or as a member of a group and in his/her relationship with the manager. These opposing views have been integrated into a systems approach to management which considers the organization to be made up of closely interrelated parts. Instead of looking separately at either the work to be done, the environment, the employee, or the manager, this approach calls for studying the organization as a whole, since an activity within any part of an organization can affect the activity of all other parts. In a hotel, for example, we cannot look at the housekeeping department and make decisions without considering the department's relationship with, and the subsequent impact of the decisions upon, other operating departments in the property. This approach recognizes that managers must look for and apply basic principles that focus upon how best to use resources to attain goals. Managers at every organizational level must make sure they are attaining objectives which are in line with the total organization's goals and missions; they must integrate their activities with those of all other departments; they must use limited resources wisely.

A contingency approach to management suggests that individual situations differ. Results of a specific practice will differ based upon the situation; that is, what works in one instance may not be effective in another. Therefore, it becomes the manager's task to identify, according to a specific situation, the technique(s) that will be best considering the particular environment, time, and personnel involved. A useful approach is reviewed as part of the process by which management decisions are made (see the discussion later in this chapter). Detailed infor-

Exhibit 1.3 The Management Loop

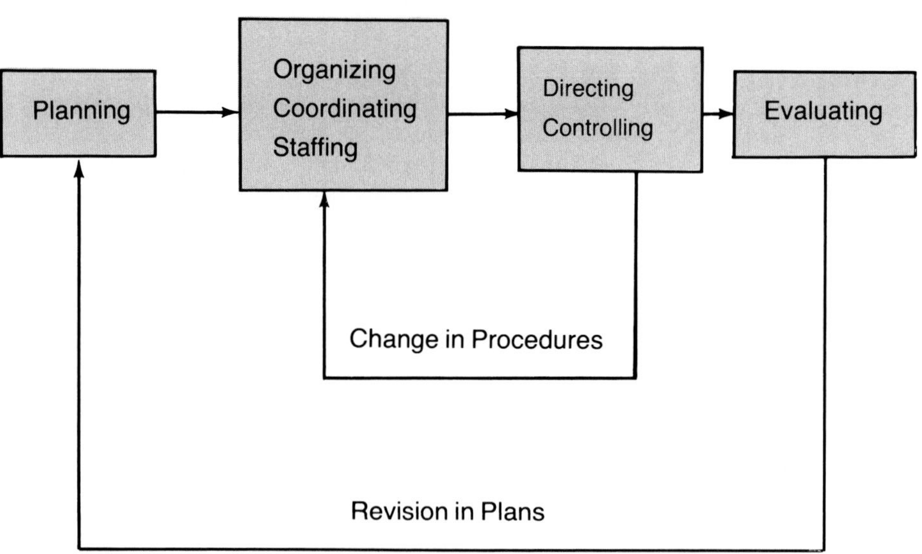

Source: Adapted from Jack D. Ninemeier, Planning and Control for Food and Beverage Operations *(East Lansing, Mich.: Educational Institute of the American Hotel & Motel Association, 1982), p. 16.*

mation about leadership techniques—including the contingency approach—is presented in Chapter 3.

A Close Look at the Management Process

The process or system of management can be discussed by separating it into components, although in practice each is interrelated. Each component or task (sometimes referred to as a function or activity) defines what a manager must be able to do—to some greater or lesser extent—as part of his/her job. Each of these components will be discussed individually. First, however, let's look at Exhibit 1.3 and note the following:

- Planning (both objectives and approaches to attain them) leads to organizing, coordinating, and staffing.
- When planning, organizing, coordinating, and staffing are completed, directing and controlling can begin.
- One part of controlling involves assessing the effectiveness of corrective actions that were taken to reduce the differences between standard plans and actual procedures. This effort may lead to required changes in procedures for organizing, coordinating, and/or staffing.
- The last task, evaluating the entire management process, as-

sesses how well objectives and plans have been met. This task may lead to revisions in plans.

Planning

Planning is an integral part of managing. The planning process begins with determining broad organizational goals that will help managers focus upon what the property is trying to accomplish. Planning continues with the statement of specific operating objectives that become the responsibility of each department. For example, top management working with department heads may develop an operating budget that specifies economic goals for the budget period. Revenue-producing departments such as rooms and food and beverage must then develop departmental budgets that will make a planned contribution toward the economic requirements of the property.

A different level of planning occurs when routine operating procedures are established. Recurring situations (such as cleaning rooms or serving food and beverage products) require standard plans that can be used each time the situation arises. These plans are often made by department heads working with other management staff (including supervisors).

Daily activities require a third level of planning. For example, personnel and equipment schedules must be developed (see Exhibit 1.1). Plans must also be generated for special events, new training programs, and other activities.

Effective planning incorporates the following principles:

1. Planning should be a formal process. It should be done as an integral part of one's job—not only when time permits.

2. Objectives must be established before plans can be developed; plans are then developed to attain the objectives.

3. Long-range, strategic planning is just as important as—and is likely to be more critical to organizational success than—short-range, daily planning activities.

4. All pertinent information should be available for consideration at the time plans are developed. (Supervisors should have available all information that concerns their areas of responsibility.)

5. Supervisors should be allowed to contribute to plans that affect their work. Likewise, employees should be allowed input to plans that affect their jobs.

6. Planning should be flexible; it should recognize that situations change and that contingency plans must be considered.

7. Planning should start at the top of the organization. Commitments to management planning should flow throughout the organization.

8. Plans must be implemented. While this is obvious, many man-

agers spend too much time on planning; they do not understand that, at the appropriate time, they must act with the best plan available.

9. Resources must be allocated for the planning task. Managers need time to plan. This implies that time will have to be allocated for work not done because of time spent in the planning activity.

10. Planning should be done at the appropriate organizational level. It is, for example, generally not a wise use of resources to have top management staff develop employee schedules for operating departments. On the other hand, only top management can develop the strategic, long-range plans necessary for strength and growth of the property.

Organizing

Organizing is the management task of establishing the flow of authority and communication between organizational levels. Further, it specifies relationships between positions in the property. An organization chart (see Exhibit 1.4) shows each position and how it relates to the others. Using organizational goals and objectives as a base, the organizing task involves dividing the work to accomplish the goals. Other organizing concerns and responsibilities are expressed in the following principles:

1. Authority should flow in an unbroken line from the top to the bottom of the organization; someone, somewhere in the organization, must be able to make a decision. Likewise, someone must be responsible for decisions which have been made and for actions which have taken place.

2. Each employee should have only one supervisor.

3. Similar activities should be grouped together to structure departments within the property. For example, activities relating to rooms can be categorized into front desk and housekeeping departments; food and beverage operations can be structured according to food, beverage, and catering responsibilities, etc.

4. Similar tasks can be grouped together to structure positions within departments (a position is a group of tasks to be performed by one person; it is also referred to as a job).

5. Line and staff relationships must be understood. **Line positions** are those which are in the chain of command. The general manager, resident manager, department heads, and supervisors are in line positions. In contrast, **staff positions** provide advisory assistance to the line. Examples include staff members in the purchasing, accounting, and personnel departments.

6. Relationships between departments in the organization must be considered; what affects one department is likely to affect

Exhibit 1.4 Sample Organization Chart for 350-Room Hotel

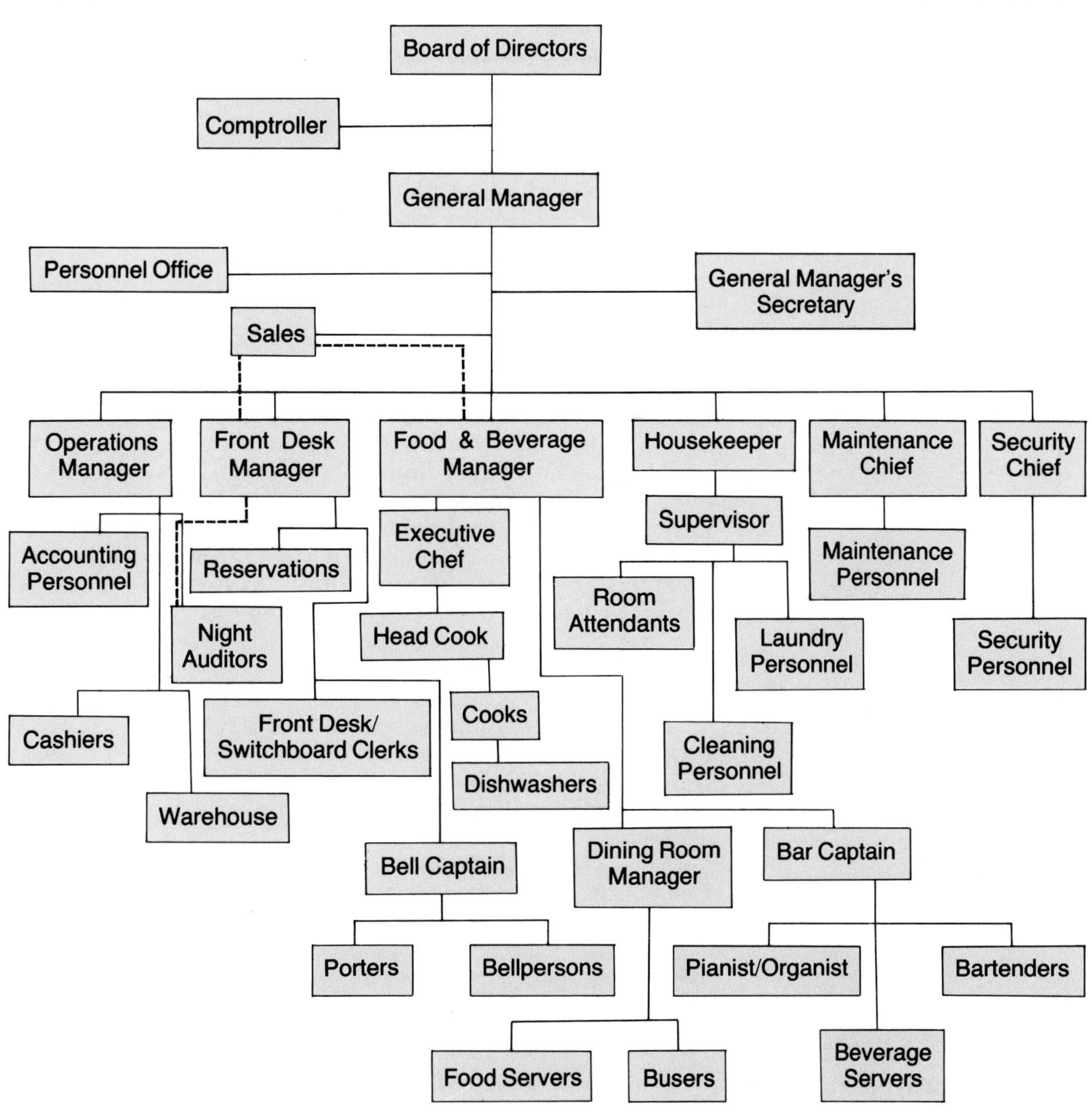

another. Consider, for example, the relationship between room check-out times and the need for room attendant staffing.

7. The organizational structure evolves through the life of the business. Changes in jobs and in the people who occupy them often generate changes in organizational structure. Organization charts and related documents must keep up with these changes.

Coordinating

Coordinating is the management task of bringing individual and group goals together in order to achieve organizational objectives. Simply put, a manager must coordinate the type and amount of resources used to attain organizational goals. Principles of coordinating include the following:

1. The number of employees which a manager must supervise impacts upon his/her effectiveness. Generally, as the complexity of a task increases, the number of employees supervised decreases (the reverse is also true).

2. Managers must have the authority (power) to enforce assignments, commands, and decisions. This authority should be delegated as necessary by top management.

3. Responsibility (the need to account to someone for the use of formal power) cannot be delegated. Thus, the front office manager who is responsible for aspects of an operating budget cannot blame his/her subordinates if budget goals are not met.

4. Generally, authority should be delegated to the lowest possible point in the organization. We have already noted that staff members appreciate the opportunity to provide input in the design of their own work. This principle is recognized when they are also given authority to influence successful work performance.

5. Channels of communication must flow freely up and down the organizational structure. Top management must be able to communicate with lower-level staff members; conversely, subordinate workers must be able to communicate with top management.

6. Procedures for interdepartmental cooperation must be practiced in order to achieve harmonious working relationships.

7. Effective managers interact with both formal and informal employee groups.

Staffing

The management task of staffing involves the recruitment of applicants and the selection of those best qualified for positions to be filled. In small operations this might be done by a manager as part of his/her ongoing work. In larger properties the staffing function is frequently performed by a personnel department. In either case the basic principles of staffing—each of which is addressed in later chapters—are similar:

1. Jobs must be defined in terms of the specific tasks that must be performed (these are incorporated into job descriptions).

2. Personal qualities needed to adequately perform specific tasks must also be considered (these are incorporated into job specifications).

3. All possible sources of job applicants should be considered.

4. Screening devices should be used to assess applicants for positions. For example, selection tests might be used to assess performance and abilities of experienced applicants. Preliminary interviews and reference checks provide additional examples of screening devices.

5. Job application forms should be used to collect required information about applicants.

6. Employee orientation and training programs should be developed and implemented.

7. Formal employee evaluation programs are an integral part of staffing activities.

8. Use of creative staffing patterns helps retain underemployed staff members.

9. Ongoing employee development programs at all organizational levels are important.

10. Decisions about transfers, promotions, and demotions are part of the staffing process.

Directing

For all practical purposes, the management task of directing is the same as supervising—the topic of this book. Directing involves what a supervisor does to oversee, motivate, train, evaluate, and discipline subordinates, whether working individually or in groups. The task of directing is complicated; it involves a wide array of activities. Each of the remaining chapters in this book focuses on some aspect of the supervisor's role in directing employees and incorporates the following principles:

1. Organizational goals are easier to attain when they mesh with goals of staff members.

2. Staff members must know what they are expected to do.

3. Orientation procedures are important and must be carefully developed.

4. Procedures for issuing orders relate to the quality of work which must be performed.

5. The process of delegation (giving formal authority to a subordinate employee) is a specific directing technique.

6. Techniques of worker motivation can have positive results; the motivation process must be productive, competitive, comprehensive, and flexible.

7. Procedures for employee discipline should include positive

reinforcement and the dispensing of punishment for wrongdoing.

8. Orders that are given should be reasonable, understood by employees, and compatible with the tasks to be performed.

9. Leadership styles should vary according to employee needs. (Keep in mind that the attitudes of management affect the attitudes and subsequent performance of employees.)

10. It is important to gain the cooperation of the people who are managed; supervisors should treat employees fairly and be honest with them.

11. Employee ideas should be solicited and, whenever possible, used.

12. Supervisors should show their appreciation to employees who perform their jobs effectively.

Controlling

The management task of controlling helps ensure that operating procedures stay on the course of attaining organizational objectives. The control process begins with establishing performance standards, continues with assessing actual performance, and then requires making a comparison between performance standards and actual performance to determine whether—and to what extent— corrective action is necessary. A final step is evaluating the extent to which corrective action has been effective. When properly implemented, controlling is based on the following principles:

1. Control cannot be accomplished until performance standards have been set; these requirements must define desired quality and quantity levels.

2. Actual performance must be assessed in a manner consistent with standard performance.

3. Allowable tolerance (variance) levels must be established for each performance standard.

4. Corrective action becomes necessary only when actual performance does not meet the standards (including variances) which have been developed.

5. Results of corrective actions must be evaluated to ensure that problems have been resolved.

6. Operating budgets should be used as a control tool.

7. Priorities should be set to resolve problems that are the most important (costly) to the operation.

8. Preventive controls are more effective than controls imposed after things go wrong.

Evaluating

In its most basic sense, the management task of evaluating considers the extent to which organizational goals established as part of the planning process are, in fact, attained. This step is frequently overlooked in many properties or it is done in a haphazard fashion. As noted earlier, an element in the control process involves the assessment of whether performance standards have been met. The management activity of evaluation is, however, much broader; it reviews all organizational goals and provides input to the restatement of goals for future periods. Principles of evaluation include:

1. Evaluation must be assigned a priority in the management of the operation; it cannot be left to do whenever there is time.

2. Evaluation helps to establish new and revised organizational objectives.

3. Evaluation is necessary to measure: (a) the degree of attainment of organizational goals, (b) employee performance, and (c) training effectiveness.

4. Input from guests and others outside the property is useful in the evaluation process.

5. Evaluation helps in the assignment of organizational resources.

6. Evaluation must be done on a timely basis, and it must be done objectively.

The Supervisor as a Decision-Maker

If your job as a supervisor involves making decisions (which it will), then you must know—and be able to apply—basic principles of decision-making. Some decisions may be relatively easy to make. For example, if you have a labor staffing guide which matches occupancy with the number of room attendants needed, it should be easy to decide how many housekeepers will be needed when an 80% occupancy rate is forecast. Other decisions will be more difficult to make. For example, how can labor costs in your work section be reduced to be consistent with the "dictates" of the new operating budget? A great deal of study, revision of standard operating procedures, training, and evaluation will likely be necessary as this decision-making process evolves.

Let's consider another—and very common—situation which requires a supervisory decision. An employee is not performing adequately. What should you—the supervisor—do? First of all, some people feel that most employee performance problems can be resolved through training. They would answer the preceding question by

Exhibit 1.5 Performance Problem Analysis Worksheet

Job Knowledge/Skill		
High 10 9 8 7	**Box A** Motivation Problem	**Box B** Resource/Job Environment Problem
6 5 4 3 2 1 Low	**Box C** Personnel Administration Problem (Selection/Transfer/ Termination)	**Box D** Training Problem

Poor 1 2 3 4 5 6 7 8 9 10 Good

Attitude

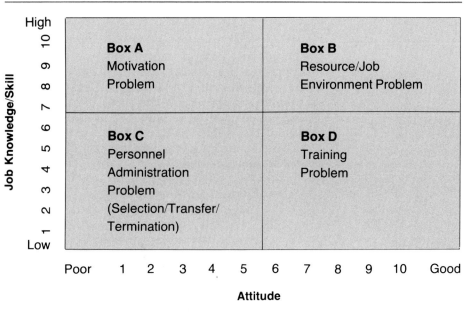

Source: Adapted with permission from John W. Newstrom and Edward E. Scannel, Games Trainers Play: Experiential Learning Exercises *(New York: McGraw-Hill, 1980), p. 33.*

suggesting training activities. However, is training always the answer? The supervisor who is able to relate concerns about employee job knowledge/skill and attitude would answer no.

Look at Exhibit 1.5, a performance problem analysis worksheet. This worksheet, which illustrates the relationship between job knowledge/skill and attitude, will help you understand how a decision relating to the employee with poor job performance might be handled. Note that an attitude scale ranging from low to high has been placed at the bottom of the worksheet. Note also that a scale ranging from low to high for job knowledge has been placed at the left-hand side of the worksheet. Let's see how it can be used in making a decision to resolve our problem. From the perspective of the supervisor, the employee might have:

- A good attitude but poor knowledge of the job or poor job skill; training may be helpful (Box D).
- A good attitude and a high level of job knowledge/skill; lack of resources or something in the environment (Box B) is likely causing the problem.
- A poor attitude but adequate job knowledge/skill; motivation (Box A) is likely to be the problem.
- A poor attitude and insufficient job knowledge/skill; problems with selection, transfer, or termination (Box C) might be involved.

We will be talking about training, working conditions, motivation, and personnel administration techniques in later chapters in this book. The point here is that you must know, understand, and apply basic principles of management as you make supervisory decisions. To the extent that you are aware of many basic techniques—just one of which was noted above—it will become easier to distinguish between and plan strategies for making decisions and resolving problems. Further, there is a greater likelihood that the decision will be the best given the circumstances of the situation.

Since all resources available to the operation are in limited supply, your job as a supervisor really becomes one of deciding how best to use limited resources to attain goals and objectives of the organization and your department and making plans to reach these goals (the "who, what, where, and when" of developing strategies). Decisions should always be made on the basis of what is best for the operation—not on the basis of what is best for oneself, what is best for the company image, what the boss wants, or what has been done in the past; while one's experience can be useful when making decisions, one must also consider the present and look to the future. Try to develop a work environment and a system of relationships with employees that encourages decision-making for the right reason—that which is best for the property. In many respects, the process of decision-making is very similar to that of problem-solving. In fact, one can view the limitation of resources as a management problem which must be resolved.

Supervisors can make decisions (and resolve problems) by using two different methods. The **programmed method** involves procedures for handling routine, repetitive situations or problems, such as how to staff for a banquet, the way in which a room should be made ready for service, and when lawn care is needed. These matters can be handled by clerical routine, through the use of standard operating procedures and policies, through organizational structures, and/or by experience. Supervisors have little freedom of action when programmed decisions must be made; the organization has, in effect, determined what to do. Positive features of programmed decisions include the following:

- They are easy to make.
- They require little time.
- They usually yield consistent results.

The **nonprogrammed** method is used for nonroutine, one-shot types of situations or problems that must be faced. This method calls for the use of judgment, reasoning, intuition, experience, and rules of thumb and the application of creative and other techniques. Nonprogrammed decisions generally involve the most significant problems. The ability to solve nonprogrammed problems actually distinguishes efficient from inefficient managers.

As you make supervisory decisions, several questions must be asked:

- What are the consequences of the decision? Generally, as the consequences of decisions become more important, more resources (such as time) should be committed to their study.

- Has a reasonable amount of time been allocated to the search for possible alternatives? As will be seen shortly, a rational approach to decision-making and problem-solving includes the generation of possible alternatives. Careful study and analysis can often yield alternatives not considered when hasty decisions are made.

- How can a *satisfactory* decision be made? Often, "real world" problems do not have more than satisfactory solutions. Supervisors often waste much time trying to find ideal solutions when they are not available.

- Is the problem easy to deal with? While some supervisors feel most comfortable working on easy problems, wise supervisors will delegate the authority to make these decisions or will make them quickly so that other, probably more important, problems can be dealt with.

- Will the problem resolve itself? Those decisions that are most important should be made first. Other problems may take care of themselves, may be dealt with by others, or may get worse. If the latter occurs, they will then receive a higher priority and the use of management time can be defended.

- Is it my decision to make? Generally, the closer to its origin that a problem is resolved, the better the decision is likely to be. A rule to be followed is to pass as few decisions as possible "up the organization" and to pass as many decisions as possible "down the organization."

Factors to consider when determining whether decisions should be passed on to higher management levels include whether other departments are affected and whether there is a major impact on your area of responsibility. Likewise, when information is only available at a higher organizational level or when there are major operating budget implications, the decision may need to be made higher in the organization. Capital outlay decisions and decisions involving precedent or organizational policy are usually made at higher management levels.

There are really three levels of organizational decision-making (see Exhibit 1.6). First-level decisions are made by top management and involve those broad situations that are most critical for success of the organization. Development of goals and operating budgets serve as examples. Second-level decisions, which might be made by department heads or supervisors, are those that affect routine operations. Examples include decisions that yield standard operating procedures and planning decisions that must be based on budgetary constraints. Third-level decisions involve routine performance matters; they may be made by the workers themselves as well as supervisors. A front desk clerk deciding which room to assign to a guest is an example of a third-level employee decision. Development of employee and equipment schedules and establishment of inventory par stock levels are examples of supervisory third-level decisions.

When supervisors make decisions, they bring three things to the de-

Exhibit 1.6 Levels of Decision-Making

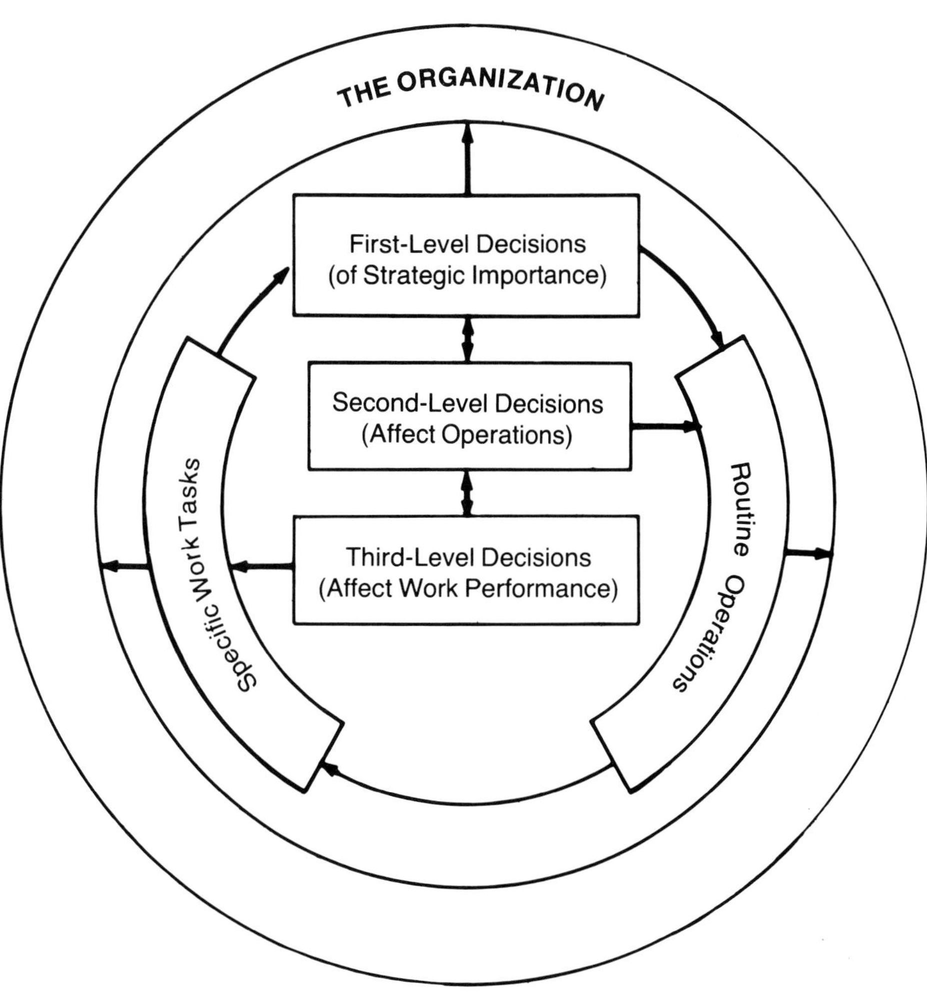

cision-making situation. These are experience, education, and common sense. Through experience one can recognize what has and has not worked in the past. If you can assess the extent to which a situation is similar (or dissimilar) to a previous experience, you have some idea about the potential results of implementing a specific alternative. The old saying "experience is knowledge gained too late" may be humorous to some, but it is a fact of life that better decisions can be made when one's background has greater depth.

Education is a critical component in decision-making. You can learn many things from many different sources that will increase your ability to analyze situations and resolve problems. For example, problems relating to ineffective supervison can be overcome by understanding and applying the principles of supervision discussed in this text.

Common sense can also be helpful in making decisions. The use of judgment, intuition, and creativity was noted earlier when nonprogrammed decisions were discussed. The "art versus science" aspect of management focuses on this point: there are times in the complex world of hospitality when one must rely on intuitive reasoning as decisions are made.

A Common-Sense Approach to Decision-Making and Problem-Solving

In making decisions or resolving problems in both business and personal situations, people cannot always be objective, spend an infinite amount of time on the situation, or think of all possible alternatives. They must use a common-sense approach—one that seeks a satisfactory rather than an ideal solution. Steps in this decision-making/problem-solving process are:

Identify and Define the Problem. What exactly is the situation? What parts of the problem must or should be resolved? It is often difficult to define the problem. For example, if two employees are bickering, you might assume it is because of a personality conflict. Rather, is it possible that there are differences of opinion about what the job description requires the two employees to do? It is a common management mistake to emphasize finding the right answer rather than defining the right problem. This is unfortunate because an accurate problem definition can focus efforts on meaningful factors for problem resolution. For example, a housekeeping problem might be defined as "the proper quantity of rooms are not being cleaned." Careful study might indicate, however, that the real problem is one of improper recruitment, selection, orientation, training, and/or supervision of room attendants. If this can be identified, meaningful alternatives for problem resolution can be generated.

Seek Alternatives to Resolve the Problem. In effect, a decision is only as good as the best alternative that is generated. Staff members who are involved in the problem situation should be asked to suggest alternatives. Supervisors will do well to involve as many resources (people, references, etc.) as possible. All too often, however, supervisors feel that they alone must make the decision without input from others. They may believe they will lose the respect of subordinate employees if input from that source is solicited. Alternatively, they may enjoy the power that comes with making decisions without their subordinates' help. Recall, however, that decisions should be made on the basis of what is best for the organization. If this premise is accepted, it follows that all alternatives from all possible sources should be generated and considered. When searching for alternatives, look to the past and consider those experiences in light of the present situation and future outlook. If one's experiences can be helpful, the search for alternatives might stop at this point. Otherwise, it becomes necessary to be creative and to generate original ideas. Again, input from others with differing backgrounds and experiences can be helpful. In our housekeeping example, study may indicate that applicants are not recruited until there is a vacancy; there is little, if any, orientation or training; and follow-up focuses upon criticism rather than helpful assistance.

Evaluate and Select an Alternative. This involves an assessment of how realistic each alternative is (in terms of both the goals of the organization and the likelihood that its implementation can resolve the problem). The alternative selected must be capable of execution, must be worth more than it costs, must have a greater probability of success than other alternatives, and should have support from affected staff. Quite often the alternative that is chosen will represent a compromise. Experimentation and research may be necessary as alternatives are evaluated and selected. In our housekeeping example, supervisors may consider ways to hire better employees and isolate specific problems which require concentrated training.

Implement the Selected Alternative. A trial period may be established to study, on a small scale, the results of implementing the selected alternative. For example, staff members in the housekeeping and personnel departments might work together in implementing techniques of orientation and training and observe whether the desired results (more rooms cleaned to higher quality levels) are actually achieved. When implementing alternatives, problems relating to resistance to change may arise. Many employees feel most comfortable when they do things as they have always done them; they resist change and defend precedents and the status quo. In these situations, supervisors must communicate with affected staff; they must explain, defend, and justify reasons for changes in procedures.

Evaluate the Effectiveness of Change. Has the problem been reduced? (In our example, are trained room attendants able to clean more rooms without reducing quality standards?) If the problem has been properly defined in a quantifiable manner, it becomes possible to measure the difference, if any, before and after the alternative is implemented. It may be necessary, as part of the evaluation process, to work out "bugs" caused by employees using new procedures. Thus, time to practice, build skills, and become comfortable with revised procedures is often in order before formal evaluation occurs.

A second part of the evaluation process concerns whether any spin-off problems have occurred because of the revised procedure(s). Since management is a process comprised of a system of closely related components, it is possible that changes in one activity will affect another. For example, general evaluation of the room attendants' training program may find that more rooms are being cleaned per hour of labor without reducing quality standards. On the surface, this appears good—the problem has been resolved. Careful study, however, may indicate that other problems—lowered morale and higher turnover levels—are occurring because room attendants feel that arbitrary productivity requirements are being forced on them. In this instance, procedures to modify behavior or, at least, a meeting to explain the process and point out to the employees that they are "working smarter, not harder" may be in order.

Selected Management Concepts

The management concepts of authority, responsibility, and delegation must be understood in order to fully comprehend how a complex management system works.

Authority

Authority is the power that a manager has to do something or to get something done. For example, a front desk manager has the authority to schedule his/her employees and a purchasing agent has the authority to order products and services within limits established by top management. In the context of our definition of management, a supervisor has power when he/she has the authority to use various resources to attain organizational objectives. There are two broad categories of authority (power): formal and informal. **Formal authority** comes with the position one holds in a formal organization. Normally, formal authority is accepted by employees who assume that those occupying selected positions have specific amounts of power. In contrast **informal (personal) authority** is the power which one has because of his/her abilities and traits. It is not formally delegated by the organization but is available to a person because of charisma, expertise, personality, assertiveness, and other characteristics.

In order to be effective, a supervisor must obviously have the power to assign work and to require subordinates to do as directed. We will resume the concept of power in Chapter 3.

Responsibility

The concept of responsibility holds those with formal power accountable for their use of that power. By accepting responsibility, individuals agree to accept the credit or blame for the way in which assignments are carried out. Supervisors are not only held accountable for their own performance, they are also held accountable for their employees' performance. Supervisors are evaluated on how well tasks assigned have been accomplished. Since a supervisor works with and through employees, he/she is responsible for their actions. If the employees are successful, the supervisor will likely be successful; if the employees are not successful, the supervisor will be held responsible for their failure. While the authority to perform specific tasks can be delegated to subordinates, the supervisor is still ultimately responsible for performance of the required work. Accountability for the action of employees is one of the most defining and critical factors in a managerial position.

Delegation

Delegation is the process of assigning authority to another person to get work done. Since no one person can do all of the work required in most organizations, the act of delegation is an obviously necessary process which must be done correctly in order for an organization to function effectively. Normally, the responsibility for specified tasks should be assigned to the lowest level of the organization at which employees have the ability and information necessary to carry out required tasks. Likewise, in order for employees to perform their assigned tasks effectively, they must be delegated the necessary authority to carry out these tasks. Therefore, while a food and beverage director may be responsible to the general manager for the attainment of economic and other departmental objectives, he/she will likely find it necessary to delegate the authority (power) to plan menus, schedule staff, purchase food, etc., to subordinate employees. As stated before, however, the director is still ultimately responsible to the general manager for the attainment of departmental objectives.

Delegation is a skill that must be learned by all supervisors. We will discuss techniques for delegation more completely in Chapter 2.

NOTES

1. This definition was suggested in Jack D. Ninemeier, *Planning and Control for Food and Beverage Operations* (East Lansing, Mich.: Educational Institute of the American Hotel & Motel Association, 1982), pp. 14-16.

2. Frederick W. Taylor, *The Principles of Scientific Management* (New York: Harper & Row, 1911).

3. Henri Fayol, *Industrial and General Administration*, trans. J. A. Coubrough (Geneva, Switzerland: International Management Institute, 1930).

4. Chester I. Barnard, *The Functions of the Executive* (Cambridge: Harvard University Press, 1938).

5. Details of Mayo's work can be found in Elton Mayo, *The Human Problems of an Industrial Civilization* (New York: Macmillan, 1953).

6. Abraham Maslow, *Motivation and Personality* (New York: Harper & Row, 1964).

7. Douglas, McGregor, *The Human Side of Enterprise* (New York: McGraw-Hill, 1960).

8. Irvin L. Heckmann and Robert L. Blomstrom, *Start Supervising* (East Lansing, Mich.: Educational Institute of the American Hotel & Motel Association, 1981), p.31.

PAGE TWO

Supervision at the Brandywine Room

"Mr. George, there was a note that you wanted to see me. I'm glad I got here early," said Stacey (hoping that Mr. George did not think she was outwardly nervous). "Congratulations," said Mr. George, "I'd like to salute our new dining room manager. You were up against some real stiff competition—the other applicants were highly qualified—but I know you will be the best for the job. Do you still want it?"

"Do I want it!" blurted out Stacey, "You bet I do. When can I start? You'll see that I learn fast."

"I'm sure you do, Stacey, but we need to start at the beginning. You've been an excellent food server and you'll be a fantastic supervisor. However, the work you'll be doing as a supervisor is different from that which you've done previously. You are going to have to learn many new job skills—a lot of which deal with people. You're an expert at dealing with our guests and I'm sure you'll be able to take many of these techniques and apply them to the management of your new staff. However, let's do it right! We'll work on this together and map out an on-the-job training program that will fit our needs. Since a supervisor is, first of all, a manager, I'd like you to read some general information about the management process. We have a little time—the promotion won't take effect for 30 days—and I think we can plan a good training program."

After a few more minutes of conversation Stacey thanked Mr. George and rushed off to work. She couldn't wait for the shift to end so that she could go home and start reading.

2 Focus on the Supervisor

PAGE THREE

Supervision at the Brandywine Room

"Wow!" Stacey thought as she looked through some management-related information Mr. George had given her. "The process of management is more complicated than I ever dreamed. About all that I ever saw the dining room manager do was dispense guest checks, make food server assignments, fill in when there was a no-show, and disappear into what seemed like a million meetings. I can't believe that a supervisor does all this!"

Stacey was concerned that the material she was reading was too general; perhaps it didn't apply to the Brandywine Room. She made lists of topics she wanted to discuss with Mr. George. He had agreed to meet with her the next day.

During their meeting, Mr. George confirmed that Stacey's new position would involve the following management tasks — especially those of directing and controlling:

1. Planning. Stacey would be responsible for special table arrangements and setups, service ideas for new menu items, new dining room decorations, and other plans.

2. Organizing. She would be making job assignments, developing procedures for food serving, and defining relationships between dining room and other staff members.

3. Coordinating. Stacey would be responsible for advising other departments of special functions which affected their activities

(such as guest count forecasts and room cleaning schedules). Likewise, as she needed to order and receive dining room supplies it would be necessary to work closely with the Purchasing Department. As she made section assignments and developed employee work schedules, she would, in effect, be coordinating the work activities of the staff.

4. Staffing. She would be responsible for hiring and training dining room employees.

5. Directing. She would spend a great deal of time directing employees. During busy times she would be "on the floor" directly relating with service staff and guests. Since *directing* means *supervising,* this was really her full-time job.

6. Controlling. Not only were there budget implications with dining room labor, but also changes in operating procedures would often be necessary to resolve problems.

7. Evaluating. Stacey would have to evaluate employees, traffic flow, and effects of problem-solving efforts, among other things.

Mr. George also made two other points: "A lot of your time will be spent in making decisions. Many of these will be made almost subconsciously (such as when to order new guest checks and how many tables to assign to each food server). You have the authority (power) to make decisions about how the dining room operates. In effect, you can delegate the authority to do a lot of different things—just as long as the job gets done."

After the meeting Stacey wondered what she was getting into. The job involved knowing a lot more than just how to wait tables and schedule staff. She had learned that the supervisor is, first of all, a manager and, while the tasks are different, the basic concepts of managing the dining room are, in many ways, similar to what managers must do at many other organizational levels in the hotel. "So," thought Stacey, "I'm now part of the management staff, I know a little bit about what a supervisor does, and I'm taking some management courses—but now I'm wondering if I'll know how to put into practice the things I'll be learning."

In Chapter 1 we defined a supervisor as an employee who, among other duties, manages the work of other people. In very broad terms, then, the general manager of the hotel, an assistant manager in the restaurant, various department heads, and those staff members who direct entry-level employees would all be considered supervisors. While individuals in all of these positions do, in fact, manage other staff members, it is more common to describe supervisors as those managers whose main functions involve the management activities (tasks) of coordinating and directing. Recall that in Chapter 1 we defined the terms *directing* and *supervising* as identical in meaning. A supervisor could, then, be contrasted with other management staff members whose primary activities involve higher-level planning, organizing, staffing, controlling, and evaluating activities. A supervisor in the hospitality industry is generally one who directs, and is responsible for, the work of entry-level employees who do not supervise others.

Levels of Management

We can focus on the supervisor by reviewing the management levels shown in Exhibit 2.1. Although most large organizations have these three levels of management, it is not possible to state for every organization which positions fall into each management level. For example, in a privately owned hotel the general manager and perhaps the assistant or resident manager would be considered top-level management. Department heads might be viewed as middle-level managers. Any other staff members whose duties, in part, involve directing the work of people could be classified as supervisory-level management.

Contrast the preceding example with a large multi-unit chain hotel. In this company's organization, there may be a board of directors, a chief executive officer (CEO), national and perhaps regional managers who would be considered top-level managers. General and assistant managers in individual properties, as well as department heads, might then be considered middle-level managers. However, for the purpose of this book, we will consider management levels from the perspective of the property; the general manager and his/her immediate subordinate (assistant general manager) will be considered top-level management. Department heads will be classified as middle-level managers. All other staff members whose duties involve the management of subordinates will be classified as supervisory-level managers.

It is therefore necessary to consider each lodging and food service property separately in order to make designations about management levels. Often, however, these distinctions are unimportant. One can view the organization chart (see Chapter 1) for a specific property and note where exactly each position fits into the total organization. As long as this is known, arbitrary distinctions such as management levels become less important.

Exhibit 2.1 suggests a second factor of importance when considering management levels. There are relatively few top-level managers, more middle-level managers, and a still greater number of supervisory-level managers in most organizations. Nonmanagement employees (who really form a base of the organization) comprise the largest staff segment in most organizations. Exhibit 2.1 also reminds us of the linking pin concept noted in Chapter 1; the supervisor is between nonmanagement employees and higher management levels. The supervisor's need to coordinate and communicate in order to keep the organization running efficiently becomes obvious.

Exhibit 2.1 Pyramid of Management Levels

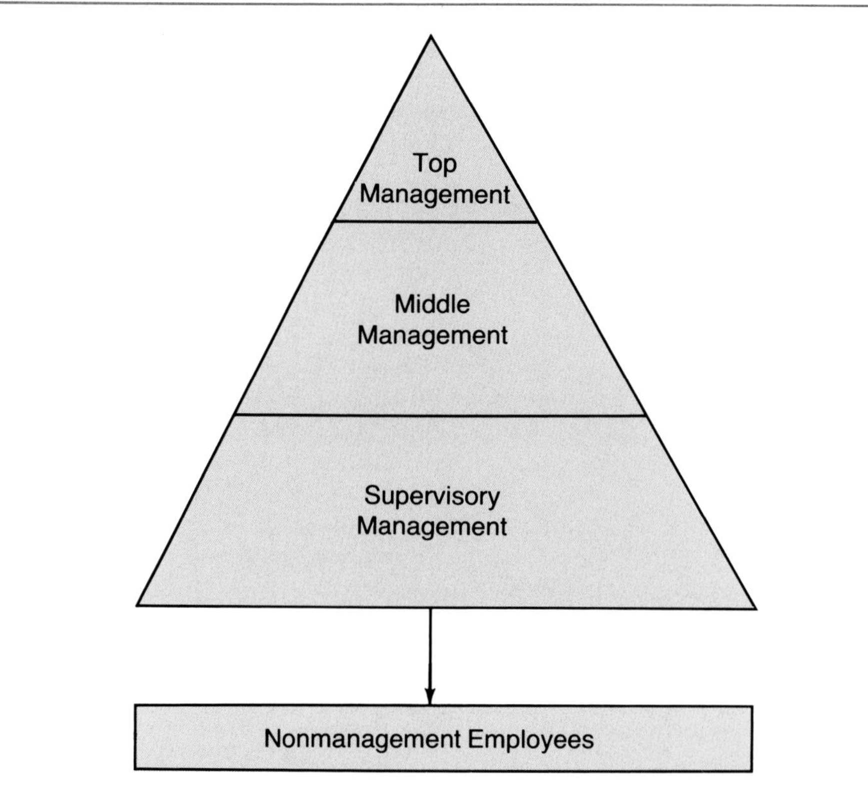

While a supervisor may spend more time in directing people than a manager at a higher level, basic principles for directing the work of people are the same. Therefore, throughout this book, as we discuss procedures for directing people, we will be focusing on supervisory-level staff members. However, with modifications as necessary, basic discussions will apply to people-related activities performed by managers in higher management levels as well.

Skills Needed for Effective Supervison

A supervisor must have three types of skills. Each is critical to effective performance on the job. A good supervisor should be able to practice each of these skills at the quality levels deemed adequate by the property.

Technical Skills

Technical skills are the abilities to perform the work of the people you supervise and the job-related activities of your position (completing required reports, making decisions about job-related matters, scheduling employees, budgeting, etc.). While technical skills are not the major factor in determining supervisory success, they are necessary. In order to train employees and direct them in their work, supervisors must know how to do the work and be able to recognize when it is being done correctly. Supervisors, however, may not be required to have the ability to perform the jobs as fast or efficiently as their employees. Should a front office manager or a floor supervisor in a housekeeping department know how to, respectively, register guests or prepare rooms as adequately and efficiently as those employees they manage? For these positions the answer may be yes; in many operations these management staff members have worked their way up from the positions they now supervise and are able to do the job as well as anyone. Alternatively, the supervisors may have gone through a company-sponsored training program or may have made a lateral transfer from another position with brief on-the-job experience to prepare them for their new supervisory position. It can be argued that supervisors must know, at least, the basic components of the subordinates' jobs, must understand job performance standards, and must be able to recognize the extent to which required quality levels are incorporated into their subordinates' work. Consider the types (sources) of power (authority) noted in Chapter 1. In order for a supervisor to have **expert** power he/she must, from the perspective of the employees, have the basic skills and ability to perform employees' work.

The ability to adequately perform the work of subordinates is more difficult as one progresses up the organizational ladder. Consider, for example, the ability of a food and beverage director to adequately do the job of a trained chef with 30 years of experience or the capability of the hotel's general manager to make management decisions required of the property's chief engineer. It is clear that a manager must have the technical skills necessary to perform his/her own work. However, performance of the work of those being supervised becomes more difficult as the subordinates possess greater levels of specialized, technical skills.

Top-level managers must carefully consider these factors as job descriptions and job specifications are developed. They must review those tasks which are to be included in the job of each supervisor. Likewise, they must know about experience and education requirements that are important in order to perform the job.

Human Relations Skills

Human relations skills are the second category of special abilities which an effective supervisor must possess. Since a supervisor must spend a great deal of time interacting with people, the ability to do this effectively becomes extremely important. Human relations skills include a wide array of abilities dealing with procedures for employee recruitment, selection, orientation, training, supervision, evaluation, and motivation. When one considers the list of human relations skills which a supervisor must possess, it becomes easy to understand that being a good supervisor can be difficult. The art of dealing with people begins with understanding your responsibility as a supervisor and continues with each topic considered in the following chapters in this book. Many supervisors in the hospitality industry have more difficulty acquiring and applying human relations skills than they do developing the technical skills which are part of their job. This, in companion with the fact that the hospitality industry is labor-intensive (the industry has not found a way to replace people with equipment; a large number of employees are needed to perform required work), suggests that the ability to interact with employees is a critical determinant of the supervisor's success.

Conceptual Skills

Conceptual abilities are the third type of skills which a supervisor must have. You must be able to visualize the entire complex system of management, each of its components, and how they relate to and affect your work. Likewise, you must know how the organization fits into the community in which it is located. Further, the ability to make wise decisions requires that a supervisor conceptualize problems and alternative solutions to resolve them. In order to do this, you must have a great deal of basic information, must be able to relate from one situation to another, and must be able to draw upon both personal experiences and those of others. It can be seen, then, that much of the supervisor's work—and required ability—goes beyond "turning to a Standard Operating Procedure and doing what it says."

Exhibit 2.2 shows the amount of technical, human, and conceptual skills necessary for all levels of management. Note that a supervisor needs more technical skills and fewer conceptual skills than a top-level manager. But managers at all levels require the same amount of human skills.[1]

Responsibilities of the Supervisor

The supervisor does not work in a vacuum. Rather, the supervisor must interact with and relate to various groups both internal and external to the organization. Some of these groups are considered in this section.

To Top Management and/or Owners

Everyone has a boss. Even the owner of a property must comply with the rules and regulations of a relatively large number of taxing, licensing, and other governmental agencies. In performing your assigned work tasks as a supervisor, you have a responsibility to your own supervisor. It is likely that this person will be influential in your progression up the organizational ladder. Beyond this, you should show respect to and accept reasonable assignments from higher management levels. In doing so, think about how you would like subordinates to relate to you. This is essentially a variation of the golden rule; you should relate to your own boss in the same way that you want subordinates to relate to you.

Further, your actions should be designed to help your boss—and the organization— achieve stated goals and objectives. Therefore, as you operate within budget limitations and company policies, transmit required records and reports, follow rules and procedures, and so on, this responsibility is being accepted.

Since the supervisor is a critical element in implementing the plans and procedures of higher management levels, a high degree of cooperation becomes necessary. There is an old saying, "If you are not part of the solution, you are part of the problem," which supervisors should con-

Exhibit 2.2 Relative Importance of Technical, Human, and Conceptual Skills

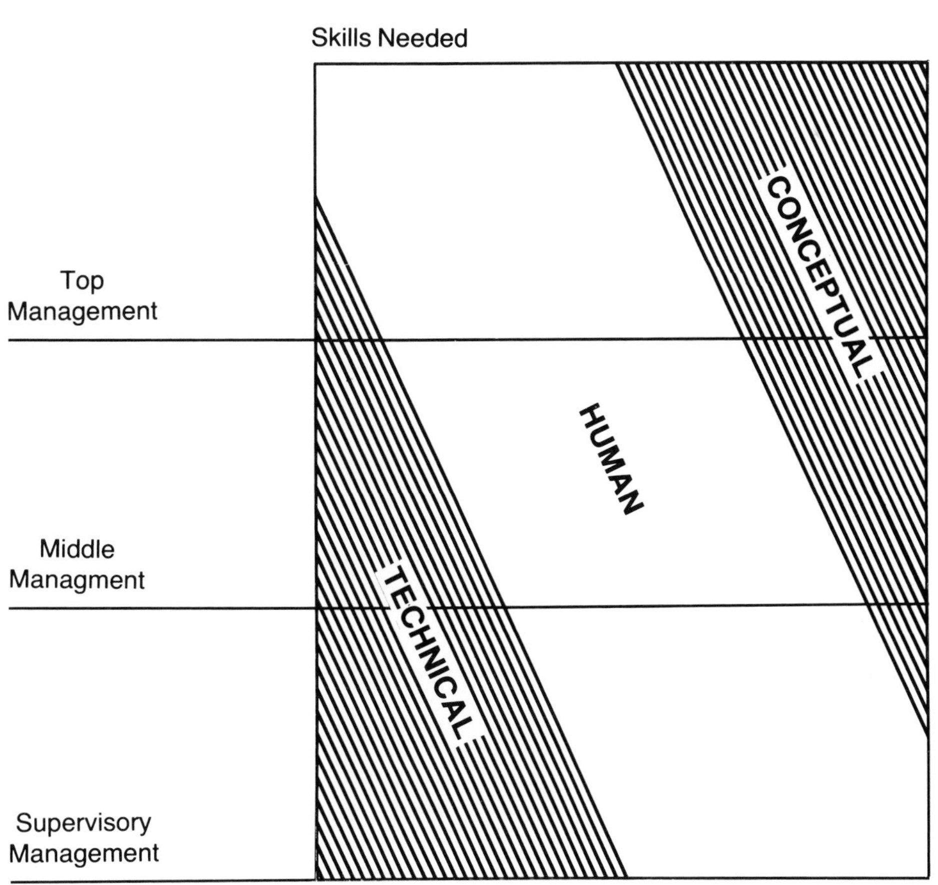

Source: Irvin L. Heckmann and Robert L. Blomstrom, Start Supervising *(East Lansing, Mich.: Educational Institute of the American Hotel & Motel Association, 1981), p. 3.*

stantly recall. As supervisors fight change, resist attempts to improve work, and otherwise hold an uncooperative attitude, this responsibility—really an obligation—is not being met.

To Subordinates

As a supervisor, you must recognize your responsibilities to the employees. First, from the human relations perspective, you must recognize—and treat—employees as individual human beings with differing backgrounds, attitudes, and needs. To the extent that this can be done, you are really helping the organization, the employees, and yourself at the same time. Other responsibilities to employees include:

- Providing a safe working environment
- Adequately representing the staff members to higher management levels

- Offering positive and fair discipline
- Being consistent and fair in all decisions that affect the employees

The need for the supervisor to provide opportunities for career development–and the required orientation, training, and personal evaluation which accompany it—must be mentioned. A supervisor who holds back employees because of concern for his/her own position is neither showing concern for employees nor exhibiting proper judgment in his/her own relationship with the organization.

To Guests

In order to meet the property's goals, products and services of the required quality and quantity must be provided. The guests' perceptions of these requirements were considered by management as goals were initially set. The supervisor has an obligation to look at the business—and his/her work—from the guest's perspective. Again, a modification of the golden rule is in order: "If I were a guest, what kind—and quality levels—of products and services would I appreciate?" To the extent that you can answer this question—and incorporate these concerns into improved job performance— you will be fulfilling responsibilities to the guests.

To the Profession

Often, as supervisors work their way up the organizational ladder, they benefit from the experiences and helpful assistance of others. There comes a time in the career of each supervisor when some of this information and assistance must be given back to others in an effort to further improve the industry. This effort should start with assistance in improving the organization. Then, when possible, assistance through involvement in professional associations, continuing education activities which extend beyond the property, and, perhaps, involvement in other community education programs becomes possible. An effective supervisor recognizes the need to assist the hospitality industry—his/her profession—in any reasonable way.

To the Public

While guests are part of the external public, it is important to highlight the need for supervisors to obey all applicable laws and regulations in both their professional and private lives. Further, safety and sanitation concerns often go beyond the immediate guest who is visiting the property. Supervisors should understand both the *letter* and the *spirit and intent* of rules and laws made for the public good. Supervisors should understand that personal, professional, and societal concerns can influence their effectiveness on the job.

To Oneself

Finally, you have a responsibility to yourself. Most of us feel good when we know that we are doing the very best possible job (the concept of self-realization was discussed in Chapter 1). We feel good when we learn, make contributions, and are able to help others. While this topic will be discussed at length in the last chapter, we can note here that supervisors should have a career plan, must sort out the strategies necessary to attain short- and long-range career goals, and should be on the right track toward attaining them.

Duties of the Supervisor

The work that is actually performed by a supervisor varies according to the position being described. It has already been noted that careful thought should be given to the tasks to be performed and that these should be incorporated into applicable job descriptions. Exhibit 2.3 indicates, in general terms, the duties performed by many supervisors. Note the extent to which relationships with people at all organizational levels are an integral part of many of the tasks. We can begin to appreciate the complexity of a supervisor's job when we recall that not only must these physical things be done but, at the same time, the supervisor is involved in human relations and conceptual activities.

Demands on the Supervisor

At the same time that the supervisor must be concerned about fulfilling many responsibilities and completing many job-related duties, there are demands and pressures being placed upon him/her from many groups. These are illustrated in Exhibit 2.4. It can be seen that the supervisor is, simultaneously, confronted with demands from governmental agencies, higher management levels, guests, internal staff departments, employees, and, if the property is unionized, union officials. The term *demanding* can certainly be added to the description of a supervisor's job.

Keys to Supervisory Success

For many years management experts searched for a list of characteristics or traits found in effective supervisors. It was thought that, through research, such factors as education, experience, intelligence, personality, etc. (even body or head size were at one time thought important), could be identified. However, just as individuals–including supervisors—are different, so are the work environments within which supervisors must manage. Therefore, if it is not possible to list a variety of characteristics that are possessed by good supervisors, what types of keys to supervisory success can be identified? The concept of leadership or effective supervision really describes a relationship that exists among people in a job situation; a person who becomes a good leader or supervisor in one situation may not be a good leader or supervisor in a different environment. Some general principles important in this discussion include the following:

1. Different employees or groups of employees respond to different types of leadership (the need to understand subordinates and to know what motivates them was introduced in Chapter 1 and will be discussed at length in other chapters). Some employees need a great deal of direction; others work best with less direct supervision. To the extent that the leadership style of the supervisor can be matched with the needs of the subordinates in a specific situation, the supervisor is likely to be more effective.

Exhibit 2.3 General Duties of the Supervisor

Production Duties
- Issue required products
- Schedule personnel and equipment
- Plan work flow
- Assign work to employees
- Evaluate work performance
- Resolve production problems
- Develop and maintain production records
- Meet production schedules

Quality Duties
- Establish performance (quality) standards
- Ensure that performance (quality) standards are met
- Develop purchase specifications
- Inspect incoming products/supplies
- Cooperate/coordinate with quality assurance, accounting, others

Maintenance Duties
- Check equipment for proper operation
- Keep preventive maintenance records
- Order necessary repairs for equipment and facility
- Maintain clean, safe, and orderly working areas

Work Improvement Duties
- Develop improved work methods
- Cooperate in implementation of new work procedures

Cost Control Duties
- Control and minimize costs
- Develop aspects of operating budgets
- Develop allowable budget variances
- Implement and use budgets as control tools
- Determine reasons for budget variance; take corrective action
- Evaluate results of operating charges

Personnel and Human Relations Duties
- Recruit, select, orient, and train employees as necessary
- Provide constant and consistent supervision
- Evaluate employees' performance
- Provide coaching and counseling assistance as required
- Assist in wage and salary administration, promotion, layoff, discharge, transfer, and related personnel decisions
- Enforce all rules, policies, and other job-related requirements
- Settle complaints, gripes, and grievances according to company and/or union requirements
- Interpret and communicate higher management decisions to subordinates; transfer employee concerns, suggestions, and criticisms to higher management
- Motivate, reward, and discipline employees
- Eliminate hazardous working conditions and practices
- Develop own skills/abilities
- Constantly work to develop cooperation between departments

Administrative Duties
- Develop and transmit required reports and/or statistics
- Participate in committees, planning, and other meetings as requested
- Assist in marketing, public relations, and publicity programs

Exhibit 2.4 Demands on the Supervisor

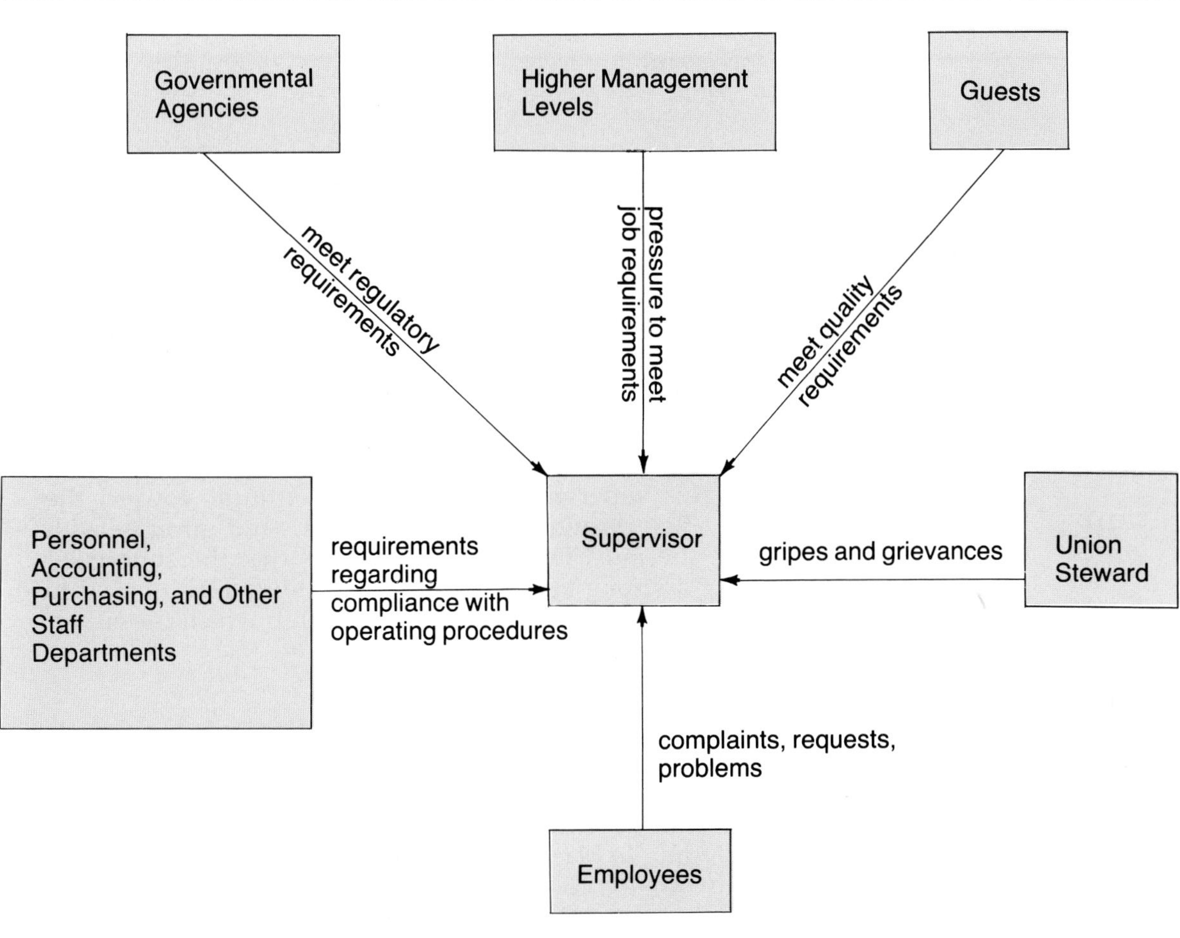

2. A supervisor must generally know the job and be good at it in order to be effective.

3. A supervisor must be closely attuned to his/her staff; he/she must be aware of the goals, concerns, and problems of the many groups with which interaction is necessary.

4. A good supervisor tends to initiate action. He/she likes to lead, is enthusiastic, and makes suggestions.

5. An effective supervisor accepts the responsibilities and duties of the job. He/she consistently puts the good of the organiza-

tion at the front of the decision-making and problem-solving process.

6. The successful supervisor is an effective communicator. The ability to talk, listen, and write is important.

7. The effective supervisor is able to withstand the demands and pressures of the job and, in fact, can use these as an incentive to do the job better.

8. The effective supervisor has a plan—and sticks to it. The plan involves organizational and professional career goals—and strategies to attain them. He/she is assertive in a search for meaningful experiences to better meet these goals.

9. The effective supervisor has a positive attitude toward the property, the position, the individuals, and groups with whom he/she must interact. This implies that the supervisor must have a strong and positive personality which is used to shape and influence the environment within which the supervisor must act.

10. The effective supervisor has a positive self-image. He/she is a positive thinker, is concerned about and recognizes self-worth and understands the contribution that he/she can make toward the organization and the profession. It is interesting to note that, according to Maslow's theory (see Chapter 1), a person is constantly striving to attain needs at higher levels; this can be a strong motivational force. This may imply that the effective supervisor has gone beyond physical, safety, and belonging needs to the point where there is a concern about self-worth and self-realization concerns.

11. The effective supervisor consistently exhibits the proper personal behavior. This implies much more than following company rules and policies. While some behavior is learned, other behavior is influenced by one's environment or is the result of common sense—which may also be a characteristic of an effective supervisor in some organizations.

12. The effective supervisor utilizes the proper leadership styles. While this topic will be discussed in Chapter 3, we can note now that an effective supervisor often makes a conscious effort to react to employees in different ways in order to recognize their individual differences. This trait is similar to that raised in point 3, except that the leadership style must be central to the entire relationship with subordinates and the work habits exhibited by supervisors.

How the Supervisor Spends Time

The supervisor has a great many things to do—and often not sufficient time to do them all. This can create a great deal of pressure on the supervisor; if he/she doesn't have time to do everything, how should priorities be set? What tasks are more important than others and should, therefore, be done first? Some supervisors react to time pressures by working harder or longer in an attempt to get everything done. Others step down to easier jobs; they find that being a supervisor isn't worth it. Still other supervisors try to avoid the issue altogether and become preoccupied with work details, become touchy about the status of "where work is," become critical of others, or look for excuses about why they aren't able to do everything that is assigned. A better approach is to critically review all work that is being done and to discard parts of tasks which don't need to be accomplished—or, at least, which can be delegated to others (this will be reviewed later in this section). Another alternative is to find ways of increasing the output of work that must be done; use of work simplification procedures (see Chapter 4) is a good place to start.

Supervisors with "too much to do—and not enough time" can also determine how time is being spent. Use of a time record sheet (see Exhibit 2.5) can be a helpful indicator. To use the time record sheet, simply make a note of exactly what you are doing at, for example, fifteen-minute time intervals during the day. Then, at the end of the day analyze these activities and make a note about whether the specific activity is:

1. a duty that only you can do.
2. a responsibility that you can delegate—at least in part.
3. a responsibility that you can delegate entirely.
4. an unnecessary activity; it can be eliminated.
5. an activity that might best be handled by another department.

Column headings in Exhibit 2.5 are numbered to correspond with each of the above findings from your analysis.

If careful analysis of the way you are currently spending time suggests that time is being wasted, or that many tasks are not necessary—or at least are not necessary for you to do—a good start at finding ways to save time for more important tasks will result.

Another tactic that is often useful in making effective use of time is, at the end of the previous workday or at the beginning of the current workday, to carefully consider exactly what must be done. In other words, priorities should be set. A good question to ask is, "Will my work or that of my co-workers suffer—or will my family suffer in any significant way—if I fail to do these specific tasks today?" Obviously, the tasks involved in those questions which can be answered yes should be done before other less important tasks are undertaken. We have already

Exhibit 2.5 Time Record Sheet

Date:

Determine appropriate category for each activity:
(1) Must Do
(2) Partially Delegate
(3) Totally Delegate
(4) Unnecessary
(5) Belongs in Another Department

Time	Activity	(1)	(2)	(3)	(4)	(5)

suggested that supervisors can save time through effective delegation. As noted in Chapter 1, **delegation** can be defined as assigning the authority to carry out specific activities to another person. Examples of activities that might be delegated include:

- Routine tasks
- Collection of information needed for a report
- Tasks that will challenge the employee to whom work is delegated
- Work that is specifically within an employee's area of responsibility
- Small parts of work assignments that fit into your own area of responsibility
- Work of a temporary nature

Supervisors must develop skills in delegating in order to attain time-saving results. It is generally best to gradually increase the amount of authority (power) that is delegated. Likewise, it is important to establish clear goals for work to be delegated. And, of course, the assignment must be clearly communicated. When delegating, it is important to give all necessary information about policies and procedures that relate to the assignment, and the employee to whom work is being delegated must clearly know the limits of his/her authority. Normally, when a person has the responsibility to make a decision, he/she should be allowed to make it. When questions arise, the supervisor should help the employee with the problem. However, help can often be of the facilitative—not directive—type.

When work is being delegated, a realistic completion date must be assigned. In the interim, follow-up reports or checkpoints can be helpful in reviewing progress being made. Supervisors who delegate should resist the temptation to require a perfect performance. Supervisors should remember that employees need time to develop the skills and experience to successfully complete the work. Likewise, supervisors should be cautioned about **reverse delegation,** which occurs when a supervisor believes that "if I won't do the job—no one will." Likewise, when employees consistently ask for assistance in areas of their designated authority and responsibility, training—not constant supervisory intervention—may be in order.

Exhibit 2.6 reviews ways of ensuring that time is effectively managed. You should study this exhibit and consider, for yourself and your own job, ways to save time.

Common Reasons for Supervisory Failure

Contrary to what many readers might think, an inability to perform technical aspects of the job is not among the top three reasons why supervisors are ineffective. The primary reason often relates to human relations matters: an inability to effectively relate with and supervise employees.[2] When a supervisor does not get along with employees, peers, or his/her boss, problems relating to productivity, morale, turnover, and other conditions are likely. As this occurs, work will not meet quality and/or quantity requirements. This affects the supervisor's responsibilities. The effect this will have in the relationship between the supervisor and the boss often leads, at the least, to a stoppage in career progression and, at the most, to demotion or discharge.

A second reason often cited for supervisory failure relates to character and personality defects. Supervisors who lack many of the keys to supervisory success are likely to be ineffective. Those supervisors with improper and/or inadequate attitudes, self-image or behavior problems, and the like are apt to be weak and ineffective. The impact of poor and/or negative attitudes must also be highlighted here. The need for a cooperative team spirit is necessary, as is the honest desire to do the best possible job both individually and through subordinate employees. We are all aware of the supervisors in our industry who don't care, those who are always looking for a job, and similar types who do not share a primary concern that organizational goals be achieved.

Lastly, an inability to perform the management tasks of planning,

Exhibit 2.6 Tips To Manage Time

1. Analyze where time is currently being spent.
2. Get to work on time, if not early, and get started without interruptions.
3. Know how to use the phone.
4. Develop schedules, stick to them, and become clock-conscious.
5. Use a "tickler" system. Remind yourself of the most important priorities.
6. Combine similar tasks and do them all at once—or, preferably, have a subordinate do them.
7. Delegate effectively.
8. Work during working hours—don't waste time, socialize, or do things that are not on your priority list.
9. Spend some time alone to plan where you want to go and how to get there.

organizing, coordinating, staffing, directing, controlling, and evaluating, which were reviewed in Chapter 1, can cause serious problems for the supervisor—and the organization. Again, the story is the same. If a supervisor is inadequate in any or all of these areas, job performance will suffer; the relationship with his/her boss and employees will deteriorate; work quality and/or quantity will be affected and the supervisor will have failed—regardless of whether he/she remains on the job.

It is interesting to note that at least two of the three reasons we have cited for supervisory failure can be prevented by learning and applying basic principles of supervision and management reviewed throughout this book. A supervisor can learn how to manage employees more effectively and to successfully perform management activities. Other technical skills necessary to perform the job can be learned–and can be improved upon—through experience. Perhaps some of the causes of negative attitudes and/or poor self-image will be removed as a supervisor becomes more proficient in other aspects of the job. To the extent that this does occur, it can be seen that education in the practice of supervision is of critical importance to all hospitality operations and to the supervisors who work within them.

NOTES

1. Irvin L. Heckmann and Robert L. Blomstrom, *Start Supervising* (East Lansing, Mich.: Educational Institute of the American Hotel & Motel Association, 1981), lesson one cassette.

2. W. Richard Plunkett, *Supervision: The Direction of People at Work,* 2nd ed. *(Dubuque, Iowa: Brown, 1979), p. 131.*

PAGE FOUR

Supervision at the Brandywine Room

A few months had gone by. Stacey had been very busy learning about and practicing the "art and science" of being a supervisor. In a way, she was glad that the dining room had not been extremely busy during her first months on the job. She had gained a little bit of time to learn the ropes and, at the same time, could reflect about what job improvements seemed necessary.

She had gone to several supervisory development meetings which the hotel was conducting for supervisors in all departments. Not only did she get to meet a lot of people—she was surprised at how common many of the most basic problems were in all departments—but she was also quickly expanding her knowledge and improving her judgment capabilities by learning about what others found that did—and did not—work in differing situations.

Probably the single biggest surprise was how different the job of a supervisor was from that of a subordinate employee. She could see now why it was that a good employee may not turn out to be a good supervisor. While she did need some technical skills, the amount of her time which was spent on human relations and administrative tasks was much greater. She also found a recurring need to understand the entire process of management—especially how the organization worked. These were things she never had to worry about as a food server.

Stacey had spent some time thinking about her feelings as an employee. What were the things that she liked—and disliked—about being a food server? Were there things that she could learn in this analysis process that could help her be a better supervisor? Also, she had become aware of how much the hotel relied on her to do things right in the dining room. She had a great deal of discretion, but realized that with this trust came the responsibility to make sound judgments about the dining room operation. Further, Stacey realized that her employees were dependent upon her for expressing their concerns to Mr. George, for treating them equitably, and for helping prepare them for advancement opportunities such as she had received. She was also aware of how much her actions could influence the guests—and she realized that her job was dependent upon guest satisfaction. There was, then, a duty to think about the guest in every decision that she made. Further, she wanted to find ways to improve the hospitality profession which had been so good to her.

While she was beginning to notice several things that weren't quite right, she had one major concern to date—and she discussed this with Mr. George. When it came right down to it, she did not know exactly what she was supposed to do. Sure, she knew what the job description said (although it was not current) and she knew what needed to be done to keep the dining room work going smoothly. But what exactly should her objectives be? What did higher levels of management in the hotel expect in terms of job performance as related to sales income, labor and supplies expense, etc.? What were the obligations which she must meet in her relationship with the employees? She needed to find this out; after all, it did affect her job performance (which she knew would be evaluated based upon the extent to which Mr. George felt she was doing good work).

Mr. George shared her concerns. He advised her that the hotel was introducing a management by objectives program for all department heads. They, in turn, would be working with subordinate staff to address this very problem. Stacey was pleased; she knew it was not just a coincidence that she, as a "freshman" supervisor, was noticing some of the fundamental problems which were now being addressed by top management.

Stacey knew she had the special abilities necessary to be a good supervisor; she had a positive attitude, positive self-image—a respect for her abilities and competence—and she knew that she could gain and retain the respect of her subordinates, peers, and, of course, her boss.

3 The Supervisor as Leader

PAGE FIVE

Supervision at the Brandywine Room

"Why is it," thought Stacey, "that I can get along with some employees very well, but I have a real problem relating to others? I'm the same person—and I try to treat all my employees the same. Isn't that the right thing to do?"

Stacey realized that her relationship with the employees was at the heart of her ability to be an effective leader. Her new career as a supervisor was really causing her to think. For one thing, she had changed from occupying a job to pursuing a career! She was taking a course in human relations at the university; also, she was continuing her conversations with her supervisor, Mr. George, and with fellow supervisors in the hotel. It seemed that many of her colleagues also had problems interacting with their staff. Many of them, however, thought nothing of it. Either they "always had problems" or "it's just part of the job—you can't get along with all the employees all the time." Stacey was not quite ready to believe these observations. She decided to concentrate her studies—both on and off the job—on techniques that can help make a supervisor a good leader.

We have emphasized that, among the many tasks of a supervisor, the need to relate to people at all organizational levels is high on the list. By far, the most frequent focus of personnel management activities is downward to the employees being supervised. A supervisor serves as the formal leader of the employees and work groups for which he/she is responsible. A supervisor's effectiveness is, in large measure, based upon the ability to direct employees in those activities designed to most effectively attain goals. A close look at the leadership process is in order.

Definition of Leadership

Leadership is the ability to attain objectives by working with and through people—both individual employees and work groups. Leadership qualities are important for every individual who must supervise subordinates. To be effective, a supervisor must have more than just power (the authority to get something done). Power is, of course, important and will be discussed later in this chapter. However, many other factors influence effective leadership ability.

In the not-too-distant past, a supervisor might have simply told an employee what to do. If the work was done, the supervisor was successful; he/she was a "good" leader. Today, however, changes in the employees' perception of the supervisor and the workplace have made this tactic less useful. Likewise, employee unions have affected the ability of supervisors to unilaterally tell employees what to do. Therefore, the concepts of leadership, direction, and supervision often imply the need to influence and request—rather than to tell—employees to undertake specific actions. The role of the supervisor is changing to that of a facilitator (one who assembles resources and provides guidance) as opposed to the "dictatorial taskmaster" of yesterday.

The process of leadership, then, implies the establishment of objectives and the attempt to influence employees—both individually and in groups—to attain these objectives.

Leadership Styles

Many supervisors try to be consistent in the way they relate to employees (recall Stacey's statement in the beginning of the chapter case that she was "the same person" in all her relationships with individual employees). It is unlikely that these supervisors would attempt to dominate some employees while using an entirely different democratic or participative approach to supervise others. However, as will be seen later in this chapter, the use of different approaches with different employees can be of benefit.

First, however, the supervisor must understand something about leadership styles and factors that suggest the potential effectiveness of their use. Likewise, of course, the supervisor must know when—and how—to use this knowledge to become a better leader. What is a leadership style? It is the combination of factors or behaviors that a supervisor uses to manage his/her employees. Let's take a look at the beliefs incorporated into some basic leadership styles. With this as background information, we will then be able to discuss strategies for effective leadership. Exhibit 3.1 recaps some of the more important points. Expanded information is presented in the sections which follow.

Exhibit 3.1 Overview of Leadership Styles

Name	Also Called	Basic Description of Leadership Style	Type of Employee with Whom It Might Be Used
Autocratic	Authoritarian or Dictatorial	Supervisor retains as much power and decision-making authority as possible. He/she is like a dictator, making decisions without consulting employees. Orders are given and must be obeyed without discussion.	New employees who must quickly learn work tasks, difficult-to-supervise employees who do not respond to other styles, and temporary employees.
Bureaucratic		Supervisor "manages by the book." Emphasis is on doing things as specified by rules, policies, regulations, and standard operating procedures. Supervisor must rely on higher levels of management to resolve problems not addressed by the ground rules.	Employees who must follow set procedures (such as accountants concerned with tax matters or purchasing staff who must comply with bidding/ordering requirements) and employees working with dangerous equipment or under special conditions.
Democratic	Participative	Supervisor involves employees as much as possible in aspects of the job which affect them. Their input is solicited; they participate in the decision-making process and are delegated much authority.	Employees with high levels of skill and/or extensive experience, employees who will need to make significant changes in work assignments (if time permits), employees who want to voice complaints, and employee groups with common problems.
Laissez-Faire	Free-Rein	Supervisor maintains a "hands off" policy. He/she "delegates by default" much discretion and decision-making authority to the employees. The supervisor gives little direction and allows employees extensive levels of freedom.	Highly motivated employees such as staff technical specialists and in some instances, consultants.

Autocratic Leadership Style

The autocratic (also called authoritarian or dictatorial) leadership style is identified with the early, classical approach to management. A supervisor practicing an autocratic style is likely to make decisons without input from staff, to give orders without explanation or defense, and to expect them to be obeyed. Often a structured set of rewards and punishments is used to ensure compliance with orders. In effect, then, the autocratic supervisor centralizes power and decision-making in his/her own position. The autocratic supervisor accepts the authority and responsibility delegated by his/her own supervisor and delegates little of it to subordinates. When this style of leadership is used, employees become dependent upon supervisors for instructions; generally employees know that they are only to act under supervision of the boss, and that no—or little—discretion in how work is to be done is permitted. The autocratic supervisor is generally task-oriented (the emphasis is on getting the work done). The wants and needs of employees are second to those of both the organization and the supervisor.

There are times when this leadership style can be effective. Consider for example, the common practice in the hospitality industry of hiring food servers and dishwashers for specific times when large business volumes are expected. The autocratic approach which says, in effect, "Here is what is to be done and here is how to do it; now go to work," might be very useful and necessary in this type of situation. Certainly, creativity would be minimized and, to the extent that employees accept this style, so would conflict.

The autocratic supervisor can be successful when he/she knows how to do the work of employees, when staff members accept this approach, and when supervision can be carried out by means of ordered and detailed instructions. However, when practiced with the wrong employees the autocratic approach can cause, at the least, verbal abuse and, more seriously, low morale levels, work stoppage, and sabotage.

One writer has suggested that the autocratic style can be effective when:

1. there are new employees who do not know tasks to be done and/or procedures to be used,
2. there is limited time and/or an emergency situation,
3. an employee does not respond positively to any other style of supervision, or
4. the supervisor's authority (power) is being challenged.[1]

McGregor's Theory X, to which autocratic leaders would subscribe, is based upon the traditional view that employees consider work as a "necessary evil" which must be done in order to obtain resources to purchase the necessities and pleasures of life.[2] Supervisors who accept Theory X believe that employees will avoid work whenever possible since they dislike it. The theory also suggests that employees must be coerced, controlled, directed, and/or threatened with punishment in order to get them to achieve organizational goals. Further, the supervisor subscribing to the Theory X approach believes that the average employee wants to be directed, wishes to avoid responsibility, and, in effect, appreciates this leadership style.

Bureaucratic Leadership Style

Plunkett refers to the bureaucratic leadership style as that in which the leader relies on the property's rules, regulations, policies, and procedures as decisions are made.[3] In his words it is "management by the book." In effect, supervisors become "police officers" who enforce organizational rules and who rely upon higher levels of management to make decisions about problems not covered in the book.

The bureaucratic supervisor is not really a leader as defined in this section. Normally, the bureaucratic style is appropriate only when all other approaches are inappropriate or when employees can be permitted no discretion in the decisions to be made. Generally, it can only be used when:

1. specialists are in charge of new equipment and/or operating procedures,
2. personnel in clerical and other office positions are being trained,
3. there is a concern for safety,
4. there is a need to carry out routine, and/or repetitive procedures.

Democratic Leadership Style

The democratic (also called participative) leadership style is almost the reverse of the autocratic style discussed initially in this section. The democratic supervisor wants to share decision-making responsibility; he/she wants to consult with the group members and to solicit their participation in making decisions and resolving problems that affect the employees. The opinions of individual employees are sought and their recommendations are strongly considered; employees are informed about all matters that concern them. The democratic supervisor tries to appeal to the employees' higher-level needs (see the discussion about Maslow's approach to motivating employees in Chapter 1). That is, the supervisor attempts to emphasize the employees' roles in the organization, tries to influence the employees' ego and esteem needs, and provides an opportunity for employees to obtain fulfillment on the job. The democratic supervisor develops plans to help employees evaluate their own performance, allows employees to provide input to the establishment of goals, encourages employees to grow and be promoted on the job, and recognizes and encourages achievement. In effect, the democratic supervisor might be compared to a coach who is leading the team.

Plunkett has suggested that the democratic supervisor must be willing to accept the number of mistakes and time delays which can occur when this leadership style is used.[4] He also notes the need for a personal commitment to the style; once employees are accustomed to it, they are likely to have difficulties working under a different approach. Employees should be delegated authority on a piecemeal basis—not all at one time—and the supervisor must have a great deal of patience as the system is used. Plunkett further suggests that the democratic style is best used with highly skilled and/or highly experienced employees, when there is sufficient time to utilize a participative approach, when operational changes are required, when group problems are being resolved, and when individual workers have specific problems.

The democratic approach incorporates many of the assumptions of McGregor's Theory Y, which proposes that employees do not inherently dislike work and do not want to avoid responsibility; they generally find work to be a natural activity.[5] Supervisors subscribing to the Theory Y approach believe that employees will respond to and appreciate procedures that encourage self-direction and self-control. Further, they believe that the employees' commitments to objectives increase as do the rewards associated with the achievement of objectives. Likewise, McGregor's Theory Y suggests that the organization loses when only limited potentials of the employees are utilized.

Laissez-Faire Leadership Style

The laissez-faire (also called free-rein) leadership style refers to a hands-off approach in which the supervisor actually does as little leading as possible. In effect, the laissez-faire supervisor delegates all authority (power) to the employees. He/she relies on the employees to establish goals, make decisions, and resolve problems. The employees are almost leaderless since the supervisor provides little or no direction and allows them as much freedom as possible. While there are relatively few times when this approach can be effectively used in the hospitality industry, it may be useful when a specialist or consultant is involved or when the supervisor lacks the experience and judgment necessary to make decisions. At best, the laissez-faire style has limited application to the hospitality industry.

Choosing an Effective Leadership Style

Leadership Styles and Decision-Making

Our discussion about leadership styles has suggested a wide range in the amount of input which employees have in the decision-making process as each leadership role is practiced. Exhibit 3.2 illustrates this graphically. As seen in Exhibit 3.2, employees have little, if any, role to play in making decisions when an autocratic leadership style is used. By contrast, a great deal of (if not total) responsibility is assured when a laissez-faire style is used.

Information about application of leadership styles to specific situations will focus further on the assistance that employees should—or can—provide as decisions affecting the job situation are made.

It is doubtful that supervisors, in their relationships with employees, actually follow any of the four leadership styles to the letter. Ideally, supervisors would know each employee and would then adapt the most appropriate leadership style for each employee and the specific work environment involved. In practice, however, this is seldom possible. After all, the supervisor is "only human"; he/she has developed attitudes, feelings, and a personality based upon a unique background which is brought to the job. This generally limits the ability to "float" between radically different leadership styles.

It is one thing to read about leadership styles and to know which to apply and when to apply it. It is quite another thing to be able to consistently interpret the situation, know which approach is best, and apply principles of the style to the unique employee and specific situation. The successful supervisor, however, does recognize that different leadership styles exist. He/she attempts to make a conscious effort to understand

Exhibit 3.2 Leadership Styles and Employee Input in Decision-Making

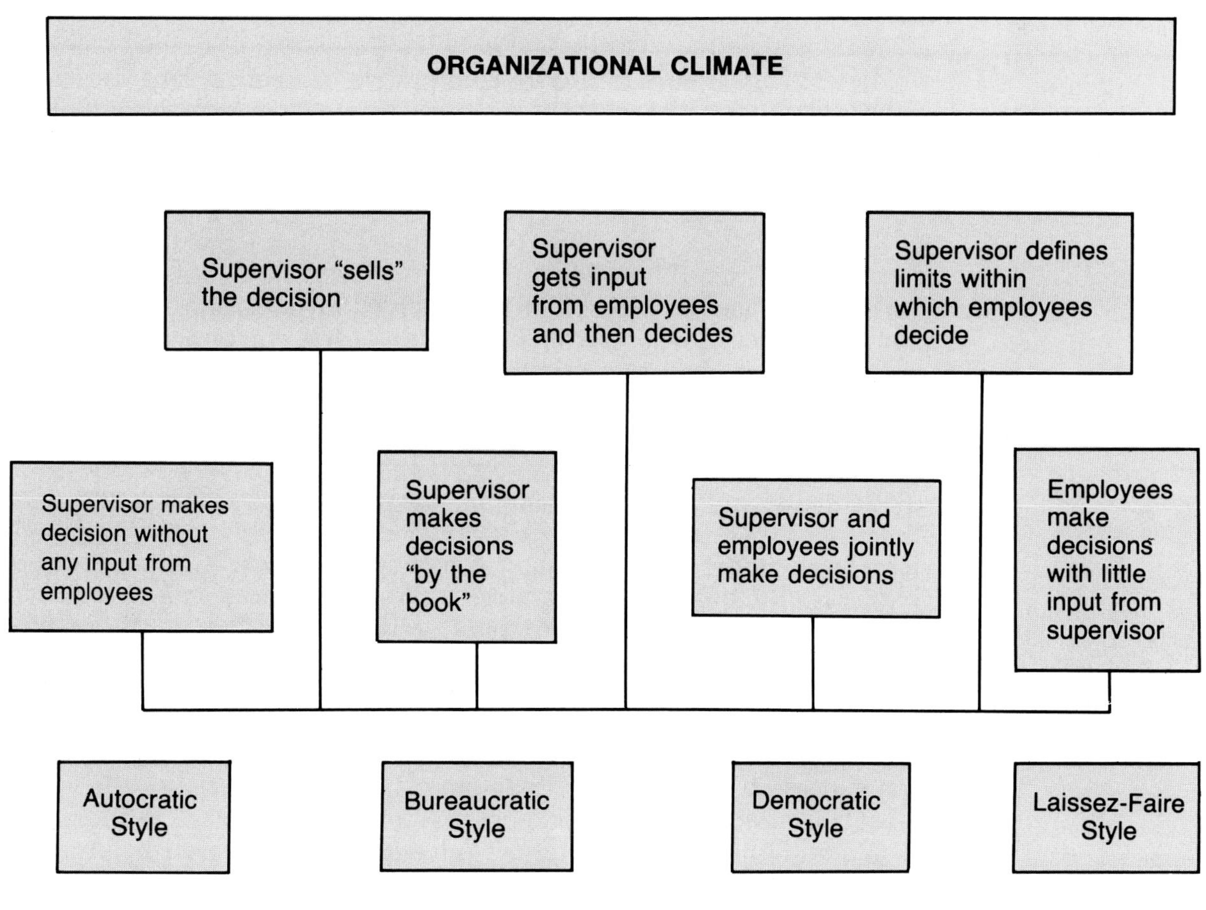

these styles and to know when each might be used. This ability comes from experience; it requires a long-term, conscious effort to practice principles of supervision when dealing with employees with differing expectations and concerns. Likewise, the effective leader recognizes that the approach used can make a difference between a team of employees who do—or do not—attain goals.

Influential Factors

Our discussion has presented basic information about several different approaches to leadership. What factors influence the choice and effectiveness of a specific leadership style? Two researchers have suggested the following:[6]

The Personal Background of the Supervisor. The supervisor's knowledge, values, and experiences will govern his/her feelings about and reactions toward employees. For example, how much input should employees have to the decision-making process? What are the supervisor's concerns about the employee and his/her ability to grow in the job and advance within the organization? How much confidence does a supervisor have in the employees? Which subordinates are, in the supervisor's estimation, able to handle delegated work, or must the supervisor hold close—and not delegate—tasks that must be completed?

Some supervisors feel more comfortable in freely delegating work. Others like to involve several employees in a team approach to defining and resolving problems. Still others like to do everything themselves. Simply put, one's inclination as to how to provide leadership is important in determining the leadership style.

What should a supervisor do in a situation where the outcome is uncertain? You should understand that when employees, rather than supervisors, make a decision or are involved in a decision-making situation, the supervisor loses some control over the outcome. Some supervisors like this challenge and break in the routine; others do not and want a very structured and predictable job situation.

Characteristics of the Employees Themselves. Employees who want independence and/or decision-making responsibility, who identify with the property's goals, and who are knowledgeable and experienced might work well under a democratic leadership approach. Conversely, employees with different expectations and experiences might require a more autocratic approach. The point is that employees are individuals with differing personalities and backgrounds; they, too, are influenced by specific factors.

The relationship between the employees and the supervisor is affected by the level of confidence and is a critical aspect of leadership effectiveness. If a supervisor is accepted, liked, and trusted, there is a greater likelihood that supervisors will be able to manage work assignments without much difficulty. Conversely, if a supervisor is not accepted, liked, or trusted, each assignment can turn into a "battle" between the supervisor and employees.

Situational Factors. The organizational climate, the work group itself, the type of work to be done, and related concerns also influence choice of leadership style. The traditions and values of the organization may influence the supervisor's behavior. Compare, for example, the organization that, through past actions and policies, stresses human relations concerns with other operations that focus on the bottom line—at the sacrifice, if necessary, of extensive employee participation in the management process. To be effective in either organization, the supervisor must at least consider, and probably must adopt, the prevailing organizational philosophy.

Size of work groups, content of interdepartmental communications, and extent of cooperation provide other examples of organizational influence on the situation within which the supervisor must lead. The ability of employees to work effectively within groups suggests one more factor related to the job environment which impacts on the usefulness of specific leadership styles.

The nature of the work and/or the problems that must be resolved must be considered. Can employees provide helpful information, specialized skills, or ideas? A particular leadership style may be appropriate

Exhibit 3.3 Job Environment Factors Affecting Leadership Style and Behavior

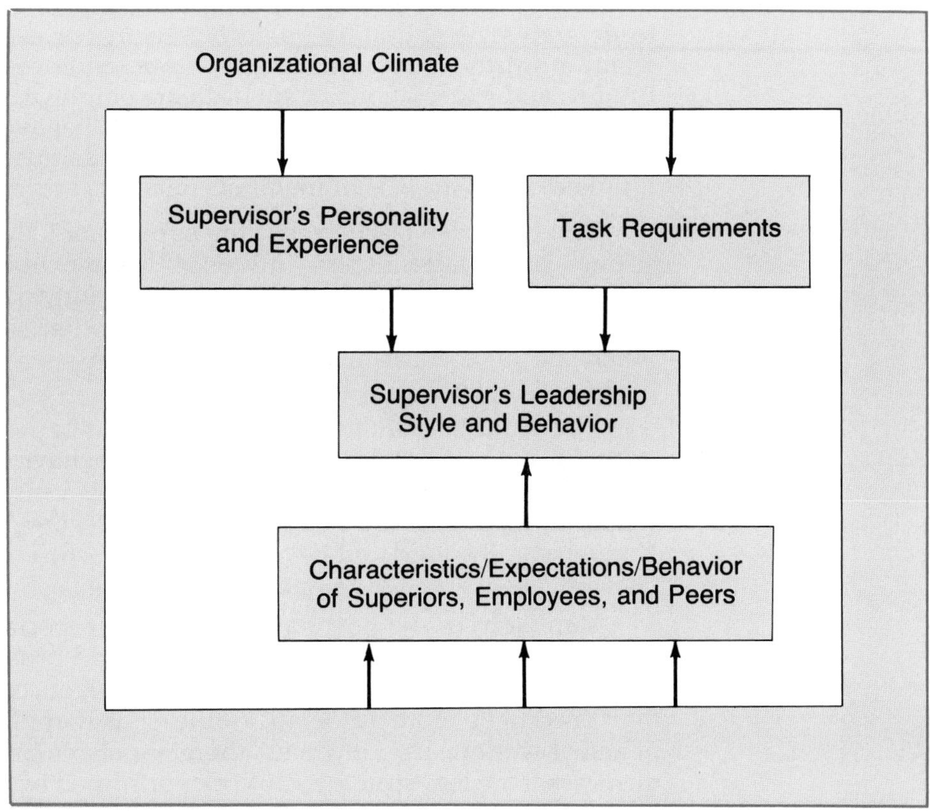

when employees can provide meaningful input, but is likely to be detrimental when they cannot.

Again, the situation itself—and all the factors within it—creates an important influence upon the choice of leadership styles.

In Chapter 2 you learned that researchers have not been able to show correlations between traits or characteristics of supervisors that separate good from poor leaders. The information we have just reviewed also indicated that no single leadership style is always the best. You should also understand that a supervisor reacts to the environment based upon his/her perception of it. If, for example, a supervisor believes upper management attitudes to be one thing (even if they are not) or required tasks to include specific activities (even if they don't), the supervisor will react to the job situation based upon these beliefs.

Factors in the job environment that affect the supervisor's leadership style and behavior are reviewed in Exhibit 3.3. The organizational climate, which is really the "personality" of the organization, affects most staff members at all organizational levels. Recall that, if the organizational climate encourages freedom of expression and creativity, supervisors are likely to behave in this manner (and to encourage their employees to be expressive and creative). Conversely, if the organizational climate is one in which there is constant effort to emphasize rules and to force compliance with standard procedures and policies, this philosophy will be passed down to lower organizational levels. The characteristics, expectations, and behavior of others in the organization (the supervisor's own boss, employees, and peers) also impact upon the supervisor's leadership style and subsequent behavior. For example, the supervisor wants rewards—not punishment—from superiors. Also, the skills, attitudes, and expectations of subordinate employees help determine how the supervisor will relate to employees and behave within the organization. Likewise, when supervisors form friendships with their peers, their influence upon these staff members must be considered.

You have also learned that the supervisor's own background—consciously or subconsciously—influences his/her choice of leadership style. If the supervisor has had success using an autocratic style, chances are that this leadership model will be used in other situations. Conversely, when the democratic approach has proven successful, there is strong likelihood that its use will be continued.

The requirements imposed by the tasks to be done will also influence the supervisor's leadership style and behavior. If, for example, the supervisor must give detailed instructions (as in training a new room attendant), this need will be reflected in the leadership style that is used. Conversely, the food and beverage director who is supervising a creative chef will likely find a different approach to be best.

Many jobs in the hospitality industry—especially those at lower organizational levels—are highly structured; procedures are carefully planned and must be consistently followed. A successful leadership style may need to be more autocratic—at least as it applies to the supervision of actual work tasks. However, there are also jobs in the hospitality industry that are less structured. Work performed by concierge staff, chefs, sales staff, and others might provide examples. For this type of work, a more democratic leadership style may be appropriate.

To the extent possible, the leadership style should be appropriate to the supervisor, to the employees, and to the work situation. A supervisor must be flexible—that is, able to select a style that is comfortable to work with and appropriate for the employee and situation in which it must be used.

Situational Leadership

You have learned something about leadership styles and factors that potentially affect their usefulness. We must now direct our attention to ways in which this information can be applied to the actual supervision of employees—either as individuals or as members of a group—in the actual work environment. Two writers have developed some interesting concepts of situational leadership which can help us see practical implications to the concepts we have just discussed.[7] Their approach considers both the amount of direction (task behavior) that the supervisor must provide as a task is being undertaken by an employee and the amount of social/emotional support (relationship behavior) that is necessary given the specific situation in which direction must be given. Let's look at these two factors more closely.

- **Task behavior** refers to the amount of one-way communication that the supervisor must provide in order to explain the "who, when, where, and how" of tasks to be performed.

- **Relationship behavior** refers to the amount of social/emotional support and two-way communication that the supervisor provides as he/she builds and maintains a personal/professional relationship with the employee.

A study of leadership styles can focus on the extent to which supervisors are oriented toward the task (job to be done) or the employee. If the supervisor is task-centered, he/she is likely to direct and more closely supervise employees to ensure that the work is being done satisfactorily. There is an emphasis on getting the job done rather than on developing and interacting with employees. If the supervisor is employee-centered, the emphasis is on motivating rather than on controlling the employees. Allowing employees participation in the decision-making process and developing professional and trusting relationships are two elements in this approach.

While many research studies do not agree, some studies have indicated that the most productive work groups often have leaders who are employee-centered rather than task-centered.[8] Likewise, effective leaders often have supportive relationships with the employees, tend to involve the employees in the decision-making process, and encourage employees to seek and attain high performance levels. While this information tends to support the need for a democratic leadership style, recall that factors in the job situation and, of course, individual differences in the employees and supervisors themselves must be taken into account.[9]

As might be expected, some supervisors attempt to direct activities by focusing on tasks to be accomplished; others concentrate on providing social/emotional support for their employees; still others use both—depending upon the situation.

Leadership styles incorporating concerns for tasks and relationships are illustrated in Exhibit 3.4. You have already learned that no single leadership style is correct; it all depends upon the situation. As suggested in Exhibit 3.4, the relationship between the amount of direction and/or social/emotional support necessary affects the leadership style which a supervisor uses.

But, what leadership style *should* be used? According to the situational leadership approach, one must consider the level of maturity of the employee or group to be supervised. The term **maturity** refers to one's ability to set high but attainable goals. In other words, it addresses the employee's level of motivation and his/her willingness to accept responsibility to undertake a specific task. Education and experience further affect the employee's ability to perform a specific task.

The procedures used to assess the maturity levels of employees are beyond the scope of this book. However, you should understand that tested, measurable procedures are available.[10] Once the maturity level of an employee is known, the supervisor has a key to understanding the most appropriate leadership style for the specific employee and task. Simply put, in regards to each task, as the employee's level of maturity

Exhibit 3.4 Basic Leader Behavior Styles

Relationship Behavior (Low → High)	Low Task Behavior	High Task Behavior
High	High Relationship and Low Task	High Task and High Relationship
Low	Low Task and Low Relationship	High Task and Low Relationship

Low ← Task Behavior → High

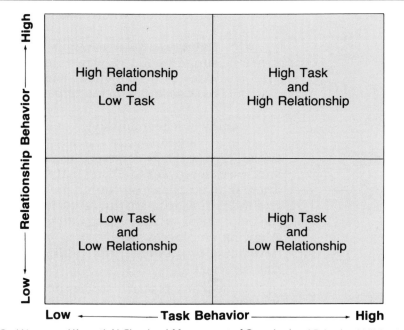

Source: Paul Hersey and Kenneth H. Blanchard, Management of Organizational Behavior: Utilizing Human Resources, *3rd ed., ©1977, p. 103. Reprinted by permission of Prentice-Hall, Inc., Englewood Cliffs, N.J.*

increases, the supervisor should reduce emphasis on the task and increase emphasis on relationship-based behavior. As the level of maturity increases still further, the supervisor can reduce emphasis not only on task but also on relationship behavior; this increase in delegation will be viewed by the employee as an indication of the supervisor's confidence in his/her ability.

Exhibit 3.5 illustrates the relationship between the employee's maturity level and the leadership style that should be used to direct the employee for the specific task to be performed. For any given situation (task), the maturity level (indicated by the range at the bottom of Exhibit 3.5) dictates the leadership style to be used. For example, let's assume that a floor supervisor believes that a housekeeper's maturity level for performing room cleaning tasks is low (in other words, the housekeeper is not motivated, not able, or lacks the required education or experience) to do the work. The supervisor's perception of the housekeeper's maturity would, then, be at a low level (this is designated as "M1" on the scale in Exhibit 3.5). This suggests that the supervisor should use a high task/low relationship leadership style as he/she directs the employee in the room cleaning task. (Note that the style "S1" is in a vertical line from the "M1" maturity level on the scale, indicating that "S1" is the appropriate style—high task/low relationship.) Therefore, the supervisor should emphasize the task and should spend most of the time directing the employee in exactly what must be done. By contrast, if the supervisor judged the employee to be at the high ("M4") maturity level, Exhibit 3.5 suggests that a low relationship/low task (delegating) leadership style

Exhibit 3.5 Situational Leadership Theory

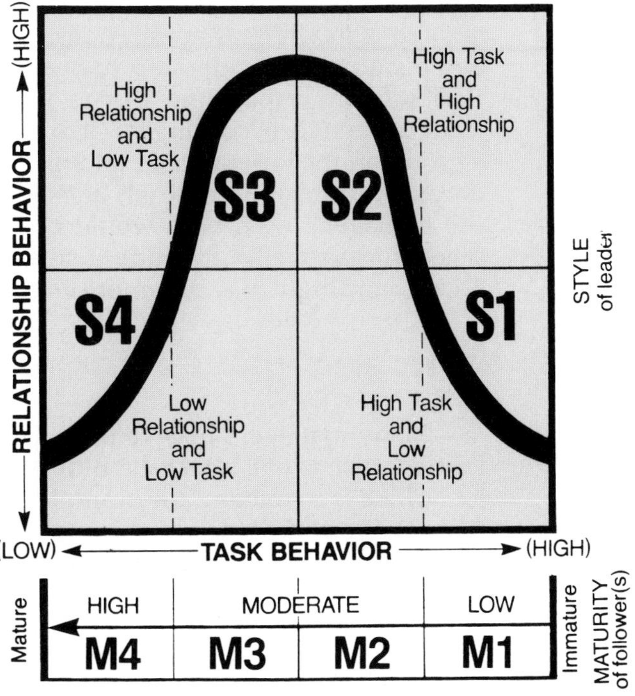

Source: Adapted from Paul Hersey and Kenneth H. Blanchard, Management of Organizational Behavior: Utilizing Human Resources, *3rd ed., ©1977, p. 167. Reprinted by permission of Prentice-Hall, Inc., Englewood Cliffs, N.J.*

could be very effective. Low relationship does not, of course, mean unfriendly or impersonal. Rather, it means there is little need for the supervisor to show emotional support or reinforcement; the employee is willing and able to perform the task without direction.

The four leadership styles illustrated in Exhibit 3.5 can be categorized as follows:

- S1 (high task/low relationship)—telling; the supervisor must tell the employee exactly what must be done.
- S2 (high task/high relationship)—selling; the supervisor must attempt to get the employee to do what must be done.
- S3 (high relationship/low task)—participating; the supervisor and employee share in decision-making.
- S4 (low relationship/low task)—delegating; the supervisor allows the employee to perform the task with little direction.

Are Leadership Styles Flexible?

Can supervisors change their leadership styles to fit the job situation? We have seen that some writers believe this is (or should be) possible and other researchers do not. If supervisors are flexible or, if they can be trained to use different leadership styles in different situations, they will be able to operate more effectively in a greater variety of job situations. If supervisors cannot vary their leadership style, the number of job situations in which they can operate effectively will certainly be limited. Some studies on leadership suggest that people do have some potential flexibility in responding to the job situation and in modifying their leadership style accordingly.[11] For example, a front office manager with a group of uncooperative employees who do not meet performance standards will probably, at least, question his/her leadership style (certainly the manager's own boss would question it). Therefore, the supervisor who can learn how to study a situation and to alter his/her leadership style accordingly may be a more effective leader.

Leadership Style and Job Performance

Many managers believe that the choice of leadership style is important because it will affect the ultimate performance of employees on the job. There is a concern, for example, that organizational goals will be better met if the "best" leadership style is used. Current research, however, is unable to consistently show this correlation between leadership style and job performance. If trained researchers cannot show a positive relationship between leadership style and job performance, what difference, then, does choice of leadership style make? In order to answer this question we must consider employee morale.[12] A summary of the relationship between leadership style, morale, and subsequent job performance includes the following:[13]

1. A participative leadership style tends to yield high employee morale.

2. High employee morale levels relate to reduced turnover rates, lower unexcused absenteeism, and fewer accidents.

3. There is no consistent and reliable relationship between morale and productivity; in other words, higher job satisfaction does not directly yield better job performance.

4. No consistent relationship can be shown between leadership style and job performance. Therefore, neither the autocratic nor democratic leadership style can be said to be superior to the other.

The summary essentially indicates that the conditions and factors which determine job satisfaction (morale) and job performance are not the same. However, one might also consider that reducing turnover, absenteeism, and accidents does yield a "back door" approach to controlling—if not increasing—job performance.

Power and Leadership Styles

Power can be defined as the authority to act or to perform; in other words, to get something done. If a supervisor has a wide variety and large amount of power available (such as the ability to reward and punish) and also has a high level of expertise (which increases acceptance by the employees), he/she is much more likely to gain compliance from the employees. By contrast, the weak leader who has not been delegated significant levels of authority (power), who does not know what needs to be done, and who is not respected by the staff will likely have less discretion. Power or authority, then, has an impact upon which leadership style can be used. In the first example above, an autocratic style might be used. This approach will clearly not work in the second example; the laissez-faire approach might be the only possible choice.

Supervisors have several potential sources of power as employees are directed:

1. **Legal power.** The ability to control others based on official position.

2. **Expert power.** The ability to control others based on possession of expert knowledge, ability, or information others do not have.

3. **Referent power.** The ability to control others because of personality, charisma, or the respect others have for them.

4. **Reward power.** The ability to control others by giving or withholding rewards.

5. **Punitive Power.** The ability to control others by penalizing or punishing them for mistakes or violations of policy.[14]

The supervisor has the responsibility to influence the employees in order to get work done, and he/she can draw on any one or a combination of these powers to do so. The types of power used will determine the leadership approach, or the way in which you lead others to get work done.

NOTES

1. Richard W. Plunkett, *Supervision: The Direction of People at Work,* 2nd ed. (Dubuque, Iowa: Brown, 1979), p. 184.

2. Douglas McGregor, *The Human Side of Enterprise* (New York: McGraw-Hill, 1960).

3. Plunkett, pp. 185-186 .

4. Plunkett, pp. 186-187 .

5. McGregor, *The Human Side of Enterprise.*

6. Robert Tannenbaum and Warren H. Schmidt, "How to Choose A Leadership Pattern," *Harvard Business Review,* May-June, 1973, pp. 162-164.

7. Paul Hersey and Kenneth H. Blanchard, *Management of Organizational Behavior: Utilizing Human Resources,* 3rd ed. (Englewood Cliffs, N.J.: Prentice-Hall, 1977).

8. See, for example, James A. Stoner, *Management* (Englewood Cliffs, N.J.: Prentice-Hall, 1978), pp. 441-444.

9. Robert R. Blake and Jane S. Mouton, *The Managerial Grid* (Houston, Tex.: Gulf, 1964). In their now famous work Blake and Mouton argue that the democratic management approach is best; it can yield improved performance, low absenteeism and turnover, and high employee satisfaction in many situations. Likewise, Rensis Likert, *New Patterns of Management* (New York: McGraw- Hill, 1961), also favors a participative management style in which goals are set and employee-related decisions are made by the worker group. His research also suggests that high producing departments tend to have supervisors who use the participative leadership style.

10. Interested readers are referred to the Learning Resources Corporation, 17594 Eads Ave., La Jolla, Calif. 92037, for detailed information about instruments used to assess maturity levels.

11. See Stoner, pp. 459-461.

12. Motivation and morale will be discussed in Chapter 11. For the purpose of this discussion, however, a workable definition of *morale* is that it is the combination of the employee's attitudes about everything that affects him/her on the job.

13. Ross A. Webber, *Management: Basic Elements of Managing Organizations*, rev. ed. (Homewood, Ill.: Irwin, 1979), p. 175.

14. Irvin L. Heckmann and Robert L. Blomstrom, *Start Supervising* (East Lansing, Mich.: Educational Institute of the American Hotel & Motel Association, 1981), p. 31.

PAGE SIX

Supervision at the Brandywine Room

Stacey had read several management books that discussed leadership styles in great depth. She had talked with her university instructor and also with her boss, Mr. George. While she assumed that all the theories and models were correct, she wasn't sure how she could apply this information in a practical way to her own situation.

She expressed these concerns to Katherine Ames (the assistant food and beverage controller). The conversation which followed made for a most enjoyable—and educational—coffee break. "You know Kath," she said, "it makes sense to me that the way I relate to my employees will affect their attitude toward me and, somehow, the quality and quantity of work which is done. But I've read—and my university instructor agrees—that there really isn't a direct relationship between employee morale and job performance. I think I understand why. An employee who doesn't like me might do good work just to show me that he can do it. Other employees might be afraid to lose their jobs because of the high unemployment rate in our town. They might work hard just to keep their jobs. I'd like to go beyond this, however, and learn how to supervise my employees in a way which will be good for them, for the Brandywine, and for me. It would certainly make my job easier."

Kath was nodding her head in agreement. "You're right, Stacey. The job that the food and beverage controllers do is very structured. Numbers have to be put together in specified ways within specified time periods. The financial information works its way into many reports used by department heads and the general manager. The reports are also sent to our regional office. I can't allow my employees to do things in their own way. When it comes to supervising the ongoing work, I have to make sure it is done a certain way. The employees are not able to make changes."

Stacey said she understood. They began talking about Stacey's employees. "It's not quite the same way in the dining room. Sure, there are rules and policies dealing with sanitation, guest service, completion of guest checks, etc., but my employees have much more latitude in how they approach suggestive selling, interacting with buspersons, doing setups, cleaning, etc. I'm trying to learn about my employees. Some really don't seem to care. With them, I need to supervise more carefully and follow up to be sure that minimum job requirements are met. Perhaps they can be motivated. I plan to talk to Mr. George about this.

"There are others, however, who are fantastic workers. They're always looking for additional responsibilities. I'm learning that it is a great help—to the Brandywine, to them, and to me—to involve these employees in making decisions about new ways to do things. Right now, for example, we're making some changes in table decorations and the way in which tables are set."

Stacey's conversation prompted Kath to think about her job situation. "You know Stacey," she said, "it seems like we're constantly designing new forms in our department. There are always special projects that seem to come up. I wonder if some of my staff members would be interested in helping me design those forms and in sharing their ideas about how we should handle those situations. I'm going to ask them. Some may not want to because they don't care, but others will be interested, I'm sure. If their ideas can be used, they will feel more appreciated. At the same time, I can get some good ideas to ease the work."

The coffee break was about over; it had been a good one for both supervisors. By talking with Kath, Stacey had been able to make a little sense out of all the "fancy" leadership theories. She knew that she couldn't change from an autocratic to a democratic leadership style in the few seconds it took to stop talking with one employee and begin interacting with another. She knew, however, that over time she could better understand her employees and improve her ability to relate to them. Kath had acquired a good idea from Stacey's conversation; she was going to try to actively involve her employees in the design of those aspects of the job which were not covered by strict rules and policies. She didn't know what would happen—or if it would work—but she was going to give it a try.

4 The Supervisor's Role in Improving Work

PAGE SEVEN

Supervision at the Brandywine Room

Stacey felt she was ready. She had been in her position as dining room manager for approximately six months. She knew what the dining room manager position involved; she knew a lot about the likes and dislikes of those staff members who had been with her for several months. (There was a turnover problem but she wasn't quite ready to tackle that yet!) She thought it was time to go to work on one problem that had bothered her ever since she was a food server—and now was the time because Mr. George had mentioned that a mandated staffing plan was only a few months away.

Basically, the major problem was that there were no organized procedures for providing food and beverage service to the guests. Sometimes the hostess provided menus, water, and coffee. At other times, this was done by the food server or the busperson. Sometimes before-dinner drink orders were requested by service staff; at other times, guests had to ask. Except when there was a rush for clean tables, there was not really a policy dictating when—or by whom—tables should be cleaned and reset.

Have you ever gone into a hotel or a restaurant and noticed things that weren't being done correctly? Did it look like the room rack system in the small hotel was disorganized? Did it appear that the system for taking food or beverage orders, serving the products, or processing guest checks for payment was awkward? Did it appear that the lobby, restrooms, and other public areas really needed attention? Why do you think that you—an infrequent visitor to the property—could notice these things, while the management staff—who work there many, many hours each week—apparently could not? Is it possible that someone from that same management staff could visit another property and notice similarly "obvious" types of things? The point is, we often do things in a certain way because we've always done them that way. We get so caught up in routines that we don't step back and take a fresh look at new ways of doing things.

People who believe that new ways are not always better are certainly correct. On the other hand, it is often possible to improve work being done in the property so that organizational goals can be better met with a reduced amount of resources expended in the process. The working conditions, required working procedures, and availability of equipment and tools in the workplace also affect work performance. In Chapter 1 we learned that problems with job performance cannot always be resolved through use of training, motivation, or personnel management techniques. Sometimes the problems relate to working conditions or the environment within the workplace itself. The concept of analyzing and simplifying work is the topic of this chapter.

In most operations the supervisor works "where the action is." Often, he/she has been promoted from the ranks of employees who daily perform the work tasks for which the supervisor is now responsible. The supervisor is the technical expert for the work assignments given to employees. It is reasonable to expect, then, that the supervisor will be able to influence which work procedures are used.

The effective supervisor accepts the responsibility to analyze work and to study ways of improving it as an integral part of his/her job. Some supervisors, however—like other people—resist change; they want to maintain the status quo and follow established precedents. Supervisors with this attitude do not take an active and assertive role in questioning how work is done with the idea that procedures can be improved.

The Philosophy of Work Analysis and Improvement

The concept of work analysis and improvement is almost as much a philosophy toward work as it is an operational technique that can help the lodging or food service property achieve increased efficiency, which yields lower labor costs. While studies differ in terms of specific findings, it is a generally accepted observation that the average hospitality industry employee is performing required work assignments only approximately 40% of the time. If this is the case, an employee being paid $5 per hour is really being paid approximately $12.50 for an actual labor hour's worth of work. It is true that many hospitality employees are more productive than the average; there are probably no hospitality operations, however, in which application of work analysis methods could not yield increased efficiency. Clearly, no hospitality operation can afford to pay for nonproductive labor hours. Since productivity levels are generally so low, and since the industry requires large numbers of employees, it is obvious that a property will benefit from supervisory efforts to increase efficiency by analyzing work and improving work procedures.

Work analysis can also benefit employees and guests. As work is done more efficiently, it becomes easier; more efficient work performance leads to higher quality products and services. With these benefits in mind, it is important that you, as a supervisor:

- Be on the alert constantly for better ways to perform jobs. This task of improving work is part of your work assignment.

- Ask your employees to think about ways to improve their jobs. After all, an employee who must consistently and routinely perform specific work tasks may well have ideas about how this work can be done more effectively.

- Realize that changes stemming from a work analysis program do not need to yield large time or cost savings. Revised procedures which yield even a few saved minutes or pennies will generate large dollar savings over a long time period. Since this is the case, the implementation of even a few small changes can have great impact.

What Is Work Analysis?

Work analysis is really a system of studying work with the idea of making employees more efficient. The purpose of work analysis is to identify and correct factors having a detrimental effect on productivity in the work system. A step- by-step approach to effective work analysis begins with selecting the jobs to be analyzed. Jobs that have never been studied, in addition to jobs involving large amounts of labor time and labor dollars, the production or provision of products or services, or consistently unmet quantity or quality standards, are particularly suited for work analysis. Others are jobs that:

- will need to be performed for an indefinite time.

- create bottlenecks.

- involve many employees performing the same routine tasks (such as registering guests, preparing for meal service, or serving guests).

- involve guest or employee complaints.

- have budget implications. Budgets and other accounting records indicate whether—and where—costs are excessive. If the standards upon which these records are based are correct, work analysis may be necessary to bring actual costs in line with expected costs.

- affect labor staffing patterns. If labor hours are excessive, if overtime is incurred, or if, for other reasons, performance standards are not met, work analysis may be in order.

- create poor environmental conditions (such as slippery floors, inadequate lighting, lack of proper equipment, etc.).
- need to be changed when revisions in working conditions are implemented (such as the installation of computerized reservation systems for the hotel or convenience food products for the restaurant). As these changes occur, a close look at how work is being done—and how it will need to be modified—is in order.

After selecting the jobs to be analyzed, succeeding steps in the work analysis process are:

Step 1 **Identify the major factors affecting the work system.** Many factors affect the way work is being done—materials, workplace design, available equipment, abilities of personnel, the work itself, work procedures, etc.

Step 2 **Collect and analyze information about current work procedures.** Often, this can be done by simple observation. If you know what *must* be done in order to meet minimum quality and quantity requirements, observe what *is* being done and note any differences.

Step 3 **Generate ideas about alternative work methods.** Generally, when work problems arise, there is more than one way to resolve them. Likewise, since work procedures and systems are generally complex, it is often difficult to pinpoint the exact reasons for observed problems. Many approaches can be used to generate ideas about work improvement methods: input from employees, review of magazine articles, conversations with other supervisors, and, of course, creative considerations of observed problems—and how they might be resolved.

Step 4 **Evaluate each method or alternative solution and select the best approach.** The method or solution to be implemented may be a compromise representing the best elements of several alternatives which have been proposed. Cost analysis, reflection on the alternatives in light of past experiences, evaluation input from colleagues, employees, and others, and related techniques can be used as an alternative is selected. (Recall the techniques of nonprogrammed decision-making which were discussed in Chapter 1.) Compliance with company rules and policies, external laws, and other requirements is also important. Cost is generally a primary concern as alternative work procedures are reviewed. It is important to remember that costs include more than just initial capital costs for any necessary equipment; operating costs, installation expenses, interest charges, insurance, taxes, etc., must also be quantified.

When analysis is done for alternative procedures not involving capital (equipment) costs, you must be sure that work of the required quantity and quality can be done in the time which is being allocated. It is one thing for an "all-star" employee to make up a room or register a guest within a specified time period; it may not, however, be reasonable to expect that an average employee—even after training and with constant supervision—can be as productive. Performance standards must be attainable in order to be useful.

Step 5 **Test the proposed work system.** A trial study may be used. With this plan, perhaps only a few employees will use the revised procedures for a specified time. During this study, closely monitor the extent to which the revised procedures are helpful. Before a formal evaluation can be done, employees need time to build speed and become familiar with revised procedures (old habits are sometimes hard to break). Further modifications to work procedures may result from this trial study.

During this step it is also important to ensure that there are no spin-off effects on other work procedures not directly involved with the work being revised. For example, revision of procedures to prepare food or to clean a hotel room may have an impact on cleanliness and quality standards that were established from a marketing perspective. A simple notation that "the work is being done quicker" would not take these marketing concerns into account.

Step 6 **Implement the revised work procedures.** After testing, and modification if necessary, revised work procedures can be implemented. Proper implementation calls for training employees in the new procedures, providing any required tools and equipment, continual supervision, reinforcement, and coaching during the ensuing transitional period. The revised procedures must be recorded in applicable standard operating procedures handbooks, training materials, and other reference works.

Step 7 **Evaluate the effectiveness of the new procedures.** The newly implemented work procedures should be evaluated against those factors initially used to judge whether a problem existed. In other words, if indicators of effective problem resolution have been identified, the evaluation phase involves assessing whether—and to what extent—these indicators are now present. For example, if a floor supervisor has determined that revised work procedures should yield an increased number of rooms cleaned with a corresponding decrease in the number of problems noted on follow-up "room ready checklists," it would be relatively easy to assess whether revised work procedures do yield desired results. If they do, it can be concluded that these procedures are effective—although routine follow-up will be necessary to ensure that old problems do not surface or that new problems do not arise. These activities are possible because the indicators (objectives of work improvement plans) are measurable. If they were not, it would be difficult to objectively assess the worth of work analysis activities.

If the evaluation step indicates that the revised work procedures do not do what they are supposed to, further work analysis activities may be necessary. It is possible, of course, for the evaluation phase to identify new problems that need to be resolved. Viewed this way, the process of work analysis is cyclical. This is shown in Exhibit 4.1, which provides a review of each of the steps involved in the work analysis and improve-

Exhibit 4.1 Continuity of the Work Analysis and Improvement Process

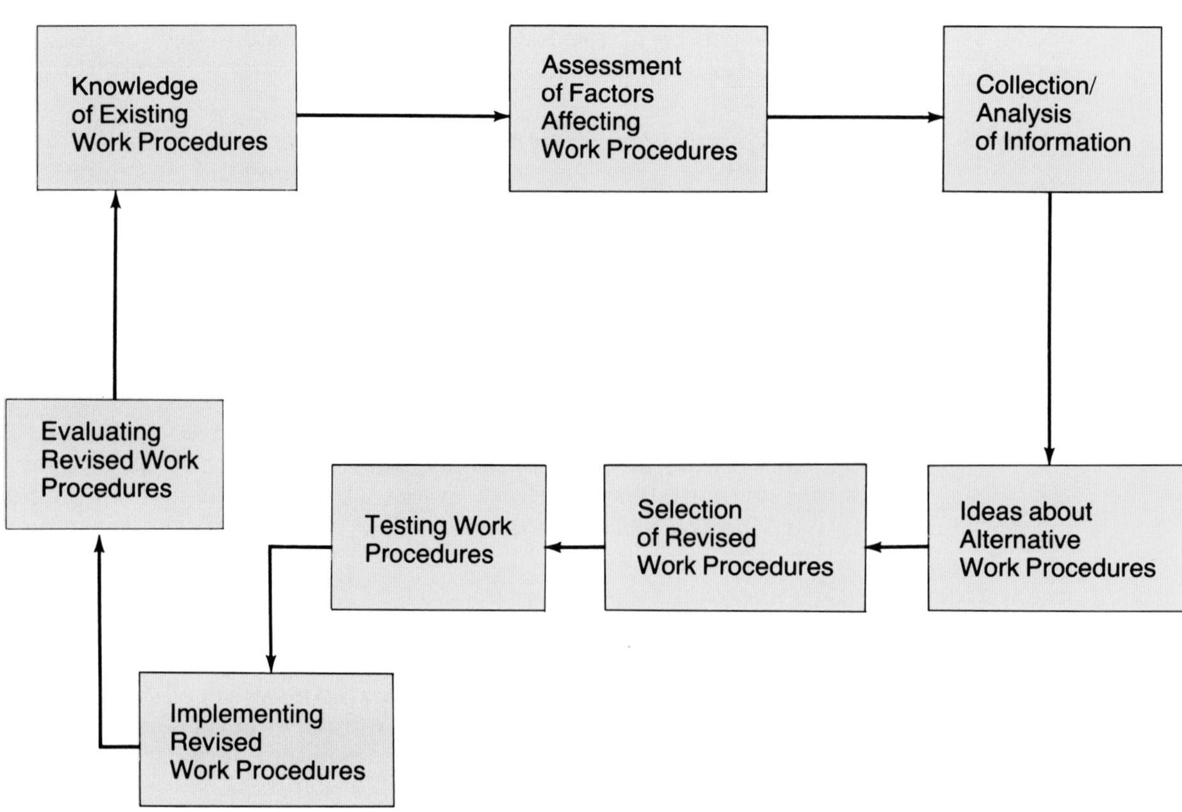

ment process. The supervisor must, first, have detailed knowledge about how existing work procedures are performed. If, for whatever reason, work output is not satisfactory, he/she must assess possible causes for the substandard work performance. As information about these factors becomes known, alternative work procedures evolve. It is at this point that, if the supervisor practices a participative leadership style (see Chapter 3), input from many sources, including employees, could be solicited. After alternative work procedures are analyzed, the best alternative must be selected. It is tested and modified, if necessary, and implemented. The revised work procedures must be evaluated to ensure that the objectives for which the work analysis was undertaken were, in fact, attained. Careful evaluation may, indeed, uncover additional problems; the work analysis process recycles.

Simple Questions Can Uncover Serious Problems

Supervisors should ask several questions as they analyze work to increase efficiency.[1]

Can the work be eliminated? Before a supervisor tries to improve a work process, the question of whether it should be performed at all should be asked. For example, must the quantity or costs of incoming products be recorded separately by food categories (meat, poultry, seafood, vegetables, etc.)? Perhaps this activity can be avoided entirely if there is no need for detailed information about incoming products on a by-food-category basis.

Can the work be combined with other tasks? For example, a dining room cashier might be able to make inventory calculations or verify time card calculations for other departments during slow periods. If so, this frees up time which other staff might use more effectively.

Are there unnecessary work delays? For example, if there is a bottleneck in the washing or repair of room linens, this can have an impact on the work performed by room attendants. The slowness of room attendants may be caused by the need to make frequent trips to the laundry department to pick up linens as they become available.

Is there misdirected effort? Can equipment perform tasks done by the employees? Should a French knife, electric slicer, or shredding attachment for a mixer be used to prepare cabbage for coleslaw? Should hand tallies of registration information be made at the front desk when computerized equipment might easily be programmed to collect such information?

Are employee skills being utilized effectively? Are high-paid employees performing work that lower-paid staff could perform? Is a high-paid chef needed to reconstitute convenience food items? Must a floor supervisor be used to fill in for room attendants who don't show up for work?

Can the job be simplified? The examples on pages 72-74 show how common problems in a food and beverage and a housekeeping department might be resolved through work simplification techniques.

Can tasks within a job be rearranged? Can a line worker plating foods on a plate assembly line for a special banquet place two items or must two employees be used? Can ceilings be cleaned at the same time that light bulbs are changed in large rooms where scaffolding is needed?

Are employees performing unrelated tasks? When, for example, a cook must also work on the serving line, efficiency may be reduced. To the extent possible, similar tasks should be grouped together into a job. An employee should be hired to perform a job made up of similar, not dissimilar, tasks.

Is work spread across work stations or employees unevenly? For example, is one front desk clerk busier than another? Perhaps tasks should be redivided.

Basically, the process of questioning work should address the concerns of what, where, when, by whom, and how work is being done, and how it should be done.

Example: Work Analysis in the Guestroom
A General Approach

The floor supervisor was concerned about excessive time being spent by room attendants in making up rooms. To resolve the problem, the supervisor decided to implement the following procedures in the work analysis process:

1. **Identify existing procedures.** Upon careful study, the floor supervisor noticed that different room attendants prepared rooms in different ways. As this occurred, some attendants did things that should not be done and others used incorrect procedures. In this instance, the first step in the work analysis process was to define exactly what tasks had to be done in order to make a room ready for resale. (It would not be uncommon for a hotel property to have a checklist of some fifty or more activities which must be performed.) Standard operating procedures—the property's "way" of performing each of these activities—needed to be established. All floor supervisors along with other management staff in the housekeeping department were asked to help determine what—and how—tasks should be done.

2. **Assess factors affecting work performance.** What room cleaning equipment was needed? What procedures were in effect to ensure that such equipment consistently operated properly? What items needed to be stocked on the housekeepers'carts? How did room attendants know when maintenance staff should be called to maintain/repair selected items? How did the size and furnishings of the room affect work procedures? After getting the answers to these questions, the supervisor proceeded to the next step.

3. **Collect and analyze information.** The supervisor noted and studied how long it took to perform all required activities, the time-consuming tasks (not directly related to cleaning the room) affecting the productivity of the department, why some room attendants took longer than others to perform the same tasks, the background (training and experience) of "good" and "bad" room attendants, and tasks that took the longest time to perform or were performed most awkwardly.

4. **Generate ideas about alternative procedures.** The supervisor knew that cleaning the bathroom and making the bed were troublesome tasks. Different ways of performing these chores (while keeping in mind the required quality and quantity standards) were tried. In the bathroom areas, different products and equipment were used along with different work procedures. Close observation of how several "good" room attendants performed these chores was helpful.

5. **Select revised procedures.** Given quality, cleanliness, and productivity standards, the supervisor selected what was considered the best alternative.

6. **Test revised procedures.** Several room attendants were trained in revised procedures and closely supervised to see what happened as these procedures were used. The revised procedures appeared to work better than existing procedures.

7. **Implement revised procedures.** As a result of the trial test, a few modifications to the revised procedures were made. Standard operating procedures were written, more employees were trained and their performance was monitored closely.

8. **Evaluate revised procedures.** On an ongoing basis, the floor supervisor evaluated the performance of room attendants. Over time, some "slippage" in how work was performed and in the quality or quantity of work was noticed. Efforts to further revise work procedures were in order.

Example: Work Analysis in the Kitchen A Specific Approach

The food production supervisor had been concerned for some time about the large amount of work necessary on Saturday afternoons. Not only was there a large amount of pre-preparation being done for Saturday evening (the single busiest dinner shift of the week), but also production staff were busy getting ready for the Sunday buffet. In fact, one preparation assistant spent almost six hours cracking shell eggs to be used for brunch omelets. The process, which had been used for many years, involved breaking eggs into a china cap (a cone-shaped strainer) and whipping them through that tool into a container used for overnight refrigerated storage. Labor costs were increasing—so was business—and there was no time for any wasted effort. Work analysis consisted of the following steps:

1. **Identify existing procedures.** The supervisor had observed the task of preparing shell eggs for many months and knew exactly how it was done.

2. **Assess factors affecting work performance.** The supervisor was aware that whole eggs were used and that small equipment items (china cap, wire whip, and various steam table pans) were also needed. She knew how the work station was laid out for the task.

3. **Collect and analyze information.** Over several weeks, the supervisor collected information about time required for various quantities of output (dozens of eggs cracked). With minor exceptions there were few ideas about how to make the current process more efficient.

4. **Generate ideas about alternative procedures.** After talking with food production staff, the supervisor developed a list of possible ideas. Could frozen whole eggs be used (which did not need to be shelled)? Could eggs be cracked into a pan with shells settling to the bottom by the time they were needed? (The egg mixture could then be poured out of holding pans into equipment for the omelet line.) As ideas were generated, they were tried. Several omelets were made with frozen whole eggs, fresh whole eggs were cracked and used without sifting through a china cap, etc.

5. **Select the revised procedures.** Based upon experience, common sense, and observation, the supervisor decided that eggs would be cracked into a pan, allowing shells to separate without the use of a china cap. This decision was made jointly with the help of several production staff members.

6. **Test revised procedures.** For two weeks one omelet line was supplied with egg products prepared with the revised method. Feedback from cooks and guests was requested. The supervisor monitored the process very carefully.

7. **Implement revised procedures.** As a result of the trial test, no modifications in the revised work procedures were deemed necessary. Staff responsible for pre-prepping the Sunday buffet were trained in revised methods for preparing whole eggs used for omelets. The preparation task was closely watched for several weeks.

8. **Evaluate revised procedures.** As a result of closely monitoring the revised work procedures, no spin-off problems were noted; there was no observable impact upon other food preparation tasks or the quality of the product being served to the guests. It was estimated that the revised work procedures saved approximately four labor hours—$25—weekly without any negative side effects.

Work Analysis and the Tired Employee

Hard work, in a physical sense, tires an employee and affects job performance (output, efficiency, and attitude). It is important, then, to find ways to make work easier from the employees' perspective. This is one objective of work analysis. The following suggestions can be incorporated with the work analysis procedures already noted in attempting to make work easier:

1. Provide adequate rest periods.

2. When possible, schedule physically easy work near the end of the workshift.

3. Recognize that heat, noise, high humidity, and other environmental problems make work more difficult. When revising work procedures, consider ways to remove these elements from the workplace or, alternatively, recognize these factors as employees are scheduled.

4. Recognize that the layout and design of the facility affects work performance. Since most facilities are already built, the task really becomes one of using the existing design as a constraint within which ways must be found to make the work easier. Nothing is gained by thinking "the job could be done more easily if only that wall were not there." Since the wall is there, the work must be revised to reduce the problems.

Use of effective work analysis procedures can make work easier for the employees and can improve products and services from the guests' perspective. At the same time, increased productivity and reduced labor costs may result to benefit the hospitality operation. Supervisors should consider these advantages and should focus upon helping employees perform their jobs in easy and time-saving ways without reducing the quality standards which have been established for the work to be done.

NOTES

1. This discussion is based on Donald E. Lundberg and James P. Armatas, *The Management of People in Hotels, Restaurants, and Clubs*, 4th ed. (Dubuque, Iowa: Brown, 1980), pp. 273-274.

PAGE EIGHT

Supervision at the Brandywine Room

It occurred to Stacey that the lack of standard procedures would give her an opportunity to practice both her leadership skills and what she had learned about work analysis and design in a recent professional development seminar she had attended.

Her first step was to call a meeting of all service staff. (Meetings had been held only infrequently; she was going to change that policy, too.) At the meeting she pointed out the problems: There were no standard procedures for serving guests. The quality of guest service was not consistent. This was a problem for service staff (some needed to work harder or faster than others) and for her (she was being asked to develop performance standards which would be used as a basis for employee scheduling). As she reviewed these points with her staff, Stacey recalled the need to explain, defend, and/or justify proposed changes to affected staff members. She then led a staff discussion about problems caused by the lack of standard service procedures. She was happily surprised to learn that several employees were also concerned about this matter. After a lengthy discussion of the problem—and some brief ideas on what to do about it—she asked the employees to think carefully about standard procedures that they would like to see incorporated into future plans. She requested that employees with ideas "get back to her" within the week.

Stacey did not really expect much input from this approach, but she wanted to give all employees an opportunity to become involved. During the next week she began listing procedures which she thought would be useful to include as performance standards were developed. She shared this list with those employees whom she knew would be concerned—and would have good ideas. Two other staff members volunteered helpful ideas; she included these staff members in her participative discussions as well.

Using this approach, Stacey was able to develop a basic list of standard serving procedures. This list was reviewed with Mr. George (he had a few suggestions to add), and she then approached two of her better employees. "I noticed that you're both working next Tuesday night. We think it will be a slow evening. I would like you to help me by looking at this list of procedures and by giving them a try during your shift next Tuesday. Will you do that?" After they agreed, Stacey sat down with the two and carefully went over the list. There were about fifteen basic procedures which she thought would lend consistency to the service style and which could form the basis for performance standards to be developed later.

Stacey met with the two staff members at the beginning of the Tuesday shift. Once again she reviewed the procedures with them and asked permission to observe them during the evening. The service personnel were flattered that she had asked and interested that she cared enough to work with them on the project. At the end of the shift, Stacey met for a few minutes with the two waitresses. They were able to confirm that most of the procedures worked very well. There were, however, three that needed some revision. They agreed to modify these procedures slightly, to try them, and to report back to Stacey at the end of their next shift.

This approach was used for several nights with several different staff members. After two weeks, Stacey felt that they had a basic set of service operating procedures which would be very effective. A series of staff training sessions was established; several of the procedures were discussed at each staff meeting. Service staff were given one week to practice the various procedures and to inform her of any problems which were incurred. Relatively few staff members had problems; when problems were indicated, they were corrected. During this time Stacey listed, in standard operating procedure format, all required tasks—and how they were to be performed. She would later develop this into formal training material to use with newly hired staff.

After the trial period, procedures were formally implemented and, from that time, were to be used by all staff members on all shifts. Stacey worked several extra shifts that week herself so that she could be present to supervise and monitor how things were going. There were several times when employees appeared to forget; brief coaching sessions helped them recall how the new procedures were to be performed.

Within approximately one month after Stacey had decided to work on the problem, she thought it had been corrected. Stacey had learned a good management lesson in work analysis and design. At the same time, she had sharpened her leadership skills, had gained more respect from her subordinates, and her ego was boosted. She was ready to tackle other problems.

5 The Supervisor as Change Agent

PAGE NINE

Supervision at the Brandywine Room

Stacey was thinking about the ease with which she was able to accomplish her first big project. The change in operating procedures for dining room service had gone smoothly. Sure, there were no big changes and certainly there were none that directly affected the "territory" or earnings of the service staff. She knew, however, that more significant changes were coming.

She had already alerted the staff that performance standards and staff planning systems were being developed. In a recent staff meeting, Mr. George had told her that department heads in the hotel were going to implement a new employee performance review program and wage and salary programs were going to be studied. Stacey knew— and in fact had told Mr. George—that there was now some employee discussion about unionization in the food production units at the hotel.

There were lots of changes around the corner. She knew that, as a supervisor, she would be actively involved in any changes which were made. She would have to implement changes imposed by management and would be obligated to inform higher levels of management about employee reactions to the changes.

"How does one learn about change?" she thought. She decided to try an approach that had worked for her earlier; she was going to speak with the instructor in her class and match that advice with practical information from Mr. George and some of her supervisory colleagues in other departments.

Supervisors are often confronted with change. Change can be mandatory or voluntary. As hospitality operations change, so do their objectives, operating policies, and organizational structures. Supervisors may be forced to implement changes mandated by top management; they may have little discretion. Recall, however, that as explained in Chapter 3, if management has practiced participative leadership, the supervisor will have had some input to the process requiring the change.

At other times, supervisors may want to implement changes to make more effective use of available resources as they strive to attain organizational goals. (Recall the techniques which Stacey Francis used in Chapter 4 to plan and implement standard operating procedures to improve service in the Brandywine Room.)

Overview: The Process of Change

Change is a continual process. It is not an activity which has an obvious beginning and end. In hospitality operations the forces of change and stability operate at the same time. The operation needs some continuity; a supervisor must assume that some things tomorrow will be like those today in order to plan effectively. Many things in the work environment, such as the facility itself, available equipment, and the basic needs of the guest, generally do not change overnight. Supervisors can consider these factors as they undertake basic management activities. Relationships among people and vested interests of the ownership of the organization are two stabilizing forces which provide some consistency in operations. Attitudes of people at all organizational levels are also difficult to change—and therefore create a stabilizing factor.

On the other hand, there are internal and external forces that promote organizational growth and change. The need to adapt to changing social, political, and economic conditions is an example. Likewise, as consumers' wants and needs change over time, adaptation to meet these needs becomes critical. As new employees enter the organization and assume leadership positions, their influence will also yield change. It can be seen, then, that external and internal forces for change are often closely linked. Organizations change to better meet the changing needs of the guests they attempt to serve. Exhibit 5.1 illustrates how external and internal pressures create the need for organizational change.

Definition

Change occurs when there is an alteration, a substitution, a new development or process, or a difference from the way things were.[1] Since each part and subsystem of the organization is closely interrelated, a change in one part, even a simple work procedure, is likely to cause change in other parts of the organizational system. When change occurs, it usually affects an initial point in the organization and a particular group of employees first. The impact of the change will be most drastic at that point, but it is likely to extend, with lesser intensity, to the entire organization and its employees.

Exhibit 5.1 Pressures for Organizational Change

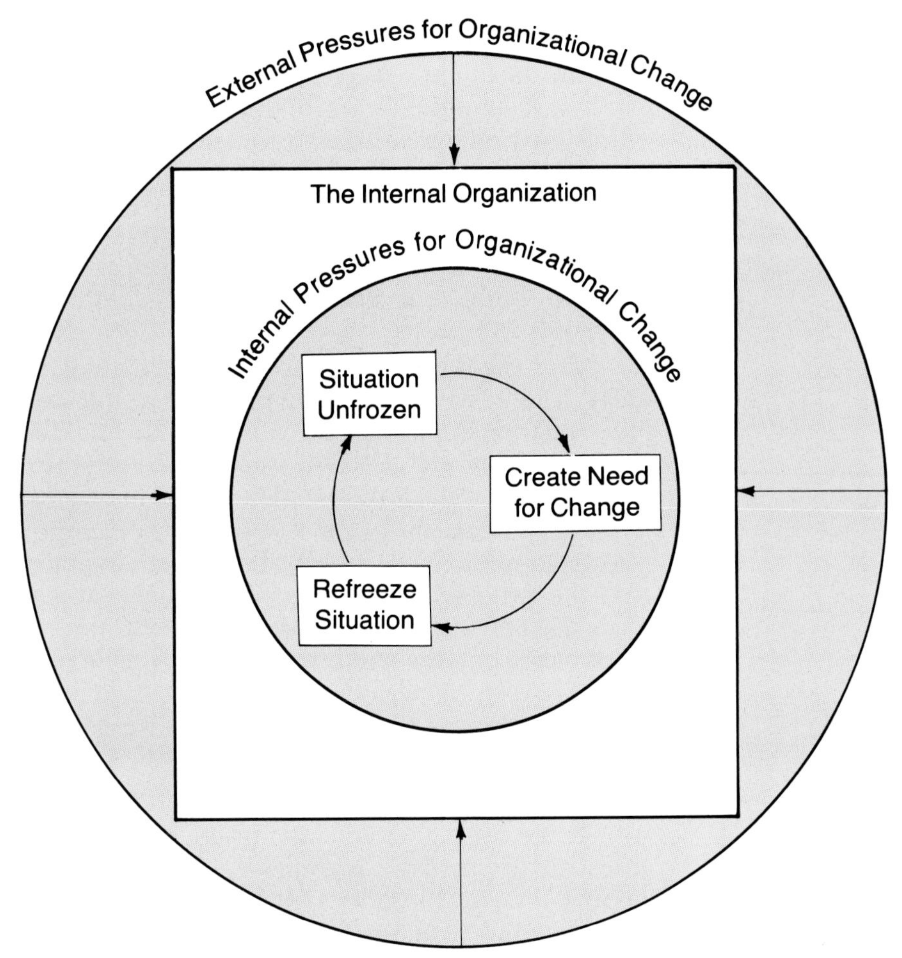

A Model for Change

Many years ago Kurt Lewin proposed a framework within which the process of change could be studied.[2] He and other researchers believed that three procedures were necessary for change to occur: first, the existing situation had to be *unfrozen;* next, the change agent (the supervisor) must work toward the desired change; then, the revised situation must be *refrozen*. This model, which is also illustrated in Exhibit 5.1, suggests that, in order for change to be undertaken effectively, it is first necessary to generate a need for change in the minds of staff members. During this process, the supervisor must show employees reasons for dissatisfaction with a current situation. A need for change might be developed by explaining reasons for it, increasing pressure for change (by using rewards and/or punishments), and/or by taking action to reduce employee resistance to change.

The process of working toward the desired change (step 2 in the model) generally requires that a supervisor attempt to modify employee behaviors and, at the same time, analyze affected policies and train staff in revised job methods and operating techniques. These tasks are easier when the supervisor has the respect of subordinates. They can also be done more effectively if the supervisor works first with those employees who are (a) highly respected by their peers and/or (b) informal group leaders. If employees are placed in job situations which confront them with new problems (or old problems which must be resolved with new methods), the process of change might, by necessity, be expedited. For example, an employee who does not want to use a new piece of equipment will likely have to use it when the older equipment is no longer available. In this instance, the employee has only two options—to continue to "fight" the equipment or to adapt by learning how, and for what, it is to be used.

After the desired change is implemented, stabilizing forces tend to create a new status quo. Lewin refers to this as the refreezing process.[3] New relationships may be established, and the new attitudes, procedures, policies, etc., become integrated with the remaining stabilized elements in the organization to define the new status quo.

While it simplifies the discussion of change to suggest that the process is comprised of three distinct parts, readers should understand (a) that the process of change is continual, (b) it is probably occurring at more than one point in the organization at the same time, and (c) that the steps of the process overlap.

A Close Look at Organizational Change

Three components of the organization can be changed: the people, the structure, and the technology. We know that each of these is closely related; a change in one is likely to affect the others. Supervisors should consider this principle when they plan change. They should recognize that it will be necessary to consider the entire organization as they plan and direct any change which, on the surface, seems to affect only one aspect. Normally, the greater the amount of change which is being planned, the greater the likelihood that other—or all—aspects of the organization will be affected. For example, consider first the implications of change on the organization when attempts are made to reach a new target market. Next, consider the impact of a new equipment item in the housekeeping or food and beverage department. In the first instance, it is likely that every department and work section within the property will be affected by such a significant change in marketing strategy. By contrast, perhaps only a few employees in a specific work station will be affected by the change in the replacement of the equipment.

Employees and Change

Supervisors often attempt to change employees' behavior by modifying their attitudes and/or improving their skills. Either changed attitudes or improved skills can create behavior change. Changes in behavior (job performance) can often result from training, reduction of environmental problems, or personnel administration activities (recall the performance analysis worksheet in Chapter 1). These efforts are frequently easier and more expedient than is the process of attempting to modify employee attitudes. As will be seen, coaching, counseling, appraisal, and related techniques may be helpful in the process of modifying employee attitudes. In working with groups, supervisors may try to change the attitudes and skills of employees through team-building activities or various types of group training programs. At the property-wide level, approaches to change employees might involve management by objectives (MBO) or various types of performance review programs which affect all employees within the organization. However, you should keep in mind that the process of changing employee attitudes will be, at best, difficult, even when techniques are applied by experienced supervisors.

Organizational Structures and Change

Organizational change can be brought about by revising chains of command, increasing—or decreasing—areas of responsibility for departments or positions, changing job descriptions, and other approaches. Organizations also can be changed through decentralization; that is, by establishing smaller, self-contained organizational units. Advantages to this approach include the increased possibility to motivate employees in the sub-unit and the ability to more carefully structure both the unit and the work of the employees within the unit to facilitate the performance of specific tasks. Another structural approach to change focuses on modifying the work flow within the organization. If the flow of work can be improved, employee productivity is likely to increase. For example, it is easy to envision how changes in the flow of work between the marketing, catering, and food and beverage departments in some lodging properties could help the management of banquet activities.

Technology and Change

New technology often creates the need for change within an organization. The many evolving computer applications for the hospitality industry serve as an example. Sometimes these changes are forced upon an organization. Today, for example, a hotel might need a modern, computerized reservations system in order to be competitive. In other instances, the organization itself desires technological change, as in the use of computerized beverage systems for added control in bar areas. Technological changes, like others, will affect personnel and structural aspects of the organization.

Reasons for Resistance to Change

Why is it often difficult to implement change? One reason is that people who feel comfortable in what they are doing will normally resist change; they want to maintain established routines. Employees are no exception; they will have a natural tendency to resist change as attempts are made to revise work procedures. The process to introduce change which we have reviewed can be effective in many instances. However, there will be employees who, for whatever reason, wish to follow precedents ("we have always done it this way—we have never done it that way") and defend the status quo. As a supervisor, you must understand the concept of resistance to change and know how to deal with it.

Economic Concerns

In some instances, change can have a severe economic impact on employees. Some employees might actually lose their jobs as organizational changes are implemented. In other situations, the employees may be greatly concerned about their job security.

Inconvenience

Changes can also mean inconvenience for employees who might have to learn new procedures, take on extra duties, and be closely supervised during trial, implementation, and evaluation periods. It is generally much easier to do things the old way than it is to be inconvenienced by changes.

Anxiety

Change often creates uncertainty and anxiety for affected employees; they feel threatened. This fear can be a major reason for resisting change. There is even uncertainty in "good news" about promotions or transfers to positions designed to train one for a promotion: "How hard will the new job be? Will I be able to do it? Will there still be a place for me in the organization if I do not succeed in the new job? What about my old friends?" These and related aspects of uncertainty hinder the introduction of change in many operations.

Relationships

As already suggested, change can threaten professional and personal relationships. Employees relate with other staff members and work groups on the job; they know about status, leaders and followers, task specialists, and other aspects of the current work groups. As changes occur on the job, patterns of personal and professional relationships may be affected. These and related social dimensions of change will influence the employees' desire to cooperate.

Control

Increased control over employees often accompanies change. We have noted that closer supervision may be required—at least initially. During such times the employees are "reminded" about "who the boss is." If change is being implemented because of needs to increase quality or reduce costs, some employees may resent the implication that the supervisor is not currently happy with worker performance.

Distrust

Employees who do not trust or respect their supervisors are likely to resist change. Perhaps changes have not been effective in the past: "Here comes another change, I wonder how long it will last!" may be a common thought. Clearly, the supervisor who tries one thing one day and another thing the next day is likely to be confronted with employees who will resist change. Some changes, however, are not initiated by the supervisor but are mandated by top management. Emphasis in the operation may change. Areas of concern today—about which changes might be proposed—may take a back seat to other priorities tomorrow. Employees recognize this and may attempt to resist change with the thought that the emphasis on the issue might "go away." The supervisor should recognize, however, that continual change, regardless of necessity, can frustrate employees.

Possible Benefits of Employee Resistance to Change

We have emphasized that employees frequently will resist change and that the effectiveness with which change is implemented is affected by the supervisor's ability to reduce resistance to change. There are, however, some possible benefits which can accrue from employee resistance to change. Consider the following:

- It forces supervisors to build a defense for change. Poorly thought-out changes might, therefore, be identified and avoided.
- To the extent that building a defense limits change, a stabilizing mechanism within the organization is provided. Impulsive decisions made by those in higher positions of authority will be tempered.
- Supervisors are required to think about the impact of a projected change on employees. In so doing, they may better satisfy individual needs and thereby help attain additional long-range objectives.
- Employee resistance to change may identify specific areas in which a change may create problems; this enables supervisors to take corrective action before more serious problems arise.
- Employees may think and talk more about proposed changes and, in the process, may better understand why they are necessary, especially when the supervisor involves the employees in coaching and counseling sessions.

Analyzing Change: The Employee's Perspective

We have been discussing reasons why people may resist change. There are, however, other times when change is desired. If, for example, employees readily see that changes will be beneficial to them personally—such as when their work may be made easier, pay raises are likely to result, or where relationships with others will be enhanced—change is not likely to be resisted; in fact, it is likely to be sought.

Change in behavior is likely to be the result of the individual's perceptions of why change should—and should not—be made.[4] For any change that is proposed, there may be, from an employee's perspective, good and bad aspects to it. Consider this example: the front office man-

Exhibit 5.2 Change: the Employee's Perspective

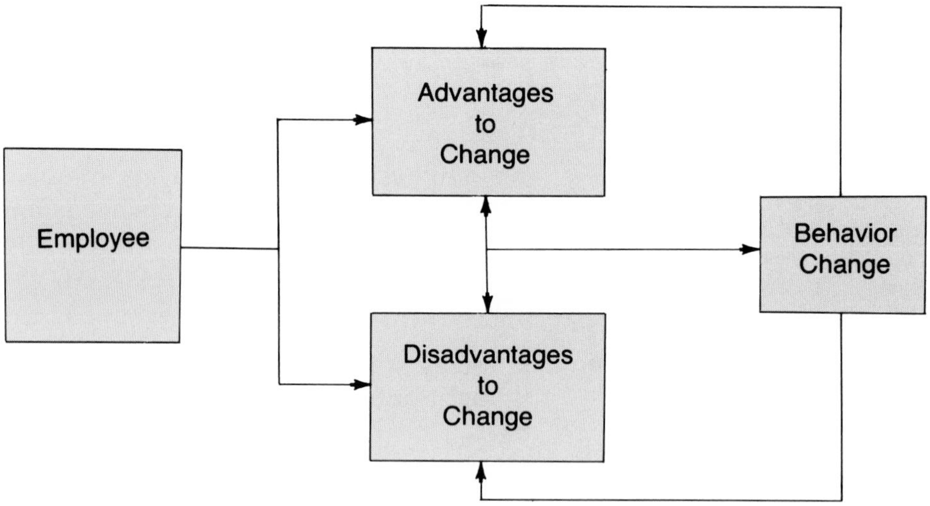

ager wants to change the way that reservations are handled. An employee might view the situation in the following way:

Advantages

1. The front office manager will like me more if I cooperate.
2. My work might be easier.
3. The way it's done now is cumbersome.

Disadvantages

1. No extra pay will result.
2. But I'll have to make an effort to learn the new procedures.
3. There's no assurance the new method will be, in any way, better for me.

The employee's view of the proposed change is, then, the result of these perceptions of advantages and disadvantages. This is shown in Exhibit 5.2. Based upon how these seem to affect the employee, some behavior will result. If the disadvantages to change are seen to be more powerful than the advantages, behavioral change is unlikely. If, however, the advantages outweigh disadvantages, change is likely. If behavior is changed, the advantages and disadvantages can be evaluated in terms of how the employee actually was affected. If the employee is, in retro-

Exhibit 5.3 Employee Response to Change

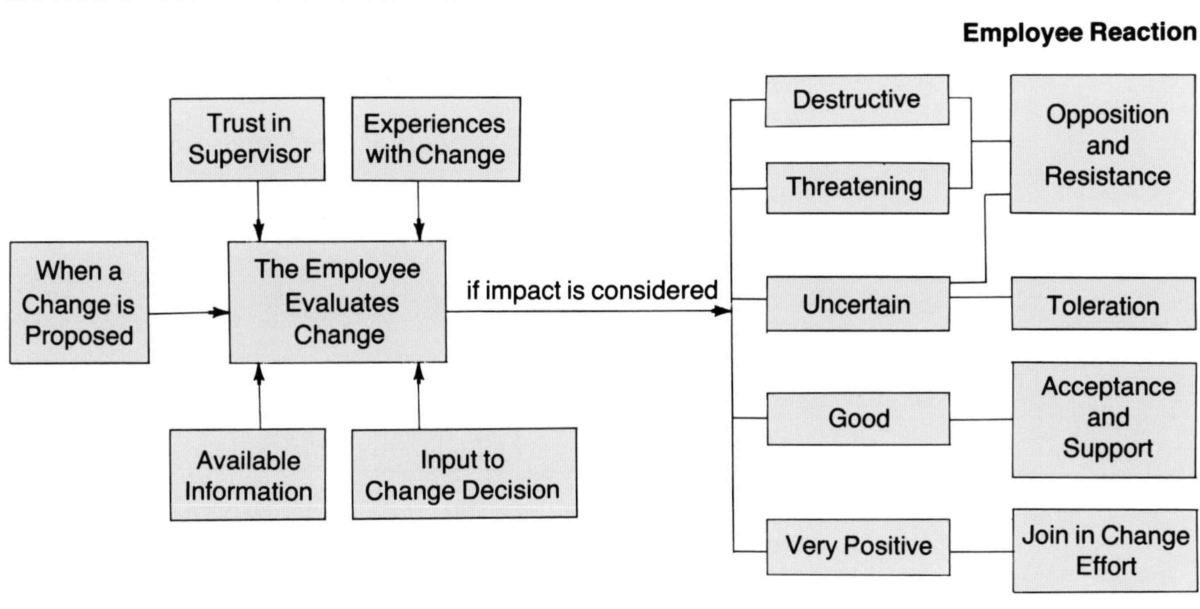

spect, favored by the change, a new status quo can be established. If, however, behavior is judged to be disadvantageous to the employee, it will not continue (or, at least, a very awkward transitional period can be expected by the supervisor).

We have seen that the supervisor has a most important role to play in gaining acceptance to change. In many instances, changes are initiated by the supervisor; on other occasions changes that are required by higher management levels must be implemented. Exhibit 5.3 reviews factors and implications that are important in determining what employee response to change will be. When a change is proposed, the employee evaluates the change based upon the:

- Extent to which he/she trusts the supervisor
- Employee's past experiences with change in the work environment
- Implications of the change, given available information
- Extent to which employee input to the change decision has been solicited

Based upon these and related factors, the employee might consider the impact of the change to be:

1. Destructive—the employee will likely oppose and resist change.

2. Threatening—the same employee reaction (opposition and resistance) can be expected.

3. Uncertain—the best the supervisor can expect is that the employee will tolerate the change.

4. Good—acceptance and support of the change can be expected.

5. Very positive—the supervisor can expect the employee to join in the change effort.

Overcoming Resistance to Change

Supervisors should recognize the many factors noted in this chapter as they develop strategies to cope with change—especially employee resistance to change. There are several techniques which can be used in an effort to overcome resistance to change.[5]

Know What's Involved

Recognize the factors involved in the change situation. The supervisor who knows his/her employees and uses this information to modify leadership styles in order to meet the needs of the situation probably has a good start. Try to look at the situation from the employees' perspective. How would you feel about it if you were an employee? What could make you feel differently about the need for change?

Encourage Employee Participation

Utilize principles of employee participation. Employees who are involved in the decision-making process leading to change will more likely accept change than those who are "kept in the dark." By making employees aware of a problem and giving them an opportunity to generate resolution methods, the supervisor is, at the least, recognizing employee concerns. To the extent that employee input can be used (with modification if necessary) to develop and select alternatives, it can also be helpful in the subsequent implementation phase (since resistance to change is likely to be lower).

Recognize Past Problems

Recognize the employees' past experience with change in the organization. If there have been problems with changes before—ideas did not work out, unexpected results occurred, employees were hurt by changes in unexpected ways, etc.—it will be difficult to convince employees that additional changes will be beneficial. Our past experiences influence our reactions to present and/or future expectations. The supervisor with a history of problems in implementing change will most likely need to gain the support of informal group leaders, or upper management levels, as change is implemented. New supervisors will do well to delay changes, if possible, for some time during which they can observe (a) existing employee relationships, (b) factors influencing the way work is being done, and (c) exactly how standard operating procedures are carried out. Time will be necessary to generate and carefully evaluate alternative procedures and plans which are to be implemented.

Accent the Benefits

Increase pressures for change. Show employees how the change will be better for them. If several employees can be won over, they can exert peer pressure, which can be a useful technique to reduce the resistance to change exhibited by other staff members.

Eliminate Problems

Eliminate resisting factors. If the supervisor can discover why employees are opposing a change, it might be possible to adjust plans to eliminate these problems. Likewise, if reasons which support the status quo are not justifiable, correct information may be helpful to educate the employees. The need to explain, defend, and justify reasons for changes—from the employees' perspective when possible—is critical to the process of implementing change.

Be Sure It's Necessary

Make changes only when necessary. "Change for change's sake" is never warranted.

Implementing Change: The Supervisor's Role

Establish Trust

Perhaps the most important factor in implementing change successfully is for the supervisor to have developed an atmosphere of trust and respect in all of his/her past experiences with the employees. Many employees are more likely to respond favorably to changes when they trust the supervisor; that is, when they agree with the supervisor's stated reasons for the change and when they also concur with his/her assessment of the employee benefits to be gained from the change. A supervisor cannot, however, develop an atmosphere of trust simply for the purpose of implementing change. Rather, a long history of honesty, fairness, and concern for employees must precede the development of a positive attitude toward the supervisor; as this occurs, the relationship will carry over in the acceptance of change.

Interact with Employees

Effective two-way communication—interacting with employees—is also important. Not only must reasons for changes be communicated to employees, but ideas about the "what, when, how, and who" for change must come from affected employees. Employees may be resisting change because of a fear of the unknown. This can be reduced or eliminated simply by providing appropriate information to those both directly and indirectly involved in the change.

Involve Employees

We have already noted that it is important for the individual employee to become involved in the change process. This must begin at the time changes are contemplated (employees may have ideas about alternatives), continues to the actual decision-making process (employee input should be solicited), and concludes with the employee's involvement in the trial, modification, and evaluation processes. The point is that some, but not all, employees may wish to become involved and, to the extent possible, these employees should become partners with the supervisor in the task necessary to implement changes.

Deal with Economic Concerns

You have learned that economic concerns about proposed change are likely to be important to employees. It is critical that supervisors understand the economic implications of proposed changes and, through effective communication procedures, inform employees about them. If employees realize there are no economic disadvantages to the change and, in fact, there are advantages for them, they will be more receptive to the change. Supervisors should practice their skills of thinking about change—and how to discuss it—from the employees' perspective. This will help identify major issues to discuss and resolve with employees.

Use Authority

In some situations a supervisor's use of authority may be helpful—or all that is necessary—to implement change effectively. Recall, for example, that if the leader has strong position power, supervises in very structured situations, and has poor relationships with employees, the use of authority may be one of the few tools available (see Chapter 3). At the very least, supervisors must be certain they have the authority (power) to make decisions and to implement changes.

Be Persuasive

In other situations, persuasive leadership techniques may be helpful. For example, during an individual counseling session the supervisor might discover reasons for employee resistance. Once these are known, problems with the employee's reasoning can be identified, proper information can be supplied, and reasons why change will be beneficial to the employee can be explained. Using this approach with informal group leaders and influential others might make them "salespersons" for the change.

Conduct Training

Employee training programs are often necessary. At the very least, new procedures and other work requirements must be explained to employees. Additionally, if the training is initiated with informational and persuasive techniques designed to reduce resistance to change, such programs can be even more valuable.

Involve Groups

Involving both formal and informal employee groups in the decision-making process is also useful. We have noted that employee participation in the change process is beneficial. This input can be generated by groups as well as individuals. Some supervisors find the technique of "buzz sessions" helpful. For example, the supervisor explains the problem to the group and solutions are solicited. All members of the group offer suggestions. Advantages and disadvantages are discussed. The results are new ideas which can be utilized, or at least considered, by the supervisor as decisions are made. Again, since the employees have been involved in the process, the decision and the subsequent change are viewed as "our" ideas–not "the supervisor's" ideas.

Exhibit 5.4 reviews helpful procedures for initiating change. As Exhibit 5.4 shows, the supervisor will need to implement change when

Exhibit 5.4 Supervisor's Steps to Implement Change

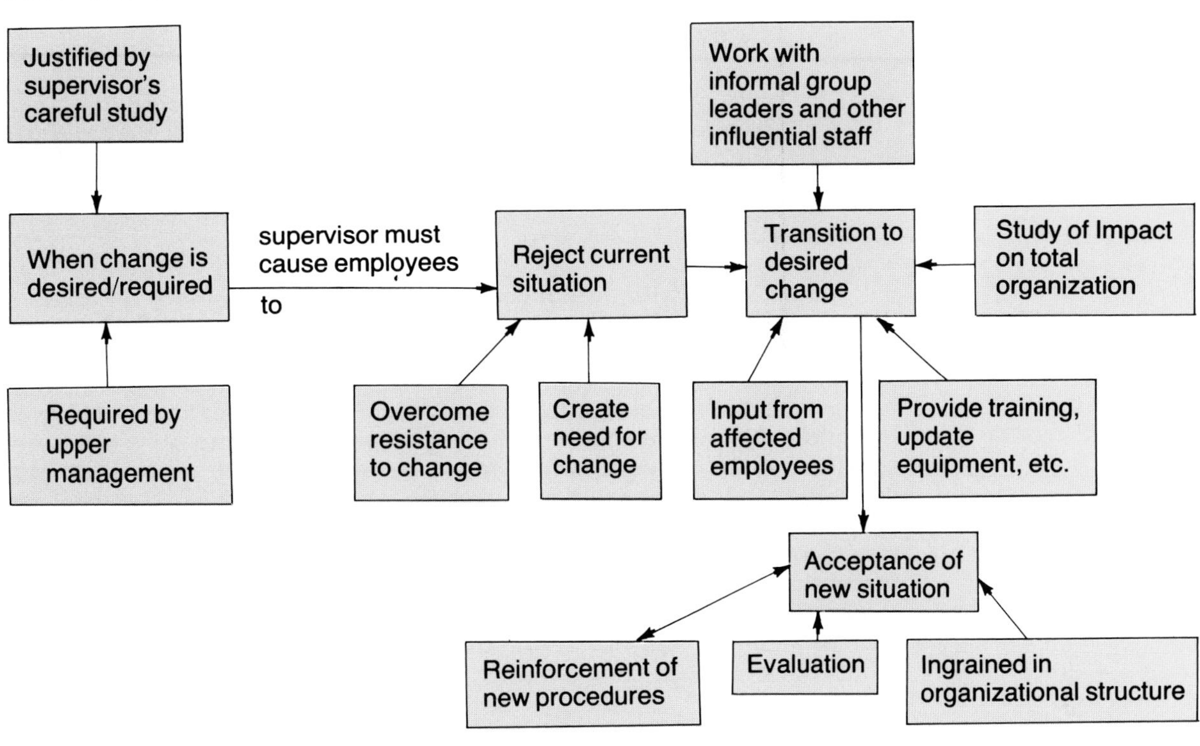

(a) he/she determines its necessity after careful study or (b) change is required by upper management. In order for change to occur, the supervisor must first cause employees to reject the current situation. This is done by practicing techniques designed to overcome resistance to change and, at the same time, by creating from the employee's perspective a need for change. Second, the supervisor must lead the employees through a transition to the desired change. This is done by working with informal group leaders and influential others, by seeking input from employees, by training, and by providing necessary equipment. Likewise, there is a need at this point to assess the impact of the change on the total organization. If this procedure can be successfully undertaken, the supervisor can gain employee and organizational acceptance of the new situation. Revised procedures must be reinforced, activities must be evaluated and, in the process, the changes become the new status quo.

Evaluation of Change

Evaluation of the changes which have been implemented serves several purposes:

- to see if the change is effective (does it yield the required results?);

- to assess whether any additional changes are necessary to increase organizational effectiveness;
- to assess whether the change has created any spin-off problems;
- to analyze the procedures by which changes have been made (perhaps the task can be simplified when the process is again necessary).

Indicators of Effective Change

Often, the evaluation of change is not easy. A primary reason is that necessary information for the evaluation is either unavailable, inaccurate, or the exact results of the change are not stated in measurable terms. For example, if changes are designed to "increase productivity," how much must the productivity increase in order for the supervisor to be satisfied with the change? The importance of stating objectives, or **indicators of effective change**, must be emphasized. The difficulty of evaluation does not modify the need for the supervisor to assume responsibility for completing it. In instances where objective measurement is not possible, supervisors can, at the least, be alert to the possibility that further change might be necessary. To the extent that differences between what is observed and what is desired can be seen, it is possible that the change has not been successful; that is, it did not accomplish what was expected.

The Change Cycle

Recall our earlier point that the results of changes become the new status quo; employee (and supervisory) resistance to change will develop in defense of the revised procedure; the entire change cycle will then need to be repeated. This process is illustrated in Exhibit 5.5. Over time, the current job situation (which is a function of the organizational structure, existing work procedures, and currently employed staff members) will be influenced by external and internal factors which will force changes in the job situation. The change process will evolve. Supervisors will need to overcome employee resistance to change, and changes will need to be implemented. This process will yield a revised job situation which will itself, over time, be influenced by external and internal factors requiring change. In this respect, then, the process is cyclical. Note also that the process occurs at different organizational levels and affects differing work procedures, staff members, and organizational levels at the same time.

The supervisor, in order to effectively perform his/her job, must make decisions and implement change. Even if these changes are good and needed—by the supervisor, the organization, and the property—they will likely be difficult to implement. The supervisor, acting in the role of change agent, must be able to reduce employee resistance to change and must use professional techniques to implement and evaluate revisions in work procedures, rules, policies, equipment, and other matters which affect how well goals are attained. Exhibit 5.6 reviews many of the factors that must be incorporated into the process by which change is managed by the supervisor.

Exhibit 5.5 The Cyclical Process of Change

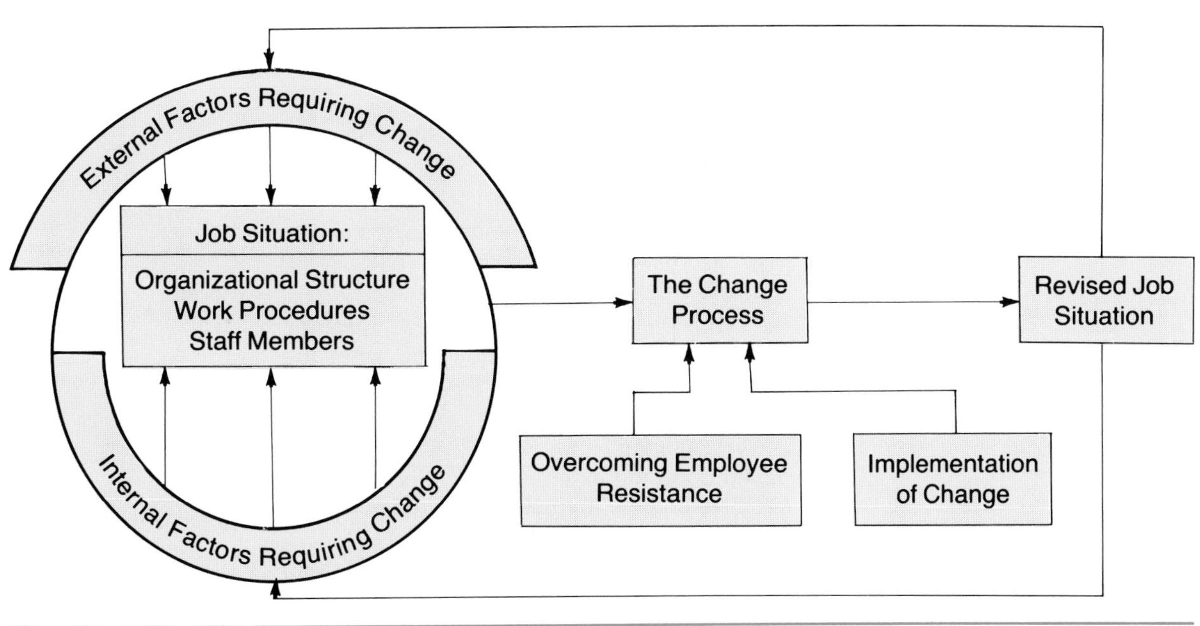

Exhibit 5.6 Supervisor's Checklist for Implementing Change

		Yes	No
1.	Is change necessary?	☐	☐
2.	Do you completely understand—from your perspective as a supervisor—why the change is necessary—and what exactly it is supposed to do?	☐	☐
3.	Do you think about possible reasons why employees might resist the change—and develop effective counter arguments for these reasons?	☐	☐
4.	Do you use an individual counseling technique to discuss the change and its implication with each affected employee?	☐	☐
5.	Do you use a persuasive technique to discover employee perceptions of disadvantages—and to counter these with information which will help employees see advantages to the change?	☐	☐
6.	Do you involve group leaders—both formal and informal—and request their help in gaining acceptance to change?	☐	☐
7.	Do you use a trial approach (test the proposed change and then modify it as necessary) rather than implement it on an "all or nothing" basis?	☐	☐

		Yes	No
8.	Do you make sure that affected employees know what must be done differently before changes are implemented?	☐	☐
9.	Do you provide carefully designed training experiences before changes are implemented?	☐	☐
10.	Do you carefully supervise employees during the awkward transitional period when changes are being implemented?	☐	☐
11.	Do you develop indicators of effective change that measurably describe what the situation should be after the changes are made?	☐	☐
12.	Do you evaluate the results of the change based upon the extent to which indicators of effective change are seen in the network situation?	☐	☐
13.	Do you try to recognize any benefits that may result from employee resistance to change?	☐	☐
14.	Do you know how to generate a need for change?	☐	☐
15.	Do you have the respect of the employees who must change?	☐	☐
16.	Do you have a good track record for implementing change with few surprises for employees?	☐	☐
17.	Do you know what other changes are occurring in the organization at this time?	☐	☐
18.	Do you know the impact of the proposed change on other departments?	☐	☐
19.	Do you have necessary training programs already planned and in place?	☐	☐
20.	Do you know whether existing work flows will be improved as a result of the change?	☐	☐
21.	Do you know whether the situation requiring change is of continuing importance to the organization?	☐	☐
22.	Are all employees permitted, to the extent possible, to participate in all activities relating to the change?	☐	☐
23.	Do you know what you can and should do to increase pressure for change?	☐	☐
24.	Do you have all the information you need to make the change?	☐	☐

NOTES

1. Robert M. Fulmer, *Supervision: Principles of Professional Management* (Beverly Hills, Calif.: Glencoe Press, 1976), p. 352.

2. Kurt Lewin, *Frontiers in Group Dynamics: Human Relations Concept, Method, and Reality in Social Science*, vol. 1, no. 1, 1947, pp. 5-41.

3. Lewin, *Frontiers in Group Dynamics*, pp. 5-41.

4. Kurt Lewin, "Group Decisions and Social Change," in *Readings in Social Psychology*, 3rd ed., Maccoby, Eleanore E., et al. (New York: Holt, Rinehart, Winston, 1958), pp. 197-211. Lewin uses the term "force fields" to discuss the impact of driving forces, which encourage change, and restraining forces, which encourage people to resist change.

5. This discussion is based on Fulmer, pp. 356-360.

PAGE TEN

Supervision at the Brandywine Room

Stacey Francis was enjoying her job as dining room manager. After several months on the job she felt she was a valued employee. Not only was she a technical specialist—she knew most everything about all positions in the dining room—but she also was becoming a good supervisor. She could perform all tasks which the previous dining room manager had performed and she was developing a list of many procedural changes which, once implemented, would make further improvements.

Stacey had realized very early in her new position that changes, even when necessary, could not be made arbitrarily. As an employee, she had seen times when proposed changes were implemented smoothly, other times when supervisors had faced real problems before implementation was possible, and still other occasions when proposed changes were withdrawn because of extensive resistance to them. Now she wondered what she could learn from these experiences that would help her to become a better change agent.

Stacey soon found herself in a situation requiring the use of techniques to manage change. A new automated data processor/cash register which had been on order for months had finally arrived. It had been hooked up, debugged, and was working well—except that Sarah, a cashier who had been in the operation for a long time, was upset. She told Stacey (and her own peers) that the new equipment was unnecessary, did not work, and slowed down the job of processing guest checks.

Stacey knew that Sarah's resistance to change was, from the property's perspective, unwarranted, and decided to resolve the problem before it got worse.

While reviewing some class notes and other materials, she came across the "Supervisor's Checklist for Implementing Change" (see Exhibit 5.6 in this chapter). She decided to use it as a base for action to modify the employee's concern about the change.

As she worked through the checklist, she saw how it could be helpful:

1. Stacey knew that the change to the new equipment was necessary. She knew about the problems caused by the use of the old cash register and she was convinced that the new equipment would resolve these problems and not cause any others (Questions 1 and 2).

2. Stacey knew that Sarah was not familiar with and was afraid of computerized equipment. Without some study and a change in current procedures, the new equipment could not be properly used. A cashier who did not know how to use it properly would certainly slow guest check processing (Question 3).

3. Stacey had coffee with Sarah and privately discussed how the new equipment actually could make work easier for her (since a lot of manual paperwork traditionally done by the cashier was now eliminated). This explanation seemed unnecessary, however, when Sarah explained that the steps for processing guest checks were confusing to her, but she did not want to let her younger peers know this. Stacey then suggested some additional training—which she herself would provide during some beginning and end-of- shift slow periods (Question 4).

4. Stacey knew that, as Sarah's supervisor, the responsibility for gaining acceptance to the change rested with her; Stacey did not need to involve others. She also knew that, unfortunately, it was not possible to use a "trial approach" to making the change. The new equipment had been installed; it had to be used (Questions 5, 6, and 7).

5. Stacey knew that Sarah had attended the training sessions given before the new equipment was "on-line"; she also recalled talking to her at a later point (but Stacey had not been told about these concerns at that time). It appeared that the training sessions should have more carefully addressed employee attitudes about the equipment—rather than focusing on skills required for its use (Questions 8 and 9).

6. Stacey realized the need to work closely with Sarah during the next several weeks. She saw that a careful step-by-step review of proper procedures—emphasizing voids and use of product keys (which the cashier had said was confusing) —was in

order. During their conversation Stacey had listed special concerns voiced by Sarah—each of which could be addressed in a short refresher session at the beginning of Sarah's next shift. Stacey believed that, once these matters were addressed, Sarah would have no difficulty using the equipment properly (Questions 10 and 11).

7. Since Stacey now knew what the problems were, she knew what needed to be done—and how to tell whether Sarah would benefit from the "mini-training sessions" which she was planning. Likewise, Stacey had learned that more explaining and employee training would be necessary as other new equipment/procedures were installed/implemented. This was, in fact, a benefit which had evolved from Sarah's resistance to the change (Questions 12 and 13).

8. Stacey was reasonably certain that Sarah was the only cashier who disliked the new equipment. From prior experience, she believed that Sarah respected her—both in terms of her professional abilities and her follow-through on promises which had been made (Questions 14 and 15).

9. Sarah had told Stacey that, in the past, there had been no surprises when other changes were implemented. This supported Stacey's belief that Sarah did, in fact, respect her (Question 16).

10. Stacey checked to confirm that no other changes were being planned which would affect the operation of the equipment. Once procedures were learned, Stacey knew they could be used for some time. Likewise, the Accounting Department had been involved in planning for the equipment, and how its output should be used, since the equipment was first suggested; that department would not be attempting to interfere with, or confuse, procedures for operation which Stacey had taught and would reteach to Sarah (Questions 17 and 18).

11. Stacey had already decided to spend additional time with Sarah to, first, go over each step in the operation of the equipment and, second, to emphasize how to deal with voids, product key, and other identified problems. This special training would begin immediately (Question 19).

12. Stacey knew that these special efforts were in order. Work flow would be improved and the dining area and entire food and beverage operation would benefit (Questions 20 and 21).

13. At the time the computerized equipment was initially pro-

posed, Stacey had talked with formal and informal group leaders; she also had conducted an employee informational meeting to discuss the proposed equipment. While there had been some discussion, the cashier now needing additional training had not spoken about any concerns. Likewise, during the intervening months between equipment order and installation, no concerns were voiced by the employee. Stacey had learned from this experience that, just because concerns are not voiced, this does not necessarily mean that the employee will cooperate as changes are implemented (Question 22).

14. Stacey was confident that there was no further need to pressure Sarah about the change. Training would resolve the problem. She was confident that she had access to all information necessary to effectively implement the change (Questions 23 and 24).

Stacey knew that she would be a better supervisor as a result of this experience. Yes, it would take time to retrain Sarah; some of this training may not have been necessary if she would have more carefully considered this cashier's—and the other employees'—concerns as the original planning evolved. She also knew, however, that change could be implemented effectively by applying human relations skills, providing training, and demonstrating effective leadership.

Part II:

The Supervisor and the Personnel Administration Process

Part I has presented background information about the supervisor and the process of management. We are now aware of the responsibilities and duties of a supervisor and about the impact of various types of leadership styles on supervisory effectiveness. We have reviewed how the supervisor undertakes work analysis and design procedures to improve work and, finally, we have seen how supervisors manage change.

It is now time to look at the supervisor's role in the personnel administration process. Large properties may have a personnel department whose responsibilities include many of these activities.

Small properties will not; more of the work will fall on the shoulders of line management staff. In either case, the supervisor must be involved.

The supervisor works with people. He/she needs the best possible employees in order to attain organizational goals. Employee recruitment and selection techniques must be designed to bring qualified, reliable employees into the property, and procedures for alerting applicants to job vacancies must be developed.

Although it happens often in the hospitality industry, employees should not be "forced into" new work positions without an introduction to the job. Employees' first impressions are likely to affect their attitudes about the job and the property. Organized orientation and training programs not only generate positive attitudes, but help the employees perform more effectively. There are many things that the supervisor can do to ensure that orientation and training are meaningful to the employees and beneficial to the organization.

The job of the supervisor includes evaluating employee performance. Detailed procedures for the design and implementation of an employee performance review must be in effect. To the extent possible, subjective methods should be replaced with objective procedures. Employees must know in advance the standards against which they will be evaluated. Traditional approaches, in which performance review programs are ineffective or nonexistent, must give way to planned activities which are part of the supervisor's ongoing responsibilities.

Wage and salary administration is central to the personnel administration process. Policies regarding wages and salaries must be fair, not arbitrary, and must be applied consistently throughout the organization. Supervisors need to be familiar with benefit programs, legal implications, and other aspects of wage and salary administration.

6 Staff Recruitment and Selection Procedures

PAGE ELEVEN

Supervision at the Brandywine Room

Stacey Francis worked in a hotel that had a Personnel Department. Therefore, many of the activities involving the recruitment and selection of staff members needed for the Brandywine Room were handled by that department. She knew that many supervisors—including herself—did not know how the Personnel Department operated. Many times the supervisors were not satisfied with the job applicants they were sent. Even when the supervisors selected the "best" applicant from those referred by the Personnel Department, they felt that there "was not much to choose from."

In her eight months as dining room manager, Stacey had to hire eight new employees to keep her staff of 35 full- and part-time dining room positions filled. During that time she had some good luck and some bad luck. When she was busy learning her new job, she did not have time to question how applicants were referred to her. Now, since things had calmed down, she wanted to learn more about it.

After discussing her plan with Mr. George and after getting a lot of basic information from him, Stacey received permission to make an appointment with Rachel Case, the personnel director. She wanted to get some general information, and she wanted some specific questions answered. Armed with her notebook pad and questions, she arrived at Ms. Case's office about five minutes before the scheduled appointment.

Supervisors must direct the activities of employees who have been recruited and selected. Careful attention must be given to the process by which these individuals are "brought on board." Applicants most qualified for positions should be selected. While this is easy to say, in practice it is often difficult to do.

Frequently, in large operations, there is a personnel department which serves in an advisory capacity to the line departments where supervisors work. Among other tasks, the personnel department helps supervisors define the type of persons needed to work in the supervisor's department. The personnel department staff can recruit applicants from many sources, administer various screening tools in the selection process, and make recommendations to line departments about applicants most likely to succeed. However, the line department—not the personnel department—should make the final selection. From that point, the supervisor must assume responsibility for orientation, training, supervision, evaluation, and related personnel activities.

The Supervisor's Role in Recruitment and Selection

We already have indicated that the supervisor has a great deal of responsibility—and several tasks to perform—in the recruitment and selection of staff. In some operations, however, supervisors depend on the personnel department. Attitudes such as: "They are going to send me who they want," "What do I know—they are the specialists at finding people," and "They do not care about my problems," etc., are prevalent in many hospitality operations. The point made earlier must be reemphasized: the personnel department should provide the supervisor whatever assistance is needed to help find the most qualified applicants for a vacant position. From that point, it is the supervisor's and not the personnel department's responsibility to make a selection.

A small hospitality operation probably will not have a personnel department. These functions may be assumed by top management staff, a specific individual within the department seeking an applicant, or by the supervisor. Whether or not there is a personnel department in the property, the basic procedures and principles which should be used are the same.

There are several important activities that are part of the supervisor's role in the recruitment and selection process:

1. The supervisor—perhaps working with the personnel department in larger properties—must define job tasks. It is important that all parties, including the applicant, know exactly what the job involves. This must start with and be the ultimate responsibility of the supervisor. The tool used to define a job is called a job description, which will be discussed later in this chapter.

2. The supervisor, working with personnel department specialists if applicable, must define the personal qualities needed for employees to perform adequately in a job. For example, the

supervisor must know if a cook has to read and perform basic arithmetic calculations when he/she works with recipes. In the housekeeping department, the supervisor should know if there are special physical abilities needed to work with cleaning equipment, move furniture, and perform similar activities. This information should be developed into a selection tool called a job specification.

3. Supervisors also must know and understand the basic procedures used in the property to recruit and select employees. What are the responsibilities of the supervisor? How much lead time is needed to fill a vacant position? What advice can the supervisor give about where to look for eligible employees? All policies and procedures required by the property for use in personnel recruitment and selection should be followed at all times.

4. In small properties without a personnel department, the supervisor might be involved in such tasks as initial interviewing, contacting references, and related selection tasks.

5. In properties with a personnel department, the supervisor should interview the top candidate sent by the department. A meeting between the supervisor and prospective employee is critical so they can discuss job-related matters and resolve pressing questions.

6. At times, the supervisor may administer selection tests. If an experienced food server is being hired, for example, he/she should be tested on carrying a loaded service tray. An experienced room attendant should be able to answer questions relating to proper procedures for cleaning bathrooms, making beds, etc.

7. The supervisor should be involved in the actual selection. Depending on the property, this may mean making a recommendation to the manager at the next higher organizational level. In any case, the supervisor's advice should be considered as the selection is made.

The role of the supervisor in selecting staff members must be active and assertive, not passive. The supervisor must get work done through the people he/she supervises. Since this is the case, it only makes sense that the supervisor should play an important role in employee selection.

Planning for Human Resource Needs

In many hospitality operations, needs are matched through use of the "warm body syndrome." Due to limited economic resources and a failure to plan ahead, personnel are not hired until a vacancy occurs or a problem arises that must be resolved by adding a new staff member. Of course, there are times when this must occur, such as when an employee quits without giving notice or business increases unexpectedly. In these situations, the supervisor has had no advance warning about the need for new or additional staff members. The pressure of time prohibits the leisurely implementation of the many procedures in the personnel selection process. When a position is vacant under emergency circumstances, literally the first "warm body" who applies for the position is hired. That is the reason many of the personnel-related problems in the hospitality industry—such as turnover, lack of trainable personnel, and problems related to accidents and absenteeism, among others—can be traced to a lack of planning human resource needs.

The first-line supervisor undoubtedly has little voice in decisions relating to the development of personnel administration policies within the property. However, to the extent that jobs are organized effectively, training programs are assembled logically to use professional procedures, and leadership styles recognize the individuality of employees, the supervisor can better help the new employee adjust to the job and perform efficiently in the shortest possible time.

Emergency Approach

A simple approach for resolving emergency recruitment/selection problems involves keeping an active file on hand of potentially eligible, prescreened employees. If applicants "walk in" looking for a job at a time when none is available, they should be allowed to fill out an application blank and participate in a preliminary interview. This practice builds a file of applicants which can become the basis for recruitment efforts when position vacancies occur. For example, if there is an emergency need for an experienced front desk clerk, persons with applications on file can be called to find out if they are interested in the position.

Long-Range Approach

Some properties use a long-range approach to planning for human resource needs. Long-range plans become important when key personnel retire or leave, when the property undertakes an aggressive expansion program, and as the property attempts to comply with equal employment opportunity/affirmative action and related programs. Long-range plans help ensure that an adequate number of qualified personnel will be available at the right time to perform needed jobs.

Human resource planning should be ongoing. The plans must be modified and updated as changes evolve. The plans must include not only an assessment of the number and type of positions which will be required, but also a review of activities such as recruitment, selection, training, performance reviews, and others that must be undertaken to meet the personnel needs of the organization.

Some of the reasons why human resource planning is necessary have already been noted. Additional reasons include:

1. The property must be able to cope with change. Job content and skill requirements change as organizations evolve. Plans are needed to ensure that these changes are anticipated and related problems resolved.

2. Frequently there is a shortage of staff, especially highly talented employees. Other organizations compete with the hospitality property for highly qualified personnel. Therefore, the lead time required to employ these staff members—or to upgrade personnel within the organization—can be lengthy.

3. Promotion and replacement programs must be planned. What must a property do to keep a highly qualified employee? How does the property go about filling the positions vacated by retiring senior executives?

4. Human resource planning is one aspect of an overall strategic planning program. In today's competitive business environment, it is critical that organizations "look down the road" to develop long-range goals and plan strategies to attain them.

5. Planning for long-range personnel needs can provide a foundation for considering all aspects of personnel-related programs such as recruitment, selection, and training.

Procedures for Human Resource Planning

Procedures in the human resource planning process apply to any category of personnel. Frequently the process is not used, or it is undertaken only for management-level staff and other technical specialists. Since it is becoming more difficult to find qualified employees at all organizational levels, careful planning of labor needs might be warranted. Because human resource planning must be linked with the overall strategic plans for the organization, an analysis of goals and plans is the first step.

Review Long-Range Goals and Plans

The organizational long-range goals and plans must be known. For example, what political, economic, social, and technological factors will affect the organization during the next few years? What are the desires of top management? What are the strengths and weaknesses of the company? What long-range strategies are necessary to attain long-range goals? When these and related questions have been answered, top management can develop objectives and operate programs to attain these aims. Once this is done, managers will have a foundation upon which human resource planning can be built.

Assess the Current Situation

After the long- and short-range plans and goals are known, an "inventory" should be taken of personnel within the organization. This may include all personnel in high management levels and other selected job categories. This inventory will be used when comparing future needs with existing levels of available human resources. The process also will enable managers to identify talented in-house staff members who should be considered for higher-level job vacancies when they occur. This kind of up-to-date information also can be useful in the organization's equal employment opportunities program.

Exhibit 6.1 Planning for Human Resource Needs

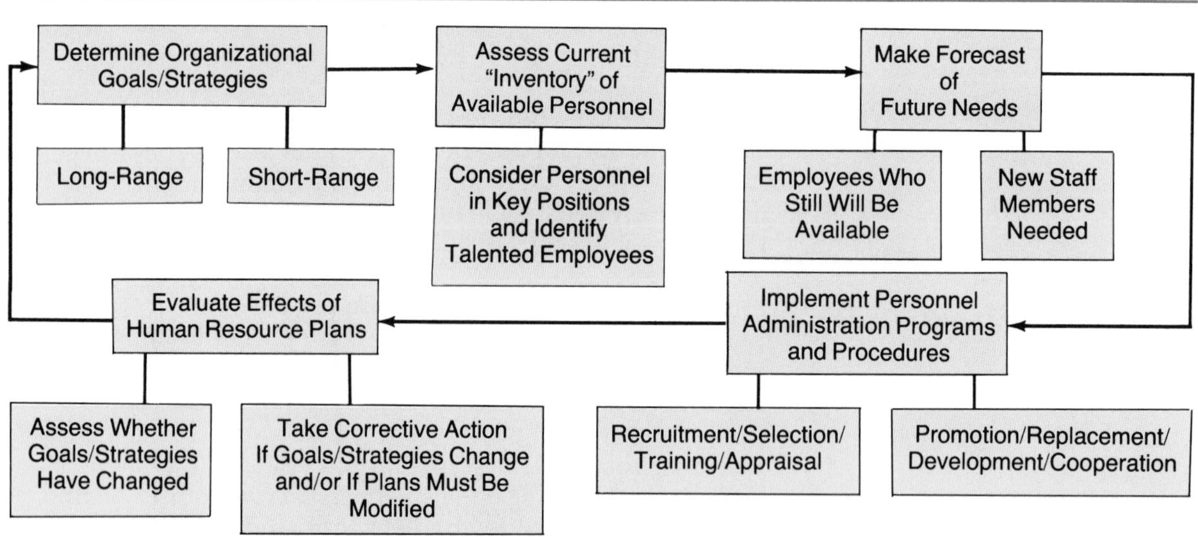

Forecast Personnel Needs

An analysis of the personnel requirements indicated in the long-range plans should determine the number and type of employees needed in various positions. The forecast should not only indicate the number of personnel needed by position, but should also review the numbers and types of employees presently with the organization who will be available during the time covered in the plan. The forecast also should specify the number and types of positions for which additional recruitment and selection will be necessary. The development of personnel forecasts involves the use of judgment and experience and an analysis of long-range budgetary implications and other key factors, such as union restraints, productivity increases, and business volume.

Put the Plan into Effect

A comparison of the current employment figures for each position with the number of employees needed will determine the number of employees who must be recruited, selected, and trained during the period covered by the plan. Procedures for undertaking personnel administration tasks must be developed and constantly modified in order to be effective and to ensure that the organizational needs outlined in the forecast can be met.

Modify the Plan

Long-range goals may have to be changed and other problems may arise which require adjustments in the strategic plan. Changes in the current number of available employees, errors in the forecast of future personnel requirements, and other possibilities confirm the need for periodic evaluation, audit, and adjustment of the human resource plan.

Exhibit 6.1 reviews the process of human resource planning. As stated earlier, supervisors may not be involved in this process. In fact, many properties do not even plan for long-range personnel needs. If this is the case, such programs may be developed in the future and some supervisory advice on the process may be warranted.

The Supervisor and Human Resource Planning

The same procedures for human resource planning at the organizational level also can be utilized with modification by a supervisor employed in a specific department or work section. It is important that long- and short-range strategies and goals of the specific work unit be known. These can then be matched with the skills represented by available personnel. If the impact of the organizational goals on the supervisor's department/work section is known, the supervisor can assess the future needs for employees for whom he/she is responsible. The same questions can be asked: How many employees currently on staff will be available in the future? How many new staff members will be needed? The supervisor should recognize that personnel administration procedures will be required to manage many aspects of the programs being planned. Procedures that are the responsibility of the supervisor should be understood, and effective communication channels should be maintained with the personnel department (see Chapter 10). As with any management effort, evaluation is necessary. Are department/work unit goals being met? Have strategies to attain them changed? Is corrective action needed to bring the supervisor's department/work unit more in line with established goals and plans?

Remember that the supervisor's job starts long before employees are on the job and ready to go to work. Developing the groundwork for finding the "best" employees is difficult; it does not just "happen." Supervisors must look beyond the current shift, month, and budget period and consider the time span used by the organization for strategic planning. What are the goals of the organization? How do they affect the supervisor and his/her work force? Once these questions are answered and the strategies to meet the needs of the department/work section are set, the supervisor is ready to deal with routine aspects of the personnel administration process.

Personnel Administration: A Key to Labor Control

This textbook focuses on one aspect of a supervisor's job—the process by which employees are directed and controlled. The process begins with staffing for the hospitality operation. Recruiting and selecting qualified personnel are critical to attaining the goals established by the property. This is true since:

- Large amounts of time must be spent in recruiting and selecting staff members.

- The abilities of employees affect the amount of orientation, training, and supervision which will be necessary.

- The quality of an employee's work, which often is affected by the attitudes and skills brought to the job by the employee, will influence guest satisfaction, which is at the heart of any effort to attain organizational goals. Employee abilities also affect the initial development of labor performance standards (see Chapter 16) which is crucial to the property's labor control program. Therefore, the relationship between effective supervision and personnel administration procedures—which begin with employee recruitment and selection—must be understood. The lodging and/or food service operation must employ the "right" individuals in the first place. Then it must provide them with additional skills and knowledge to perform on the job.

Personnel administration problems probably would not be great if one, or a few, employees could do all the work. However, there is too much work for the management staff and/or several assistants to do, so it becomes necessary to divide the work. This principle of specialization is important to the successful supervision of employees. Few employees can be "good at everything." Therefore, the operation must hire specialists, such as food and beverage servers, room attendants, front desk clerks, and others to perform a small part of all the work that has to be done. Once staffing begins, these questions must be asked:

- What work must be done?
- When must the work be done?
- Who must do it?
- How much can one person (specialist) do?
- What is the relationship between each of the specialists?
- How many and what type of specialists are needed?

When these and similar questions are answered, the development of effective supervision techniques has begun.

Development of Job Descriptions

One of the first steps in planning the operation is development of job descriptions. A job description lists all the tasks and related information which make up a job or a work position. For example, a steward's job may involve washing dishes, pots, and pans plus cleaning floors and straightening out storage areas.

A job description provides the basis for organizing work and is useful in training personnel. It also is used as the basis for developing organization charts (discussed in Chapter 1). A job description should be task-oriented. It is written for a *position* not a *person*. In other words, the supervisor developing job descriptions should not consider: "I have a front desk clerk named Sally. What does she or should she do?" Rather, the supervisor should consider: "What tasks can I reasonably expect *any* front desk clerk to do?" Currently employed staff may not be employed in the future. Rotation of shifts, promotion, and continued changes within jobs also suggest that it is not wise to plan/define job tasks on a personal basis.

Exhibit 6.2 Sample Job Description For Room Attendant

Room Attendant

Job Summary

Performs routine duties in the cleaning and servicing of guestrooms and baths under close supervision of Housekeeper, Housekeeper Assistant, or Inspector.

Work Performed

1. Removes soiled linen from beds to be changed, carrying it with soiled bath linen to linen room; separates and counts soiled linen, calling amount of each kind to attention of the Housekeeper, Linen Room Supervisor, or Linen Room Attendant who fills out itemized records; procures fresh linen at linen room or from Linen Room Attendant.
2. Makes beds: Turns mattress over, placing thick, quilted pad on top of mattress; spreads bottom sheet on bed, tucking it in well at sides and head; adds top sheet, tucking it in at the foot and, from the foot, half-way up each side; places blankets and spread on sheets, tucking in blankets but not spread; shakes pillows and puts on clean slips; places pillows at head of bed with open end facing away from door.
3. Removes debris and maintains cleanliness of furnishings: Picks up paper from floor, removes and empties trash in wastebaskets, wipes mirrors and door frames with damp cloth; dusts furniture, light fixtures, window sills, and baseboards; vacuum cleans carpet at regular intervals; arranges furnishings in proper position.
4. Cleans bathrooms: Scrubs basin, bathtub, outside of toilet, and tile floor with damp rag and abrasive powder, using scrub brush and cleanser to remove difficult stains; completes cleaning by wiping up washed surfaces with damp cloth; cleans glassware, such as shelves and mirror, with moist cloth; applies metal polish to bathroom fixtures with damp cloth, washing it off with hot water and restoring polish by rubbing with dry cloth.
5. Replenishes supplies: Places clean towels on racks; places proper quantity of pens, stationery, blotters, soap, ink, and tissue in rooms.
6. May, upon specific instructions from Housekeeper, perform additional services, such as cleaning lounges, lobbies, and restrooms.
7. Reports to Housekeeper rooms cleaned, rooms occupied which have been cleaned, rooms vacant and in good condition, and unusual conditions or furnishings requiring repair.

Equipment Used

Wall brush, cleaning and scrubbing brushes, carpet sweepers, dust pan, uniform.

Vacuum cleaner: An ordinary electric vacuum cleaner, or one attached to pipes leading from a central vacuum pump.

Relation to Other Jobs

Promotion from: Bath Attendant

Promotion to: Inspector, Linen Room Attendant, Housekeeper, Housekeeper Assistant

Transfer from and to: Parlor Attendant, Ironer

Job Combination

The duties of this job may be combined with those of the Day Housekeeper, Parlor, Bath, or Linen Room Attendants.

Special Qualifications

This is usually a beginning job for which no experience is required.

A job description should be written for *all* management and submanagement positions. Writing job descriptions does not have to be

Exhibit 6.3 Sample Job Description for Food Server

JOB TITLE: Food Server

IMMEDIATE SUPERVISOR: Dining Room Manager

JOB SUMMARY:

Waits on dining room guests, obtains orders, and serves when food is prepared. Cleans and sets up assigned tables when guests have departed. Must have a knowledge of menu prices, daily specials, and all menu items. Refills condiments at the end of each shift.

DUTIES:

Greets guest at assigned tables and ensures that each guest has a dining room menu. When the guest is ready, obtains the meal order and gives to kitchen personnel for preparation. Obtains the food when prepared, delivers order to respective guest, and then moves on to service another table.

Suggests cocktails and obtains cocktail orders from guest.

Returns to each assigned table periodically to ascertain whether additional items are desired. When guests have completed their meal, a dessert is suggested and the check presented.

Removes dirty dishes and silverware, placing them in respective bus trays.

Prepares tables (or counter) for service by wiping them clean, setting clean linen, glassware, and silverware in the proper places, and placing condiments in an attractive fashion. May concentrate all his/her efforts on service during rush periods.

Refills all condiments and food server station supplies at the end of each shift.

SPECIFICATIONS AND PREREQUISITES:

Requires a basic knowledge of menu prices and the composition of food and beverage menu items.

Requires familiarity with all daily specials and with proper placing procedures.

EDUCATION:

Open

SKILLS:

Ability to carry and balance service tray on shoulder. Must have legible handwriting.

PHYSICAL:

Must be neat in appearance, possess a pleasant personality, and correct posture. Must possess a valid Health Card.

Courtesy: Mississippi Management, Inc.

---

time-consuming or difficult. Brief statements are sufficient. Sample job descriptions for two selected positions are shown in Exhibits 6.2 and 6.3. They provide illustrations of ways to write job descriptions which explain what the job is about. They are not meant to be used as is. The job description for each position must fit the exact needs of the specific property.

Job descriptions should describe all tasks which are or might be considered part of the job/position. In general, a complete job description will answer several important questions for each position within the lodging or food service operation:

- What, *exactly*, are all the tasks which a worker in this position must perform?
- Who supervises a worker in this job?
- What other factors clarify what this position involves and how it relates to other positions within the property?

A job description is used for several purposes:

- It tells supervisors and employees which tasks are the responsibility of each position. For example, who receives food deliveries—the food service supervisor or the cook? Who cleans the lobby—the housekeeper or the bellperson? Knowledge of this information can resolve many feuds regarding "who should do what."
- It explains how each position in the department relates to other positions in the department. It lays the foundation for the communication, authority, and responsibility processes.
- It provides the basis for organizing positions into work sections so that effective labor control systems can be implemented.
- It helps with employee recruitment. An employee considering a job wants to know what the position involves. Task requirements of the job are listed in the job description.
- It provides supervisors with an overview of tasks involved in all positions which they oversee.
- It is helpful in developing the property's organization chart.

Job descriptions should be combined into a personnel manual. Since jobs do change, descriptions should be updated to provide a current view of all tasks involved in each position.

Developing Job Specifications

A job specification indicates the personal qualities needed to successfully perform tasks which make up a work position (as outlined in the job description). Job specifications should be simple and not overstate needs for the position since:

- Experience and other unnecessary requirements will increase labor costs. Supervisors must pay more for more highly qualified personnel.
- Overqualified personnel tend to lose interest in the job, while underqualified employees are unable to perform the job.
- It becomes more difficult to find personnel when qualifications

for positions become more detailed since there are fewer applicants with the specific qualifications.

Job specifications should not *understate* the needs for the position. Personnel without training, education, and experience for the position will not be able to perform the work, at least not as quickly as more qualified personnel. Employees want to perform work at the expected quantity and quality levels, but will not be able to do so if they are underqualified. Frustration and job discontent lead to many work-related personnel problems.

In some areas, labor market conditions may require supervisors to take anyone who applies. Properties in some locations cannot recruit enough qualified applicants. When this is the case, training (see Chapter 7) becomes extremely important. Operations that use effective personnel procedures will be better able to attract and retain qualified staff than those which function in a less professional manner.

Job specifications should be written for tasks covered in job descriptions. They should not be developed around personnel currently employed in that position. Do not ask: "What is Joe's background?" Instead, consider what qualifications are needed to perform tasks outlined in the job description to a minimal level of acceptance. A job specification for the position illustrated in Exhibit 6.3 is incorporated at the bottom of the job description.

Factors that might be included in a job specification—other than required education, experience, knowledge, and training—may include physical skills, communication abilities, and equipment skills, among others.

The job specification identifies which applicants for vacancies are eligible and should be considered for the vacant positions. Job specifications set acceptable standards for employment in the property. Only individuals who possess the personal qualifications outlined by the job specification should be considered for employment. The job specification also may help identify existing staff who should be considered for advancement to more responsible positions (if only "qualified" personnel are eligible, allegations of employee favoritism are reduced).

Developing an Organization Chart

A "picture" of the positions in the lodging or food service operation is presented in an organization chart. The chart shows the relationship between various positions and answers questions such as: "How do I fit in?" "Who is my boss?" and "Who is above me and below me in terms of job responsibilities?"

The organization chart is developed by aligning similar positions into sections and then building sections into departments. The chart is developed by considering top and middle management positions and then slotting in other positions by sections. Unlike the development of job descriptions and job specifications, the supervisor will have less input in the development of the organization chart. However, a review of aspects relating to the supervisor's work sections is necessary and the supervisor should make recommendations about the positions of immediate concern to him/her.

A sample organization chart for a moderate-sized hotel was presented in Chapter 1 (Exhibit 1.4) for illustration purposes only. An organization chart must reflect the specific relationships between positions in the individual property.

The organization chart keeps the sections and positions straight in the property. A copy of the chart should be included in the employee handbook and should be referred to as disputes between personnel, positions, and/or sections may arise. The organization chart also is useful in developing channels of communication. If an employee has a complaint, to whom should he/she talk?

Just as job descriptions and specifications change, so do organizational structures. Therefore, organization charts should be updated so they always reflect the current relationship between positions and sections within the organization.

Formal and Informal Organizations. The organization chart we have discussed outlines formal, "on paper" relationships between positions. Supervisors must understand, however, that there also is an informal organization which may (and often does) differ from the expressed, formal organization. While an organization chart may suggest that a dining room manager supervises buspersons, for example, in practice each food server may have his/her own busperson—at least during busy periods. Actual procedures performed on the job should be *known* and understood. Supervisors must understand the informal organization and be able to work within it to attain organizational goals.

Procedures for Hiring Qualified Employees

The staffing tools already covered—job descriptions, job specifications, and organization charts—provide the basis for developing effective supervision programs even before employees are hired. Once these tools are developed, supervisors will know the positions needed within the operation, tasks to be performed in each position, personal qualities needed by successful employees for each position, and the way positions relate, formally and informally, to each other.

Recruitment Procedures

Employee recruitment is the process by which applicants are sought and screened as to their suitability for positions in the property. The process involves announcing job vacancies through proper sources and evaluating applicants to determine who should be considered for available positions. The employee selection process begins with recruiting and ends with hiring. As noted earlier, the supervisor of the vacant position should be directly involved in the recruiting and selecting of staff since he/she has first-hand knowledge about what exactly must be done. The recruitment process entails attracting qualified applicants for the positions. The exact tasks to be performed by the successful applicant will be known since the position will be defined in the job description.

Sources of Employees

There are several possible sources which can be used to recruit employees for hospitality operations:

Friends/Relatives of Current Employees. There are advantages and disadvantages to considering for employment friends and relatives of existing staff members. One advantage is that employees know the job requirements and "what it is like to work for the property." If employees have favorable impressions of the workplace, they may be "good salespersons" to recruit others. Current employees also have relationships with many of the same types of people who would be good candidates for vacant positions.

A possible disadvantage is that when several friends or family members work for the same operation, what affects one may affect all. For example, if one of the group is disciplined, the entire group may react negatively. These factors should be considered when decisions are made regarding recruiting and selecting friends and family of existing employees.

Promotion of Current Employees. Development of a "career ladder" program in the property may be possible. With this plan, a good employee can be trained for a series of progressively more responsible positions. Good employees are hard to find and should be encouraged, through opportunities for advancement, to stay with the operation. An example of a career ladder might be to advance a food service worker to an assistant cook position, and, after training and experience, on to a cook position. Lateral transfers from one section of a department to another section or department are also possible. Advantages of internal promotion/transfer may include building morale, encouraging existing employees to perform better with hopes of promotion, and encouraging employees to remain with the property because of the possibility for promotion.

Remember that training (see Chapter 7) is needed not only for new employees. Supervisory development programs must be continuous because there are many areas to learn in a position and work requirements for a position may change. Supervisors must keep in mind that employees who are successful in one position may not be effective in the job they accepted as a promotion. Continuous employee development programs can be helpful in screening employees for promotion.

Other Sources. Applicants for vacancies may be recruited from newspaper advertisements. Public and private employment agencies also are helpful in locating applicants. Government agencies and groups which work with and train handicapped and disadvantaged persons also may be employment sources. Some properties have reported much success in hiring trainees from these sources—especially for entry-level positions. Colleges, universities, vocational schools, and secondary schools with distributive education programs also are possible sources of new staff members.

Information about Applicants

Information about persons applying for positions must be collected. The following are sources of information.

Job Application Form. The job application form provides basic informa-

Exhibit 6.4 Sample Form for Preliminary Job Application

PRELIMINARY APPLICATION

Date ________________

Name ______________________________ Phone Number ________________

Address ____

Position Applied For: ____________________________________

Part Time or Full Time? __________________________________

Are You Working Now? ___________________________________

Current or most recent employment:

Company Name	Address	Job Title	Dates	Salary

Previous Employment:

Company Name	Address	Job Title	Dates	Salary

Why are you seeking employment? ______________________________

Give Names and addresses of three references:

1. ____

2. ____

3. ____

Courtesy: Mississippi Management, Inc.

tion to assess whether the applicant meets minimum job qualifications. Information contained on the completed form indicates how well the applicant meets qualifications listed in job specifications. The form should be simple and should only require information that is important in considering job suitability. Examples of general types of information include:

- Name
- Address

- Education
- References
- Experience
- Physical problems which hinder job performance

Some properties may find it advantageous to use a preliminary application for job applicants who "walk in" without being recruited. Basic information collected on the form can be helpful in deciding whether the applicant should be contacted and the formal application process initiated when a job opening occurs. A sample preliminary application is shown in Exhibit 6.4.

Care must be taken in structuring questions included in application forms because there are federal, state, and some local laws that deal with age, race, and other types of discriminatory practices in hiring. Exhibit 6.5 is a guide developed by the Michigan Department of Civil Rights that lists employment questions which may be discriminatory and ways of avoiding the problem. Since laws and their interpretations vary among states, a lawyer should review your employment application, related personnel forms, and interview procedures to ensure that there are no violations of current antidiscriminatory laws or their spirit and intent.

A sample job application form is included in Exhibit 6.6. Revisions may be needed to adapt it for use in a specific operation. The form shows basic information that is necessary in assessing an applicant's suitability for a vacancy. There are several advantages to using formal job applications. These include:

- Testing the applicant's ability to read and write, if these qualifications are important in performing the job.
- Providing basic information for use in deciding which questions to ask at a subsequent employment interview.
- Indicating the past experiences of the applicant which may provide a clue to whether the current vacancy fits within the applicant's career plans.

Interviews. A preliminary interview should be conducted to assess the applicant's attitudes and to inform him/her about the property and job. This interview normally is conducted by the personnel department in a large property or the department manager in a smaller operation. Additional information is obtained in these interviews about applicants who, as suggested by the completed job applications, should be considered for the vacant position. A preliminary interview enables the personnel manager or person with this responsibility to directly evaluate the applicant.

If the supervisor is not included in the preliminary interview, he/she should meet the eligible applicants before a final selection is made. The supervisor must be involved in the selection process and the preliminary

Exhibit 6.5 Pre-Employment Inquiry Guide

SUBJECT	LAWFUL PRE-EMPLOYMENT INQUIRIES	UNLAWFUL PRE-EMPLOYMENT INQUIRIES
NAME:	Applicant's full name. Have you ever worked for this company under a different name? Is any additional information relative to a different name necessary to check work record? If yes, explain.	Original name of an applicant whose name has been changed by court order or otherwise. Applicant's maiden name.
ADDRESS OR DURATION OF RESIDENCE:	How long a resident of this state or city?	
BIRTHPLACE:		Birthplace of applicant. Birthplace of applicant's parents, spouse or other close relatives. Requirement that applicant submit birth certificate, naturalization or baptismal record.
AGE:	*Are you 18 years old or older?	How old are you? What is your date of birth?
RELIGION OR CREED:		Inquiry into an applicant's religious denomination, religious affiliations, church, parish, pastor, or religious holidays observed. An applicant may not be told "This is a Catholic (Protestant or Jewish) organization."
RACE OR COLOR:		Complexion or color of skin.
PHOTOGRAPH:		Requirement that an applicant for employment affix a photograph to an employment application form. Request an applicant, at his or her option, to submit a photograph. Requirement for photograph after interview but before hiring.
HEIGHT:		Inquiry regarding applicant's height.
WEIGHT:		Inquiry regarding applicant's weight.
MARITAL STATUS:		Requirement that an applicant provide any information regarding marital status or children. Are you single or married? Do you have any children? Is your spouse employed? What is your spouse's name?
SEX:		Mr., Miss or Mrs. or an inquiry regarding sex. Inquiry as to the ability to reproduce or advocacy of any form of birth control.
HEALTH:	Do you have any impairments, physical, mental, or medical which would interfere with your ability to do the job for which you have applied? Inquiry into contagious or communicable diseases which may endanger others. If there are any positions for which you should not be considered or job duties you cannot perform because of a physical or mental handicap, please explain.	Inquiries regarding an individual's physical or mental condition which are not directly related to the requirements of a specific job and which are used as a factor in making employment decisions in a way which is contrary to the provisions or purposes of the Michigan Handicappers' Civil Rights Act. Requirement that women be given pelvic examinations.
CITIZENSHIP:	Are you a citizen of the United States? If not a citizen of the United States, does applicant intend to become a citizen of the United States? If you are not a United States citizen, have you the legal right to remain permanently in the United States? Do you intend to remain permanently in the United States?	Of what country are you a citizen? Whether an applicant is naturalized or a native-born citizen; the date when the applicant acquired citizenship. Requirement that an applicant produce naturalization papers or first papers. Whether applicant's parents or spouse are naturalized or native born citizens of the United States; the date when such parent or spouse acquired citizenship.
NATIONAL ORIGIN:	Inquiry into languages applicant speaks and writes fluently.	Inquiry into applicant's (a) lineage; (b) ancestry; (c) national origin; (d) descent; (e) parentage, or nationality. Nationality of applicant's parents or spouse. What is your mother tongue? Inquiry into how applicant acquired ability to read, write or speak a foreign language.
EDUCATION:	Inquiry into the academic vocational or professional education of an applicant and the public and private schools attended.	
EXPERIENCE:	Inquiry into work experience. Inquiry into countries applicant has visited.	
ARRESTS:	Have you ever been convicted of a crime? If so, when, where and nature of offense? Are there any felony charges pending against you?	Inquiry regarding arrests.
RELATIVES:	Names of applicant's relatives, other than a spouse, already employed by this company.	Address of any relative of applicant, other than address (within the United States) of applicant's father and mother, husband or wife and minor dependent children.
NOTICE IN CASE OF EMERGENCY:	Name and address of person to be notified in case of accident or emergency.	Name and address of nearest relative to be notified in case of accident or emergency.
MILITARY EXPERIENCE:	Inquiry into an applicant's military experience in the Armed Forces of the United States or in a State Militia. Inquiry into applicant's service in particular branch of United States Army, Navy, etc.	Inquiry into an applicant's general military experience.
ORGANIZATIONS:	Inquiry into the organizations of which an applicant is a member excluding organizations, the name or character of which indicates the race, color, religion, national origin or ancestry of its members.	List all clubs, societies and lodges to which you belong.
REFERENCES:	Who suggested that you apply for a position here?	

*This question may be asked only for the purpose of determining whether applicants are of legal age for employment.

Source: Michigan Department of Civil Rights

Exhibit 6.6 Sample Job Application Form

APPLICATION AND EMPLOYMENT RECORD

AN EQUAL EMPLOYMENT OPPORTUNITY EMPLOYER.

To Applicant: We deeply appreciate your interest in our organization and assure you that we are sincerely interested in your qualifications. A clear understanding of your background and work history will aid us in placing you in the position that best meets your qualifications and may assist us in possible future upgrading.

PERSONAL Date ____________

Name ____________ (Last) (First) (Middle) Social Security No. ____________

Present address ____________ (No.) (Street) (City) (State) (Zip) Telephone No. ____________

Do you have any physical condition which may limit your ability to perform the particular job for which you are applying? ____________ If yes describe such condition ____________

Position(s) applied for ____________ Rate of pay expected $______ per week.

Would you work Full-Time______ Part-Time______ Specify days and hours if part-time ____________

Were you previously employed by us?______ If yes, when? ____________

List any friend or relatives working for us ____________ (Name(s))

If your application is considered favorably, on what date will you be available for work? ____________ 19______

Are there any other experiences, skills, or qualifications which you feel would especially fit you for work with our organization? ____________

RECORD OF EDUCATION

School	Name and Address of School	Course of Study	Check Last Year Completed	Did You Graduate?	List Diploma or Degree
Elementary		X	5 6 7 8	☐ Yes ☐ No	X
High			1 2 3 4	☐ Yes ☐ No	
College			1 2 3 4	☐ Yes ☐ No	
Other (Specify)			1 2 3 4	☐ Yes ☐ No	

MM - P2 (10/81) (Turn to Next Page)

interview provides this opportunity.

Prior to the interview, the supervisor ought to read the application, resumé and other information about the applicant. The preliminary interview allows the supervisor to assess the abilities, attitudes, and com-

List below all present and past employment, beginning with your most recent

I

Name and Address of Company and Type of Business	From		To		Describe the work you did	Weekly Starting Salary	Weekly Last Salary	Reason for Leaving	Name of Supervisor
	Mo.	Yr.	Mo.	Yr.					
Telephone									

II

Name and Address of Company and Type of Business	From		To		Describe the work you did	Weekly Starting Salary	Weekly Last Salary	Reason for Leaving	Name of Supervisor
	Mo.	Yr.	Mo.	Yr.					
Telephone									

III

Name and Address of Company and Type of Business	From		To		Describe the work you did	Weekly Starting Salary	Weekly Last Salary	Reason for Leaving	Name of Supervisor
	Mo.	Yr.	Mo.	Yr.					
Telephone									

IV

Name and Address of Company and Type of Business	From		To		Describe the work you did	Weekly Starting Salary	Weekly Last Salary	Reason for Leaving	Name of Supervisor
	Mo.	Yr.	Mo.	Yr.					
Telephone									

V

Name and Address of Company and Type of Business	From		To		Describe the work you did	Weekly Starting Salary	Weekly Last Salary	Reason for Leaving	Name of Supervisor
	Mo.	Yr.	Mo.	Yr.					
Telephone									

May we contact the employers listed above?__________If not, indicate by No. which one(s) you do not wish us to contact __________

PERSONAL REFERENCES (Not Former Employers or Relatives)

Name and Occupation	Address	Phone Number

—2—

patibility of the applicant for the position.

The applicant should be encouraged to ask questions about the position and property. After the interview, the applicant ought to be told the next step in the application procedure. The supervisor should take notes at this time to record accurate information resulting from the interview which will help in making a hiring decision.

VETERAN OF U.S. ARMED FORCES	SERVICE BRANCH	DATE DISCHARGED & FINAL RANK	SELECTIVE SERVICE CLASSIFICATION OR RESERVE STATUS
☐ Yes ☐ No			

Describe hobbies, special interests, awards and activities: (Omit reference to organizations/activities which have racial, religious or sex identification) ________

DO NOT ANSWER ANY QUESTION CONTAINED IN THE BLOCKED-OFF AREA UNLESS THE EMPLOYER HAS CHECKED THE BOX NEXT TO THE QUESTION. A check box indicates that, for the position for which you are applying, the requested information is needed for national security laws, a bona fide occupational qualification, business necessity or other legally permissable reasons.

To Applicant **READ THIS INTRODUCTION CAREFULLY BEFORE ANSWERING ANY QUESTIONS IN THIS BLOCKED-OFF AREA.** The Civil Rights Act of 1964 prohibits discrimination in employment practice because of race, color, religion, sex or national origin. P. L. 90-202 prohibits discrimination on the basis of age with respect to individuals who are at least 40 but less than 65 years of age. The laws of some States also prohibit some or all of the above types of discrimination, as well as some additional types, such as discrimination against the physically handicapped.

☐ How long have you lived at present address? ________

☐ Previous address ________ (No. Street City State Zip) How long did you live there? ________

☐ Are you over the age of eighteen? ________ If no, hire is subject to verification that you are of minimum legal age

☐ Sex M ________ F ________ ☐ Height ________ ft ________ in ☐ Weight ________ lbs

☐ Marital Status Single ________ Engaged ________ Married ________ Separated ________ Divorced ________ Widowed ________

☐ Date of Marriage ________ ☐ Number of dependents including yourself ________ ☐ Are you a citizen of the U.S.A.? ________

☐ What is your present Selective Service classification? ________

☐ Indicate dates you attended school

Elementary ________ (From To) High School ________ (From To) College ________ (From To)

Other (Specify type of school) ________ (From To)

☐ Have you ever been bonded? ________ If yes, on what jobs? ________

☐ Have you been convicted of a crime in the past ten years, excluding misdemeanors and summary offenses? ________ If yes describe in full ________

☐ Do you have any physical defects which preclude you from performing certain kinds of work? ________ If yes, describe such defects and specific work limitations ________

☐ Have you had a major illness in the past 5 years? ________ If yes, describe ________

☐ Have you received compensation for injuries? ________ If yes, describe ________

Employer may list other bona fide occupational questions on lines below.

☐ ________

☐ ________

PRE-EMPLOYMENT STATEMENT

I certify that to the best of my knowledge the foregoing statements and medical history information given by me are true. I understand that if I am employed, any misrepresentation or omission by me herein will be sufficient cause for dismissal from this Company. I also authorize any investigation of the above information for purposes of verification. Furthermore I agree that during the course of my employment any accounts which may be owning by me to the "Company" may, at the discretion of the "Company" be withheld from my salary. I also agree and understand that if employed by the "Company" my employment is for no definite period of time and may, regardless of the date of payment of my salary, be terminated at any time with the customary notice as prescribed by law either by myself or by the "Company", without necessity on the part of either for showing special cause for such termination. I consent to taking any pre-employment physical examination if required by the "Company" or such future physical examinations as may be required by the "Company".

May we contact present employer? ☐ Yes ☐ No

________ DATE ________ SIGNATURE

3

Check Applicant References. All references, especially business/professional sources, provided by the applicant should be checked.[1] This is to verify information contained in the application form and to attempt to "draw out" information about the applicant's work and personal habits which would be known by the reference.

Telephone conversations with past employers also can help provide

PERSONS TO BE NOTIFIED IN CASE OF ACCIDENT OR EMERGENCY

NAMES	ADDRESS	CITY	STATE	PHONE

APPLICANT—Do not write on this page
FOR INTERVIEWER'S USE

INTERVIEWER	DATE	COMMENTS

REFERENCE CHECK

*Position Number	RESULTS OF REFERENCE CHECK	*Position Number	RESULTS OF REFERENCE CHECK
I		IV	
II		V	
III			

*See Page 2

Courtesy: Mississippi Management, Inc.

information during the screening process. A previous employer will need less time to talk on the telephone than to write a letter. Therefore, he/she may be more cooperative and provide "sensitive" information that might not be written in a letter. This is when a personnel department manager or person with this responsibility can inquire about eligibility for rehire and when discussions might occur about dependability, honesty, and other characteristics.

If the past employer directs a larger operation, he/she may not know detailed information about the applicant. If this is the case, inquiries may be made directly to the applicant's previous supervisor. The same questions which would be asked of the employer should be asked of the supervisor.

If appropriate, the past employer or supervisor may be asked about any health problems or injury claims that occurred while the applicant was employed at the firm. (Information about pre-existing health conditions and injuries can affect future workers' compensation claims.) Background on personal problems, alcohol or drug addiction, or other difficulties might be obtained. This information may have a bearing on the applicant's reliability, dependability, and job performance.

Employer references may be more helpful than personal references since the applicant probably will note only friends or other persons who may give a biased recommendation. Past employers may provide more objective observations. If an employer provides negative information, the manager may discuss the matter with the applicant. There may be additional information that the applicant may want to be known. The applicant then can "tell his/her side of the story."

Applicants who will handle cash can be bonded. The bonding company provides an application that must be completed. Through an independent background check of the applicant, the bonding company may uncover information that makes the applicant unbondable without higher payment rates. If this happens, the manager may question the applicant's suitability for the position.

Selection Tests. Applicants who have passed the initial screening process of application review, interview(s), and reference checks may be given selection tests. Selection tests are controversial in the personnel field. Caution must be used in giving written aptitude or psychological tests. In some cases, the courts have ruled that such tests discriminate against minorities. Also, it may be difficult or impossible to show a direct relationship between test scores and job performance. Therefore, before administering such tests as a screening procedure, employers should confer with legal counsel.

Formal selection tests are not frequently utilized by small hospitality operations. Use of some physical means to determine an applicant's suitability for employment may be wise. An applicant for a cook's position which requires previous experience may be required to prepare one or more food items by using a standard recipe. Likewise, an experienced front desk clerk should be able to explain how a room rack is organized. These simple tests would quickly prove worthwhile if they affirmed or questioned an applicant's statements written on the application form and made at subsequent interview(s).

Some facilities use the U.S. Department of Labor's General Aptitude Test Battery (GATB) exams which, for selected positions, can provide evidence of an applicant's aptitudes for performing work that is required in the position. (Contact the local employment service for further information regarding the GATB tests.)

Some firms use lie detector (polygraph) tests when considering applicants for certain positions, such as handling cash, because it is believed that through the tests applicants may reveal information or tendencies which would affect the selection decision. Experience indicates that polygraph tests may or may not be useful. Accuracy depends in large measure on the abilities of the test technician. From a legal perspective, test findings may not yield supportable reasons for making selection decisions. Properties considering the use of polygraph tests for any purpose should contact an attorney, state labor department, or the U.S. Department of Labor for current legal advice and specific information regarding polygraph tests.

Medical Examination. The medical examination may be the last step in the selection process. Since there is some expense that probably will be borne by the operation, the exam should be required only of those applicants who have agreed to accept the position. State and/or local regulatory agencies may require medical exams for food handlers. (This is an excellent idea even if it is not required.) Insurance companies may require medical examinations before new employees can be covered by property-sponsored insurance programs.

Legal Concerns. Equal employment opportunity regulations prohibit discrimination on the basis of race, color, religion, sex, or national origin in recruiting and hiring employees. Other laws also prohibit discrimination against handicapped persons and others for employment purposes. Traditionally, these groups have not received equal treatment in the labor market. Wage rates have been lower, promotion opportunities have been fewer, and unemployment rates have been higher with these groups than with others. To counter these problems, Congress passed the Civil Rights Act of 1964. (Title VII of that act is labeled "Equal Employment Opportunity.") This act, as amended, provides much of the authority for today's laws dealing with equal employment. Executive orders addressed to organizations dealing with the federal government and signed by President Lyndon B. Johnson in 1965 banned employment discrimination based on race, color, religion, sex, or national origin. Other employers also should be aware of the standards because implementation of affirmative action programs may be required of an employer as a result of settlements with the Equal Employment Opportunities Commission.

The basis for these laws does not deal with management's "intentions," but with the results of its actions. The 1967 Age Discrimination in Employment Act, as amended, prohibits discrimination because of age for persons at least 40 but less than 70 years of age. In regard to various employment measures, including hiring and pay, employers dealing with the government must use affirmative action to recruit, hire, and advance qualified handicapped persons. While this is not mandated for other organizations, many hospitality properties, for example, have had great success in hiring mentally and physically handicapped persons for selected positions.

These and related laws have had a significant impact on personnel activities in organizations. Top management must be committed to equal employment opportunity programs, in their requirements as well as their spirit and intent. Managers must communicate this, along with necessary policies and procedures, to lower-level management staff who administer personnel-related programs. Directors also must set definite goals and plans which address concerns about recruiting/selecting minority workers. Many state antidiscrimination laws, which contain enforcement regulations, are very explicit in prohibiting certain types of recruitment advertising and pre-employment requirements.

While planning a selection process, care must be taken that employment application forms do not include illegal questions and that unlawful inquiries are not made during pre-employment interviews. While employment tests may be administered, they must not be designed or used to discriminate against minorities.

Although there are many detailed regulations that hospitality operations have to meet, and these will vary depending on the state where the property is located, it is still necessary to select the "best" employees. The organization will be hurt by arbitrary factors which exclude candidates who otherwise would be positive contributors to the organization's work. Therefore, it is important to match work to be done with the best applicant available to do the work. Discrimination not only is illegal but it is an extremely ineffective management procedure.

The Selection Decision

The selection decision should be made after consulting all concerned parties. As previously noted, these include at least the section or department head and the supervisor of the prospective employee. The decision should consider which applicant among several is the best suited for the position. This procedure implies that time has been allowed to recruit as many applicants as possible for the vacancy. Such a procedure is much better than the alternative of recruiting only one person and then using selection procedures to "ensure" that he/she is capable of doing the job.

Applicants rejected by the property should be informed. If an applicant may be eligible for a future vacancy, permission to keep the application and supporting information should be requested. If there are other positions for which he/she may be qualified, the applicant should be told. If the applicant is not, and probably will not be, eligible for work within the property, this should be recorded. Personnel with job selection responsibilities have an obligation to be fair and honest in all dealings with current employees and persons who desire to be employees.

Evaluation of Recruitment and Selection Procedures

Periodic evaluation of business activities and goals is important for good management. Evaluation of recruitment and selection procedures may examine the following questions:

1. Are policies and procedures developed and consistently used?

2. Why are job applicants denied work? (An analysis of equal employment opportunity procedures is justified here.)

3. What impression, if any, do agencies supplying job applicants to the property have about recruitment and selection procedures being used?

4. How many persons have applied for each job vacancy?

5. What sources of job applicants are used?

6. Are current job descriptions, job specifications, and organization charts available to help in the selection process?

7. Of the employees who are hired, how many are discharged during the probationary period? How many resign?

8. What amount of employee turnover can be traced to poor selection decisions? How well does a supervisor's predictions of a new employee's success actually relate to this factor?

9. Do applications, interviews, and related selection forms meet requirements of current laws and regulations on nondiscrimination in employment?

Procedures for Employee Termination

Effective recruitment and selection procedures help bring the "best" applicants to the job, and the use of basic supervisory principles helps retain these employees on the job. However, given the high turnover rates experienced by the hospitality industry, supervisors should recognize that, for a variety of reasons, some staff members will terminate their employment. Separation may, of course, be initiated by the property, as in the case of disciplinary action, or, more commonly, because of the performance of the employee.

Supervisors must follow consistent procedures when employees leave. Through exit interviews (also called employee separation interviews), supervisors can attempt to determine reasons why employees leave the organization. When there is "nothing to lose," employees are much more likely to be frank about their reasons for leaving. Supervisors often can learn much that will help improve the job and related working conditions to minimize future turnover rates. Conducted properly, exit interviews can be very helpful in identifying organizational problems which will then lead to major improvements in the way the organization interacts with its employees. A sample format for an employee separation interview is shown in Exhibit 6.7.

Depending upon the property, other paperwork may be important to help ensure an orderly update and close-out of the employee's personnel files. For example, Exhibits 6.8 and 6.9 show, respectively, a sample form for giving notice of termination to an employee and a personnel action form used to recap termination procedures implemented by various departments within the property.

Exhibit 6.7 Sample Form for Employee Separation Interview

EMPLOYEE SEPARATION INTERVIEW

Our company, like all businesses today, is concerned with the rate of employee turnover. When any employee is forced to make a job change, it represents an added expense to the employer plus a certain amount of confusion in the department from which the employee left. We are working towards making our organization an outstanding place to work and would sincerely appreciate your frank appraisal and honest answers to the following questions. This report is confidential and used for research purposes only.

Name	
Supervisor	Department

I. Please indicate below the reason you decided to leave your employment with us.

1. ☐ Another Job	8. ☐ Return to School
2. ☐ Dissatisfied with Supervisor	9. ☐ Dissatisfied with Company
3. ☐ Leaving City	10. ☐ Salary
4. ☐ Pregnant	11. ☐ Transportation
5. ☐ Marriage	12. ☐ No chance for advancement
6. ☐ Released	13. ☐ Lack of Work (Boredom)
7. ☐ Short Time Temporary	14. ☐ Other (Explain below)

____

____

____

____

II. 1. Was your job accurately explained to you at the time of your employment? ☐ Yes ☐ No

2. Did you receive accurate job instruction? ☐ Yes ☐ No

3. Was your pay adequate for the job you were doing? ☐ Yes ☐ No

4. When difficult problems came up in your work, or things went wrong, how free did you feel about asking questions?

☐ Not Free At All ☐ Reasonably Free

☐ Immediate Supervisor Hard To Approach ☐ Completely Free

5. What is your opinion of the Company's general working conditions?

☐ Good ☐ Fair ☐ Poor

6. Did you understand the importance of your job? ☐ Yes ☐ No

7. How long did you work with us? ________ Years ________ Months

8. Did you feel a part of the Company? ☐ Yes ☐ No

9. Would you tell us what you liked about your job?

____

____

10. How would you rate your Supervisor?

☐ Does Excellent Job ☐ Below Average

☐ Satisfactory ☐ Poor

MM P5

Comments: ____

____

____

11. Is there anything the Company could have done, other than salary, to make your stay a more lasting one?

____

____

12. Is there anything else you would like to say?

____

____

____

____

____
Employee's Signature

____

Interviewer ________________________________ Date __________

____

____

Courtesy: Mississippi Management, Inc.

NOTES

1. This section is based on Jack Ninemeier, *Food and Beverage Security: A Systems Manual for Restaurants, Hotels and Clubs* (Boston: CBI, 1982).

Exhibit 6.8 Sample Termination Notice

TERMINATION NOTICE TO EMPLOYEE

Name ____

Address ______________________________________ Phone ________

Person to contact if we need to locate him/her: ____________________

____ Phone ________

This is to advise you that since your last date of employment with this property is __________, your group insurance will be cancelled effective that date, unless you complete the necessary forms by the above date to convert your coverage to a private plan.

This is to advise you also that all other fringe benefits extended to employees by this property are cancelled, effective the above date.

Please be certain to provide us with a permanent address for the purpose of forwarding any forms or information to you at a later date.

All of the above statements were explained.

______________________ ______________________

Employee Department Head

____

Witness

Courtesy: Mississippi Management, Inc.

Exhibit 6.9 Sample Termination Report

PERSONNEL ACTION: TERMINATION

Name of departing employee: ______________________

Last day of work? ______________________

Uniforms & other inn property accounted for? ______________________

Location of uniforms & inn property ______________________

Reason for employee leaving (in detail) ______________________

____

____

Does this employee have to be replaced? ______________________

If yes, when? ______________________

What action is being taken to get a replacement? ______________________

____

____

Did you explain that group insurance is cancelled as of the last day of work? ________

Did you explain the effect of termination on the profit sharing plan? ____________

____

Signature of Department Head

____

Department

1 Copy to Secretary
1 Copy to General Manager (Day of Departure)

Courtesy: Mississippi Management, Inc.

PAGE TWELVE

Supervision at the Brandywine Room

Stacey arrived several minutes early for her appointment with Rachel Case, the personnel director. As she was waiting in the reception area, the door opened and she overheard Ms. Case say to a staff member who was leaving: "You're right. Our job in the Personnel Department would be much easier if we could get the cooperation of the staff members in each department. We do have a big communication problem here."

"How coincidental," Stacey thought, "the personnel director and one of her staff members are, at this very moment, concerned about the very thing that I want to discuss." Her thoughts were interrupted when Ms. Case greated her. "It's nice to see you, Stacey. I've been following your progress since you started here almost four years ago. How does it feel now to be a big shot?"

After talking briefly with Ms. Case, Stacey brought up the reason for the meeting. "I'm here because as a supervisor, I'm not exactly sure what the Personnel Department does or what I should be doing as new employees are hired. I've talked to several other supervisors and they have similar questions. I've also spoken to my boss, Mr. George, who told me some things that I just do not see being practiced. It was his idea that I talk with you. If you can help me to better understand the process, I can do my job much more effectively. Also, if you need help, I might be able to get the word out to other supervisors about what I hear."

"Stacey," said Ms. Case, "I was just discussing this very matter. Let me share with you a rough draft of an outline for a talk I am going to give to the next Executive Council Meeting. I would like to know your reaction to it as a supervisor."

Outline of Talk for Executive Council Meeting

Subject: Relationship Between Personnel Department and Line Departments
Recruiting and Selecting New Staff Members

1. The Personnel Department is responsible for helping a line department find the most qualified applicants for vacant positions. A line department, in turn, has a responsibility to provide information which will help the Personnel Department. The final selection of an applicant rests with the line department.

2. Line departments can help the Personnel Department. The line department provides job descriptions and specifications to

the Personnel Department. Even though changes always occur on the job, we seldom revise job descriptions or specifications. We are recruiting new employees with outdated job information. Often there is a big difference between what we tell the applicants about the job and what work must really be done in the position. The same concern applies to job specifications. As work is changed, equipment is purchased, etc., this changes the personal qualities needed to effectively perform the job. Yet, many times, the Personnel Department does not know this. The department often looks for employees with knowledge, skills, and abilities outlined in outdated job specifications. Other personal attributes about the applicant are important but we don't know them. We must get this kind of information in order to find the best applicants for the job.

3. The Personnel Department receives little lead time for recruiting applicants. We realize that emergencies occur, but there are times when line departments have advance notice of upcoming vacancies. We should be informed of these.

4. Personnel in line departments often have good ideas about recruiting prospective applicants. Yet they do not tell us, and we continue using the old and often ineffective sources.

5. Line departments could "advertise" position vacancies among their own employees. Perhaps these staff members have ideas about where to look or even know specific individuals who would be eligible and would like to apply.

6. Many times personnel in line departments say they are too busy to interview a lot of applicants. They just want us to send down one or two of the best. The selection process would be more effective if line department staff would make finding the best applicants a top priority. They may have to interview several candidates for vacant positions.

7. While the Personnel Department is not perfect, we do think that we are "experts" in recruiting employees. Line departments might consider this and ask us our opinion regarding applicants being considered for the position. Not only could the line deparments talk with us, they also could more carefully review all of the information about applicants that we gather.

8. There may be simple, inexpensive, and easy tests which line departments could give applicants who are supposed to have work experience. Many times, this is not done. Supervisors often think they can tell a "good" applicant from a "bad" appli-

cant. Sometimes they feel that they don't have time to ask more than a few questions, and certainly don't have the spare time to give a test.

9. A lot of the work done by the Personnel Department in recruiting excellent applicants is undone when these people are hired. Inadequate orientation programs "turn off" new employees. Our records indicate that a majority of employees quit within the first months of being employed. This means that:

    a. selection procedures are poor.

    b. orientation and training procedures are inadequate.

    c. a combination of poor selection and training could be the cause of extensive turnover rates among newly hired employees.

    Some of the blame for turnover and other employee-related problems might rest with the line department.

10. Line departments could benefit by asking for advice and assistance in such employee-related matters as wage and salary compensation, development of training programs, implementation of employee performance reviews, motivation, and related programs. However, many departments don't seek help. We are an untapped resource within the organization.

As Stacey read through the outline, she was impressed with (a) the personnel director's helpful attitude, (b) the Personnel Department's ability to provide assistance in hiring, and (c) the importance that the Personnel Department placed on the line department and supervisor in recruiting and selecting employees. "Ms. Case, I think this outline is excellent. After you share it with the Executive Council, I hope they will let their management staff, including first-line supervisors like me, know about it. As for me, I would like to volunteer the Brandywine Room as a place for you to begin work. I want to revise my job descriptions and specifications. Will you help me? Also, I'm not very happy with our orientation program for new employees. I agree that initial contacts with new staff members affect their attitude and length of service with the property. Will you help me design a new orientation program?"

Stacey and Ms. Case learned a lot about the operation of each other's department during the meeting. Ms. Case was pleased that Stacey would allow her staff to "practice what they preach." The assistance given in the Brandywine Room could be a model to interest other supervisors in using effective personnel management procedures to improve their operations.

7 Staff Orientation and Training Procedures

PAGE THIRTEEN

Supervision at the Brandywine Room

About a week after her meeting with the personnel director, Stacey met with the personnel director's assistant. She obtained lots of ideas about how to update job descriptions and job specifications. At the same time, she was introduced to a lot of resource material that she did not even know was available within the hotel. The Personnel Department had assembled many current books and trade magazines dealing with all phases of management and supervision. They were available for any interested staff member.

There were two major problems which Stacey wanted to address. First, she was concerned that new employees were not being properly oriented to the job. (Could that be a reason why employees were "turning over" so quickly?) Also, she was slowly but surely introducing new work procedures in the Brandywine Room. Implementation of these procedures required employee training. The only experience that Stacey had with training was acquired when she was a trainee food server. From an employee's perspective, she did not think "showing everybody how to do things once and then expecting them to do it" was very effective. She felt that the training materials in the Personnel Department, along with lots of "friendly advice" from that department and her own boss, Mr. George, would be very helpful.

As a result of proper employee recruitment and selection techniques, the best employees are hired. How these employees view their new jobs—and how well they perform—depends on the quality and extent of the orientation and training programs which the property provides. The primary responsibility for orientation and training rests with the supervisor. In many properties, employees are brought in to work when needed, introduced to their fellow employees in the work station, and turned over to a senior employee for on-the-job training. This in itself is not effective orientation.

An effective orientation program properly sets the scene for the relationship between the new staff member and the property. The orientation process is very important. It may cost several hundred dollars to replace entry-level employees. Costs are incurred for recruitment, overtime pay for existing staff during the search for a new employee, training, increased breakage and lowered productivity during the training and job learning process, and forms processing. It may, likewise, cost thousands of dollars to replace middle or top management personnel. These costs increase labor costs and, to the extent that they can be reduced as a result of an effective orientation program, economic benefits can be seen.

Introducing the Employee to the Workplace

Much—perhaps 90%—of all turnover occurs within the first few weeks and months of employment (in many operations, approximately one-half of the initial turnover occurs within the first month). This indicates the importance of the employee selection program and the property's first work relationships with the employee (the orientation process). Doesn't high turnover during the early period of employment suggest that the recruitment and/or orientation process is inadequate?

When employees first begin working they are often very enthusiastic and highly motivated. They *want* to do their jobs exactly as shown; they want to meet their supervisor's expectations. It is up to the supervisor to build on this initial desire so that the new employee will perform effectively on the new job.

An inadequate orientation program makes new employees think that the supervisor does not care for them and that they have not found a good place to work. It is this negative feeling, which can quickly overcome the initial good feelings about a new job, that a proper orientation program is designed to counter.

Orientation Procedures

Effective orientation builds proper relationships between the new employee and his/her supervisor, co-workers, and, in general, the entire operation. Orientation entails a number of steps, many of which are designed to make the new employee feel welcome, comfortable, and eager to learn the new job. Other steps involve such administrative necessities as completing forms. One of the first things you may have to do is provide the new employee with withholding tax, insurance, and other work documents. The employee will have concerns about these matters. You share these concerns by making the forms available and by helping the new employee understand how to complete them (in large operations this may be the responsibility of the personnel department). Employee payroll forms, work files, etc., should be established as soon as this and related information is available.

Another of your first duties should be to review the job with the new employee. How does it relate to other jobs? Where is small equipment located? How is large equipment operated? You should carefully think about—and provide answers to—all questions which you would have if you were the new staff member. A comprehensive employee handbook (see Exhibit 7.1) can help with this task. The handbook, which should be given to each new employee, should review policies and procedures and answer such questions as when are breaks taken, when is payday, what is the policy about eating on the job? The handbook should be written specifically for the property so that it provides accurate information about actual policies, programs, and procedures. In some properties, the first page of the handbook is a tear-out form which employees must sign and return to their supervisor within the first several weeks of employment. They are, in effect, signing a statement indicating that they have read the handbook and agree to abide by all personnel policies and other practices outlined in the document.

The person's work station must be defined, and any uniforms, tools, or other small equipment which the property provides should be assembled before the new employee arrives. This and other procedures suggest that an effective orientation program requires planning. To help with the actual on-the-job orientation, one experienced employee (a mentor) can be assigned to work closely with the new employee if you are unable to do so. This staff member, who should be available to answer general questions, might be the trainer (discussed later in this chapter) or another experienced person who has a genuine interest in helping the new employee feel comfortable.

Employees should understand the specific tasks of their job as outlined in the job description. They should also be told about promotional opportunities in the organization. ("Success" stories of current employees are helpful.) A review of planned career progression possibilities is also useful here. For example, can a dishwasher advance to steward, or an assistant preparation cook to assistant line cook? Can a housekeeper advance to a floor supervisor or related position?

The new employee should be given a tour of the property. Work stations can be identified, and personnel can be introduced as they are encountered. Special attention should be given to the introduction of the new employee to his/her peers (co-workers in the same work section). Also, these co-workers should be informed in advance that the new employee will be starting work. The employee should be carefully introduced to his/her work station; other features (water fountain, time clock, employee restrooms/lockers, etc.) can also be pointed out during the tour.

By this point, you should be aware that orientation efforts cannot take place in five minutes. Likewise, it is not normally effective to schedule a new employee's first workshift during the property's busiest time of day or week. Simply put, it takes time to perform required orien-

Exhibit 7.1 Sample Table of Contents for Employee Handbook

TABLE OF CONTENTS

Welcome to Our Company

About Our Company
- Our Philosophy
- What We Do
- Our Organizational Structure

About Your Earnings
- Your Salary
  - Salary Grades
  - Salary Review
  - Cost of Living Increases
  - Pay Periods and Pay Days
  - Payroll Deductions
- Other Benefits
  - Holidays
  - Vacations
  - Sick Leave
  - Maternity Provisions
  - Insurance Programs
  - Educational Assistance
  - Employee Honor Awards

Important Policies to Help You
- Probationary Period
- What to Do If You Cannot Come to Work
- Personal Appearance
- Overtime
- Job Problems
- Access to Personnel Records
- Recognition
- Use of Time Clock
- Rest Periods
- Before/After Work Requirements
- Employee Lockers
- Packages

Career Challenges
- Promotion from Within
- Equal Employment Opportunities
- Training Opportunities
- Employee Development Program
- Career Progression Paths
- Employee Appraisal Programs

We know you'll like us, welcome to the team!

tation activities. The supervisor or other staff members "with a million things to do" will not have the time to properly introduce the new staff member to the property and his/her new co-workers.

When your primary role in orientation is completed, the person who will be working closely with the new employee can take over. He/she should show the new employee exactly what must be done. Patience and understanding (empathy) are needed at this point. If at all possible, you should visit with the new employee at the end of the first workshift. Questions can be answered and, in the process, concern about the new employee's well-being and future with the property can be expressed. An informal meeting with the new employee (and the experienced staff member assigned to him/her) might be scheduled several days later to assess how well the training process is progressing. It should be made clear to the experienced staff member that all possible assistance should be provided and that the supervisor should be informed about any problems which occur.

All of the preceding procedures in an employee orientation program will help instill a positive, favorable impression on the new staff member. They will help eliminate confusion and uncertainty as the new employee learns about the job and as you learn about the new employee.

Orientation Checklist

An orientation checklist itemizes all activities to be undertaken and all information to be reviewed at the time of orientation. It has several advantages. First, since it is developed before the new employee arrives (and is used for all employees), it requires the supervisor and other management staff to give advance thought to the type of experiences with which the new employee will become involved. Second, it provides for equal treatment of all new employees; when following the checklist, all supervisors and new employees do the same things, and new employees are, essentially, exposed to the same basic job information.

The checklist also serves as a reminder for supervisors. Without a checklist it is easy for a busy supervisor to overlook one or more of the many activities in the orientation program. Finally, the checklist requires supervisors to conduct a thorough orientation (they must sign the checklist at the completion of the orientation to affirm that all activities have been completed). The checklist formalizes the orientation process; the presence of a checklist signed by the supervisor assures top management that orientation policies and practices are being followed. (An example of an orientation checklist is shown in the case study at the end of this chapter.)

A point made several times earlier is relevant to the job orientation process: Put yourself in the place of the new employees. How would you like to be treated during this most important time?

The Supervisor and Employee Training

Training is important for both new and current employees. It can be used to teach or improve job skills, broaden knowledge, and modify behavior or attitudes. Training is critical to the success of the hospitality operation, which is only as good as its employees. Training that involves "shoving" a new employee into the work station, letting him/her watch what is happening, and then, with little supervision, putting the employee right to work is not effective. Improperly trained employees increase costs and create guest dissatisfaction. Supervisors must establish work procedures which incorporate the most cost-effective and guest-centered methods and must train employees to perform work in the way that it is supposed to be done.

Developing and using a training program need not be difficult; it does take time (probably less time when the new employee closely meets personal qualifications outlined in the job specification). Training is, essentially, the process of improving one's ability to do required work. Using "where the employee is now" as a starting point, training continues with presenting information to the employee and involving the employee in experiences that will help him/her meet quality and quantity performance standards. A final aspect of training involves continual coaching to help the employee solve problems, make decisions, and become more involved in planning for and performing required work.

Initially, training costs money. Employees being trained are less productive and require more supervision. They also make more mistakes. However, effective training is worthwhile since trained employees become more productive and are better able to do their work. Therefore, labor costs can be reduced and guests will be happier because they are receiving the quality of service, food, and other products which the property has planned that they receive.

Employees must know how to perform, at a minimum quality level, each of the tasks required to do their jobs. A timetable for mastery of each task should be developed. The training program, outlined by task, time, and sequence, should be reviewed with the employee.

Characteristics of a Good Trainer

Training can be used to teach knowledge and skills.[1] It can also be helpful in modifying behavior or improving attitudes. Success of the training program is dependent upon both the ability of the trainer and the willingness of the trainee to learn. Generally, the new employee is willing and anxious to learn about the new job. This suggests that the trainer plays a critical role in training success. (Success is attained when the trainee has learned and can do what has been taught.) A good trainer has the following characteristics:

Desire to Teach

A desire to teach. A trainer who enjoys helping employees learn will probably enjoy training.

Knowledge

A thorough working knowledge of the job. While the trainer need not be an expert, he/she must be able to explain and demonstrate the required job tasks.

Ability

The ability to convey understanding. The trainer must be able to communicate effectively.

Patience

Patience. The trainer must be objective and patient; he/she cannot be easily upset.

Sense of Humor

A sense of humor. A trainer who can interject humor at the proper time develops a bond that makes training easier.

Time

Time to train. Trainers must be provided time to train; they should not just train "when they get around to it."

Respect

Respect from trainees. Without respect for the trainer, the trainees will gain minimal benefits from the training.

Enthusiasm

Enthusiasm for training. The trainer's enthusiasm is likely to carry over to the trainees themselves; this can make training more effective.

Basic Principles of Learning

Training is, in effect, any activity that results in learning. In a job related situation, training (learning) pertains to acquiring knowledge of skills, or modifying behavior or attitudes, in order to perform more effectively on the job. Since most hospitality employees (and trainees) are adults, basic learning principles that are incorporated into training programs must recognize ways in which adults learn best.

The Desire to Learn

First of all, trainees must want to learn. They should have a strong motivation to learn new skills or acquire more knowledge. Likewise, trainees will learn only when they believe there is a need to learn. Most trainees are practical. They want to know how training activities will help them. Therefore, early in training sessions, trainers should defend the need for training. This defense should be part of initial training activities.

Learning by Doing

Trainees learn by doing. Passive learning (reading, listening, etc.) is much less effective than active learning—when the trainees participate in the training. Also, training should focus on realistic problems. Trainees must be shown how the information being presented applies to specific situations in which they are involved.

The Effect of Prior Experiences

The trainees' prior experiences will affect their learning. Employees come to training programs with differing backgrounds into which training experiences must be integrated. These past experiences will affect their ability to learn and the way they relate to the training. You should understand that trainees learn best in an informal training environment. The traditional "classroom" approach to training will likely be ineffective in most hospitality industry situations. Trainees should be treated as professional colleagues—not as subordinates or children.

Training Methods

Using a variety of training methods strengthens the training presentation. Demonstration, use of audio-visual aids, role playing, and related activities in which trainees can become involved can supplement the more traditional lecture method. The focus of training should be on providing guidance rather than grades. Trainees want to know how well they are doing. However, they have a greater need to know whether they are learning correctly and the extent to which they understand basic ideas presented in the training.

Learning is more likely to take place when several other guidelines are followed as training programs are planned:

- Training activities should not exceed the trainees' span of attention. Do you like to think about one specific thing for several hours at a time? Your answer is probably no. Training activities should be kept short and should be spaced over a period of time. Rest periods should be scheduled when necessary.
- Trainees learn at varying rates of speed. Trainers should recognize this, have patience, and provide additional information to those who need it.
- Accuracy is more important than speed during initial training sessions. Important points emphasized in training should be repeated.
- An entire job should be shown before it is broken down into its smaller parts. Individual job tasks should be practiced only after the trainee understands what the entire task involves.
- Trainees should know what will be required of them as a result of the training. The trainer should hold the trainees responsible for a measurable amount of achievement. The trainees should have a chance to evaluate their activities relative to expected achievement levels.

The Training Process

The training activity should be viewed as a process; there is a sequence to be followed as training activities are undertaken. Each of these steps are reviewed in this section. As you study this information, recall the performance analysis procedures described in Chapter 3; not all problems can be resolved through training. Assume, through a problem identification and analysis process, that lack of training, and not working conditions or other factors, is found to be the cause of the problem. Recall also that training is not only needed to resolve operating problems; it is also needed to teach new staff members about required job procedures and to instruct current employees in revised procedures. Training should be implemented in the following sequence.

Define Training Needs

There are several ways to tell when training might be necessary. Common job-related problems such as guest dissatisfaction, low morale, high levels of waste, low productivity levels, excessive employee grievances, or accidents provide some evidence that training may be necessary. Supervisors can determine these and related types of training needs by simple observation, analysis of guest and employee complaints, study of fluctuating business levels, inspections, or through feedback from employees and others.

Set Priorities

After determining that a training program is necessary, priorities must be established. Since there are expenses involved in training, it is unlikely that extensive training programs covering all observed problems can be undertaken at the same time. The most important training needs must be identified and addressed first.

Consider Costs

Costs are an important concern when training programs are being considered. Obviously, a training program must be worth more than it costs. Problems being addressed by the training must be reduced to a point where training can be justified. As training priorities are established, supervisors should consider not only what the training costs are but also what costs will be incurred if training is *not* provided. Obviously, those problems which have little overall effect on the total hospitality operation should not be given as high a priority as are those which are visible, occur frequently, and significantly affect the attainment of organizational objectives.

Plan the Training

The process of training involves a great deal of upfront planning. In order to evaluate training effectiveness (what has been learned), the trainer must first know the employee's level of performance before training begins. The trainer will then know that training was effective to the extent that performance after training more closely approaches requirements than was the case before the training was undertaken.

Develop a Job List

Once the decision to train has been made, the supervisor, perhaps working with interested and experienced employees, must prepare a **job list**. This notes all tasks that an employee must perform as part of the job. It includes every activity that the employee will be expected to master during training. A sample job list for a reservations clerk is shown in Exhibit 7.2.

Develop a Job Breakdown

The next step in the job analysis activity required to plan training programs is to develop a **job breakdown**. This tool specifies the task to be performed and indicates what is needed to accomplish the task. The job breakdown further lists the steps required to do the task and the procedures for performing each step in the task. It also provides additional information necessary to fully explain what the job involves. A sample job breakdown, telling how to help guests make food and beverage selections, is shown in Exhibit 7.3.

As a result of the job list and job breakdowns, supervisors and trainers will have a clear understanding of exactly what and how tasks are to be performed. This information provides the foundation for procedures and other requirements which must be taught as part of the training process.

Exhibit 7.2 Sample Job List for Reservations Clerk

JOB LIST

POSITION: Reservations Clerk — DATE PREPARED: 00/00/00

TASKS: Employee must be able to:	J.B. Number*
1. Identify room status	64
2. Identify room rate structures for both individual and group bookings	65
3. Determine the physical status of any given room from front office controls	66
4. Operate reservations telephone	67
5. Take and process telephone reservations	68
6. Take and process reservations through correspondence	69
7. Take and process reservations from the 800 number	70
8. Take and process in-person reservations	71
9. Use the reservations filing system	72
10. Etc.	

This is a partial job list. The list developed for a specific property should include all tasks to be performed.

*Job Breakdown Number.

Source: Lewis C. Forrest, Jr., Training for the Hospitality Industry *(East Lansing, Mich.: Educational Institute of the American Hotel & Motel Association, 1983), p. 42.*

Define Training Goals

After the job is analyzed, broad training goals must be defined. Normally, training is designed around the ability to *do* rather than to *know* something. Knowledge for its own sake is not a common training goal; rather, trainers must define exactly what the trainees should be able to do and how well they should be able to do it as a result of the training.

Select Trainees

Training can be conducted for both new and experienced employees. While new employees must frequently be taught many skills and much information as they begin to work, experienced employees also need training (or retraining) as problems arise and as procedures change. Many employees are ineffective because they do not know what to do, how to do it, or why it should be done, rather than because they do not want to do quality work. Therefore, supervisors must train all employees who can benefit from it regardless of their length of service with the property.

Establish Performance Objectives

Performance objectives state exactly what the training is designed to accomplish. Each task on the job list and outlined in the job breakdown should have accompanying performance objectives. These will indicate skill levels that employees must meet following training. Objectives, then, should not be general, they should address specific tasks.

Develop the Training Program

After specific training objectives are established, the training program can be defined. Skills to be developed should be arranged in logical order. Materials must be prepared or assembled. The training must be

Exhibit 7.3 Sample Job Breakdown

JOB BREAKDOWN

Job Breakdown #36: The ability to assist guests in making food and beverage selections
Equipment needed: Guest check, pen (guests will already have menus and wine list).

WHAT TO DO	HOW TO DO IT	ADDITIONAL INFORMATION
1. Approach the table.	1. Stand erect. Look at the guests, smile, and greet them pleasantly. Introduce yourself. If you know their names, use them when you greet them. Be courteous.	1. You "win" the table by your first contact when you are pleasant and personable.
2. Take cocktail order.	2. Suggest a cocktail or appetizer wine. Be sure to get the complete details of the order such as on-the-rocks, straight up, extra olives, etc. Remember which guest ordered each cocktail.	2. Most guests know which drinks they prefer. Be prepared to make suggestions if appropriate. Do not push your personal preferences. Do not act surprised when a guest orders some nonstandard drink.
3. Serve cocktails.	3. Place a cocktail napkin in front of each guest. Serve all beverages from the right with the right hand when possible. Place cocktail glasses on napkins. Do not ask who ordered each drink (you must remember). As each drink is served, state what it is, such as scotch and water, double martini, scotch on-the-rocks, etc.	3. Knowing "who ordered what" shows that you care about the order. Guests feel the special treatment when you repeat their order as you serve their drink.
4. Check back for a second cocktail.	4. Be courteous and bring the second round if ordered, following the same procedure as the first round. Remove all first round empty glasses and napkins. Put down new napkins and serve the drinks.	4. Check back when drinks are approximately two-thirds consumed.
5. Take the food order.	5. Ask the guests if they are ready to order. Explain the chef's specialty and answer any questions about the food. Take orders beginning with the ladies when possible. Suggest appetizers, soups, or salads as appropriate to help them plan a complete meal. Proceed to the male guests. Be sure to inform the guests of the approximate cooking times of selections that may require some wait for preparation.	5. Guests expect you to know about the food. When you are asked a question and do not know the answer, do not bluff. Go to the kitchen or manager and find out the answer. Then go back and tell the guest. Suggesting menu items helps a hesitant guest make the decision he/she really wanted to make in the beginning. It also creates sales. Communicate with the guest in this very important step. It is more than taking orders. It should be "menu planning."

(Continued)

(Continued)

WHAT TO DO	HOW TO DO IT	ADDITIONAL INFORMATION
6. Take the wine order.	6. Ask: "Have you chosen a wine?" When you are asked to help, ask whether the guest prefers red or white, dry or semi-sweet, etc., to get some idea of his/her preferences. Then, point out two or three choices that fall within the characteristics described. The guest can choose according to price or other factors. Excuse yourself from the table and assure the guest that you will be right back with the first course.	6. Know the wine list. Always be careful to recognize the timid guest who is a novice at selecting wines. Be prepared to coach them through a selection process that will meet their needs. Experienced wine drinkers will usually know what they want to order and will not expect much assistance. This is not the time to feed your ego by demonstrating your technical wine knowledge and intimidating the guest. Be confident, but be courteous.

Source: Forrest, pp. 45-46.

organized to cover all areas where improved performance is required. **Training plans** and **training lessons** must be developed (see Exhibits 7.4 and 7.5). Each training plan outlines a series of sessions—each of which relates to objectives developed for the training program. A training plan is, simply, an outline of all aspects of the proposed training program. Training lessons are developed after training plans are constructed. These tools outline the specific activities that should take place during each session described in the training plan. The training lesson, then, indicates activities required for trainees to attain performance objectives developed for the lesson.

Select Training Methods

A final step in planning for training involves the selection of training methods. There are many possible methods; these are described in more detail later in this chapter.

Prepare Trainees

A trainee should have at least a basic understanding of what the job involves before being confronted with a training program. Trainees like to know what to expect; the "mechanics" of the training sessions must be explained. Likewise, employee ideas which have been selected earlier in the planning process can often be helpful.

Trainees must be allowed time to participate in training activities. This is far different from a traditional practice in the hospitality industry which squeezes training in with other activities. Employees must understand that training is not punishment. They must realize that it is not a waste of time or an insult to their intelligence.

Exhibit 7.4 Sample Group Training Plan for Front Desk Clerks

TRAINING PLAN

General Goal: To improve the performance of front desk clerks

Specific Performance Objectives: At the conclusion of the training, trainees will be able to:

1. Register guests according to procedures outlined in the company's procedures manual.
2. Assign rooms according to guest requests for type of accommodation and be able to "up-sell" rooms.
3. Verify guest identity and credit according to established policies.
4. Make correct entries and adjustments on guest folios.
5. Satisfy special guest requests.
6. Respond to guest complaints according to property policies and guest relations practices.
7. Check out guests and handle all approved forms of payment.

Performance Standards: Employees must perform each job according to specifications in applicable job breakdowns.

Employees Involved (names): G. Harris, M. Taylor, B. Williams, B. Conners, H. Snyder, T. Schmidt, H. Bernstein, J. Tyson, K. Evans, B. Atwood, F. Fisher, P. Harnett.

Date	Time	Location
9/14/80	2:00-3:00 p.m.	Cherry Room, Front Desk
9/15/80	2:00-3:00 p.m.	Cherry Room
9/16/80	2:00-3:00 p.m.	Cherry Room
9/17/80	2:00-3:00 p.m.	Appleblossom Room
9/18/80	2:00-3:00 p.m.	Cherry Room, Front Desk

Methods of Instruction (by session) and Assignment of Trainer:

Session #1 Lecture/Discussion, Role Plays ....(Obj. 1-3) J. Jones
Session #2 Demonstration, Conference ....(Obj. 4) J. Jones, A. Smith
Session #3 Lecture/Discussion, Panel........................(Obj. 5) J. Jones, T. Doe S. Tyler, M. Beck
Session #4 Role Play, Case Studies ....(Obj. 6) J. Jones, A. Smith
Session #5 Demonstration ....(Obj. 7) J. Jones, A. Smith

Equipment Needed (by sessions)

Session #1 Folios, reservation examples, chart of room types, rate card, job breakdowns #301, #302, and #303
Session #2 Folios, posting equipment, job breakdowns #304
Session #3 Guest relations policies, guest services handbook, job breakdown #305
Session #4 Guest complaints policy, guest services handbook, job breakdown #306
Session #5 Folios, cash register, cashiering manual, credit card imprinter, credit card vouchers, cash bank, job breakdown #307

Training Room Setup (by sessions):

Session #1 Schoolroom, podium, flip chart
Session #2 Auditorium, demonstration around posting machine at the desk, flip chart
Session #3 Schoolroom, head table with 3 chairs, flip chart
Session #4 Rounds (4 per table), flip chart
Session #5 Schoolroom, demonstration around cash register at the desk, demonstration and practice of credit card procedures in classroom

Audio-Visual Requirements: Flip chart in classroom each session

Class Rules: No planned breaks due to length of sessions (1 hour each).
Smoking is permitted in classrooms.
Smoking is not permitted in Front Desk area during demonstrations.

Evaluation

Session #1 Knowledge test of check-in policies and procedures; performance testing of role plays
Session #2 Performance tests of posting operations
Session #3 Knowledge test of guest relations and guest service policies and procedures
Session #4 Performance tests of role plays; attitude assessments of case situations
Session #5 Performance tests of cashiering and check-out operations

Special Notes or Reminders: Block rooms for training at least 2 weeks prior to first session.

Source: Forrest, p. 176.

Exhibit 7.5 Sample Training Lesson for Guest Relations

TRAINING LESSON

Objective: The ability to handle guest problems that arise at the front desk.

Content	Process	Who	Time
1. Identify five guest problems that have arisen during the past month.	Brainstorm. List problems on flip chart.	Total group	10 min.
2. Discuss ways that the problems could have been prevented or solved.	Brainstorm. Each group take one problem which has been identified in (1) above.	Small groups (3-4/group)	20 min.
3. Compare approaches used by different groups.	Spokesperson from each group reports steps that could have been taken.	One person from each group.	10 min.
4. Identify principles for preventing or solving guest problems.	Brainstorm key points that each group presents.	Facilitator leads with group participation.	10 min.
5. Review organizational philosophy related to handling guests and compare with principles and techniques identified by the group.	Presentation with group participation.	Facilitator presentation with group suggestions.	10 min.

Source: Forrest, p. 178.

Conduct the Training

The actual "mechanics" for conducting training programs vary by the type of training method which is used. Details about several possible training methods are reviewed later in this chapter.

Evaluate the Training

Evaluation is necessary to determine the extent to which training has accomplished its objectives; that is, to what extent employees are more able to perform their jobs as a result of training experiences. Two components of training must be evaluated:

1. The training method which has been used

2. The actual results of the training program

Combined, these two aspects of evaluation help determine whether the training was successful and whether it should be repeated. Evaluation helps supervisors assess whether progress is being made toward attaining objectives established for training activities.

Coach and Counsel Final steps in the basic training process often involve coaching and counseling. The former activity involves a constant review, reinforcement, or reminder to the trainees about what was learned in the training program. Counseling, while not as directly related to training, may become necessary when training is not effective. Both coaching and counseling techniques are reviewed later in this chapter.

Training Methods for Individual Employees

Training programs in the hospitality industry have traditionally emphasized individual, one-on-one, on-the-job training (OJT) programs. With this plan, employees "tag along" with an experienced employee and are taught procedures while watching, talking with, and helping the experienced staff member. The concept of individualized training is excellent. In practice, however, these training programs are often ineffective because they are improperly conducted. The four-step training method incorporates simple procedures which can be used for OJT programs:

Step 1 **Preparation.** Procedures for preparing OJT programs are the same as those for planning and preparing any other type of training. (We have noted the need to develop job lists and job breakdowns, to write training objectives, prepare the trainee, and select a trainer.)

Step 2 **Presentation.** After the trainer has been selected, the training programs have been developed, and trainees have been selected and prepared, the actual training process can begin. First of all, job breakdowns should be used as a guide. Share these with the trainee so that he/she will understand what exactly must be done on the job. After reviewing how a task should be done, demonstrate how to do it. Speak in simple terms, take adequate time, and be patient. Characteristics of good trainers and the procedures for training which were reviewed earlier become important concerns at this point. After a procedure has been demonstrated, it should be repeated to help the trainee understand the process.

Step 3 **Practice.** After the trainee is familiar with the job, he/she should attempt the task alone. The trainee should be required to repeat the demonstration and explain what is being done. Allow time for practice, and provide coaching as necessary. For example, you might compliment the trainee for correct performance or make suggestions for improved performance.

Step 4 **Follow-up.** After completing steps one through three, the trainee should be able to perform the job task alone. Continue to observe the employee to make sure the job is being done correctly. You should provide positive reinforcement and feedback to help the employee better perform his/her job and, at the same time, develop a positive attitude toward training.

On-the-job training is not the only individualized training method. Three others are also discussed.

Other Individualized Instruction Methods

Individualized instruction involves custom-tailoring the instructional needs of a specific trainee. It may include independent study, team teaching methods, computer-assisted instruction, and other techniques. These methods have great potential for training staff members at higher levels of the organization. Therefore, supervisors might want to know about them.

When individualized instruction is used, the trainer responds to the trainee's specific needs, checks progress, and offers assistance as required. Further, the trainee generally perceives that the training is personalized to meet his/her specific needs. The trainee can progress according to his/her own efforts, and his/her performance and preferences have some effect in determining the training sequence.

Other benefits are that the trainee can determine how much assistance or interaction is necessary and which resources are best suited to his/her needs. Generally, the trainee will believe that performance standards are attainable and relevant. After all, he/she provided some assistance in their development.

As a final step, the trainee must be evaluated against his/her own potential and on his/her progress toward attaining learning goals.

Learner-Controlled Instruction

Learner-controlled instruction (LCI) is a specialized form of individualized training that is used for management training in some multi-unit food service and lodging operations. It differs from a traditional training approach in that the trainee manages and controls the learning process. It is, then, an application of both directed learning and individualized instruction. Learning outcomes are expressed in performance terms. LCI programs make use of contract learning techniques. The learning environment becomes the actual job situation. Learning is indicated by demonstrated mastery under specific conditions; feedback about performance and progress must be provided on a continuous basis. The LCI trainee controls the pace and sequence of learning activities; he/she can bypass required learning activities by demonstrating a mastery of necessary behavior. This approach to training is relatively new in the hospitality industry. It shows great promise, and it is possible that supervisors aspiring to higher organizational levels will, at some time in their careers, be exposed to this innovative training alternative.[2]

Correspondence Courses

Individuals who are interested in self-improvement can take correspondence courses on subjects applicable to the hospitality industry. Such courses are available from the Educational Institute of the American Hotel & Motel Association, the National Institute for the Foodservice Industry, and the American Management Association.

Correspondence courses are taught with materials that trainees read and study alone, on their own time. Trainees complete examinations and submit them for feedback and final credit to the organization that is offering the course. Correspondence courses are appropriate for adults because they are self-paced, individualized, voluntary, and self-directed. An unlimited number of employees within an organization can be enrolled concurrently, yet each person proceeds at his/her own pace. Since correspondence study employees complete the training on their own time, employers do not have to pay employees for the training, and correspondence or home study does not take time away from the job. Also, in order to add realism to the training, the employees can practice applying what they are studying while they are at work.

Coaching and Counseling Procedures

Often, supervisors do not think that they have time to discuss, on a one-on-one basis, job-related or personal problems which affect their staff members' performance. On the other hand, earlier chapters have indicated the need to get to know employees in order to gain their cooperation and confidence. Supervisors should, then, give a priority to meeting with each employee privately on a routine basis to (a) discover how the employee believes he/she is doing on the job and (b) to jointly assess areas for future development. This topic will be discussed further when we consider employee performance reviews (see Chapter 8).

Some employee meetings may directly relate to a follow-up of training activities. When supervisors use coaching techniques they are really providing extended job training. **Coaching**, the process of providing feedback to an employee, reinforces knowledge and skills that have been developed through training. It can also help correct and further develop job skills. When coaching employees, the supervisor needs to assess reasons why training has not yielded long-range job performance improvements. Was the training ineffective? Is there an "attitude" or related problem which keeps the employee from performing the job correctly? A questioning process can be used to reach a mutual agreement about what actions will be taken to resolve job-related problems which have been observed. Let's see when coaching might be helpful:

Immediately after training, employees generally are able to properly perform the tasks that were covered in training sessions. Over time, they may forget and/or become confused about some procedures which they once knew. Coaching is needed to refresh their memories of how to perform these procedures correctly. By coaching, you show patience and understanding to the employee who is faced with recalling a wide range of job information and techniques presented in training.

Normally, coaching is problem-oriented; it must focus upon problems which the employee faces when trying to perform the job. Sometimes the coaching activity may involve no more than pointing out an error and working with an employee to correct it at the job-site. At other times, however, a formal interview might be necessary. Sometimes, in fact, an extensive pre-interview evaluation is necessary in order to adequately consider the employee's performance, the possible reasons for problems, and strategies to deal with them.

Counseling, in contrast to coaching, focuses more upon the attitudes or feelings of the employee than it does upon the inability of the staff member to perform specific aspects of the job. The wise supervisor recognizes that the employee is faced with the same personal concerns both on and off the job. Few supervisors, however, are trained psychologists. Many times, the best approach for a supervisor to take when he/she is aware that an employee has (or seems to have) a personal problem is to suggest specialized professional counseling. This approach is far better than the well-intentioned supervisor who, because of the lack of knowledge about how to deal with special personal problems, actually causes greater difficulty for the employee.

There are times, however, when a patient and concerned supervisor can serve as a confidant, give common sense advice or, at least, suggest alternatives which might provide personal assistance to an employee. The matter of dealing with personal problems, then, must be of great concern to the supervisor. Often, the effectiveness of a counseling interview depends upon the relationship of trust which has been established. The supervisor must assure the employee that everything discussed will remain confidential. Likewise, an atmosphere must be established in which the employee will feel able to discuss any matter without fear of offending or alienating the supervisor. Generally, a counseling session is best conducted by using a nondirective approach in which open-ended questions are utilized. Interviewing techniques are discussed in more detail in Chapter 10.

NOTES

1. This section, and much of the remaining chapter, is based on Lewis C. Forrest, Jr., *Training for the Hospitality Industry* (East Lansing, Mich.: Educational Institute of the American Hotel & Motel Association, 1983).

2. Readers interested in more detailed information about learner-controlled instruction are referred to Forrest, pp. 110-125.

PAGE FOURTEEN

Supervision at the Brandywine Room

Stacey appreciated the help she was getting from her contacts in the Personnel Department. By putting together bits and pieces of information from several supervision and management books, Stacey had developed a new employee orientation checklist. She was anxious to share it with Mr. George. "Wouldn't it be great," thought Stacey, "if something that I developed could be used throughout the hotel?"

After a brief review of the checklist, Mr. George told Stacey he was impressed and wanted to show the list to the Executive Council (which was comprised of the general manager, the assistant general manager, and department heads).

Stacey received permission to use the checklist in the Brandywine Room. She decided to do a test-run with several new employees so that she could become aware of any modifications that might be necessary.

New Employee Orientation Checklist

Name of New Employee: ____________________ Position: ____________

Department: ____________________ Supervisor: ____________________

Date Hired: ________________

Instructions — Initial and date when each of the following activities are completed.

Part I — Introduction

- ☐ ____ Welcome to new position (give your name, find out what name the employee prefers to be called, etc.)
- ☐ ____ Tour of property
- ☐ ____ Tour of department work area
- ☐ ____ Introduction to fellow employees

Part II — Discussion of Daily Procedures

- ☐ ____ Beginning/ending time of workshift
- ☐ ____ Break and meal periods
- ☐ ____ Uniforms (responsibilities for, cleanliness of, etc.)
- ☐ ____ Assignment of locker
- ☐ ____ Employee meals (if any)
- ☐ ____ Parking requirements
- ☐ ____ First aid and accident reporting procedures
- ☐ ____ Time clock or "sign-in log" requirements
- ☐ ____ Other (specify)
- ☐ ____
- ☐ ____

Part III — Information About Salary/Wages

- ☐ ____ Rate of pay
- ☐ ____ Deductions
- ☐ ____ Pay periods
- ☐ ____ Overtime policies
- ☐ ____ Complete all payroll withholding, insurance, and related forms.
- ☐ ____ Other (specify)
- ☐ ____
- ☐ ____

Part IV — Review of Policies and Rules

- ☐ ____ Safety, fires, accidents
- ☐ ____ Maintenance and use of equipment
- ☐ ____ Punctuality
- ☐ ____ Absenteeism
- ☐ ____ Illness
- ☐ ____ Emergencies
- ☐ ____ Use of telephone
- ☐ ____ Leaving work station
- ☐ ____ Smoking/eating/drinking
- ☐ ____ Packages
- ☐ ____ Vacations
- ☐ ____ Other (specify)
- ☐ ____

Part V — Employee Handbook/Related Information

☐ ____ Received and reviewed
☐ ____ Review of employee appraisal process
☐ ____ Review of organization chart
☐ ____ Review of job description
☐ ____ Review of department's responsibilities
☐ ____ Review of all benefit plans
☐ ____ Discuss performance standards/expectations
☐ ____ Discuss career path possibilities

Part VI — Miscellaneous Orientation Procedures (Review all other areas covered with the new employee)

____

____

____

I certify that all the above activities were completed on the date indicated.

____________________	____________________
Employee	Date
____________________	____________________
Supervisor	Date

Later that day, on one of Stacey's visits to the bookshelf in the personnel office, Rachel Case (the personnel director) called Stacey in to show her something. "Stacey," she said, "take a look at this. A friend of mine from The Twin Towers Hotel across the city gave me a copy of a checklist for training which was developed by his property. Since I know you are interested in this topic, I thought perhaps you would like a copy. Do me a favor, OK? Take a look at it and let me know from your perspective as a supervisor what you think. I'd be especially interested to know whether these points are practical, which should be done by a supervisor, and which are the most important to consider when putting together a really effective training program."

Stacey was elated. For the second time today she was having an opportunity to share her ideas with top management staff in the hotel. Likewise, for the second time, there was a possibility that her ideas could have hotelwide implications. "Sure," Stacey said. "I would like to take a look at the training checklist. I'll be very happy to give you my comments about it. I'm glad you think enough of me and my ideas to ask for my comments. Do you mind if I put some of the ideas to use?" She knew what the answer would be and she thought to herself, "Being a supervisor is fun, especially when you are in a position to make a difference."

Checklist For Effective Training

Part I: Recruit, Select, and Orient "Trainable" Employees

☐ 1. Responsibilities for recruitment and selection are clearly separated between personnel (staff) and the user (line) department.

☐ 2. Final selection decisions are made by the user department.

☐ 3. Personnel needs are planned for when possible; an active file of potentially acceptable candidates is maintained.

☐ 4. All company policies regarding hiring are closely followed.

☐ 5. Job descriptions—which list major job duties and personal qualities needed by employees to successfully perform the job—are used as part of the selection process.

☐ 6. Applicants are recruited from all possible sources.

☐ 7. All applicants are required to complete an application form.

☐ 8. An initial applicant interview is used to screen potential employees.

☐ 9. All managers and supervisors are trained in effective selection and interviewing techniques.

☐ 10. The manager/supervisor who will be responsible for the new employee is involved in the selection decision.

☐ 11. All references are checked.

☐ 12. Selection tests (written and/or performance) are used, where applicable, as part of the screening process and selection decision.

☐ 13. All new employees are given a thorough orientation to their new job:

- ☐ information about the company is provided
- ☐ benefits, pay, etc., are explained
- ☐ the organization of the company—and where the employee "fits in"—is explained
- ☐ working conditions—breaks, meal periods, training schedules, etc.—are outlined
- ☐ company rules and regulations are discussed
- ☐ the new employee is introduced to the work group
- ☐ uniforms, lockers, special equipment, etc., are provided
- ☐ an employee handbook is given to the new employee

Part II: Planning for Training

☐ 14. Job-related training is presented to every employee.

☐ 15. A job list is developed for each position. It indicates all skills and abilities which an employee must perform as part of the job.

☐ 16. Employees who perform the job are involved in preparation of the job list for their position.

☐ 17. Job breakdowns are used to break down each task on the job list. Each task is defined in terms of:

- ☐ a performance-based statement to describe the task
- ☐ tools and materials needed to do the task
- ☐ steps in performing the task
- ☐ how each task step is to be performed
- ☐ any additional information which is needed

☐ 18. Experienced management, supervisors, and employees are involved in developing job breakdowns.

☐ 19. Job descriptions are written around the job breakdown information.

☐ 20. Job performance standards which indicate quality and quantity requirements for each task identified in the job breakdowns are specified.

☐ 21. Work simplification procedures are utilized to ensure that work being analyzed is being performed as efficiently as possible.

Part III: Basic Principles of Learning are Incorporated Into Training

☐ 22. Learning activities are planned to involve the trainee's sense of hearing, seeing, tasting, smelling, and touching.

☐ 23. Trainees are shown the personal benefits of training and learning.

☐ 24. Training maximizes trainee participation in accordance with performance objectives.

☐ 25. The training must relate to the trainees' experience.

☐ 26. An informal training environment is utilized.

☐ 27. A variety of training methods is utilized.

☐ 28. Trainees are objectively informed of their training progress.

☐ 29. Training periods do not exceed the trainees' attention span.

☐ 30. Training sessions are spaced over time rather than concentrated into long sessions.

☐ 31. Training takes into account the learning speed of the trainees.

☐ 32. Training stresses the right way to do things in a step-by-step approach and incorporates repetition into the process.

☐ 33. Cooperation—*not* competition—between trainees is built into the training process.

☐ 34. Trainees know exactly what is expected of them when training begins.

☐ 35. Trainers are qualified to conduct the training.

☐ 36. Training is adapted to the needs of the individual trainee.

☐ 37. Trainees are able to practice what has been learned.

Part IV: Individual Training is Effectively Designed and Implemented

☐ 38. On-the-job training is properly planned.

☐ 39. The trainer is selected, based on skills and interest, and is prepared for the training:

- ☐ training objectives are written
- ☐ training methods are determined
- ☐ training timetables are established
- ☐ training locations are selected for effective results
- ☐ necessary materials and tools are collected

☐ 40. The trainee is prepared for training:

- ☐ reasons for training are explained
- ☐ the knowledge and experience of the trainee are assessed

- ☐ 41. The training is presented in an effective manner:
  - ☐ procedures are explained and demonstrated
  - ☐ the trainer speaks in simple terms, takes adequate time, is patient, and recognizes and utilizes principles of learning (see Part III)
  - ☐ the trainee repeats the training to demonstrate learning
- ☐ 42. The following are used where applicable:
  - ☐ audio-visual aids
  - ☐ individualized instruction techniques
  - ☐ learner-controlled instruction (LCI) techniques
  - ☐ correspondence courses
- ☐ 43. The trainee is coached as necessary after training to ensure that proper procedures are learned and utilized.

Part V: Group Training Methods are Effectively Designed and Implemented

- ☐ 44. The group trainer is prepared and qualified to train. He/she:
  - ☐ knows how to lead the group
  - ☐ asks and answers questions
  - ☐ uses props and training aids to facilitate the training
  - ☐ practices techniques to build confidence within the individual trainees
- ☐ 45. Group training is properly planned; the four-step training method is used to facilitate planning.
- ☐ 46. Various group training techniques are used where applicable. The following methods are used as appropriate:
  - ☐ lecture method is limited to use when retention of details is not essential
  - ☐ demonstration method is widely used for basic skills training
  - ☐ conference method is used when the training objective involves problem solving
  - ☐ seminar method is used for upgrading the knowledge and skills of experienced employees
  - ☐ panel methods are used for presentations by in-house and outside resource people
  - ☐ role playing is used for interpersonal skills training
  - ☐ case study method is used to teach situational analysis techniques
  - ☐ simulation method is used to develop and refine skills
  - ☐ project method is used with experienced employees for upgrading systems
- ☐ 47. The group is properly oriented to the training which will take place.

- ☐ 48. Techniques to control the group—and the learning which is to take place—are utilized.
- ☐ 49. Handouts are used where applicable.

Part VI: Developing the Training Program

- ☐ 50. Training needs are assessed.
- ☐ 51. Broad training goals are defined.
- ☐ 52. Specific and measurable training objectives are defined.
- ☐ 53. A training plan is developed for the department. It determines:
  - ☐ what must be learned and by whom
  - ☐ how much is to be learned
  - ☐ when it should be learned
  - ☐ where the training will take place
  - ☐ what training methods will be used
  - ☐ what evaluation methods will be used
- ☐ 54. Training lessons are developed based upon the training plan. They tell:
  - ☐ the objective (outcome) for each lesson
  - ☐ what the trainer must do
  - ☐ how the trainer should do it
  - ☐ other information of help to the trainer

Part VII: Evaluating the Training Program

- ☐ 55. Methods used to undertake training are evaluated.
- ☐ 56. Training results are evaluated.
- ☐ 57. Measurable information is collected as part of the evaluation process.
- ☐ 58. Evaluation information collected is properly interpreted.
- ☐ 59. Evaluation information is used by the manager/trainer responsible for training.
- ☐ 60. Training evaluation focuses upon the learning process. It includes:
  - ☐ what you want to know
  - ☐ where and how information will be obtained
  - ☐ by whom the information will be collected
  - ☐ how information will be analyzed
  - ☐ what the information means
- ☐ 61. Information collected as part of the evaluation process is accurate, measurable, and objective.
- ☐ 62. Evaluation occurs before, during, and after training.
- ☐ 63. Training evaluation is undertaken using a variety of methods. In use are:
  - ☐ questionnaires

- ☐ interviews
- ☐ case studies
- ☐ planned observations
- ☐ study of records
- ☐ tests

☐ 64. Tools used to evaluate must be:

- ☐ valid—the tools measure what needs to be evaluated
- ☐ reliable—the tools adequately measure all subject matter or trainees
- ☐ objective—the tools provide a tangible basis for evaluation
- ☐ practical—the tools recognize time, cost, and convenience
- ☐ simple—the tools are simple to use and easy to understand, administer, and summarize

☐ 65. Evaluation generally makes use of simple, numerical counts, percentages, and averages to summarize and interpret the information in understandable terms.

Part VIII: Trainer Guidelines for Speaking and Writing

☐ 66. Trainers know exactly what is to be said.

☐ 67. Trainers look at the person(s) to whom they are speaking when possible.

☐ 68. Trainers ask trainees if they understand what was said.

☐ 69. Trainers listen and hear trainees in order to evaluate understanding of what is said.

☐ 70. Trainers recall educational backgrounds of listeners/readers when developing training materials.

☐ 71. Trainers use short sentences; written statements are precise.

☐ 72. Trainers recognize that physical obstacles (noise, lighting, temperature, etc.) can be barriers to learning.

☐ 73. Trainers control the training and do not let trainees' actions/responses interfere with the training.

☐ 74. Trainers adequately defend, justify, and explain concepts taught in order to overcome resistance to change.

☐ 75. Trainers think as they speak to avoid losing their thoughts and their audience.

☐ 76. Trainers avoid jumping to conclusions, hearing what they want to hear, or acting with prejudice.

☐ 77. Trainers are well organized

Part IX: Coaching and Counseling Procedures

☐ 78. Coaching procedures are used to provide feedback to trainees as an extended part of the training.

☐ 79. Counseling procedures are used to help employees with one-on-one problem solving, encouraging them to seek solutions on their own.

☐ 80. Employees are encouraged to get involved in appraising problems and outlining possible alternative solutions.

☐ 81. Employees are encouraged to take an active role in coaching and counseling sessions.

☐ 82. Managers do more listening than speaking while coaching and counseling.

☐ 83. Procedures for effective use of directed (focused) and nondirective (allowing employees to explain what is meant) interviews are well known and properly utilized.

Part X: Training Resources

☐ 84. Trainers make maximum use of a wide variety of resources as training is planned and implemented, including:

- ☐ colleges and universities
- ☐ vocational and technical schools
- ☐ continuing education and extension programs
- ☐ externship work programs
- ☐ trade associations
- ☐ sales representatives
- ☐ equipment manufacturers
- ☐ Chambers of Commerce/other civic groups
- ☐ Small Business Administration/Small Business Institute
- ☐ libraries
- ☐ professional training societies
- ☐ labor unions
- ☐ apprentice programs
- ☐ competitors
- ☐ special counseling services
- ☐ community service organizations
- ☐ general training programs
- ☐ outside consultants
- ☐ governmental agencies
- ☐ packaged training programs

8 Evaluating Employee Performance

PAGE FIFTEEN

Supervision at the Brandywine Room

Ever since Stacey Francis had been at the Brandywine Room, she had been concerned about the process used to evaluate employees. She remembered that in many conversations she had with food servers before she became dining room manager, the performance review process was considered "just a joke." The annual evaluation frequently amounted to nothing more than a five-minute talk with the dining room manager. The review focused on selected negative incidents that took place since the last review. Few, if any, constructive comments resulted from the sessions. It seemed as though the supervisor only conducted the evaluation because it was required by hotel policy. So, the supervisor just "went through the motions."

Stacey knew that much good could come from employee evaluations, if they were done properly. These ideas had been reinforced by conversations with Mr. George and her friends in the Personnel Department.

Now that she was dining room manager, Stacey was determined to improve the evaluation process in her department. The first step was to find out what she could do. With Mr. George's permission, she again visited Rachel Case, the personnel director.

The process of evaluating employees is integral to the supervisor's job. Some evaluation takes place informally on a daily basis. These judgments occur when the supervisor interacts with employees and assesses the quality of their work. However, a more formal evaluation also is needed to provide a structure for informing employees about their work performance.

Defending the employee evaluation is easy. The "golden rule" method of supervision, discussed throughout this text, also applies here: Would the supervisor like to know how his/her work is being judged by department managers? The answer probably is yes. The supervisor, like his/her subordinate employees, has basic concerns about job security and performance. Employees, too, would like to know how their boss, the supervisor, assesses their work and what improvements might be made.

The Supervisor's Role in Performance Reviews

As part of the responsibility of directing staff members, the supervisor must assume a role in their evaluation. There is, however, no "hard and fast" rule about what this role should be. Let's look at some examples.

In one property, schedules of front desk clerks may cross several workshifts that are staffed by different supervisors. The employee's immediate superior, the shift supervisor, will be a different person depending on what shift the employee works. Therefore, no single supervisor can adequately review the employee's performance. Who, then, should review the performance of the front desk clerk? Depending on the organization of the department, there may be an assistant front office manager who is responsible for this task. Alternatively, the front office manager may assume this role. When a large property has many front desk clerks, the department head (front office manager) may not be able to handle this responsibility without a great deal of input from the assistant front office manager and several front office supervisors. In smaller properties, however, the shift supervisor may report directly to the front office manager. When this occurs—especially where there are few front desk clerks to be evaluated—the responsibility for performance reviews could rest with the department head (front office manager).

Let's look at an example of employee evaluation in the kitchen operation. Who should evaluate the work of an entry-level dishwasher? While that employee's supervisor may be a "head dishwasher," he/she may have few administrative responsibilities. Perhaps he/she only directs the physical work of employees. The supervisor may spend most of his/her time washing dishes along with the other dishwashers. A more effective way to handle evaluations would be for the boss of the head dishwasher, who might be the executive steward, to conduct performance reviews in the dishwashing department.

In these examples, the employee's immediate supervisor may not be directly responsible for the evaluations. Who handles that function depends on the size and structure of the property. Let's look at a third example. Who should supervise the work of the dining room manager in the hotel or restaurant food service operation? In most instances, this would be done by the supervisor's immediate boss, especially if he/she is the food and beverage director. (In our case study of the Brandywine Room, Stacey Francis, the dining room manager, has an immediate boss, Mr. George, who is the food and beverage director and is responsible for her evaluation.)

Role Depends on Operation's Size, Structure

Several factors have been identified from these three examples. First, an employee's immediate supervisor may not be the staff member who ultimately conducts performance reviews. The size of the operating department also is a factor. As the number of employees within a department increases, it is more difficult for the department head to make evaluation decisions. At the same time, there probably are more intermediate level managers/supervisors who can assume responsibility for this task. We now understand that the supervisor's responsibilities may determine whether or not he/she undertakes employee performance reviews. While the department head ultimately is responsible for employee evaluations, the authority to do this may be delegated to a subordinate depending on the structure of the specific organization.

When a supervisor has total authority and responsibility to evaluate employees, he/she must recognize and use performance review principles. If the department head or another manager assumes these obligations, the employee's immediate supervisor must: (a) be able to answer employees' questions about the performance review process, (b) provide information on the evaluation process to the person doing the performance review, and (c) understand the results of the performance review. The supervisor should know, for example, that the evaluator and the employee agree on problem areas that need improvement. A supervisor also should help the employee, through on-site supervision, training, coaching, and counseling, to improve those job-related activities that were graded poorly during the evaluation session. The supervisor also can comment on the employee performance review process. Perhaps the evaluation procedures can be improved. As the supervisor becomes aware of techniques that may improve the evaluation process, he/she can pass ideas on to management officials who are responsible for developing and implementing performance review programs.

Remember that the supervisor, too, must be evaluated by his/her boss. No matter who assumes ultimate responsibility for employee performance reviews, the supervisor is very involved in the process.

Development of Procedures

The same procedures for performance reviews should be used throughout the property. Each department and/or supervisor should not establish independent rules, procedures, and policies for conducting a performance review. In a large property with a personnel department, the basic design of the program may be developed by that department. Suggestions from the general manager, department heads, and other top- and middle-level managers should be included in the performance review process. In smaller properties, the owner/manager often will assume the responsibility for developing a program, while using advice from the management team.

Union Input

Employee unions have a voice in decisions that relate to performance reviews. If the results of the review process are tied to a wage-salary-benefits program, there definitely will be input from employee unions. (Detailed information about the supervisor and employee unions is found in Chapter 15.)

Benefits of Performance Reviews

Recognize Individual

Performance reviews can benefit the employee, supervisor, and organization.[1] For example, a performance review helps recognize individual employees. By focusing attention on the employee and by giving him/her an opportunity to help design work, the performance review provides a forum for recognizing the worth of the ideas contributed by the employee.

Identify Strengths, Weaknesses

Performance reviews help identify employee strengths and weaknesses. As the evaluator identifies employee strengths, he/she can compliment the employee. This makes the employee feel good and is a way to boost an employee's ego and esteem. Conversely, employee weaknesses can be identified and improvements in job performance can begin.

Report Progress

Performance reviews help employees involved in training programs know how well they are doing. Trainers also will know how effective the training program has been. Just like employees who want to know how they are doing on the job, supervisors and managers also must know how effectively their departments/sections are managed and to what extent organizational goals are being attained. Information stemming from employee performance reviews helps answer these questions.

Provide Basis for Coaching, Counseling

Performance reviews provide the basis for coaching and counseling employees who are experiencing job-related problems that were identified during the performance review session. Employees then can be coached in ways to resolve these problems. Personal problems also may surface during performance reviews. The evaluator may offer assistance or refer troubled employees to professionals who can provide required help.

Provide Basis for Wage/ Salary Decisions

Performance reviews also provide the basis for determining wages and salaries. When wages, salaries, merit increases, and bonuses are linked to job performance, employee evaluation sessions provide information that is helpful in making wage/salary decisions. Although employee unions may have critical interests in compensation matters, wage and salary adjustments should focus on job performance as well as employment seniority. (See Chapter 9 for additional information about compensation programs.)

Justify Job Actions

Justification for job actions results from effectively conducted evaluation sessions. Competencies of employees, which are recognized during performance reviews, can be strong factors that influence promotions, transfers, and other positive job actions. The inability to complete work can lead to demotions, terminations, or other negative job actions. Supervisors must constantly attempt to objectively evaluate employee competence. This can be accomplished through the performance review process and will have an impact on plans to further direct the work of the employees. (Remember that union concerns on these issues must be noted.)

Identify Problems, Needs

Performance review sessions, if done effectively, will identify job-related problems. This information can be useful in determining the need for training programs. If the review process indicates that some employees are deficient in several skills, for example, a group training session may be needed. On the other hand, individualized training programs or coaching sessions may help resolve specific problems with staff members.

Improve Management

As evaluators focus on an individual employee's work output, they should be aware of performance goals and the extent to which these are or are not being met. When supervisors interact with employees and discuss their strengths and weaknesses, they should consider the implications of these findings on their management styles and practices.

Improve Relationships

Performance reviews can help improve employee-management relationships. The evaluator and the employee must work together as they undertake the performance review process. When they become partners in this effort, team building begins. Relationships can develop so that the evaluator and the employees can learn what the other believes and how either party will react.

Performance Standards and the Review Process

Since the performance review process focuses on the employee and how well he/she works, the evaluator must know the employee's responsibilities and the levels of acceptable performance. Remember that in Chapter 7 supervisors who planned training programs were urged to develop lists that identify all tasks in a job and job breakdowns that indicate specific procedures for performing each task. Another step required the identification of performance standards for each task. The evaluator must know the employee's tasks and expected performance level. This information forms the basis of the review. The performance standard can be compared with the employee's actual performance. The difference between the two levels represents the improvement employees are expected to make in order to bring their work "up to par."

Planning for performance reviews is time-consuming. If training programs have been developed properly, however, much of the effort to undertake performance reviews will have been completed. With this insight into the performance review process, you should understand why simple evaluations consisting of "calling the employee in and talking it out" are not effective. The major emphasis in a properly conducted performance review is to explain how the employee's performance can be improved so that the quality and/or quantity of work can be brought closer to standard or expected performance. At the same time, the employee has a chance to tell the evaluator about factors in the job environment—including the supervisor, working conditions, and tasks to be performed—that, from the employee's perspective, also can be improved.

Performance Reviews and Employee Potential

The term **employee potential** means the best possible job that an employee can do. Actual work often falls short of the optimal performance level. There are at least two ways that employee potential relates to performance reviews. The evaluator must assess whether employees doing substandard work (work that does not meet required quality and/or quantity standards) can actually do better. Some staff members may be overemployed—not capable of performing required work. On the other hand, employees who are not working up to their potential can be helped through the performance review process.

A second area of employee potential concerns the abilities of employees to be promoted to a higher organizational level. Persons conducting performance reviews should consider this factor as the review process is undertaken. Evaluation of an employee's potential is enhanced when employees who are being considered for a promotion are given additional responsibilities that would be part of their new job. As the review process unfolds, the evaluator then can look at performance in these areas of added responsibility as well as in the ongoing work performed by the staff member.

When performance reviews indicate that employees are not working to their potential, the supervisor can implement motivational and human relations techniques to encourage the employee to perform at higher levels. In fact, the supervisor and/or evaluator who can determine that an employee can do better work already has taken the first step to understanding the employee. Some supervisors assume that employees always work to their best abilities. These supervisors view substandard work as the result of inability rather than conditions in the job environment which may inhibit the work. (This situation was addressed in Chapter 1 in the discussion on performance analysis problems.)

Approaches to Performance Reviews

Many methods of performance reviews have evolved over the years. This section will consider some of the more common types.

Comparative Methods

Comparative methods of performance reviews involve comparing employees to each other. There are four types.

Simple Ranking Method. The evaluator classifies employees in order from the best to the worst. This is done subjectively on the basis of overall performance.

Alternative Ranking Method. This is a modification of the first method which requires several steps. First the evaluator places the best employee at the top of the list and the worst employee at the bottom. The evaluator then selects the second best employee and puts him/her second from the top of the list and places the second worst employee second from the bottom of the list. This process continues until all employees have been included in the ranking list.

Paired Comparison Method. A third example of the comparative approach requires the evaluator to rank each employee from best to worst only in terms of a single factor, such as overall performance, quality of work, or receptivity to new ideas. Employees are "matched" not only with each other but also to specific factors that are important to an effective job performance.

Forced Distribution Method. With this approach the evaluator can assign only a certain number of employees to each of several categories being considered. For example, the supervisor may be permitted to rank only 10% of the employees as "superior" and 10% as "unacceptable." He/she then is forced to place a required percentage of the remaining employees in categories such as "above average," "average," and "below average."

A distinct disadvantage of these performance review methods is that the evaluator must compare employees with each other. It is unlikely that, in the hospitality industry, all workers supervised by one person perform identical tasks. Therefore, it becomes very difficult—if not impossible—to use these methods consistently, fairly, and objectively. Some of these techniques could be used with other methods. When used alone, comparative methods have serious limitations.

Absolute Standards Approach

Under the absolute standards approach, the evaluator assesses each employee's work performance without regard to other employees. Generally, there are three popular methods by which absolute standards can be incorporated into performance reviews.

Critical Incidents Method. With this method, the supervisor or other manager who is responsible for the evaluation keeps a "diary" of incidents that indicate good and bad job performance. These situations, often grouped to represent a dimension of the overall performance, are used to compile a review of each employee. When using this kind of evaluation, remember that a "diary" should be kept during the entire interval between reviews. This will avoid the unfortunate tendency to "write something down" immediately before a review is conducted. You should not dwell on negative incidents. While these are important, the positive aspects of an employee's performance should be considered. A sample of a critical incidents format is shown in Exhibit 8.1.

Weighted Checklist Method. With this technique, checklists are developed by supervisors and others familiar with the jobs of employees who are being evaluated. The checklist is weighted to represent the relative value of good and bad aspects of performance. A sample of a checklist format is shown in Exhibit 8.2.

Exhibit 8.1 Sample of Absolute Standards Evaluation: Critical Incidents Method

Instructions: Provide examples of employee activity in regard to each of the following. Indicate positive and negative incidents.

Name of Employee: ____________________

Activity	Date	Observed Activity
Follows Directions		
Work Quality		
Makes Suggestions		

Signature of Supervisor: ____________________ Date: __________

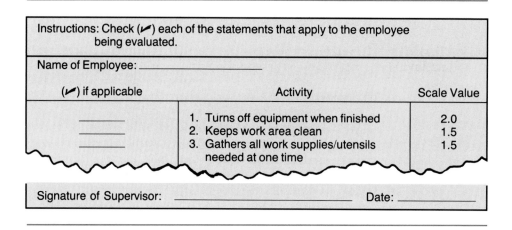

Exhibit 8.2 Sample of Absolute Standards Evaluation: Weighted Checklist Method

Instructions: Check (✔) each of the statements that apply to the employee being evaluated.

Name of Employee: ____________________

(✔) if applicable	Activity	Scale Value
______	1. Turns off equipment when finished	2.0
______	2. Keeps work area clean	1.5
______	3. Gathers all work supplies/utensils needed at one time	1.5

Signature of Supervisor: ____________________ Date: __________

Forced Choice Method. The forced choice method requires the evaluator to select one statement that describes how the employee performs on factors considered important for successful job performance. A sample of a format used in a forced choice method of performance review is shown in Exhibit 8.3. Many hospitality operations use the forced choice method in their performance evaluation process. The number of work factors addressed in this method may vary; consideration should be given to specific tasks that are important to a position.

Exhibit 8.3 Sample of Absolute Standards Evaluation: Forced Choice Method

Instructions: Check (✔) the box for each factor which exemplifies the quality of work performed by the employee.

Name of Employee: ____________

FACTOR	PERFORMANCE				
	Excellent	Above Average	Average	Below Average	Unacceptable
KNOWLEDGE OF JOB	Understands all aspects of work	Understands almost all aspects of work	Understands basic aspects of job	Has fair job knowledge	Has poor job knowledge
WORK QUALITY	Very accurate and neat	Seldom makes mistakes	Work normally acceptable	Work often unacceptable	Work seldom meets quality requirements

Signature of Supervisor: ____________ Date: ____________

Management by Objectives Method

When a management by objectives (MBO) method is used, the manager conducting the evaluation works with the employee to determine a set of goals. They also consider how goals are to be reached and establish procedures for evaluating goal attainment. Procedures in a management by objectives plan consist of four steps:

1. Goals are set for the employee to attain by the next evaluation.
2. The employee is given time on the job to master tasks needed to attain goals. (Provisions for training, coaching, and other developmental activities should be built into this plan.)
3. The actual goals attained are compared to the original goals during a subsequent evaluation. Reasons for goals not being met are explored. The evaluator solicits the employee's reactions to the level of goal attainment and the actions that should be taken.
4. New goals and new strategies for attaining them are developed for the next evaluation period.

Readers should recall that job lists and job breakdowns developed for training programs are helpful when employee evaluation is conducted. The evaluator and employee agree on the specific tasks that have been performed well and those activities where additional effort is needed. A copy of this material can be given to the employee for use in practice sessions to gain mastery of the requirements.

Exhibit 8.4 Job Descriptions and Performance Evaluations

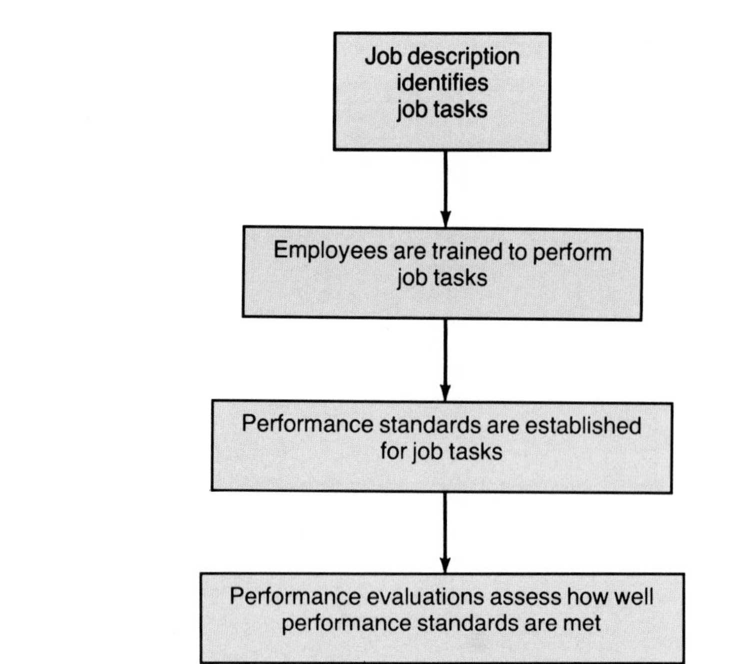

Direct Index Approach

The direct index approach quantifies the tasks and measures the employee's performance. For example, a receiving clerk could be evaluated against the actual number of products received that were unacceptable. (This would be compared to records of the number of product returns initiated after supplies were in inventory.) Or, the clerk could be evaluated against the number of times that stock shortages occurred because he/she failed to inform the purchasing department according to required operating procedures.

Job Descriptions and Performance Reviews

What do job descriptions have to do with performance reviews? A job description is used at the start of the hiring process while performance reviews occur after staff members are trained and working. Yet, both are integral to the personnel evaluation process.

Remember that job descriptions identify the tasks that must be performed. An employee should be trained to perform each task up to the performance standard established for it. Since performance reviews partially focus on the quality of work performed, the job description becomes the basis of the review process. Let's look more closely at its relationship to the evaluation process, as illustrated in Exhibit 8.4.

Exhibit 8.5 illustrates a form for conducting performance reviews. Note how each task is specifically identified and how the evaluator is expected to work with the employee in identifying and developing plans to resolve problems. The result of this process should be an employee who is better able to perform the job for which he/she was hired.

Exhibit 8.5 Performance Review Appraisal Form

GUEST SERVICE REPRESENTATIVE

PERFORMANCE APPRAISAL

PLEASE PRINT — Effective: 3/15/80

EMPLOYEE: ____________ SUPERVISOR 1: ____________

DATE: ____________ SUPERVISOR 2: ____________

INSTRUCTIONS: Please answer the questions listed in this section with a check mark (✓).

YES if: The individual's performance is totally acceptable.

NEEDS IMPROVEMENT if: The individual's performance is acceptable, but substantial improvement could be achieved.

UNACCEPTABLE if: The individual's performance is totally unacceptable.

I. SERVICE TO GUEST PROVIDED	YES	NI	UN
Are guest requests handled in a manner which provides for guest satisfaction?	☐	☐	☐
Are guest mail, packages and messages processed to provide prompt notification and delivery to guests?	☐	☐	☐
Is guest information treated discreetly?	☐	☐	☐
Room numbers?	☐	☐	☐
Names and addresses?	☐	☐	☐
Does the representative willingly and efficiently aid the guest in determining reservation needs?	☐	☐	☐
Does the representative offer to make system reservations for the guest?	☐	☐	☐
During registration?	☐	☐	☐
When the guest is checking out?	☐	☐	☐

SUPERVISOR'S COMMENTS:

EMPLOYEE'S COMMENTS:

II. PROCEDURES FOR GUEST ARRIVAL AND CHECK-IN FOLLOWED	YES	NI	UN
Are guests acknowledged in a timely manner?	☐	☐	☐
Are guests greeted in a friendly, positive manner?	☐	☐	☐
Are guests registered promptly and efficiently?	☐	☐	☐
Does the representative follow Holiday Inn policies and procedures for completing the registration card?	☐	☐	☐
All entries complete and legible?	☐	☐	☐
Time stamped and initialed?	☐	☐	☐
Does the representative notify guests paying by check of the hotel's check policy?	☐	☐	☐

III. PROCEDURES FOR REGISTERED GUEST FOLLOWED

	YES	NI	UN
Is all guest account information filed promptly and accurately?	☐	☐	☐
Folio?	☐	☐	☐
Registration card?	☐	☐	☐
Switchboard information slips?	☐	☐	☐
Room rack slips (if applicable)?	☐	☐	☐
Reservation cards?	☐	☐	☐
Credit card vouchers?	☐	☐	☐
Travel vouchers?	☐	☐	☐
Charges posted to the folio?	☐	☐	☐
Are the name and room number verified before charges are posted to the guest folio?	☐	☐	☐

SUPERVISOR'S COMMENTS:

EMPLOYEE'S COMMENTS:

IV. PROCEDURES FOR GUEST CHECK-OUT AND DEPARTURE FOLLOWED

	YES	NI	UN
Are guests' names repeated to assure the correct account is being pulled for check-out?	☐	☐	☐
Are inquiries made of the guest about recent charges which may not appear on the folio?	☐	☐	☐
Is the folio presented to the guest for review?	☐	☐	☐
Can the representative promptly locate the pertinent information and satisfactorily substantiate charges posted to the folio?	☐	☐	☐
Does the representative perform guest check-out procedures in an accurate and timely manner?	☐	☐	☐
Are sincere and friendly parting remarks always extended to the departing guest?	☐	☐	☐
Are departmental policies adhered to in checking out groups or tours?	☐	☐	☐

SUPERVISOR'S COMMENTS:

EMPLOYEE'S COMMENTS:

IX. PERSONAL CONDUCT MAINTAINED	YES	NI	UN
Does the representative comply with department conduct policies?	☐	☐	☐
Does the representative adhere to security and emergency procedures?	☐	☐	☐
Is the required name badge worn when on duty?	☐	☐	☐
Is the uniform worn as required?	☐	☐	☐

X. MAINTAINS INFORMATION AND COMMUNICATION SOURCES	YES	NI	UN
Does the representative notify the housekeeping department of late check-outs and room changes?	☐	☐	☐
Are check-outs promptly communicated to the housekeeping department?	☐	☐	☐
Does the representative communicate with the food and beverage cashiers the status of charge totals?	☐	☐	☐
Is the room rack updated promptly upon receipt of room status reports from the housekeeping department?	☐	☐	☐
Follow-up on discrepancies completed promptly?	☐	☐	☐
Are maintenance requests completed accurately?	☐	☐	☐
Copies distributed promptly?	☐	☐	☐

SUPERVISOR'S COMMENTS:
EMPLOYEE'S COMMENTS:

XII. DEPARTMENTAL EFFICIENCY AND SERVICES MAINTAINED	YES	NI	UN
Does the representative actively seek out work to be accomplished during slow periods?	☐	☐	☐
Are new assignments accepted and performed willingly?	☐	☐	☐
Does the representative maintain a continuous high level of work activity?	☐	☐	☐
Does the representative willingly aid in keeping desk area clean, neat and uncluttered?	☐	☐	☐
Does the individual work effectively with others to provide the best possible service to guests?	☐	☐	☐

SUPERVISOR'S COMMENTS:
EMPLOYEE'S COMMENTS:

EMPLOYEE DEVELOPMENT PLAN

PLEASE COMPLETE THIS ENTIRE PAGE.

Is this employee interested in moving into another job, either by being transferred or promoted? ____________

If yes, what? ____________

What does the employee need to learn to do so that he/she would be qualified for this job?

____

____

____

ACTION PLAN Please list in order, the development steps needed to qualify the employee for the desired job, or improve performance in the present job. Enter start and finish dates.	START DATE	FINISH DATE	ON SCHEDULE YES	ON SCHEDULE NO	COMPLETED CORRECTLY

During the next evaluation, indicate the employee's progress by completing the "On Schedule" and "Completed Correctly" columns for each development step.

Please list below all new skills learned during the last period. The action plan from the last evaluation should provide useful information to help you complete this.

____

____

OVERALL PERFORMANCE RATING

☐ GOOD - Quality and quantity of performance is consistent with expectations for the position. Performance is steady, adequate and of consistently good quality. Employee is clearly succeeding in position and progressing in personal development at an acceptable pace.

☐ MARGINAL- Quality and quantity of performance is not consistent with the expectations for the position. A significant number of the duties need improvement. The employee can remain in the position on the expectation that performance will improve.

☐ INADEQUATE PERFORMANCE - Quality or quantity of performance is at an unacceptable level. Employee cannot remain in the position unless immediate and dramatic improvement in performance occurs. Specific plan for correction is required.

Please mark the appropriate evaluation period:

☐ 90-day ☐ Mid-year ☐ End of year

Signature of:

Employee ____________

Supervisor 1 ____________

Supervisor 2 ____________

Courtesy: Holiday Inns, Inc.

Common Problems with Performance Reviews

Performance review methods can be classified in two ways. One, the trait approach, identifies qualities or traits that are required for effective performance. The individual is rated against a profile of desirable traits. Procedures and forms are developed to eliminate bias by the evaluator. This approach, however, does not focus on the employee's job performance. When used alone, this approach is of little help in reviewing job performance abilities.

The second basic approach considers goals and focuses on employee performance. If the evaluator and employee mutually define the factors to be considered in the evaluation, then performance goals can be developed. Once quantified, an employee's performance can be measured against the earlier performance to assess how well goals have been reached.

In addition to not focusing on performance factors that distinguish a "good" from "bad" employee, there are other common problems with performance reviews. Consider the following:

Use of Incorrect Procedures. In some hospitality operations there are few, if any, organized procedures for conducting performance reviews. Sometimes, reviews may be used only as a form of disciplinary action—not as an opportunity to gain the benefits of evaluation.

Use of Ineffective Forms. When evaluation forms do not recap factors that relate to job performance, such as focusing instead on popularity or personality traits, the review forms may cause problems with the process.

Lack of Performance Reviews. Some hospitality operations conduct no reviews at all. When important operating and employee decisions are made without information that can be gained from reviews, problems result.

Inadequate Management Abilities to Conduct Performance Reviews. Evaluators and supervisors may not have the knowledge or skills to adequately plan or conduct employee performance reviews. They use poor procedures which yield poor results.

Use of Complicated Performance Review Systems. When procedures and/or forms are too complicated, difficulties arise. Some evaluators may not know how to complete forms. Others may not know how to use information gained from reviews to plan improvements with the employee.

Irregular and/or Infrequent Reviews. When reviews are held irregularly and/or infrequently, benefits to be gained from a continuous review process are lost. Employees want—and supervisors should provide—continuous feedback on how employees can improve job performance.

Fear of Offending Employees. Some evaluators and supervisors may be afraid of offending employees by telling the truth during the performance review sessions. This is unfortunate because supervisors have a responsibility to be honest and to provide employees with the help they need to become better workers.

Comparisons of Employees. Some evaluators have a tendency to compare one employee's performance with that of another. (Several of the performance review methods previously noted require that this be done.) While this approach sometimes can be helpful, remember that the most effective comparison is between what the employee is expected to do and how the employee performed on the job.

Failure to Use Performance Review Information. In some hospitality operations, performance review procedures may be instituted and forms may be completed, but nothing else is done. Some evaluators may complete performance review forms without consulting the employee. Neither of these approaches is acceptable. Employees must be actively involved in the performance review process. To have any meaning at all, information developed from these reviews must be used to improve the employee's performance.

Failure to Follow Up on Performance Reviews. To be effective, information gathered from performance reviews must be put to use. A review should not be conducted and then forgotten until the next review. Follow-up supervision, coaching, and counseling can be done between performance reviews to keep employees "on the track" of improving job performance.

Overemphasis on Errors. Some evaluators become so concerned that an error may occur in the evaluation process that they fail to implement a performance review program, or they develop so many safeguard procedures that the process becomes unwieldy. Evaluators should acknowledge that errors will exist. Differences in judgments about employees and other problems will arise. Managers must recognize that greater problems will occur if a performance review system is not implemented. Design of procedures that are reasonably free from human errors should be attempted.

Concerns about Fairness. An effective manager tries to be fair and just in all interactions with employees, including performance reviews. Some evaluators may be concerned that negative information resulting from reviews will become part of the employee's permanent personnel record. This data could affect the employee even after problems have been resolved. One way to overcome this problem would be by maintaining the negative information in a separate file. This critique would not be part of the permanent record, but could be used for planning and implementing performance improvement programs and then be discarded.

Procedures for Developing and Implementing Performance Review Programs

A set of requirements and procedures should be incorporated into performance review programs. While they must fit the needs of the specific hospitality operation, there are basic points that should be addressed. These include:

Establish Objectives for Review Activities. Performance reviews normally are designed to improve the employees' job performance and recognize basic human relations concerns.

Establish Factors for Judging Performance. Tools used in developing training programs can be helpful here.

Determine Who Will Be Conducting Performance Reviews. This person probably will be a department head in a smaller operation or a supervisor or intermediate management staff member in a larger operation. Whenever possible, the employee's immediate supervisor should perform performance reviews or, at least, have an integral part in them.

Determine the Frequency of Performance Reviews. These reviews should be conducted at least twice yearly. More frequent reviews can often be helpful, especially for new employees. In some hospitality operations, performance reviews are conducted during a specific month. For example, semi-annual reviews may be held in July and December. In other properties, reviews may be conducted at six-month intervals beginning when the employee first started work. With this plan, the evaluator conducts reviews on a year-round basis. With this approach, the evaluator does not have to recall detailed procedures for conducting performance reviews.

Develop Procedures for Incorporating Employee Participation. Employees should be given as much freedom as possible to participate in the performance review process. They should be allowed to react to the evaluator's opinions, to offer a "defense" to any problems, to help plan goals for the next evaluation period, and to offer any opinion/advice about the job situation during the review.

Establish Appeal Procedures. Employees who believe that the performance review was administered unfairly should be allowed to appeal to the next management level. If this is not done, the credibility of the entire review process will be in jeopardy. Normally, procedures for an appeal can be handled through a clearly stated policy.

Develop Follow-up Plans. Activities to be implemented after the performance review is completed should be defined. Traditionally, interim evaluations and other types of follow-up assistance are possible.

Inform Employees about the Performance Review Program. They want to know what aspects of the work will affect them, and performance review programs will be high on their list of concerns. There should be no secrets about how the program is to be implemented. Employees should be informed about the specifics of the program. This can be handled through orientation conversations, employee handbooks, and discussions as the need arises.

Use Effective Interview Procedures. The supervisor must talk with the employee as the performance review process is undertaken. Therefore, the supervisor should understand the basic techniques of verbal communication and interview skills that are discussed in Chapter 10. Some important procedures are specifically applicable to performance review interviews. For example, employees must be told when the performance review will take place. In some properties, copies of the supervisor's evaluation forms are provided so employees can evaluate themselves. These completed forms can provide a basis for discussion during the performance review. Even when this does not occur, employees must be told about the structure of the evaluation.

The emphasis during the performance review should be on a two-way communication process that permits the supervisor to help the employee develop goals to be accomplished by the time of the next review. At the close of the performance review, there should be mutual agreement about areas where the employee is performing well, where improvement is needed, and specific action plans to improve performance. The interview process should not end until there is agreement about these points. When the review is completed, the supervisor must complete any required paperwork. Information frequently is required for the employee's personnel file and often is used as wage and salary decisions are made.

NOTES

1. This section is based on Lewis C. Forrest, Jr., *Training for the Hospitality Industry* (East Lansing, Mich.: Educational Institute of the American Hotel & Motel Association, 1983), pp. 286-288.

2. Forrest, pp. 291-296.

PAGE SIXTEEN

Supervision at the Brandywine Room

"Hello, Stacey," Rachel Case said as Stacey entered the personnel director's office. "What can I do for you?"

Stacey began to explain her concerns about improving the employee performance review process in the Brandywine Room. After a few minutes of conversation, Ms. Case pulled out the standard operating procedures section of the hotel's handbook which outlined requirements for performance reviews.

"Stacey," she said, "this is another example of how communication problems affect the relationship between the Personnel Department and other operating units. We have developed what we believe is a very acceptable performance review process. However, it's up to the individual working units to administer the program. Over the past few years, the performance review process in your unit probably has not been done correctly. One or two procedures were overlooked one year. If no concerns are voiced, the process further deteriorates the next year to the point where the review process becomes rather meaningless. I'll tell you what, why don't you look this over and see if the procedures are acceptable? Then, let's work together to develop some performance review forms that are applicable to the specific positions in the dining room you supervise."

Stacey was happy about the cooperation that she was getting from Ms. Case. During the next few days, she made a list of the procedures that already were part of the performance review policy at the hotel.

1. Performance reviews were to focus on factors which were important in good job performance. Each of these factors were to be identified and addressed in a performance review form designed for a specific position. The focus of the evaluation should be on how well the employee performed the required job tasks, and not on how well the employee's work compared to others.

2. Performance reviews were to be conducted twice annually beginning with the time of the employee's hiring.

3. Employees were to be informed about all aspects of the performance review at the time of employee orientation. The supervisor was to go over the performance review form which would be used to evaluate the employee, and a copy was to be given to the employee.

4. Performance reviews were to be conducted in private. Before beginning the review, the dining room manager was to fill out specific parts of the form, being careful to compare the employee's ability to perform each task with the required performance standard. A comparison of one employee to another was not acceptable.

5. In addition to considering specific factors, a supervisor was to write a brief essay statement about the employee. During the employee performance review, the supervisor was to go over each point on the form with the employee, who was encouraged to ask questions, seek additional information, and provide insights as to his/her views about each point.

6. The final part of the performance review process required the supervisor and employee to construct an employee develop-

ment plan. This document would provide an action plan indicating steps needed to improve the employee's performance in the present job. Both the employee and the supervisor were to sign this form, with a copy being given to the employee while the original copy was retained for personnel records.

7. Information stemming from the employee performance review was to be passed on to other staff members for input in the wage and salary administration process.

8. Employees were encouraged to make suggestions about how the performance review process could be improved.

9. Employees were urged to appeal to the food and beverage director, Mr. George, any time they disagreed with the evaluation procedures and/or findings.

10. All management staff in the Food and Beverage Department were to meet at least annually to discuss ways that the performance review process could be improved.

Stacey thought that the updated version of the Brandywine policies and procedures manual was nearing completion. After several weeks of working with Personnel Department representatives, Stacey had a good working copy of a performance review form for the food server position. Stacey was going to get permission from Ms. Case to use it. She would distribute it to all affected staff members, explain what it meant, and start evaluating employees the way that the hotel wanted it done.

9 The Supervisor and Wage and Salary Administration

PAGE SEVENTEEN

Supervision at the Brandywine Room

Apparently, the "people who count" around the hotel were getting to know Stacey. The memo she received said:

OFFICE OF THE PERSONNEL DIRECTOR

TO: Stacey Francis
FROM: Rachel Case

You may know that the hotel has decided to review its wage and salary administration program for all entry-level staff members. I invite you to serve on a committee that will recommend ways to make the compensation program more equitable for employees in your department. Please let me know about your availability to serve on this committee. We will have a meeting next Wednesday at 10:00 a.m.

Stacey quickly realized that she knew nothing about making wage and salary decisions. She assumed that minimum hourly wages were determined by law and that employees with greater seniority should be paid more. Was that correct or equitable? She didn't know. By serving on this important committee, she could learn more about the way these decisions were made. "At the same time," Stacey thought, "I could learn more about the operation, and that would make me a better supervisor."

Personnel at all levels in any organization are concerned about the wages and salaries they receive. Principles for managing wages and salaries must be understood and practiced by management staff at all levels of the operation to avoid potential problems.

A first-line supervisor in the hospitality industry probably won't play a critical role in the initial establishment of wage and salary rates. Normally, these activities are the responsibility of the personnel and/or accounting departments, with input from top management staff. A number of external factors also affect decisions about compensation administration.

Operationally, there are few reasons why supervisors should be involved with these details. First of all, planning compensation programs takes a great deal of time. The supervisor might better spend this time in his/her direct area of responsibility. Second, wages and salaries paid throughout the organization must be fair. Many departments and positions are part of most lodging and food service operations. A supervisor generally can only relate facts and assist in compensation planning for those positions which he/she directly supervises. A person with a view of the entire organization must be involved in matters that affect all staff members. Finally, there can be a great deal of mathematics and budgetary concepts which determine fair compensation rates for employees. This information is beyond the expertise of most supervisors and other management staff who don't possess highly technical and specialized backgrounds.

Therefore, the supervisor's role in compensation administration generally relates to determining what impact the proposed plans have on the department, and interpreting, defending, and communicating these plans to the employees. The supervisor should inform upper management about possible inequities, misunderstandings, and problems that must be resolved so the plan can be administered equitably within the department.

A Close Look at Wages and Salaries

Employers think of wages and salaries as a cost of doing business. The term **wage** refers to pay given employees whose compensation is based on the number of hours worked. Most entry-level employees, who are under the control of many supervisors, are paid by the hour at a specific rate. The gross pay these employees earn rises as the number of overtime hours they work increases. By contrast, the term **salary** applies to pay that is based on a specific period of time, such as a week or month. Salaried personnel receive the same amount of pay regardless of the number of hours worked. However, current fair wage and salary laws require that nonexempt salaried employees must be compensated for time worked over a base number of hours. These laws are complicated and changing. Specific questions about "overtime" pay for salaried employees should be addressed to officials in state and/or federal fair wage and hour law departments. In addition to the differences in pay calculations for waged and salaried employees, another distinction may be made. Salaried employees often are considered to be in a higher status position than waged employees. With increasingly attractive benefit plans for waged employees, however, many of the differences between salaried and waged workers in fringe benefit programs, such as paid sick leaves and generous vacation plans, no longer warrant such a distinction.

Compensation administration—also called wage and salary administration—describes the process by which effective policies and reasonable methods for studying and managing employee pay programs are developed and implemented.

Few hospitality firms have "thrown out" all their pay plans and started over as plans were developed. Rather, current levels of pay often evolve over the years. These are based on a number of rational and subjective factors. Large, multi-unit hospitality operations may have corporate-level specialists whose work primarily involves developing and administering compensation programs. Other operations are more likely to develop their programs over time and base them on a large number of factors that are internal and external to the organization. These will be described in this chapter.

Goals of Effective Wage and Salary Programs

Compensation programs are developed for several purposes. Properly developed pay policies and structures can help with employee recruitment programs. Hospitality operations must be competitive in their pay rates to attract the most qualified job applicants. In this context, the term **competition** refers not only to other hospitality operations but also to any other employer within a local area who is recruiting from the same kind of people. For example, cooks can be hired not only by hotels and restaurants but also by a wide variety of institutional operations. Therefore, employees in some entry-level positions may find jobs in businesses other than hospitality services. In contrast, an experienced front desk manager or catering department manager may have specialized skills primarily applicable to the hospitality industry. In these cases potential competitors are likely to be other employers in the hospitality industry.

Wages, salaries, and benefits paid to employees constitute labor costs that are of primary concern to hospitality managers. Procedures developed for compensation programs (such as maximum pay rates, merit plans, and administration of benefits) help keep labor costs under control. When reasonable pay for specific positions is established and the number of positions and necessary job skills are known, supervisors can become responsible for the labor costs that are incurred. Many employee-related problems can be traced to inequities in compensation programs. If a fair wage and salary program is implemented, these problems can be minimized. Some pay plans recognize employee performance. In this respect, pay can be considered an important motivating factor. Many managers believe that employees who work harder and produce higher quality work than other employees should receive a higher wage. In many hospitality operations, however, seniority seems to be rewarded more than performance. Employees with more years of service tend to be at high ends of pay scales—regardless of their performance. Pay plans that benefit operations will be examined later.

Factors Affecting Wages and Salaries

Many factors affect the pay rates assigned to positions in the hospitality organization. Supervisors who know and can explain these to their staff may resolve problems resulting from a lack of understanding about basic wage programs. Consider how the following factors can affect compensation rates:

Rates Paid by Competitive Firms. Managers in many hospitality operations compare their pay rates to those paid by other properties. The concept of supply and demand seems to work well in many areas of wage and salary administration. As the number of eligible applicants decreases, wage and salary rates increase. The reverse also is true. When properties find that they are unable to attract and/or retain qualified staff members, compensation plans, in part, may be the reason.

Economic Condition of the Operation. The property's ability to pay will affect the level of wages and salaries offered by the operation. Firms that generate high profit levels often pay staff members more than firms experiencing economic difficulties. Properties in economic "trouble" may be unable to pay wages and salaries that attract the best applicants. This may contribute to ongoing operating problems which create poor economic conditions.

Cost-of-Living Factors. Many operations—especially those that are unionized—incorporate cost-of-living allowances (COLA) into their pay phase. Pay rates may change as consumer price indexes—a measure of inflation—change. Employees generally feel that these plans are easily administered and understood. Employees want to keep up with the cost of living. As inflation raises prices, the consumer's purchasing power decreases unless wages keep pace with this rate. Many employers have concerns about COLA plans because wage increases are not tied to performance or productivity.

Productivity Levels. Manufacturers generally tend to pay higher wage rates than do operations with lower productivity levels. The hospitality industry is well known for its low productivity—work output relative to hours of input. This may explain why hospitality industry pay rates are often low. Constant or reduced productivity levels matched with high inflation rates cause problems for hospitality employers. This often leads to a scaling down of increases in wage and salary rates.

Employee Bargaining Power. Employee unions are a definite factor in determining wage rates for their members. Effective unions are often able to raise pay rates faster than productivity increases would warrant. While this benefits the union members, it can cause severe problems for the organization. Annual earnings of unionized workers generally are higher than those of their nonunion counterparts.[1] Hospitality managers at all levels must learn to effectively deal with and interact with unions. This topic is discussed at length in Chapter 15.

Requirements of the Job. Job requirements are important factors in determining wage and salary levels. For example, those jobs requiring greater amounts of skill, effort, and responsibility should pay more than others requiring lesser degrees of abilities and fewer duties.

State and Federal Labor Laws. Most hospitality operations are covered by the Fair Labor Standards Act, as amended. This law and many state laws require that minimum wages in specific amounts be paid to covered employees. Equal pay laws require equal pay for equal work. Discrimination against minorities, women, and others is prohibited.

Several of the preceding factors influence wage and salary levels at any given property. A property's ability to pay, for example, must be matched with supply and demand in seeking specially skilled personnel. Awareness of these factors can be used to discuss wage and salary administration principles.

Principles of Wage and Salary Administration

Hospitality administrators should recognize and prioritize several principles as they decide on and implement pay plans. First of all, there must be a plan. Differences in pay between and within positions should be based on specific factors that are consistently applied in all situations. Prevailing wage rates also must be considered. Managers must recognize the need to compete with other organizations as they recruit and retain staff members. As noted earlier, the law of supply and demand is critical to the development of pay plans.

Plans must consider specific positions—not employees. Normally pay rates should be established for a position. An employee assigned to the position then will receive the pay associated with it. This plan provides for more consistency and fairness than does a plan in which pay scales are based on personal qualities and preferences of employees. Equal pay provisions are important. When jobs have equal difficulty and require equal abilities to perform them, pay should be the same.

Hospitality operations want to retain the best qualified staff. To do this, compensation plans with pay ranges, wage incentives, and fast promotion tracks may be in order.

Employees and the union must know how the wage administration program works. The supervisor's role is critical in accomplishing this.

Job Evaluation and Pay Rates

Several types of evaluation procedures can be used to determine the pay rates for specific jobs within the property. Job descriptions, which note required tasks, and job specifications, which list personal qualities needed to perform the job successfully, form the basis of the job evaluation process. The question to be answered in the evaluation is: "What is the job worth to the organization?" When done correctly, the job evaluation process can be time-consuming and complex. There are, however, simplified systems that can be used with reasonable accuracy.

Exhibit 9.1 reviews the general process of job evaluation. Job descriptions and specifications form a basis of information for a job evaluation/rating process. As a result of this analysis, pay rates for specific jobs

Exhibit 9.1 General Process of Job Evaluation

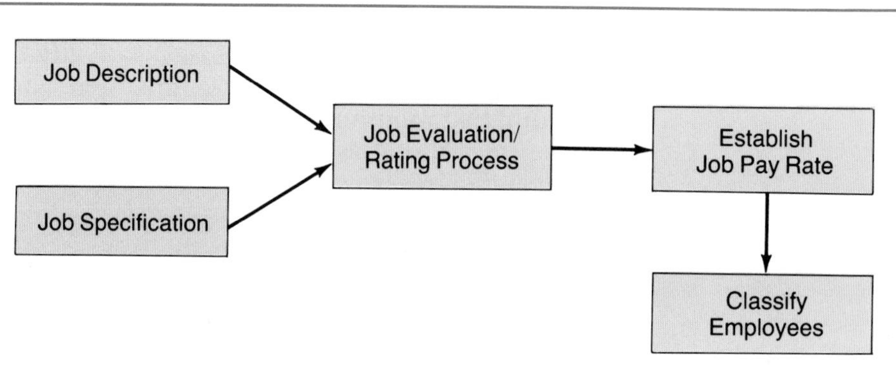

are established. Employees are classified according to the job they perform, and the applicable pay for the job becomes the employee's compensation.

When jobs are evaluated and rated, several points should be noted. First of all, jobs—not the employee performing the job—should be rated. When possible, the judgments of several people should be used to evaluate and rate jobs. Job descriptions and specifications—which form the basis of the evaluation process—must be current and accurate.

Methods of Job Evaluation

Several methods of job evaluation exist. Each has advantages and disadvantages. You should be aware of the basic methods and understand when they may and may not be used.

Simple Ranking Systems. With this plan, job descriptions and specifications are studied. Decisions are made about the job requirements for each position. Then, the job positions are ranked from low to high. Exhibit 9.2 shows a possible job-ranking order in a food and beverage department of a small hotel. Neither Exhibit 9.2 nor any other exhibits/statistics in this chapter are meant to suggest industry standards or guidelines. Information is presented only for illustrative purposes. Specific information must be developed for the individual property.

In most operations each position already will have applicable wage rates. The ranking process judges whether the rates are equitable and provides information for future wage and salary adjustments. After the ranking is established, a committee of management personnel can review it and make adjustments to correct any inequities.

Although simple, the ranking method does have several disadvantages. For example, it is a very subjective process. Judgments often are based upon prevailing wages rates. The process does not indicate which positions have more—or fewer—job requirements. As the number of jobs to be ranked becomes greater, more difficulty is encountered.

Grade Description System. This evaluation method requires that jobs be divided into pay groups (grades). Definitions are written for each group

Exhibit 9.2 Possible Job Ranking Order for Food and Beverage Department in Small Hotel

	Position
	Food and Beverage Manager
High Job Requirements	Chef
	Assistant Food and Beverage Manager
↓	Restaurant Manager
	Dining Room Manager
	Cook
	Bartender
Low Job Requirements	Food/Beverage Server
	Dish/Pot Washer

(grade). Each job then is classified into a specific grade. The basis for this information comes from current job descriptions. A committee often is used to make these job evaluation decisions. A large number of jobs within the organization can be studied when using the grade description system. Special attention is given to duties, skills, abilities, responsibilities, and other factors which differentiate jobs. After each job is evaluated, it is classified into grades which represent different pay levels that range from low to high. A review of descriptions for a specific job helps match the job with the grade schedule that corresponds best with the job. The pay attached to the job is assigned to the grade.

Point System Method. The use of a point system is a popular and more objective method of job evaluation. This system involves developing a list of job factors or characteristics that relate to the skill, effort, responsibility, and conditions associated with the job. Each factor is divided into degrees so that an assessment of the relative weight of that factor can be determined for a job. If experience is an important factor, for example, it might be subdivided into: (a) 0-6 months, (b) 7-12 months, (c) 13-16 months, (d) beyond 16 months. Points are then assigned to each degree. The job evaluation committee studies each job relative to all factors—and degrees of each factor—that have been established. Points are allocated to each factor/degree and are totaled to determine the total number of points. This represents the job score, which dictates a particular wage and salary grade. The grade becomes the basis for compensating employees in the position.

The point system, while more complex, is an effective job evaluation method because various factors that affect the job are studied individually. The consistent assignment of points helps make the plan more objective.

Factor Comparison Method. This method, the most complex of all, is actually a combination of the simple ranking and point systems. Jobs are

Exhibit 9.3 Possible Step-Rate Plan for Hourly Worker in Specific Position

Position: Cook—Hourly Rate

	Months				
Entry Rate	6	15	24	36	Maximum
$5.15/hr.	$5.45	$5.85	$6.35	$6.85	$7.10

Exhibit 9.4 Possible Performance and Seniority-Based Step-Rate Plan for Specific Position

Position: Cook—Hourly Rate

Performance Level	Months Pay Rate Per Hour					
	Entry	6	15	24	36	Maximum
Excellent	$5.15	$5.45	$5.85	$6.35	$6.85	$7.10
Above Average	5.15	5.35	5.55	6.00	6.35	6.80
Meets Standards	5.15	5.25	5.35	5.55	6.00	6.35

rated by comparing them with each other and using a point system to quantify specific factors within the job. Details of this system are beyond the scope of this book.[2]

Salary Increases

After a basic pay structure has been established, procedures for determining wage/salary increases must be developed.[3] There are a number of possibilities. When a **flat-rate plan** is used, each employee assigned to the same job receives the same pay increase, regardless of seniority or performance. This plan has limited usefulness, but it is found in some unionized organizations. When a **step-rate plan** is used there are various fixed pay levels,which are usually based on seniority, for the same job. An employee can progress from one step to another within the pay range based on seniority—unless performance is not satisfactory. Exhibit 9.3 shows a possible step-rate plan for an hourly worker. Performance and seniority variables may be introduced into a step-rate plan. An example is shown in Exhibit 9.4. With this approach, compensation can be tied to the performance review process. (See Chapter 8 for additional information.)

Exhibit 9.5 Possible Performance-Based Pay Increase Guidelines for Specific Position

	Position in the Salary Range Before the Raise			
Performance Level	1st Quartile	2nd Quartile	3rd Quartile	4th Quartile
Outstanding	16% 6-9 months	14% 9-12 months	12% 12 months	To Maximum 12 months
Exceeds Standards	14% 6-9 months	12% 10-12 months	10% 12 months	No Raise
Meets Standards	12% 9-12 months	10% 12 months	No Raise	No Raise

Example: Amy was hired as an experienced front office manager high in the second quartile of her position's salary range. As an outstanding performer she can expect a raise of 14% after completing 9 to 12 months on the job. If her performance was just meeting the required position standards she would have to wait 12 months for a raise of 10%.

Source: Clifford Slade, "How to Design a Pay Plan for Hotel Employees," Lodging, *November, 1981, p. 48.*

As noted earlier, **cost-of-living allowance (COLA) plans** are tied to an inflation measure such as the Consumer Price Index (CPI). Normally, COLA plans are found in union contracts. From management's perspective, COLA plans are not good because they often are very expensive in periods of high inflation and do not relate to productivity increases.

Compensation under **performance or merit plans** is, as the name suggests, based on different levels of job performance. A performance appraisal must be completed to measure different levels of accomplishment. Employees generally approve of these plans if the performance review process that is used to determine merit increases is viewed as being fair and objective. There are several variations of performance or merit plans. One example is shown in Exhibit 9.5.

Other Issues

The many alternatives for job evaluation and development of compensation plans suggest that these efforts can be quite complex. There are many other factors which need to be considered as a total compensation program is developed.

For example, when should wage and salary increases be given? Possibilities include: (a) employee service anniversary dates, (b) the same date for all employees—such as semi-annually, and (c) varying dates according to job performance. In operations where seniority is recognized as critical to effective performance, the employee's service anniversary date seems to work well. On the other hand, the budgeting process is easier when a calendar date plan is used. Semi-annual plans help ensure that the property keeps up with compensation plans offered by competitive companies. Frequent but smaller raises may encourage employees to continue their high performance. When pay raises are coordinated with performance reviews, employees may see the relationship between performance and frequency—or amount—of raises.

Exhibit 9.6 Average Cost of Benefits as a % of Payroll

Company provided pensions, medical and life insurance	12.1%
Paid vacation, holidays, sick leave	9.5%
Government required payments (FICA, workers' compensation, etc.)	9.0%
Paid break time and lunch periods	3.5%
Other benefits (profit sharing, thrift plans, bonuses, etc.)	2.5%
TOTAL	36.6%

Source: Slade, p. 49.

Employees can be compensated by methods other than wages and salaries. For example, profit-sharing programs provide opportunities for rewarding employees. Many of these programs have income tax implications which must be considered. Where an employee or group of employees directly controls productivity, the use of production bonus (incentive) plans can be effective. Some properties offer special cash awards for significant efforts which go above and beyond the scope of the job. There are other examples of programs that do not permanently add to the base pay levels but provide extra compensation as well as recognition for employees.

Fringe benefit programs in many hospitality operations have recently become major expenses. These programs are integral to the wage and salary compensation plan.

Managing the Benefits Program

Employee benefits—also called fringe benefits—can be a very large expense. Exhibit 9.6, which was compiled by the U.S. Chamber of Commerce in 1979, indicates that costs of benefits average more than 36% of base payroll expense. Hospitality operations must be aware of the tremendous expense created by attractive benefit programs. There also are several types of low-cost or no-cost benefits which can make a benefit package more attractive:

- **No-cost benefits.** Examples of benefits which may not cost money include group purchase plans where employees may order items from company suppliers at the company rate. Flexible working schedules may be possible with some jobs and would be considered a job benefit by many employees.

- **Low-cost benefits.** Employee meals are an example of this type of benefit, while discounted room rates or complimentary rooms for employees are another possibility.

Informing Employees about Benefits

Even the best compensation program will be harmed if employees are not informed about it. Managers should tell employees about compensation and benefit programs at the time of new employee orientation. Copies of the benefits program should be provided.

Employees also may be provided annually with a statement of benefits and base pay. This information can detail all aspects of the compensation program so that employees are reminded about the specifics of the plan and how it works. Detailed information also should be provided to supervisors who can relay this information to employees at the time of training, evaluation, and other activities.

NOTES

1. U.S. Department of Labor, Bureau of Labor Statistics. *Selected Earnings and Demographic Characteristics of Union Members*, 1970. Report 417, Washington, D.C., U.S. Government Printing Office, 1972.

2. Interested readers are referred to Dale S. Beach, *Personnel: The Management of People and Work*, 4th ed. (New York: Macmillan, 1980), pp. 574-578.

3. This section is based on Clifford Slade, "How to Design a Pay Plan for Hotel Employees," *Lodging*, November, 1981, pp. 45-50.

PAGE EIGHTEEN

Supervision at the Brandywine Room

Stacey was pleased that Ms. Case thought enough of her abilities to seek her service on the hotel's Compensation Review Committee. The committee's existence was an excellent example of how the company could incorporate human relations and employee participation concerns in its dealings with staff at all organizational levels. After reading material about wage and salary compensation, Stacey began to understand its complexities.

At the committee meeting, the chairperson—who was the head of the Accounting Department—explained that the committee met annually to review wages and salaries and to consider procedures used to assess pay levels for each department. The committee currently was reviewing wages paid to hourly personnel in the Food and Beverage Department. The chairperson also explained that the group would not "throw out all existing wage rates" and start over. Rather, they would review the job rating scales in light of any changes in job descriptions and differing opinions of committee members to ensure that the wage base was still current.

Stacey began to appreciate the importance of job descriptions. She already knew about their use in staff recruitment and training programs, and was aware of their value in conducting employee performance reviews. At this time of wage and salary considerations, job descriptions and specifications were necessary again. Stacey vowed that she would never permit job descriptions for the Brandywine Room to become obsolete.

Each committee member was given a handout that listed in rank order the job requirements for positions in the Food and Beverage Department. (The list was similar to that illustrated in Exhibit 9.2.) Committee members outlined changes in the job descriptions for waged employees and discussed whether changes in the rank order were required because of modifications made during the year in tasks covered by each job description.

As a result of this process, one position—that of head bartender—had grown in importance during the year. A management task of issuing beverages and taking inventory had been added to the position's responsibilities. Because of this, the committee recommended that the pay for bartenders be raised to compensate for these additional tasks. After all, a primary purpose of the Compensation Review Committee is to eliminate inequities.

Additional analysis suggested that responsibilities for the host/hostess position decreased during the year because some bookkeeping duties no longer were necessary. The purchase of a sophisticated, computerized cash register system had eliminated these responsibilities. The committee realized that it would not be fair to reduce the pay for employees in this position. Rather, it chose to recommend that the pay rate be raised more slowly for employees in that position until the inequity was eliminated. The committee also recommended that all new employees hired for the host/hostess position be paid at the new—and appropriate—pay scale.

Before the meeting adjourned the committee discussed the need to inform all employees more effectively about all aspects of the compensation program. Also emphasized was the supervisor's role in conducting orientation programs, circulating information about salary plans developed by the Personnel and Accounting Departments, plus training employees and answering questions as part of the daily supervisory process.

Stacey left the meeting having learned a great deal about wage and salary administration. She also realized that hotel officials were trying to be fair and equitable in their treatment of this most basic employee concern. Sure, there were problems. Subjective decisions were necessary and Stacey did not agree with every decision the committee made. However, she did think that, without exception, the hotel managers were trying to reward employees for acceptable job performance through fairly administered, reasonable compensation programs.

Part III:

The Supervisor in Action: Activities for Successful Leadership

Supervisors in the hospitality industry must know how to communicate effectively. Speaking, writing, acting, and listening will not be effective unless basic communication techniques are practiced. The supervisor also must learn how to motivate employees. Motivation comes from within the employees. The supervisor cannot tell the employee to be motivated. Yet, a supervisor can take steps to encourage employees who want to help the hospitality organization attain its goals.

The supervisor must learn how to discipline employees. Discipline can be positive if it reinforces correct actions and attitudes. Discipline also can be negative if it is used solely to punish employees for wrongdoing. A discipline program can be easy to implement, and should be part of the "arsenal" of management tools used by every supervisor.

Conflict inevitably will arise in a hospitality operation, which can be healthy if it creates opportunities to examine procedures. But conflict also can be very harmful. In either case, supervisors must be able to effectively manage and resolve conflict.

The supervisor must know how to manage individuals and groups. An understanding of basic human relation techniques, the formation and working of groups, and the ways leaders can be influenced helps the supervisor in his/her efforts to work with individual employees and groups of staff members.

There are many activities that a supervisor must perform successfully in order to be an effective leader. Each of these topics will be reviewed in Part III.

10 The Supervisor and the Communication Process

PAGE NINETEEN

Supervision at the Brandywine Room

Stacey Francis had just returned from a monthly meeting of the local hotel and motel association. She particularly enjoyed this session. The featured speaker discussed communication and the important role it plays in helping supervisors manage employees. She learned a lot of things that were going to be a great help. Stacy knew that other supervisors in the hotel who had not been present at the meeting would benefit from the information. She had a great idea: "I'm going to volunteer to make a presentation to the hotel supervisors at their upcoming meeting. I have to write a paper for my management class at college anyway, so I'll write it on communication. Besides, in the process of studying for the presentation and paper, I'll learn a lot more about communication. I already know that it's important in my job as supervisor, and that I should know as much about it as I can."

Communication is the process by which information is exchanged. We all know that we communicate when we talk. What about when we say nothing? Our actions, or lack of them, also "say" something. We also listen and write; both are forms of communication. Many people believe, since they have been speaking, listening, and writing all their lives, there is nothing to learn about the topic: "We are able to communicate so what is the problem?"

In reality, the communication process—its procedures and techniques—is rather complex. All of us can improve our communication skills. How often do we have difficulty getting our message across and blame this on communication breakdowns or communication problems? To be successful in any business, including the hospitality industry, you must be an effective communicator.

We have noted throughout this book that the supervisor is "the person in the middle" who must represent upper management levels to lower organizational levels while acting on behalf of his/her own employees in relations with others in the organization. In many respects, the act of representation is one of communication. In Chapter 1, several management activities were described. One such activity—coordination—is almost the same as communication. As the supervisor represents employees to different levels of the organization and coordinates use of the property's resources, he/she is involved in the communication process.

Several points should be clear. The supervisor must be an effective communicator in order to be a successful leader of his/her employees. Further, communication by a supervisor is more than just speaking. Completing a report, scheduling employees, nodding your head in agreement, and shaking your fist in anger are examples of communication.

Some Myths about Communication

Before studying how the communication process works, several misunderstandings should be cleared up. There are several common myths that influence how people think and react to the communication process:[1]

1. *People communicate only when they consciously want to communicate.* In fact, people cannot control their communication time. If a supervisor ignores a situation or does not respond to it in a timely manner, these actions still convey messages to people concerned about the situation.

2. *Words have the same meanings to everybody.* This myth suggests that words have specific meanings which are understood identically by everyone. Actually, words have meaning based on a person's experiences with them. What does this mean: "I want my order of chickens cut in half." Does the purchaser want half as many chickens as were received in the last order? Or, does he/she want the same number of chickens, with each chicken cut in half before delivery? Supervisors should realize from this and many other similar examples that words mean different things to different people.

3. *Words are the primary vehicle of communication.* Many people believe they cannot communicate without speaking or writing. In fact, many messages are nonverbal—words aren't used. We all have heard the old saying "actions speak louder than words." How we look and act, and what we do as we speak or listen are very effective communication devices.

4. *Communication is a one-way activity between the sender and receiver of the message.* This myth suggests that the communication process is a one-sided activity of "telling people something." Effective supervisors talk *with* employees rather than *at* employees. Problems occur when the supervisor *tells* an employee, rather than *communicates* with an employee. Therefore, communication is a two-way process in which feedback helps clarify and give meaning to a message. **Feedback** is any reaction by the listener to the sender's verbal and nonverbal messages. Because of feedback, message senders realize how well they are communicating. If feedback is effectively interpreted, the sender knows whether—and to what extent—the message has been understood.

5. *The message we communicate is the message that will be received.* You should not assume that a listener or reader will get the message exactly as it was sent. There may be a different interpretation. We have already noted that words have different meanings. In addition, a person's interpretation of our words and actions—even if they are beyond our control—influence the message that is received.

6. *There is no such thing as too much information.* Certainly, too little information is not good, but neither is too much information. For example, problems arise when a lot of paperwork must be generated. Time is wasted informing employees about things that do not affect or interest them. "Information overload" occurs when employees receive too much information. The supervisor's concern should be with the *quality* of communication rather than the *quantity* of communication.

The Communication Process

The communication process must be understood so supervisors can effectively use techniques designed to enhance their communication abilities. The most important elements in the communication process are illustrated in Exhibit 10.1, which will be discussed in this section. The purpose of communication is to transmit messages from one individual (the sender) to another (the receiver).

The sender is responsible for assembling the message so that the message is accurately conveyed. While communication is a two-way process, the sender has the primary responsibility to create understanding. To do this, the sender must look at the message being developed from the perspective of the receiver. As the sender develops the message, however, he/she is influenced by perceptions. The sender has specific skills, attitudes, abilities, and experiences which form and modify the perception of what is being communicated. Some important skills are the sender's communication abilities. These can be developed so messages can be transmitted more effectively.

Exhibit 10.1 The Communication Process

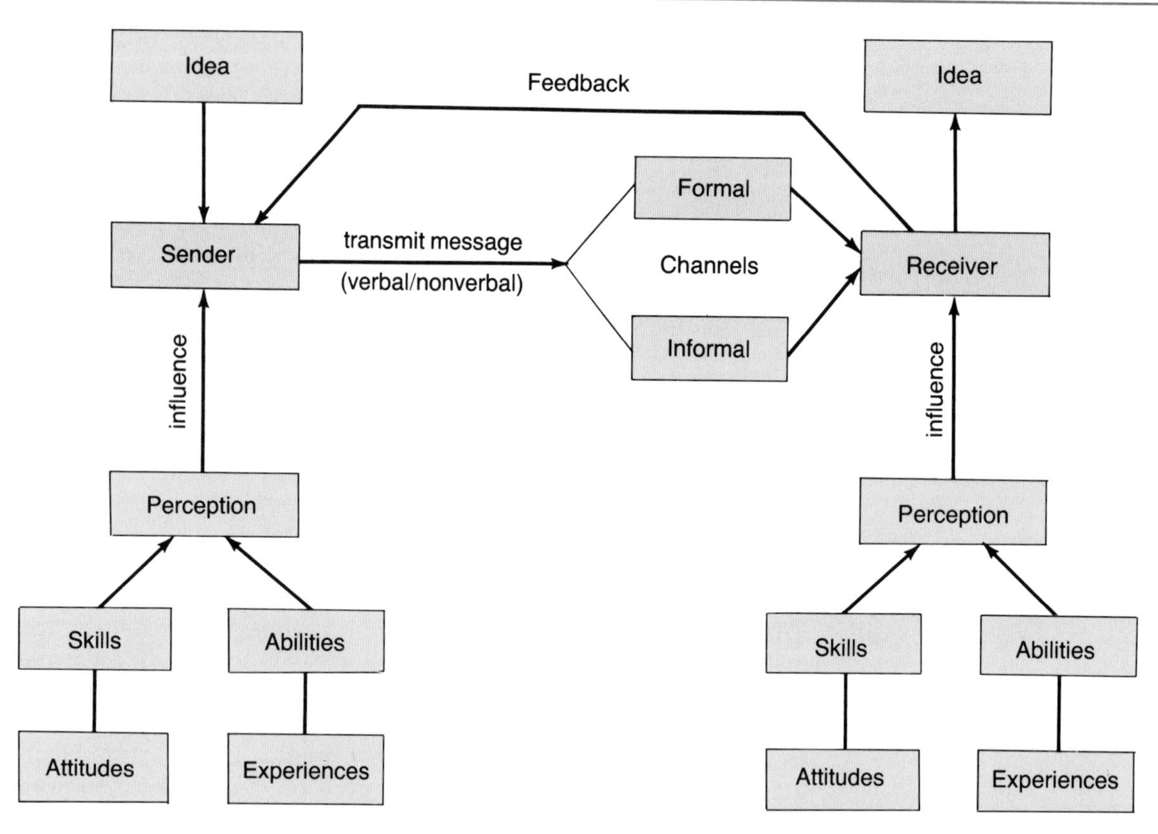

The message is comprised of verbal and nonverbal symbols. As already explained, a verbal message often is accented with nonverbal expressions, gestures, and actions. Nonverbal communication will be discussed later in the chapter. A written message can be transmitted in a way that adds further meaning. For example, an important message is hand-carried to the receiver as opposed to being routed through the organization's internal mail system.

Note that in Exhibit 10.1 the receiver also is influenced by his/her perceptions as the message is being decoded. The receiver's perception is influenced by the same factors— skills, attitudes, abilities, and experiences—that affect the perception of the sender.

Feedback relates to the reaction a receiver has about the message that was transmitted. There may be an agreement or disagreement, questions, or statements. Feedback may be written or oral, and may take place formally or informally. Whatever the form, the sender will do well to seek and use feedback in evaluating the extent to which the receiver understands the message.

Viewed as a process, communication is complex and is comprised of several interrelated parts. You should begin to see how the effectiveness of message transmittal can be influenced by many factors.

Considerations in Selecting the Communication Method

A message can be transmitted in a written or spoken manner. Factors to consider when selecting a communication method include:

Feedback

- The need for immediate feedback. If immediacy is vital, oral communication would be more effective than written.

Resistance

- The potential problem of the receiver resisting the message. If you anticipate resistance, a written message is best.

Proof

- The need for proof of the communication. If proof is necessary, written communication is best.

Accuracy

- The need for significant accuracy in the message. Here again, written communication might be best.

The use of both oral and written communication methods is often best. It is common, for example, to follow up a conversation with a written memo. A written communication can be hand-carried to the receiver so that some explanation can be given upon delivery.

Formal and Informal Communication Channels

Formal Channels

As noted in Exhibit 10.1, communication channels can be formal and informal. An effective communicator uses both. Examples of formal communication channels include:

- Downward channels—communication formally flows down the organization through job instructions, policies, rules, and procedures.
- Upward channels—information flows up the organization as supervisors inform higher levels of management about work which has been performed, problems which are encountered, ideas about future plans, and the need for changing policies and procedures.
- Horizontal channels—there is a need, especially in large organizations, for communication to move horizontally in order to coordinate tasks, solve problems, share information, and resolve conflicts.

Informal Channels

Informal channels of communication must be understood and used by supervisors. The "grapevine" can be very effective in spreading messages quickly throughout the organization. Often, the grapevine is a faster channel of communication than the formal channels. It also can be a fairly accurate indicator of problems or concerns.

Some supervisors may pretend that the grapevine doesn't exist. They may use the same strategy while denying awareness of informal groups (see Chapter 14). There are times, however, when supervisors should use the grapevine. For example, the grapevine is a good way to disseminate information about social events, or to gain informal reactions to proposed policies and procedures.

Three Special Communication Skills

There are three basic skills which, if properly developed, can help the supervisor become an effective communicator.

Analyze Receiver

First, the supervisor must learn how to analyze the person receiving the message. This chapter already has pointed out that each of us comes to the communication situation with different perceptions. We will learn about the need to recognize individual differences of employees as we discuss motivation (Chapter 11). The ability to recognize "where the receiver is coming from" is a special skill that good communicators have developed. Attempting to understand how the receiver will react, what can influence him/her to better accept the message, and how to communicate so the correct message will be received are reasons for analyzing the receiver.

Use Feedback

A second communication skill involves using feedback as a barometer of understanding. Questions such as: "Do you understand?" "Do you have any questions?" "Do you know what I said?" do not always produce useful feedback. There is no one way of obtaining accurate feedback. It depends on the situation. Effective feedback should be specific—not general; it should consider the needs of the sender and receiver. A message should be directed toward something that the receiver can control if feedback is to be effective. Frustration can be created if a person is told about an individual facility, problem, or matter over which the person has no control. Feedback should be timely; it should occur at the earliest opportunity after the message has been transmitted. Both the sender and receiver should get feedback about the other's perception of the message, which should be tailored to the individual.

Make the Message Meaningful

Understanding how messages can be made meaningful is a third communication skill. We send and receive messages according to our past experiences. The way we interpret messages also is influenced by our backgrounds. Therefore, the entire approach used to form and communicate the message must take past experiences into account.

Overcoming Barriers to Effective Communication

Many things can happen that decrease the effectiveness of communication. If supervisors are aware of these barriers, strategies for working around them can be helpful.

Different Perceptions, Interests

One barrier to effective communication already has been discussed in this chapter. That is the difference in perceptions between the sender and receiver of the message. If the sender or receiver isn't interested in the topic of the message, there can be a serious reduction in the effectiveness of the communication. Perception and lack of interest are related. How else could one party believe the matter is important while the other party does not share the interest? Use of attention-getting statements at the beginning of the message might help counter this problem. A better approach is to motivate the individual to be interested. This can be done by presenting information in a way that illustrates benefits to the disinterested party.

Lack of Knowledge

A third communication barrier occurs when either the sender or receiver does not have the knowledge to understand the message. Remember to match the message with the other party's knowledge, skills, ability, and experiences. A similar problem occurs when one party is so knowledgeable that he/she makes assumptions that have no meaning to the other person. The communicator who attempts to know the other person and uses feedback skills can help reduce these problems.

Emotions

Emotions of either the sender or receiver can create communication barriers. Objective and rational communication is difficult, if not impossible, when emotions become involved. Emotions do not have to be obvious to create obstacles in communication. Deeply rooted emotions can affect the perception of messages being sent or received.

Personality

The personalities of the people involved in the communication process also can create barriers. We are often influenced by another person's personality to the point that we accept or reject communication without reason. Personalities of a group are just as important as are those of individuals. Reasons for problems that appear to stem from personality or attitudinal differences should be explored and resolved, if possible.

Appearance

The appearance of the person or the way the message is presented provide additional examples of communication barriers. We are impressed or distressed by how a person looks, speaks, and acts. A person's poor verbal skills will influence us. Written messages that "don't make sense" or appear sloppy affect the presentation.

Prejudice

Prejudice is another communication barrier. We can be prejudiced negatively or positively about people or situations. An example of negative prejudice is disliking people because we have an irrational attitude toward them. Defending the status quo, because we like things the way they are, is an example of positive prejudice. Either type of prejudice causes dismissal of potentially good ideas. Prejudice is a barrier which is very difficult to eliminate. Education, discipline, and conflict resolution techniques, which will be discussed in this book, are possibilities for handling prejudice.

Distractions

Distractions that occur when the message is transmitted create communication obstacles. Noise, inadequate lighting, people, and temperature are a few examples. Any factor that upsets our defenses also is likely to upset the clear transmission of messages.

Others

The list of communication barriers can continue. If the sender's ideas are disorganized or if the sender does not know exactly what he/she wants to say, other problems arise. Poor listening habits, which will be discussed later in this chapter, create problems. Communication suffers when we have difficulties deciding on what we want to do and say. Language problems are a final barrier to effective communication.

Effective Communication Procedures

Now that we have discussed some of the technical aspects of the communication process and know what to look for as we develop our communication abilities, let's look at some specific techniques for practicing the art of communication.

Effective Speaking Skills

The supervisor uses speech to judge reactions to people and things, question activities that occur in the job situation, and provide answers to questions, among other activities. Exhibit 10.2 lists 27 traits and qualities that are frequently associated with effective oral communication. These factors are important when a supervisor speaks to one person or a group of persons, participates in formal interviews, and conducts performance reviews.

As can be seen in Exhibit 10.2, the list of characteristics associated with effective speaking is lengthy. The art of speaking is not easy. The supervisor who can inject many of these characteristics into his/her speaking will be more effective than his/her counterpart who cannot.

The following techniques can help you improve your speaking skills:

1. *Plan what you are going to say.* Know the purpose of your message and "speak to it" as you talk.

2. *Organize what you are going to say.* Identify the main points, and make sure they are addressed.

3. *Keep in mind your purpose.* Try to cover the main points that you must address. Don't ramble or introduce any part of the message that is not necessary.

Exhibit 10.2 Traits and Qualities for Effective Speaking

1. Self-confidence
2. Knowledge
3. Articulation
4. Pleasing voice quality
5. Sincerity
6. Control of emotion
7. Fluency
8. Friendliness
9. Reasoning
10. Empathy
11. Open-mindedness
12. Trustworthiness
13. Personal appearance
14. Honesty
15. Understanding
16. Humility
17. Concern for listener
18. Responsiveness
19. Awareness
20. Humor
21. Forcefulness
22. Sensitivity
23. Personal magnetism
24. Character
25. Spontaneity
26. Tact
27. Intelligence

Source: Adapted from Richard Husmand, et al., Business Communications: Strategies and Skills *(Hinsdale, Ill.: Dryden Press, 1981), p. 261.*

4. *Concentrate on the listener—not yourself.* The main objective is to communicate—not to project a better image of yourself.

5. *Be enthusiastic.* Speak your message in a way that will transmit your enthusiasm.

6. *Provide sufficient information to back your statements.* Doing this will enable the listener to concentrate on the message and not question its accuracy.

7. *Consider the listener's background.* His/her perceptions will affect how your message is received.

8. *Use language that the listener will understand.*

Listening

Many supervisors spend more time listening than doing any other type of communicating. Supervisors who learn to listen will have a better understanding of employee attitudes and morale. Employee complaints about "management not listening to me" also will be reduced. When supervisors learn how to listen effectively, they are better able to gain work-related information, to be more effective in interpersonal relationships, to obtain needed information for making good management decisions, and to respond appropriately to messages they hear.

Several techniques can be used to improve listening ability. These include:

1. *Listen for the central idea that the speaker is trying to convey.* (Remember that in discussing speaking skills, we noted the

need to identify and clearly communicate central ideas.) When the speaker is organized, listening becomes easier than when rules for speaking are not followed.

2. *Focus on what the speaker is saying.* It is easy to get distracted when someone is talking. When this occurs, listening ability is diminished.

3. *Don't be influenced by your emotions.* The old saying "we hear what we want to hear" expresses this concern very well. This problem is difficult to avoid. As a first step, recall that everyone's perceptions are influenced by factors that are specific to the individual. To avoid this problem, try not to immediately evaluate the speaker's comments. This permits time for more objective reasoning about the speaker's message.

4. *Don't "turn off" a speaker because the message sounds familiar, strange, or unimportant.* The speaker probably has a good reason for attempting to communicate with you. Remember the importance of taking into account the other person's perceptions as the communication process evolves.

5. *Avoid listening for specific facts.* Facts presented by a speaker are only part of the total message. Be aware of the "hidden agenda" which may be a very subtle but important part of the speaker's message.

6. *Make sure you understand the speaker's ideas before developing arguments against them.* If you concentrate on countering the speaker, then listening to what is being said becomes more difficult.

7. *Make the best of uncomfortable physical environments.* There are few places in a food service and lodging operation where the environment is totally acceptable for effective communication. If distractions are too great, try to continue the communication at another place or time.

8. *Look for special meaning in the speaker's message.* Try to sort out those parts of the message that are most important to you.

9. *Be aware of the speaker's nonverbal communication.* Often the real message can only be understood when implications of nonverbal communication are considered. The use of "body language" will be discussed later.

10. *Don't "turn off" information that is complicated or difficult.* Listen to the information and use feedback ("I do not understand." "Can you say that in another way?") to help the speaker know that communication has not been effective.

11. *Judge the content of the message—not its delivery.* Problems

with the speaker's voice, rate of speaking, and pronunciation should be overlooked as much as possible. The meaning of the message is most important and that is the purpose for careful listening.

12. *React fairly and sensibly to the message.* Allow the speaker to finish. You usually will have an opportunity to respond.

13. *Take notes only if the information will be needed in the future—and it is too detailed or specific to be recalled.* Otherwise, do not.

Writing

Supervisors must write as part of their management activities. Formal and informal reports must be written, records of significant activities must be maintained, and written replies to memos and instructions often are required. There are guidelines that you can follow to improve your writing ability.

1. *Consider the reader when you write.* Readers will understand the message based on their perceptions, and perceptions are influenced by a person's experiences, skills, abilities and knowledge. The personality of the reader also influences how effectively the message is communicated.

2. *Since writing does not allow for immediate feedback, consider how to judge the effectiveness of the communication.* Checking with readers and encouraging them to contact the writer are ways to increase feedback.

3. *The written message must be clear.* There is a trade-off between writing a message quickly and writing it clearly. That trade-off is accuracy.

4. *A simple message is best.* As with any type of communication, the purpose is to communicate, not to impress the receiver. Big words, specialized jargon, and fancy sentences are not necessary and often hurt the communication.

5. *Make sure that the central idea is clear and concise.* The reader should not have to hunt for it. Often an introductory paragraph that emphasizes the "what, who, why, where, when, and how" of the message can help.

6. *Keep the message as short as possible.*

7. *Be tactful.* Some readers may be offended at material that we consider harmless. Use of sexist language (business*man*, chair*man*, etc.,) may be offensive. Remember that the main point is not whether you—the writer—are offended but whether the reader will be.

8. *Try to be personal.* Focus on the reader's concerns—not just yours. There is a common saying that *I* is the most often used word in the English language. True or not, the point is that messages should emphasize *you* (referring to the reader) not *I* (referring to the writer).

9. *Written messages should not contain grammar and format problems.* Supervisors are busy people; they are not English teachers. However, writing must be reasonably problem-free to be clearly understood. For this reason, it is important to review and evaluate your writing before disseminating the message.

10. *Avoid overloading the same sentence or paragraph with too many thoughts.* The message is easier to understand if the writer covers each topic individually.

11. *Be positive when you write.* For example, consider the different implications between "Do Not Enter" and "Please Use the Front Entrance." While both of these messages have the same meaning, they express very different ideas about the relationship the writer is developing.

Interviews: A Special Type of Communication

Supervisors conduct many types of interviews. There are interviews with job applicants or with employees for disciplinary reasons and performance reviews. All the speaking and listening skills apply to an interview situation. Other principles also are important. Since the reasons an interview is conducted are critical to the supervisor's—and organization's—success, a supervisor should learn to be an effective interviewer. An interview is conducted for a specific purpose, so it is more formal than a normal conversation. Interviews have a clear structure—a beginning, body, and end— with each participant (the interviewer and the interviewee) having specific roles to play.

Open-Ended Questions

There are two types of questions that can be asked in an interview: open-ended and closed questions. **Open-ended questions** permit the person being interviewed to respond freely in an unstructured manner because the questions are broad and require more than a few words in reply. Examples include: "What are your feelings about this position?" "What do you like—and dislike—about your job?" "What are the main problems you face as an employee?" From the supervisor's perspective, use of open-ended questions has several advantages: (a) there is a greater opportunity to obtain meaningful information from the interviewee, (b) these questions are easier to answer and are not threatening to the employee, and (c) they suggest that the interviewer is interested in the employee.

There are, however, certain disadvantages. Open-ended questions take more time, and getting a record of the answers as well as controlling the interviewee is difficult.

Closed Questions

Closed questions are restrictive and call for a very brief response. Examples include: "Do you like your job?" "Did you read the application form?" "Who referred you to our property?"

From the supervisor's perspective, advantages of closed questions include: (a) little training is required to phrase and analyze questions, (b) less time is needed for the question and response, (c) the answers are easy to quantify, and (d) the supervisor can more effectively control the interview process.

There are disadvantages. Closed questions often provide little information, retard the communication process, and provide less opportunity for the employee to provide additional information.

The Interviewing Process

Interviews of any type can be conducted in five specific steps.

Plan for the interview. Planning involves: (a) assessing reasons for the interview, (b) considering the type of information to be solicited, (c) developing information about the interviewee and the subject to be discussed, (d) determining the type of structure to use, (e) determining questions to be asked, (f) deciding when and where the interview should be conducted, and (g) formalizing the schedule with the interviewee.

Reduce the Interviewee's Tension. Establish a pleasant relationship with the interviewee. Greeting him/her, making "small talk" at the beginning of the interview, and/or discussing matters of mutual interest are examples. The purpose of this step is to make the interviewee feel comfortable and establish a rapport that will help make the rest of the interview process more agreeable to both parties.

State the Purpose of the Interview. Often the purpose of the interview is obvious, such as with a job applicant. At other times, that is not the case and a basic introduction to clarify any misconceptions about the purpose is in order.

Ask Questions. The actual business of an interview is accomplished through the asking and answering of questions. If effective planning has been done, you will have a written or mental list of questions to be asked. This step in the interview process consumes the most time. Take notes or be sure that you understand—and have a record of—the most important points developed during the interview.

Review and Summarize What Was Said. Add your conclusions and discuss follow-up activities, if applicable.

Interview Styles

There are two types of interview styles: directive and nondirective. Between these two extremes are many styles that vary in the amount of freedom and control which distinguish the two basic styles. When a supervisor uses a **directive** interview style the emphasis is on control. Little time will be spent during the preliminary part of the interview to establish an agreeable relationship between the supervisor and the interviewee. Most questions will likely be of the closed type, and answers will likely be recorded. Questions are prepared in advance, and a checklist type of format may be used.

By contrast, the **nondirective** style of interviewing relies almost exclusively on open-ended questions. Time is permitted to establish rapport. While the supervisor may have a general list of concerns to be addressed, much control of the interview is assumed by the interviewee. Interviewers must have a great deal of skill and experience to use this approach. If not, much time will be used without producing any certain results. This type of interview can be effective in seeking opinions, assessing attitudes, and soliciting general information.

Nonverbal Communication: Body Language

You have learned that supervisors communicate in ways other than speaking. Writing is the best example of nonspoken communication. Actions are examples of nonverbal communication. Another term for this kind of exchange is **body language**—the concept that you can effectively communicate through body actions. Consider how a smile is a friendly gesture, a frown is a negative response, a wink can say hello, while a nod of the head can signify agreement—if up and down—or disagreement—if side to side.

There are many other examples of body language, such as fingers forming symbols— "V" for victory or circles for "OK." Think about eyes and what they can "say." Contrast the receiver of the message "looking straight into your eyes" with intense interest and another receiver gazing around the room while you are talking. The manner in which legs and arms are held can communicate a message. When crossed, they almost convey a feeling of protecting oneself. Yet, when they are in a neutral position, it can suggest receptivity to the message. Body language accurately describes an important way we communicate.

Personal space is another component of body language. How do you feel when a person stands within a few inches of you before he/she begins speaking? Contrast that with the person who stands at a distance and tries to converse with you. How do you feel about a person who is seated at a raised desk looking down at you?

When people tap their fingers, twitch an eye, or scratch an ear, are they "saying" that they are nervous? How about the person who is pacing the floor or biting his/her fingernails? While there are many more examples, the point is that we truly do "speak" in ways other than through written and spoken communication. Body language and similar actions are often subconscious ways of telling someone something about ourselves or our situations. The effective supervisor knows how to read body language and how to be sure that, through his/her actions, the right message is communicated.

NOTES

1. This discussion is based on Richard Husmand, et al., *Business Communication: Strategies and Skills* (Hinsdale, Ill.: Dryden Press, 1981), pp. 21-25.

PAGE TWENTY

Supervision at the Brandywine Room

Stacey was developing a presentation on communication for an upcoming supervisory development program. Actually she was accomplishing two things at once: developing an outline for her college paper that contained information she could use for her presentation. In this case, she thought, there would be no difference between the "real world" and what was being discussed in her academic program.

Stacey reviewed her outline:

1. Supervisors must be effective communicators.

2. Information is power. When a supervisor aids or blocks the flow of information to and from employees and superiors, he/she is taking on important responsibility.

3. Supervisors must develop and analyze information along with providing a spark of energy to start the information flowing up the organization chart.

4. Supervisors must learn how to "communicate with themselves." They have to understand their perceptions and recognize the effect they have on their decisions and on the communication tools they use.

5. When speaking, supervisors must think and plan ahead, use language and examples that listeners will understand, utilize feedback to monitor the listener's understanding, and clarify the message when necessary.

6. Since supervisors may spend more than half their time listening, they must know how to listen correctly. Important listening principles are: (a) give your full attention so you will understand the message accurately; (b) listen for meaning, not just for words; (c) keep an open mind; (d) realize that whatever the speaker is saying, it may have meaning for you; (e) analyze what has occurred for any subtle meaning; (f) ask for specific examples when questions arise; (g) repeat information to confirm that you understood what was said.

7. Supervisors must have effective writing skills. Some tips include: (a) keep sentences short, (b) use simple words and write simple sentences, (c) avoid unnecessary words, (d) write the way you speak, (e) write to express—not to impress, (f) evaluate and rewrite the material before it is circulated.

8. Supervisors must be effective readers. To do this: (a) read material that is absolutely necessary for the job, (b) understand why you read what you do, (c) sort out unnecessary reading, (d) read trade magazines, journals, and other business-related information.

9. Supervisors must practice nonverbal communication skills. As supervisors, your actions are constantly observed. The way you walk, stand, gesture, smile, and dress can make a difference in your communication ability. Set an example for your staff in terms of promptness, work habits, and positive attitudes, among other qualities.

10. Supervisors must clearly specify what they expect employees to accomplish.

11. Supervisors should identify and explain how the employees' and the organization's objectives are related.

12. Supervisors must know how to conduct one-on-one interviews. This means you must: (a) understand the objective of the interview; (b) know as much as possible about who is being interviewed (all available information must be assembled and studied); (c) attempt to make the interviewee feel comfortable; (d) make all arrangements regarding time, place, and available facilities; (e) have an open mind and be prepared to listen carefully; (f) address all concerns and cover all required parts of the interview in proper sequence; (g) ensure that questions relate to what the interviewee knows; the questions should be short, clear, and specific and the interviewee should be allowed enough time to think of responses; (h) summarize the interview to ensure understanding; (i) take time to record appropriate notes as soon as the interview is completed.

13. The supervisor should sometimes use the "grapevine" to accomplish communication objectives. Monitoring the grapevine will help assess how employees feel about almost any job-related matter. As concerns are identified, the supervisor should provide information that will resolve problems before they become serious.

14. Many factors can create barriers to effective communication. These include a poor choice of words, status, misunderstandings, prejudices, improper attitudes, and environmental interference, among others. Basic common sense can be effective in overcoming these barriers. For example: (a) face-to-face talks are better than other types of communication, (b) an under-

standing of body language will help, (c) use of simple, clear, and appropriate language is necessary, (d) important points should be repeated, (f) understanding of the other person's perceptions—and what influenced them—can be helpful, (g) proper physical locations for communication activities are important.

15. A supervisor can help improve communications in the organization by being willing to discuss job-related matters with employees, encouraging employees to "say what is on their mind," and using other channels of communication, such as counselors, suggestion systems, and opinion surveys.

16. Supervisors must do all they can to ensure that communication paths in the organization do not become distorted. Much accuracy in communication is lost as it passes through the many organizational layers.

17. Supervisors must know how to communicate effectively with their colleagues in other departments as well as with their superiors and employees at levels above and below them in the organization.

Stacey realized that it was difficult to say everything that needed to be said about communication in a short presentation. She found it ironic that she was having difficulty "communicating about communication." She knew, however, that use of common sense was the basis of many techniques designed to improve communication abilities. An important first step, she realized, was for her colleagues to understand that many organizational problems stem from the inability of supervisors to communicate effectively. At the least, her session would identify this potential problem, she figured. If she could motivate her colleagues, procedures and techniques for effective communicating could be learned and used on the job.

11 The Supervisor and Motivational Techniques

PAGE TWENTY-ONE

Supervision at the Brandywine Room

Stacey had wondered about the high levels of employee turnover at the Brandywine Room almost from the first day she had been employed as a food server. In her college classes in hospitality management she had learned that employee turnover was an industry-wide problem; it almost seemed that "short-timers" were a fact of doing business. She had also learned that high turnover rates could indicate motivation and morale problems.

Stacey had known a lot of food servers whose story was often the same; they were hired because of an emergency (someone had quit and there was no one to replace him/her). Dining room employees had all kinds of priorities besides working at the Brandywine, and there were a lot of big and little things that seemed to irritate some of them while they were on the job. Stacey felt it was time to look at employee turnover. She knew that if she could tackle this problem successfully, it was unlikely that any problem would arise that she wouldn't be able to handle.

She decided to do two things. She was going back to her college books and her instructor to get some basic information. Second, she was going to attend the employee motivation sessions which the hotel was offering for supervisors during the next two weeks. Surely, between the combination of "academia" and the business world, she could get some answers that would help make the employee turnover problem a thing of the past at the Brandywine Room.

Definitions

Motivation is a state or force within an individual that makes him/her act in a way designed to achieve some goal. Taking this broad definition and putting it into the context of supervision in the hospitality operation, we might say that **motivation** is what the supervisor does to encourage and/or influence other people to take necessary action. This is different, however, from the supervisor who establishes a goal dealing with "what I will do to motivate my employees." Motivation is, in fact, an internally generated force or drive within the individual which provides an incentive for him/her to act. (Remember our discussion in Chapter 1 about human needs—and how they create internal pressures to satisfy those needs.) What the supervisor *cannot* do, then, is to *motivate employees*; what he/she *can* do is provide the conditions and interests that will encourage the employees to do what they want to do. The secret to this approach is to mesh the goals of the employees with those of the hospitality organization in developing plans and strategies to attain them. If this can be done, the employees and the organization can benefit. The supervisor's role is really one of encouraging the employee to become motivated.

The supervisor, as he/she practices principles of motivation, must interact with people other than employees. There may be times when the supervisor must get peers and even superiors to see things his/her way. This further suggests that a traditional definition of motivation, such as "convincing employees to want to do required tasks," is not broad enough.

At least one writer emphasizes the relationship between motivation and teamwork.[1] In the labor-intensive hospitality industry where large numbers of employees must work closely together to attain organizational goals, teamwork is very important. With this background then, **motivation** can also be considered as a process which attempts to replace goals of individual employees with those of a group (such as the work team in a specific section or department, or the entire hospitality organization).

While there are many definitions of motivation, most include the concept of goals or objectives. The process of motivation begins with establishing goals and continues with taking actions to attain them—or at least come closer to meeting them. As this process is undertaken for ourselves as individuals, we are talking about self-motivation.

It can be seen that to establish goals for a group (such as a team of employees), the goals must be mutually agreeable. Is it possible to establish goals that provide outcomes desired by employees, employee groups, supervisors, higher levels of management, and the entire organization? In practice, goals (of either work groups or the organization) frequently are not even defined. In other situations, defined goals are not mutually compatible with individual employees, employee groups, and/or other levels of the organization.

Simply stated, in order to have motivated employees, the supervisor must ensure that well-defined objectives have been established and that these are compatible with the needs of all concerned parties within the operation.

The Organization and the Motivated Employee

Why should the hospitality operation want motivated employees?

The answer should be obvious. Organizational goals cannot be effectively attained unless employees work together. The need for teamwork in the hospitality industry has been noted throughout this book. To emphasize a point made earlier, supervisors should realize that their job is not just to "motivate an employee." All employees come to the work situation motivated to attain goals which they have already established. How can the supervisor blend the goals of the organization with those of the employee?

Morale and Productivity

One goal of the supervisor's efforts to develop a motivated staff can be to increase employee morale. **Morale** can be defined as the feelings an employee has about all aspects of the job (work to be done, supervisors and peers, the organization, and working environment). There are many benefits to be gained from building high morale. However, to dispel a common myth, researchers have not consistently been able to find a positive correlation between high morale levels and productivity. High employee morale levels do not always yield high productivity levels.[2]

Organizations, of course, desire high productivity levels without corresponding decreases in work quality. As this occurs, economic objectives are better met. As noted in Chapter 3, leadership styles and the job situation may affect productivity. An employee might dislike his/her boss and perform adequately because he/she needs the job, because there is a need to show the supervisor that "I can do it," or because the employee is intimidated when assigned work is not done. In each case, the employee's morale (attitudes toward work) can be low, yet productivity can be high (or at least satisfactory).

Morale and Turnover, Absenteeism, Accidents

If productivity and morale cannot be equated, does this mean that high morale levels are immaterial to organizational success? Researchers have found that the answer is no. There are proven relationships between morale levels and turnover, absenteeism, and accidents.[3] We can argue that as these factors become less of a problem, productivity is likely to increase. This "back door" approach to relating morale levels and productivity well suits the needs of our discussion. Regardless, however, the advantages of reduced turnover include lowered recruitment and selection costs, reduced orientation and training costs for new employees, fewer problems with work quality and related job problems during orientation periods, and the like. As absenteeism is reduced, the organization realizes fewer scheduling and emergency problems and a reduction in overtime costs. As accidents decrease, personnel-related problems, insurance costs, and product problems also decrease. Therefore, even if the direct relationship between morale levels and productivity cannot be established, certainly an indirect relationship can be shown.

Let's reconsider our definitions of motivation. As we think of how an organization will benefit from motivated employees, it becomes obvious that there is a need to consider the personal goals of the staff members and to do what is possible to ensure that the goals of both the employee and the operation are compatible. When an employee desires to accomplish the same thing that his/her employer does, the work can become interesting and challenging. The employee is more likely to accomplish work that the organization requires. Staff members are more willing to cooperate with the supervisor in the task of attaining goals. Synthesis is more likely to occur; that is, the output of the group is likely to be greater than the combined output of individuals working alone. Personnel-related problems that otherwise would require discipline, training, coaching, or more specific supervision will likewise be reduced.

The concept of **negative motivation** should also be considered in our discussion. Simply put, the term refers to a situation in which the employee's needs actually are in conflict with the goals of the organization. When this occurs, such problems as sabotage, work slowdowns or stoppages, and attempts to turn other employees against the organization can arise.

Perhaps the reasons motivated employees are important can be better seen by looking at this question from the opposite perspective. What are the disadvantages of motivated employees? The answer is simple—there are none. So often in the process of supervision it is necessary to consider the pros and cons of alternatives being considered. If a matter as important as motivation—which affects all employees and the organization—generates no negative aspects which need to be countered, the answer to the question, "Is it important to motivate employees?" is obvious. The answer is yes, and the supervisor has an important role to play in this effort.

The Supervisor and Motivation

The supervisor can do much to develop motivated employees (those who have goals in harmony with the hospitality operation). Certainly it is not possible to order employees to change their goals or to have a high morale level. However, the supervisor can attempt to develop a climate in which employees will want to work *with*—rather than *against*—the organization. This can be accomplished by practicing basic principles of human relations, communication, and supervision.

The supervisor interacts with employees constantly throughout every workday. He/she, more than any other management staff member, is likely to influence the employee's feeling about the job. The blending of personal and organizational goals can only come as a result of the supervisor's long-range actions which yield the proper work environment.

Providing Motivational Conditions

In order to provide conditions for an employee to become motivated, the supervisor must understand the wants and needs (goals) of the employee. The supervisor must, to the extent possible, recognize personal concerns as work is being assigned and supervised. Organizational tools such as organization charts, job descriptions and specifications, job lists, and job breakdowns all tend to make work requirements rigid and uniform. This need for consistency is good from the organization's perspective but, at the same time, the supervisor must find ways within the restrictions established by these and related personnel tools to allow employees to meet personal goals on the job. If this sounds difficult, it should—because it is.

Exhibit 11.1 What Do Employees Want from Their Jobs?

Factors	Rank Given By	
	Employees	Supervisors
Full appreciation of work done	1	8
Feeling of being in on things	2	10
Help with personal problems	3	9
Job security	4	2
Higher wages	5	1
Interesting work	6	5
Promotion in the company	7	3
Personal loyalty of supervisor	8	6
Good working conditions	9	4
Tactful discipline	10	7

Source: Adapted with permission from John W. Newstrom and Edward E. Scannell, Games Trainers Play: Experiential Learning Exercises *(New York: McGraw-Hill, 1980), p. 121.*

There is little, if anything, that a supervisor can do to control the employee's life off the job. The employee does, of course, bring personal goals and concerns with him/her to the work situation. The case is again made for the supervisor to get to know the employee. In addition to personal concerns, there are other factors that occur on the job which influence the employee. Some of these are within the control of the supervisor. Examples include job security, working conditions, job tasks to be performed, and the like.

Frequently there is a vast difference between what the supervisor believes the employees want and what employees actually do want from their jobs. These differences are shown in Exhibit 11.1. Thousands of workers across the country were asked to rate the factors which most affected their morale. Likewise, supervisors were asked to indicate what they believed were most important to their employees. It is interesting to note that the top three items cited by employees are the last three cited by supervisors.

What does this mean? First of all, these findings suggest that supervisors may not know what their employees want from their jobs. Second, these findings suggest that the factors judged most important by employees are within the control of supervisors. Further, the findings indicate that, in terms of Maslow's hierarchy of needs (see Chapter 1), employees appear to be motivated by factors which affect their esteem and belonging needs. By contrast, supervisors view employees' needs to center on physical and safety concerns. Can't we begin to question how supervisors can work so closely with employees over relatively long periods of time and not have better ideas about what their needs and desires are?

The way in which the supervisor relates with formal and informal employee work groups (see Chapter 14) will also affect whether employees become motivated to work with the supervisor in the pursuit of organizational goals.

Personal characteristics of the supervisor must also be taken into account. The supervisor must, first, be concerned about the need to provide conditions within which the employees can become motivated. Second, he/she must practice leadership styles that meet the demands of the specific situation, and must implement policies and procedures that recognize employee goals and needs. The supervisor who shows appreciation, involves employees in decisions which affect them, and has the skills and abilities to supervise is more likely to be able to motivate employees than is his/her peer who is unable and/or unwilling to practice the skills.

How can a supervisor tell if employees are motivated to attain organizational goals and/or if morale levels are high? Common-sense observations can help; sophisticated studies are not always necessary. Consider the following:

1. Are there excessive costs, excessive waste, and quality control problems?

2. Are there a large number of gripes and grievances? Are accidents, turnover, or absenteeism excessive?

3. Is there a general lack of cooperation?

4. Are employees disrespectful to supervisors and unconcerned about the company?

If the answer to each of these and similar questions is yes, the supervisor should begin to recognize that morale problems may be the cause. Fortunately, there are supervisory actions which can eliminate these types of problems when they are caused by morale factors.

Before any of this can be done, however, the supervisor must first be aware that there is a problem. From our discussion of the supervisor as a decision-maker (see Chapter 1), we know that this step must precede the generation of alternatives and the remaining components in the decision-making process. Therefore, in the context of motivation, as the supervisor observes employee-related problems, the alternative of improving motivation and morale levels should be considered. Recall that in Chapter 1 we emphasized an approach to reviewing performance-related problems to assess whether training, changes in the work environment, use of motivational techniques, or implementation of personnel management efforts might be most helpful. If motivation-related problems are defined, the supervisor must ensure that observed problems do not stem from the use of improper management techniques.

In addition to a purposeful effort to apply techniques of motivation, we must also recognize that supervisors must use a great deal of common sense or intuition as they interact with employees. A supervisor might be only partially conscious of the fact that an employee acts in a certain way. Likewise, an individual may not know why he/she acts in a specified manner. Regardless, experienced supervisors may sense that a problem exists and know what to do about it.

The Employee as an Individual

In order for motivational efforts to be successful, it is absolutely necessary that the supervisor understand the individual(s) with whom he/she is trying to work. A successful motivator knows what it takes for an employee to be motivated. As stated earlier, the task must begin by knowing the employee and having at least an idea of, or sense about, the inner goals which affect his/her behavior. In Chapter 1 we noted that all individuals, regardless of their differences, have certain basic needs which they strive to meet. Many different theories have been offered to suggest what these needs are. The supervisor must have some understanding of the basic factors that influence employee actions. Exhibit 11.1 reviewed some of these factors and attempted to answer the question, "What drives a person to action?" If the supervisor can develop an understanding about these and related factors, he/she will be on the way to understanding the causes of human behavior. With this knowledge, plans to blend employee and organizational concerns and objectives can be developed.

Needs and Behavior

Exhibit 11.2 outlines the basic causes and courses of human actions. Essentially, behavior begins when an individual feels (perceives) a need. This need is then directed into behavior designed to attain that need. If the need is met as a result of the behavior (the goal is attained), this will affect the individual's perceived needs; he/she is likely to modify behavior in order to meet new needs. If, on the other hand, the actions taken to attain goals are ineffective, there may be a revision in either the needs or the behavior. As a result of these additional actions, needs (goals) may be met; this will influence future needs and subsequent courses of action. Alternatively, the needs still may not be met. Normally, frustration will result and the individual will have to modify his/her needs since they cannot be met.

An example of these concepts may clarify the relationships. Suppose that a supervisor is directed by his/her boss to attain a specific economic goal (for example, to keep labor costs within the specified limits); suppose also that the supervisor is in agreement with this goal. He/she will develop plans and procedures and otherwise exhibit behavior designed to meet this goal. If the goal (maintain the specified labor cost) is met, this will influence the supervisor's next concerns. For example, perhaps he/she will turn priorities to another cost or, alternatively, work to reduce labor costs still further.

If, on the other hand, the need to minimize labor costs is not met (the goal has not been attained), the supervisor has two choices: revise the original need ("it is not possible to meet the labor cost goal") or use different labor-saving approaches in an attempt to reduce labor costs. The result of these actions may be to meet the labor cost goal (which, again, will influence future needs and courses of action). Alternatively, perhaps even the additional actions will not yield desired results. In this event, other courses of action are possible. At some point, however, if labor costs cannot be reduced, the needs (goals) of the supervisor will require modification.

This process is not as difficult as it may seem. The main point is that an individual's perceived needs give rise to courses of action (behavior) designed to meet those needs.

What needs do human beings have? As individuals, we are all different but, at their most basic levels, individual needs are the same. In the context of Exhibit 11.2, then, if an individual perceives that a basic need is not being met to a level he/she judges to be a satisfactory minimum, behavior designed to meet that need may result. As this occurs, the individual will strive to meet higher levels of need.

While this description of the role of needs in causing behavior (action) has been simplified, it can provide the game plan for a supervisor's motivational efforts. He/she must first discover what is causing an employee to act. To the extent that these causes do not yield behavior consistent with organizational goals, there is a need to change the individual's needs and/or courses of action.

Changing Employee Attitudes

An **attitude** is a preset idea that causes an individual to react to other individuals, events, or things in certain ways. Recall that, earlier in this chapter, we defined morale as a reflection of the combination of attitudes which an employee has toward the job situation. An attitude is an outcome of one's past experiences. Attitudes are formed by feelings based upon experiences and, at some point, they work their way into our personalities. It is difficult to change attitudes.

As a supervisor attempts to motivate his/her staff, there may be a need to consider the employees' attitudes. The supervisor normally must be concerned about creating opportunities that will result in behavior change. This is an ongoing part of the supervisor's job. The objective, of course, is to discover opportunities for more effectively blending organizational and employee goals. An individual does not hold an attitude which he/she does not feel is good. It is only from someone else's vantage point—in this case, the supervisor's—that the attitude is viewed as poor, or negative. Attitude modification involves the following sequence of events (these are illustrated in Exhibit 11.3):

Becoming Aware of the Undesirable Attitude. Often this is observed through improper performance or behavior on the job. (Refer to the performance problem analysis worksheet in Chapter 1.) Consider, for example, the supervisor who observes an employee performing a task incorrectly. The supervisor has provided training, coaching, and follow-up and is convinced that the employee knows how to perform the task properly. What is the problem? Perhaps it is an outward sign of a negative attitude held by the employee. The relationship between poor attitudes and an employee who is not motivated should be clear.

Determining the Reason(s) for the Attitude/Performance Problem. Discussions with the staff member might indicate why the problem exists.

Exhibit 11.2 Needs, Behavior, and Goals

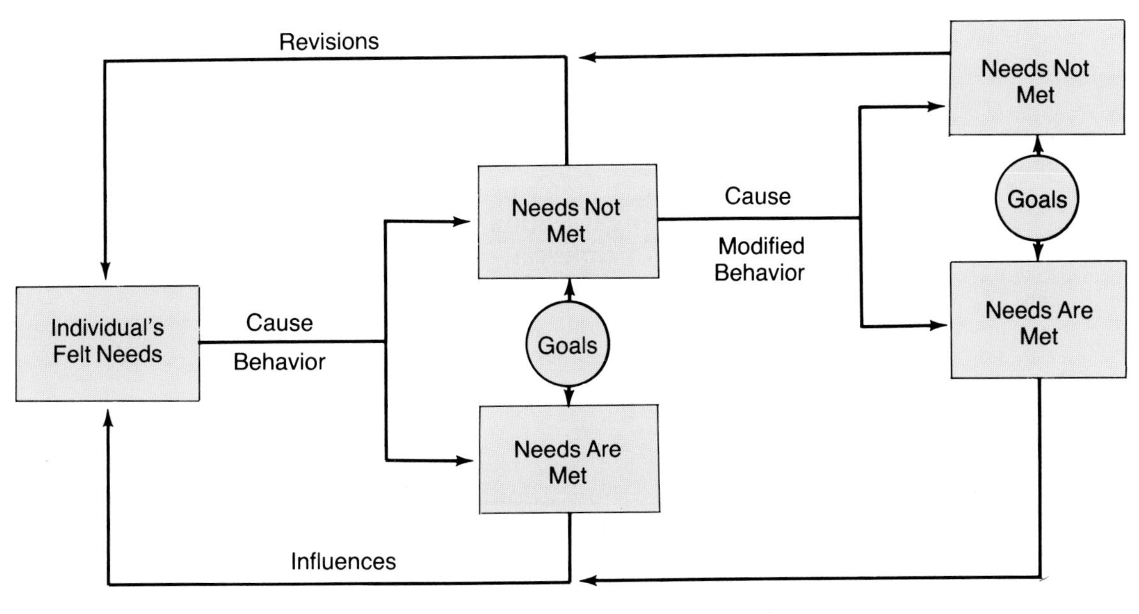

Exhibit 11.3 How a Supervisor Modifies Employee Attitudes/Behavior

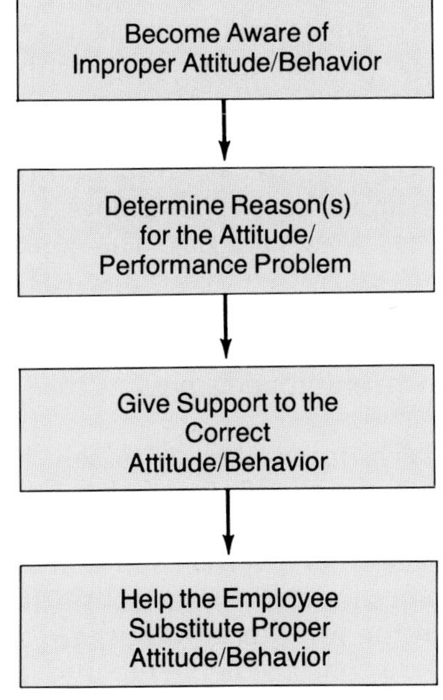

Giving Support to the Correct Attitude/Behavior. If, for example, there are incorrect reasons for the employee's behavior, these should be pointed out. The provision of correct information and the use of objective communication can be helpful.

Helping the Employee Develop a Proper Attitude/Behavior. As the employee sees that his/her perception of the situation is incorrect, it is likely that the employee will replace the improper attitude/behavior with a proper one. As this occurs, the supervisor not only corrects a problem but, at the same time, may bring the employee's feelings more in line with those of the organization. The combination of these types of behavior changes over time can yield motivated employees whose needs and goals become more similar to those of the organization.

Other Motivational Strategies

There are other motivational strategies that supervisors can use besides the identification and modification of undesirable attitudes. Consider the following:

Communication Techniques. Security, belonging, and recognition needs can all be satisfied, at least to some extent, by effective communication. For example, you can get to know your employees, give praise when due, and talk about rewards. Conversely, the ineffective use of communication can be a detriment to employee motivation practices.

Management Approaches. Various leadership styles also help (or hinder) motivational efforts. Redesigning jobs, when possible, can be helpful. The use of such techniques as job rotation, job enlargement, job enrichment, and flex-time (in which, to the extent possible, workers develop their own work schedules) provide other examples.

Behavior Modification Techniques. Briefly, this approach suggests that you must reinforce employee actions which are desirable and discourage those activities which are not. The concept of rewards and punishments will be discussed further in our discussion of discipline (Chapter 12).

Sales Techniques. Act as a salesperson; explain, defend, and justify the needs, from an employee's perspective, for policies and procedures.

Listening Techniques. Listen closely to employees to determine what they desire.

The Employee's Perspective. Put yourself in the employee's place to determine his/her individual needs and to assess how these things can be provided on the job. Recall that there are many ways to look at and do things. Make a concerted effort to understand the employee's viewpoint. This forms the foundation for developing strategies to change attitudes and to help staff members become motivated. If you can find out what

Exhibit 11.4 Principles of Motivation

1. **Compatibility with objectives.** People being motivated must (a) have clearly defined objectives, and (b) these objectives must be in concert with those of the organization.
2. **Motivational flexibility.** The type and degree of motivational efforts must be varied.
3. **Multi-directional force.** The manager must be the driving force behind the motivational efforts.
4. **Management maturity.** The type and direction of motivational efforts must change as the organization matures.
5. **Self-motivation.** Motivational efforts by the supervisor must be designed to yield self-motivation.
6. **Effective communications.** There must be an open and trustful atmosphere based upon respect in order for motivational efforts to be effective.
7. **Employee participation.** Employees must be able, to the extent possible, to be involved in matters which affect them.
8. **Credit and blame.** The supervisor must give credit to employees when due and accept responsibility to share blame when problems occur.
9. **Authority, responsibility, and accountability.** To motivate employees, a supervisor must give them the authority and responsibility necessary to perform their work and must, at the same time, hold them accountable for effective performance.
10. **Conscious self-motivation.** The most effective type of motivation comes from a serious and deliberate effort by the individual employee.
11. **Genuine respect.** A supervisor cannot be an effective motivator until he/she genuinely respects employees, recognizes their rights, and accepts their capacity for self-direction.

makes employees act or think as they do, you gain some insight into what will be necesary for change to occur.

Human Relations Skills. Practice the "art and science" of human relations; that is, develop and maintain good working relationships and actively solicit employee input.

Goal Identification. Make sure that the organizational goals which you are attempting to blend with the goals of the employee are, in fact, property goals and not your own personal goals.

Other Approaches. Recognize that there are different approaches which can be used to assist staff members. If one does not work, try another. This is much better than dismissing further attempts to provide motivational opportunities when initial techniques are ineffective.

Motivational techniques and strategies are summarized in the principles of motivation noted in Exhibit 11.4. A review of these principles will highlight many of the specific concerns about motivation that we have identified. As they can be incorporated into motivational strategies, there is an increased likelihood that motivational efforts will be successful.

Motivational Factors

Job Interests

If an employee is interested in his/her work, increased motivation may result. The employee may be motivated to remain on the job, participate in creative tasks, and better identify with the operation's goals. Obviously, interests vary among employees; a person's interests are a function of his/her background, personality, intellect, attitudes, and other characteristics. Supervisors should understand that what will interest one employee may not interest another. The supervisor's challenge, then, is to know what employees desire and find a way to incorporate their desires and interests, whenever possible, into ongoing work.

Identification with Property

Those employees who identify with the organization, believe in it, and agree with its purposes, policies, and goals, will be better able to help the organization than will other employees who are motivated only by rewards and punishments. Normally, the desired behavior can be influenced most effectively when the employees accept and agree with the purpose of the organization.

The new employee orientation process is an excellent time to begin acquainting employees with work requirements. Often, if employees are led to believe that they should perform in a specific way, they will attempt to meet the behavior expectations. Over time, these performance standards and policies may be accepted by employees as their own.

Subconscious Motivation

We have noted that many employees do not know, or at least cannot verbalize, their goals or needs. Much motivation is subconscious. For example, some "high energy" employees may perform work to their highest level of ability because they fear rejection if they do not produce. In fact, they may not even be aware that they are seeking approval from their peers. There are some positive aspects of subconscious motivation. For example, employees are less likely to be defensive about attempts of the supervisor to assess their inner needs. Likewise, employees can focus their attention and concentration on job-related concerns.

Is Money a Motivator?

Many supervisors and employees in the hospitality industry believe that money is the primary—or at least a very important—motivator. Is this true? Since money is a symbol, it has different meanings to different people. For example, to employees concerned about meeting basic physiological needs, money really means food, health care, clothing, shelter, etc. At higher levels of need, money might be equated with status, power, or prestige. Therefore, like other aspects of this topic, it is difficult to generalize about the use of money as a motivator.

As noted in Chapter 1, Herzberg has considered the use of money as a motivator in his maintenance and motivation theory.[4] This research labels economic factors (wages, salaries, benefits, etc.) as maintenance elements. That is, these factors will not create employee motivation; however, if they are not present they can cause dissatisfaction. "The best a business can hope for by providing these factors is that the average employee will put forth an average commitment in time and effort at his or her job."[5] If this is correct, economic factors are not, in themselves, motivators (those conditions within the work situation which are necessary to yield above average commitments from employees and which help provide the means for employees to achieve a greater satisfaction of their personal needs on the job).

Achievement and Motivation

Classic studies by McClelland have suggested that achievement (the desire to succeed) can be a motivating factor in some individuals.[6] McClelland also traced the possibility of increasing achievement potential through training. His studies suggest that achievement-motivated supervisors might be able to strengthen their own performance and motivation (and/or that of their employees) through training efforts.

Employees with high achievement needs can be motivated by challenging and competitive job situations. They often like to accept responsibility for problem-solving activities, set reasonably high performance goals, and actively solicit feedback about their efforts.

High needs for achievement, then, correlate with subsequent job performance. Supervisors should seek out high achievers and give them opportunities to satisfy these needs on the job. Employees will be motivated and, at the same time, the hospitality organization will benefit from their improved performance.

Competition and Motivation

Competition between employees, if it is fostered deliberately by management, can be effective only in certain situations. As a motivational technique, it must be used with caution; generally, it must be combined with other strategies that are not associated with manipulation and destructive conflict. Competition can help employees focus on goals. There is a difference between natural competition that evolves in a job situation and that which is purposely planned by managers.

There are at least two problems involved in purposely planned competition. Most employees, by definition, are average; this implies that competition will only be beneficial to relatively few employees. The remaining employees may become frustrated. Second, employees often are rewarded for seniority on the job rather than for merit. To the extent that this situation exists, competition will not yield benefits that would be possible if the best employees were rewarded. Likewise, competition between work groups normally should be discouraged, since it puts work teams at odds with each other when, in fact, they are both attempting to attain the same organizational goals.

Analysis of Motivational Problems

The concept of management control requires the supervisor to define expected performance, assess actual performance, and identify differences, if any, between them. A performance problem exists when an employee's behavior is substandard, but this type of problem is not always caused by a low level of motivation. A motivation problem exists when the difference between standard and actual results is due to a lack of effort rather than to a lack of ability, training, or other factors. To determine whether performance problems result from low motivation levels, supervisors should answer the following questions.

1. Does the problem relate to communication? Does the employee understand what is expected? If he/she does not, a more effective communication process is necessary.

2. Does the problem require training? If it does, training should be conducted before motivational problems, if any, can be assessed.

3. Does the problem relate to an inability, after training, to do required work? If this is the case, the employee may be untrainable. Transfer, demotion, or termination may be in order (and the selection process should be reviewed to determine why the employee was hired).

4. Are other job-related problems evident? If there are undesirable conditions in the job situation (inadequate tools, inferior operating procedures, etc.), the problem may be the lack of opportunity, not motivation.

If the problem is found to be due, at least in part, to a lack of motivation, the supervisor will need to apply the principles of motivation discussed in this chapter and throughout this book.

Summary: What Employees Want from Their Jobs

This discussion reviews some employee-related concerns that can be incorporated into ongoing strategies of employee motivation.

- Employees are individuals; every staff member brings a different perspective to the job which is the result of differing experiences, education, common sense, and environments.

- Each employee is at the center of his/her own concerns; a primary interest is to satisfy needs, ambitions, desires, and goals. These are basic concerns that all human beings have.

- An employee wants to satisfy basic needs. These relate to survival and security concerns and a desire to belong, to generate positive feelings from within and from others, and to be self-fulfilled. The supervisor who can discover what the employee is trying to accomplish—and can help him/her do it—will be helping the employee in a way that will have spin-off benefits for the organization.

- Most employees want (a) fair and consistent company policies in matters which affect them; (b) management staff they can respect and trust; (c) adequate working relationships with superiors, subordinates, and peers; (d) acceptable salaries and working conditions; (e) appropriate job security assurance; (f) favorable job status.

- There are other factors which, when present, can help to satisfy and motivate employees. These include: (a) challenging work, (b) work that yields a sense of personal accomplishment, (c) the expression of appreciation for good performance, (d) increased responsibility and the chance to grow in the job, (e) the feeling of importance and making a contribution to the organization, (f) participation in job-related matters that affect the employee.

- For many employees, more challenging and interesting work will be possible if supervisors practice job rotation (moving employees into other jobs which they are capable of performing), job enlargement (increasing the number of tasks that are part of the job), and job enrichment (changing job tasks in order to make them more interesting and challenging).

- Most employees appreciate opportunities to make decisions about their jobs. Supervisors can seek their help in defining problems, suggesting alternatives, and/or evaluating the results of their decisions.

To the extent that the question, "If I were an employee what would I want from the job?" can be answered with elements not now present in the employee's job, potential areas in which a job can be improved will be identified. Professional supervisors recognize and, to the extent possible, provide those things which, from an employee's perspective, will make the job better.

NOTES

1. Jud Morris, *The Art of Motivating: a Guide to Getting More Accomplished Better Through Others* (Boston: Industrial Institute, 1968), p. 29.

2. Ross A. Webber, *Management: The Basic Elements of Managing Organizations*, rev. ed. (Homewood, Ill.: Irwin, 1979), p. 175.

3. Webber, p. 175.

4. Frederick Herzberg, et al., *The Motivation to Work* (New York: Wiley, 1959).

5. Samuel C. Certo, *Principles of Modern Management, Functions and Systems* (Dubuque, Iowa: Brown, 1980), p. 358.

6. David C. McClelland, *The Achieving Society* (Princeton, N.J.: VanNostrand, 1961).

PAGE TWENTY-TWO

Supervision at the Brandywine Room

As she read, thought, and talked about employee motivation, Stacey began to understand that the turnover rate in the Brandywine Room was likely caused by a motivation problem. She thought she had a fairly good understanding of motivation, and she felt ready to apply what she knew to improving motivational conditions.

The basic problem, as she saw it, was to find a way to satisfy the employees' basic needs while they were performing their jobs and addressing goals established by her, Mr. George, and top management at the hotel.

She began her efforts by scheduling staff meetings to give employees a chance to air their concerns. She made it a point to visit personally with all of her staff members on a frequent basis. She used these opportunities to discover "where they were coming from." She remembered her earlier review of leadership styles and made a renewed effort to practice different styles with different employees based upon her understanding of what would be best from their perspective. She gave added responsibilities to those employees who wanted them; she attempted to draw into the decision-making process other staff members who appreciated this approach. Within her limitations, she tried to redesign work to recognize special interests of the employees.

Stacey implemented a job rotation program designed to give employees a fresh look at different jobs, reduce boredom, and help Stacey ensure that, through cross-training, qualified personnel would be available to perform specific jobs when emergencies arose.

Stacey also began to develop job enrichment programs (which would increase the employees' responsibilities in planning and performing work as well as in decision-making) and job enlargement programs (which would increase the variety of tasks employees were to perform). She knew existing job descriptions would need to be revised to reflect these changes.

Stacey talked with Mr. George about beginning the development of a management by objectives (MBO) program on a trial basis in the dining room. With this plan, she would decide mutually with the employees exactly what they were to accomplish within a given period. Mutually determined goals might range from plans to resolve observed performance problems to personal/professional growth activities for the employees.

While the concept of flex-time could not be used in the traditional manner, she did ask employees to give her schedules which best met their needs and, when possible, she incorporated these requests into the work schedules as she developed them. Stacey knew that, in some cases, rewards and punishments could be part of a motivation strategy, but she knew little about these techniques (and she vowed to resolve this problem).

Stacey implemented many communication techniques as she conducted her group meetings and individual conferences. She channeled information "coming from the top" to employees, and she provided feedback to employees about acceptable—and unacceptable—job performance. She was developing a group of employees who were willing to help her improve dining room operations. She hoped they would serve as a barometer of employee concerns and provide appropriate, timely feedback.

As a final effort, Stacey realized that her effectiveness in improving the conditions for motivation could not be judged unless there was a benchmark of information to use for comparison purposes. With the help of the Personnel Department, she began to collect and make use of turnover information. This data was also being collected for some of the other departments. She thought it would be helpful to compare turnover rates of the dining room not only with previous periods, but also with the rates of other departments in current periods. Since many of the personnel policies, organizational philosophies, and procedures were the same, she felt that higher than average turnover rates in her department might be reflective of either inadequate selection, orientation, or training efforts, or to her shortcomings as a supervisor. She knew that being aware of a problem was the first step in resolving it. If turnover rates or other factors suggested that her supervisory skills were inadequate, she would take whatever steps were necessary to correct the problem.

12 The Supervisor and the Disciplinary Process

PAGE TWENTY-THREE

Supervision at the Brandywine Room

Stacey's efforts to apply motivational techniques seemed to be paying off to some extent. Now that she, with the help of the Personnel Department, was gathering statistics about turnover rates, she could measure her progress. Since she had learned that absenteeism and accidents were related to morale levels, she was developing and reviewing statistics on these factors as well. Unfortunately, however, Stacey still had problems with some employees. Even after training, coaching, strict supervision, and repeated reprimands, some employees still refused to comply with rules and policies and follow standard procedures. She knew from her study of motivation that attitude problems might be the cause. Stacey was attempting to learn the reasons for the employees' attitudes so she could help them see faults in their thinking.

There were times, however, when this long-range approach to problem-solving wasn't sufficient. Stacey needed to learn the principles of employee discipline so she could put them into practice when necessary. Stacey had been a supervisor long enough to realize that the best wage/salary program or the most useful communication and motivation techniques would not "work" with every employee. Back to the books! Back to her supervisor, Mr. George! Back to her college professor! Back to the Personnel Department! Stacey was grateful that she had a number of resources to help her learn how to supervise effectively.

Discipline is necessary in any organization. Members must control their desires to achieve individual goals that override the "common good." Employees must follow reasonable rules that are established by managers so mutually developed goals can be attained.

Most employees understand and accept policies and rules. They also will meet, or honestly try to meet, performance standards. There often is a small minority of employees, however, who will not cooperate. Disciplinary procedures are needed to modify these employees' behavior and communicate to all employees that reasonable rules and procedures must be followed. In effect, discipline is an extension of motivational techniques.

What Is Discipline?

Discipline is an attempt to modify employee behavior. In a positive sense, discipline includes activities that correct, strengthen, and improve employee performance. Discipline also relates to the necessity of complying with rules and policies and following procedures. In this sense discipline is a positive process, which is similar to coaching a team.

More commonly, discipline is perceived as a negative process, referring to punishment for wrongdoing. While the negative aspects of discipline are well known to most supervisors, many do not consider the positive, or preventive, aspects of discipline.

Given the definition of positive discipline, all supervisors should be actively involved in efforts to correct, strengthen, and improve employee performance. To do this, qualified employees must be brought to the job, orientation and training programs must tell them what has to be accomplished, and follow-up coaching, communication, and motivational techniques must be used effectively. Viewed in this manner, discipline is more than punishing an employee for wrongdoing.

Since one of the supervisor's tasks is to prevent wrongdoing, he/she occasionally may have to punish employees who will not follow reasonable rules. When this occurs, other employees must be made aware of this action to reduce the likelihood that they will break rules.

The Supervisor and Employee Discipline Programs

Leadership

An effective supervisor must develop skills in disciplining employees. Some supervisors have this ability. They are tactful in dealing with people and have common sense. These supervisors just "know" how to work with employees to gain cooperation. Others resort to punishment, a negative discipline, to get cooperation. Another type of supervisor is the one who does nothing when rules are broken. (Leadership styles were discussed in Chapter 3.) Still others "rule with an iron hand" and, in effect, "dare" employees to break rules so that punishment can be dispensed.

Positive vs. Negative Approaches

In many hospitality operations, the "big stick" approach to discipline has been replaced with positive approaches. Unionization movements also have helped reduce this negative approach. Because of the severe competition for employees in the hospitality industry, many supervisors view work from the employees' perspective, in the hopes that turnover rates and other personnel-related problems will decrease. Effective supervisors realize the serious drawback to negative discipline: employees only do the minimum amount of work in order to avoid punishment. Working merely to avoid punishment is not the attitude supervisors want to instill in employees.

Many people who get into trouble do so because they only think of immediate needs, and ignore long-range plans. When this is the case with employees, punishment may not deter their spontaneous thinking.

Some employees will respond only to negative discipline. However, as emphasized throughout this book, a supervisor must know the employees' needs and react to them with the appropriate management styles.

The positive approach to employee discipline requires leadership to develop a spirit of cooperation among employees. When this occurs, employees will obey and follow reasonable rules and procedures because they want to—not because they fear punishment.

For any disciplinary program to be effective, employees must know the job requirements. Part of the supervisor's role is to provide this information through orientation, training, coaching, supervision, and personal example. Rules and other requirements must be fair, reasonable, and consistent. As noted earlier, there are many techniques that supervisors can use to implement a positive discipline program. Even the employee handbook, which lists policies and procedures, is an integral part of the disciplinary program (see Chapter 7). Employee work groups, which will be discussed more fully in Chapter 14, provide further disciplinary assistance.

A Close Look at Rules and Regulations

Reasonability

We have noted that one objective of employee discipline is to gain compliance with reasonable rules and regulations. Many hospitality operations have lots of rules and regulations—"red tape." Others do not. The number and types of rules will vary according to the philosophy and leadership styles of the top management staff. The rules that will cause "trouble" and be broken often are those that do not make sense to employees. Therefore, it is important to review rules, especially those frequently broken, and be sure that they are reasonable. Once this is confirmed, supervisors should explain and justify these rules to employees. If employee attitudes toward the rules can be improved, disciplinary problems can be reduced. Employees working in organizations that have too many rules often feel that management is saying: "Employees are not intelligent and mature enough to discipline themselves. We must issue rules." This type of management attitude can create problems.

Enforcement

Once rules or policies are developed, they must be enforced. Management's credibility drops when this does not happen. Consistent enforcement of rules helps employees know that these requirements have

Exhibit 12.1 Types and Frequency of Employee Disciplinary Offenses

Offense	% of Total Offenses
1. Absenteeism, tardiness, leaving early	9
2. Dishonesty-related	13
3. Incompetence or negligence-related	11
4. Illegal strike or restriction of production	9
5. Drinking-related	5
6. Trouble with other employees	10
7. Insubordination-related	29
8. Miscellaneous rule violations	14
	100%

Source: Hoyt N. Wheeler, "Punishment Theory and Industrial Discipline," Industrial Relations *15, no. 2 (May 1976): 239.*

value, as far as management is concerned. When supervisors are consistent, employees feel more secure. This is done when rules are uniformly enforced. Reasonable rules and procedures set the parameters within which employees must work. Rules also indicate areas where employees do and do not have discretion. Reasonable rules are important elements in the organization's basic management—and discipline—program.

Reasons for Disciplinary Problems

Specifying the types and numbers of discipline problems that arise in hospitality operations is difficult. While some companies may collect this information, no industry-wide statistics are available. Exhibit 12.1 shows the types of disciplinary cases that reached arbitration during the early 1970s. While these cases do not represent the hospitality industry specifically, it is doubtful that the disciplinary problems noticed in the hospitality industry differ greatly from these. Exhibit 12.2 lists other types of offenses that occur regularly in lodging and food service operations.

When do disciplinary problems occur? This is hard to answer when policies and procedures are not written. Larger operations and those that are unionized are more likely to have written rules than are their small, non-unionized counterparts. Rules and regulations that tell what should be done when there is a disciplinary problem should be recorded and communicated to the employees.

Four Causes

What are causes of disciplinary problems? Research indicates there are four classifications of possible causes of disciplinary problems: those relating to (a) inadequate aptitudes and abilities, (b) inadequate knowl-

Exhibit 12.2 Other Examples of Discipline Problems

Minor Problems

1. Failure to report accidents/injuries
2. Leaving assigned work areas without permission
3. Unauthorized breaks/rest periods
4. Gambling
5. Unauthorized selling
6. Smoking-related problems
7. Time clock violations

Serious Problems

1. Purposeful destruction of property
2. Immoral, indecent, disgraceful actions
3. Carrying weapons
4. Falsifying records

edge and skills, (c) personality and motivational problems, and (d) troublesome environmental factors.[1]

To reduce the reasons for specific disciplinary problems, the supervisor must be a good communicator. He/she must talk with and listen to employees. Sometimes, the supervisor will have to dig below the surface to identify the real problems. Once identified, these difficulties can be addressed by using the motivational concepts discussed in Chapter 11.

There are two major types of unacceptable behavior:

1. The result of a purposeful decision made by the employee, such as stealing, willful damage to equipment, and lying.

2. Behavior beyond the control of the employee that stems from lack of training, improper tools, poor supervision, or other conditions.

Unacceptable behavior that is *within* the control of the employee must be handled through effective disciplinary action procedures. Unacceptable behavior that is *beyond* the control of the employee is really the supervisor's problem. He/she simply is not doing an adequate job of helping the employee meet the requirements of the job and the organization. In this case, supervisors should look at themselves and the organization to see whether root causes of employee discipline problems might be the result of their actions.

Procedures for Disciplinary Action

Disciplinary programs must be designed effectively so they can yield positive benefits for the hospitality operation. If not, they can create serious problems in poor human relations, lowered job performance, legal/

union difficulties, and personal problems for the supervisors and the employees involved. Normally, the employee's supervisor is directly, or at least actively, involved in the disciplinary process. Some supervisors may ask their bosses to be involved in disciplinary programs. This is not advisable, however, because the supervisor loses an objective source of power and authority.

As the amount of punishment increases for policy and procedural infractions, other levels of management become involved. For example, a supervisor may not be able to reprimand an employee and place a written report in the personnel file. He/she also may not be able to discharge an employee without approval from managers in higher levels of the organization.

In unionized operations (see Chapter 15), union officials also are involved in many aspects of the discipline program. The result of some disciplinary actions may be mediation or arbitration by an outside disinterested party.

A number of important principles should be recognized when programs for employee discipline are designed. These include:

1. Policies, rules, and procedures must be developed for all aspects of the operation—not just on a department or section basis.

2. Managers and employees should be involved in decisions that result in policies, rules, and procedures.

3. Policies, rules, and procedures should be written and included in employee handbooks. This information should be explained during orientation and other supervision activities.

4. In the United States, there is a principle of law that states: "an individual is presumed innocent until proven guilty." This also applies to employee discipline cases. The burden of proof that an infraction has occurred rests with the supervisor.

5. Policies and rules should be enforced on a consistent basis.

6. Policies, rules, and procedures should be reasonable, fair, and just from both management and employee perspectives.

7. All circumstances in specific situations should be taken into account. Remember the previous discussion of whether problems resulted from purposeful actions by the employee or whether the problems were beyond his/her control.

8. Custom or practice in many hospitality operations calls for progressive penalties. For example, the first infraction may result in a spoken warning. A second occurrence may require a written warning. The third occurrence may require a written warning with notice in personnel records. Demotion and discharge

may result if the problems continue. Approval from higher levels of management for these last infractions may be required.

9. Appeal procedures should be designed and incorporated into the discipline process. When a supervisor has made a disciplinary decision, the route of appeal normally would be to the supervisor's boss. In unionized operations, these and other aspects of the disciplinary process are covered in the bargaining agreement.

10. Supervisors must prepare for effective disciplinary action. A hasty "bawling out" of an employee is not likely to modify behavior over the long term. Thoughtful consideration of disciplinary actions will help the supervisor defend his/her action, if necessary. The supervisor also should observe the situation to ensure that it is a disciplinary problem and not one of training or motivation.

11. Timing is important. Punishment, when necessary, should be given soon after the infraction has occurred.

12. Employees should be informed of major changes in policies, rules, and procedures before they are implemented. There should not be any "surprises."

13. Consistency in action is important. This applies not only to enforcing rules but also to providing equal punishment for the same offense.

14. Discipline should be administered objectively. Personal and other biases should be eliminated.

15. After the supervisor is certain that disciplinary actions are justified and correct, he/she should proceed with confidence and firmness. Neither a doubting attitude nor arrogance is in order.

16. Whenever possible, a supervisor should reprimand the employee in private.

17. A supervisor should not threaten, argue, or display anger. He/she should criticize the employee's behavior—not the employee him/herself.

18. Once disciplinary action has been taken, follow-up is necessary to ensure that problems are resolved.

19. The supervisor should attempt to re-establish a friendly and professional relationship with the employee soon after the disciplinary action has occurred.

20. As part of the performance review process (see Chapter 8), an employee should be told when his/her work is inadequate and how it can be improved.

21. Supervisors who are new on the job should not "start off easy" so employees will like them and later enforce the rules. Employees will "test" new supervisors. Therefore, rules and policies should be enforced from the time that a new supervisor is in the position.

22. Supervisors should keep records of all employee discipline actions.

Procedures for Disciplinary Interviews

When employees must be punished for wrongdoing, the supervisor must comply with all applicable rules and policies as negative disciplinary actions are taken. Frequently, routine problems can be handled at the time of employee performance reviews. After all, the identification of problems and agreement on ways to resolve them are important aspects of the employee appraisal process. There are times, however, when a punishment is the most effective way to encourage compliance with reasonable rules and policies. How should this be done?

Let's consider the concept of progressive discipline that was noted earlier. Spoken warnings should precede written reports. As with other types of interviews, the supervisor first must obtain and verify, if possible, all information regarding the incident before the disciplinary interview takes place. The interview should be conducted in private, focusing on problems viewed from the property's and employee's perspectives. The employee should be allowed to state his/her view of what happened. Then, the supervisor and the employee should work together to develop a mutually agreeable conclusion. At the end of the interview session, the supervisor should summarize what has occurred and review the corrective action plan. When properly handled, this process—which involves working with the employee to find a mutually agreeable resolution to the problems—is a very effective tool in the disciplinary process.

NOTES

1. J. Clifton Williams, *Human Behavior in Organizations*, 2nd ed. (Cincinnati, Ohio: Southwestern, 1982), p. 483.

PAGE TWENTY-FOUR

Supervision at the Brandywine Room

Stacey had gained much information from her study of the disciplinary process. Perhaps the most important fact she learned was that the objective of employee discipline is to emphasize and reinforce compliance with reasonable rules and procedures—not just to punish employees for wrongdoing. As she looked at the Brandywine's employee discipline program, she could see many problems that needed to be corrected. For example, only a very few of the many policies and rules that employees were required to know were expressed in writing. She recently had been involved in a conversation with an employee who said, in effect: "If the hotel has certain personnel policies that are required of all employees, why are they consistently enforced in some departments—such as the Brandywine Room—and completely ignored in others?"

This, Stacey thought, was a legitimate observation. She could understand how employees would think it was unfair to enforce a policy in one department but not others. Stacey also sensed a need for cooperation between hotel departments as she "fine-tuned" the discipline process within her own department.

When Stacey visited the Personnel Department, she found that the situation regarding employee discipline was similar to other matters she had investigated. Many of the principles had been incorporated into policies and procedures which the hotel had developed. The problem was due to the hotel's decentralized operation. Implementation of procedures was, for the most part, left to the discretion of department heads. Over time, enforcement had eroded to the point where many people did not know that procedures existed or, if they did know, they weren't sure about the details. Therefore, Stacey was not really a "pathfinder" in designing an employee discipline program. Rather, she was "reinventing the wheel" and knew that the best way this could be done was by obtaining the information and reimplementing it.

Stacey found where she could combine the hotel's policies on employee discipline with principles of communication and motivation. She had a chance that afternoon to practice her skills. A food server who had not been at work for the past two days had finally reported. He was a relatively new employee and had been through the employee orientation and training programs which Stacey had helped reorganize. During his short time with the Brandywine, he had shown signs of becoming an excellent worker. What was the problem?

Stacey called him into her office for a private conversation and showed him a copy of the front page of the employee handbook that he had signed. (At that time, he said that he was aware of and understood all rules and policies and had consented to comply with them.) One dealt with the need to call in if the employee was going to be absent. Stacey was prepared with facts about his violating the absenteeism rule. She stated the facts in a simple and straightforward manner.

"Tom, you know we have a rule about calling in if you can't come to work. You didn't do this the last two days. What happened?" His explanation dealt with "personal problems that he couldn't discuss." Stacey responded by saying: "Well Tom, this is the first time that this has happened. I want to tell you why we have this rule." (Stacey then explained, defended, and justified—in great detail—the reasons for the rule and the terrible problems that resulted when it was violated.)

She confirmed that Tom understood the rule and its importance. She then asked his advice about what she—as a supervisor—could do to help him comply with the rule. Tom couldn't offer any suggestions but, in a story that followed, he explained some family matters that had been troubling him. He also explained that he really wanted the job, liked the work and the people, and that he would appreciate her understanding. They agreed that if the problem ever recurred, he would call and give Stacey ample opportunity to find a replacement. Further, he volunteered to work some shifts the next week that she was having difficulty filling. They agreed to this plan and decided to have another conference in a couple weeks to see whether any other problems were occurring and, if so, what to do about them.

During the interview, Stacey remained calm and did not talk to Tom as if he were a child. She conceded that Tom may not have understood the importance of the rule. (Perhaps, Stacey thought, she was not clear in the orientation session.) Yet, she sternly insisted that this rule be followed, and offered to help him resolve any job-related concerns he had. Stacey was pleased with Tom's offer to help her with scheduling problems and thought this was a sign that he was a concerned and interested employee.

Stacey, of course, was going to supervise and watch Tom closely during the coming weeks. She made a mental note to show concern for him and his family. As a further clue on how to approach him in ongoing motivational efforts, Stacey noted that he was reacting to basic insecurities that stemmed from problems with his family.

13 Procedures for Conflict Resolution

PAGE TWENTY-FIVE

Supervision at the Brandywine Room

Stacey had been on the job as dining room manager almost a year and felt that the Brandywine Room was becoming a better place to work. There were still lots of things she wanted to do, but she had set priorities to first handle concerns that would meet the dining room's overall goals. Stacey now was coming face to face with two difficult problems that involved relationships with colleagues—not with employees.

Both of her problems were different. In one instance, Stacey was having difficulties with the chef, her counterpart in the kitchen, about requirements for the timing of orders and presentation of meals. At the same time, the supervisor of the laundry wanted to change times for having clean table linens available. The problem with the chef confused her employees because they didn't know whether to listen to Stacey or the chef. This troubled Stacey because she was aware of the management principle that an employee should have only one boss. Changes in the laundry schedule would mean that the dining room tables for the breakfast shift would need to be set in the morning by workers on the early shift and not by the afternoon shift workers at the end of their scheduled time, as was the current practice.

These were big problems, and Stacey realized it was time to address them. She started refreshing her memory about conflict management by reviewing her college reference materials. Then, she made an appointment with Mr. George.

A conflict occurs when there are opposing views about a situation and what must be done about it. A conflict can arise between individuals at any organizational level in the hospitality operation. It also can occur within an individual, between individuals and groups, between groups, and between organizations.

All operations will have conflict; it is almost a fact of life. A supervisor must know how to manage conflict just as effectively as he/she manages resources. Disagreements occur between people—whether as individuals or members of groups and organizations— and a supervisor must manage people.

Conflict can be as simple as a difference in opinions or as complex as lengthy "battles" over matters of significant importance to the property.

Left alone, conflict can cause serious problems that slow down the achievement of goals. Properly managed, some types of conflict can be constructive and helpful in meeting organizational goals. The "loyal opposition" type of conflict purposely injects concerns into the operation to help it identify and resolve problems.

Two Views of Conflict

A traditional management view holds that conflict is avoidable and is caused primarily by management errors. Advocates of this view believe that proper design and management of organizations can prevent conflict. This view suggests that staff members who create disharmony within the organization should be identified and removed from the staff. This view further holds that, because conflict disrupts an organization and prevents optimal performance, it should be eliminated in order for the property to reach its goals.

By contrast, there is a current view that conflict is unavoidable. There are many causes, including management errors as well as differences in goals, ideas, and values among staff members. Under this view, some conflict does detract from—but other conflict can contribute to—an organization. The task of the supervisor, therefore, is to manage conflict and ensure that it does not detract from optimal performance of an operation. A moderate level of opposition may be necessary.

One example of how conflict can be helpful occurs when two department heads must share limited resources, such as money in an operating budget. If there were no conflict, nothing would be done differently. This may be good or bad for the organization. However, as conflict over the limited funds occurs, the entire budget allocation process may be analyzed. Done properly, the entire operation could benefit. The analysis should identify the department with the greatest need or where the funds could be utilized most efficiently.

This example shows that not all conflict is bad. Disputes can occur because of honest differences of opinion over what should be done. In these cases, rational approaches to management of conflict can yield positive results for the organization.

Types of Conflict

There are several types of conflict that affect hospitality operations. Supervisors must learn how to deal with them.

Conflict Within an Individual. An employee or even a supervisor can experience mixed feelings about what he/she is supposed to do, how it is to be done, and about differences between personal and organizational goals. When this occurs within employees, the supervisor should be aware of the conflict and deal with it through training, coaching, performance reviews, attitude development, and other techniques discussed in this book.

Conflict Between Employees. When two employees disagree because of "personality problems" or differences in job requirements, a conflict arises. This situation is common in all food service and lodging operations. Depending on the degree or visibility of the conflict, the supervisor may have to serve as an objective third party until compromise or resolution is reached.

Conflicts Between Individuals and Groups. Conflicts can arise as individuals must conform to formal or informal requirements imposed by the group. This will be discussed further in Chapter 14.

Conflict Between Groups in the Same Organization. This is a common type of discord which frequently develops when groups have opposing ideas about one group's role versus the other group's role in attaining organizational goals.

Conflict Between Organizations. Our free enterprise system, for example, focuses on economic competition between commercial operations. This type of conflict often is beneficial because it may lead to new technologies, products, and services in addition to a more efficient utilization of limited resources.

The Supervisor: A Conflict in Roles

The supervisor is often a study in conflict. Many times, he/she has been promoted from the ranks of employees whom he/she now must supervise. Therefore, the supervisor's attitudes may be similar to those of the employees and he/she may share their wants and needs. Upon promotion, the supervisor must assume a leadership role and must impose the property's policies and procedures upon employees who formerly were his/her peers. Problems about friendships and professional relationships must be resolved. Even though the supervisor may identify more with employees, he/she is now "management." Conflict can develop depending on how the new supervisor adapts to the position.

Sources of Conflict

Conflict within an organization can develop from several sources, such as:

1. Relationships between supervisors
2. Relationships between employees
3. Relationships between the top and other levels of management
4. Competition between line and staff personnel
5. Competition between different departments within the property
6. Competition between employees and management
7. Disagreements between individuals in the organization

We have noted one of the reasons these individuals and groups become involved in conflict: the need to share the limited resources of a hospitality operation. When limited resources are allocated among departments, some units will get less than they need or want. Building levels of cooperation and trust is difficult when managers/departments "fight" each other for a "fair share" of the resources. There are numerous other reasons.

As organizations evolve, there are different opinions about goals. Management and other staff may view their areas or objectives as more important than others. Consider the goals of the food and beverage department and those of the rooms department. What is the relationship between these two profit centers? Which department constitutes how much profit and how is this determined? How are cost plans developed? This example illustrates how easily management staff in one department could think its efforts are more important than those of the other unit. This would be harmful to the hospitality organization.

When two or more departments depend on each other to complete their work, conflict can develop. Recall the problems of Stacey Francis in the case study at the beginning of this chapter. The dining room staff cannot complete its work without the cooperation of the laundry department. Similarly, the laundry department cannot finish its work until the soiled linen is brought from the dining room and other areas.

Conflicts may develop as supervisors set goals that are seemingly incompatible. For example, the supervisor concerned about minimizing labor costs may tightly schedule employees, while the marketing department, which is interested in increasing sales, is concerned about the possible effect this can have on guests.

Differences among employees because of work, personal attitudes, opinions, educational backgrounds, experience, and age can cause problems when varying perceptions are brought to bear on the same situation.

Exhibit 13.1 Managing Conflict: Conflict or Cooperation?

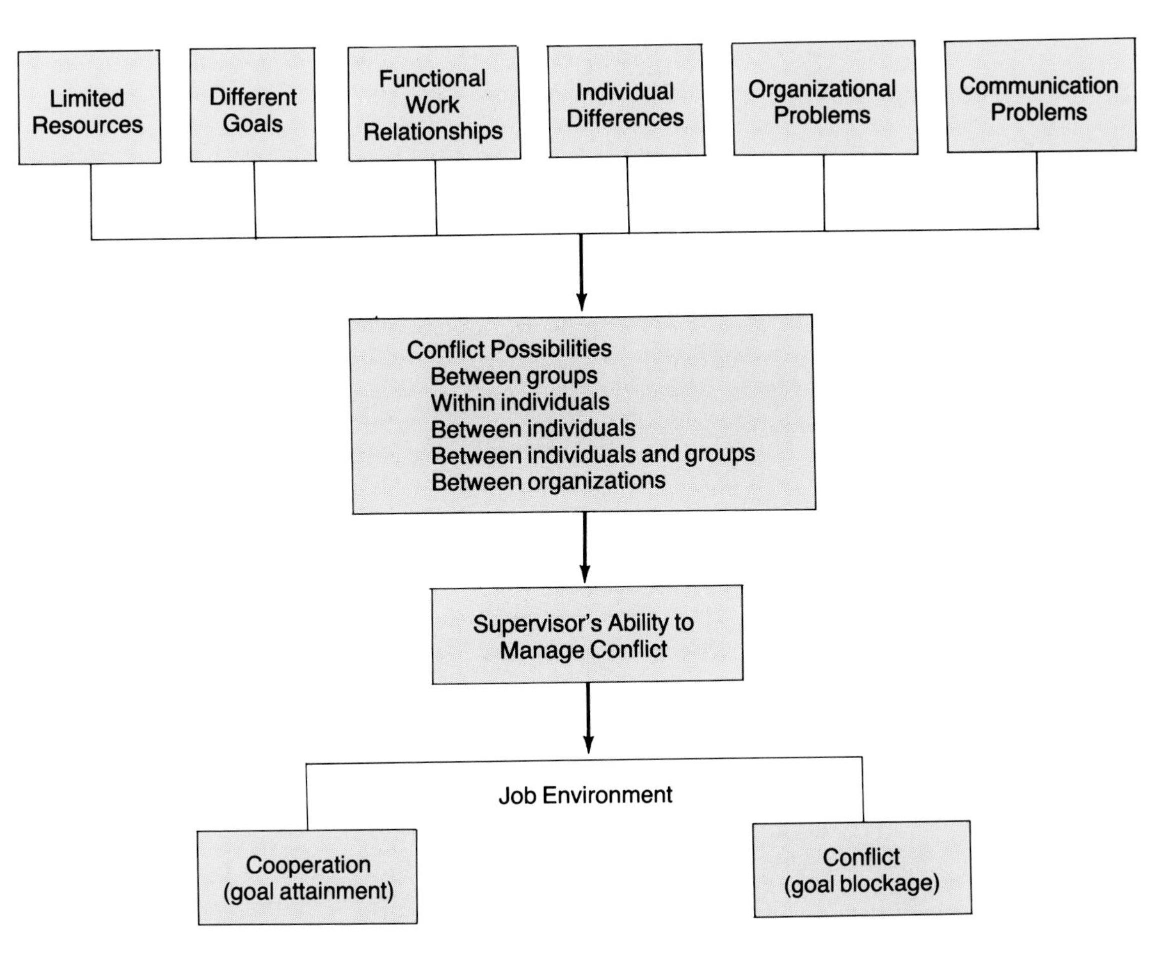

Organizational structures and communication problems can cause conflict. When work responsibilities and position relationships are not clearly defined, disagreements develop. Conflict resulting from communication—or the lack of it—is often at the root of problems within the hospitality operation.

Other potential sources of conflict include overlapping job responsibilities, interruptions in the flow of work, and "personality clashes."

Exhibit 13.1 illustrates the supervisor's role in managing the complex situations in which conflict may arise.

At times, conflict should be encouraged if better ideas are generated because people are required to clearly explain their views. Employees also can be given an opportunity to generate new alternatives in some conflict situations. When discord hinders the attainment of organizational goals, it should be repressed. (Techniques for doing this are noted later in this chapter.)

Exhibit 13.2 Possible Outcomes of Conflict on an Organization

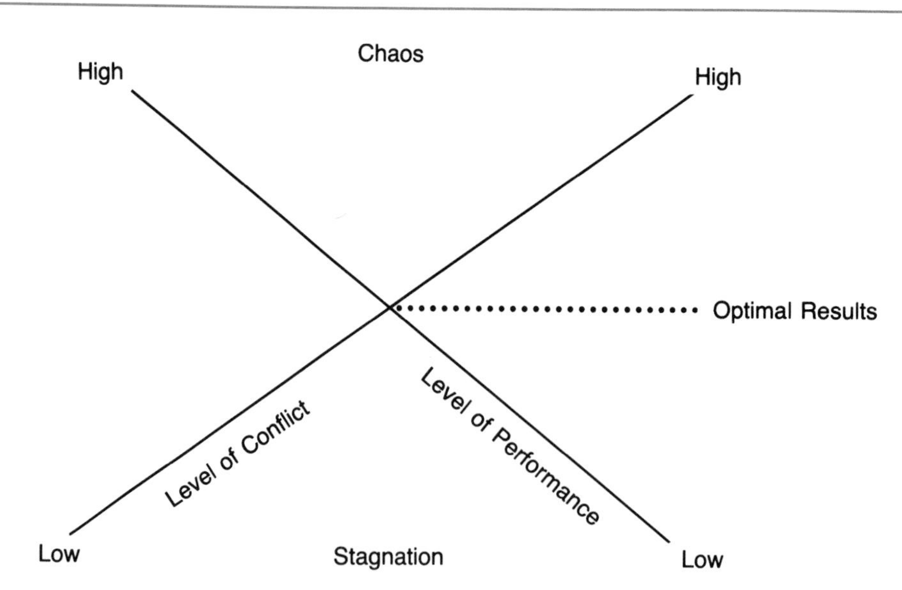

Results of Conflict

We have noted that conflict is caused by the opposing views of two or more individuals and/or groups. Frequently, this is not good for the organization because, in a competitive situation, someone must win and someone must lose. A better way to resolve conflict is through cooperation. The conflicting individuals or groups should work together to resolve problems so organizational goals can be reached. In this chapter, when we discuss the management of conflict we are stressing that managers should try to resolve the problem through cooperation so that the organization and the opposing parties can benefit from the experience.

Exhibit 13.2 shows possible outcomes of conflict on an organization. When there are low levels of disagreement and performance, the organization is stagnant; little is being accomplished and organizational goals are not being achieved. When there are high levels of conflict, chaos and disruption result because of differences in goals and how they should be achieved.

There is a point in the levels of conflict and performance where optimal results are achieved. But, there is no "magic formula" for identifying this point. Supervisors must try to attain goals and realize that at some point conflict actually can help performance. Beyond this point, however, it will be disruptive. The supervisor's task is to foster honest and objective opposition that will help the organization and prevent disruptions which occur when the good of the employee or group is placed before the good of the organization.

Conflict and Group Competition

Competition between employees generally should be avoided, but at times hospitality managers purposely generate competition between employee work groups, such as between housekeepers on different floors or dishwashers on different shifts. Results of such conflicts include:

1. Group members form closer relationships—sometimes to the exclusion of others not immediately involved in the group.

2. Individuals who can help the group attain its goals become leaders. These informal leaders often have authority to move the group toward its own goals and away from those of organization.

3. Members perceive of their group as "good" and the other group as "bad." Differences rather than similarities betwen groups are accented.

As an alternative, hospitality managers would be wise to consider competition between internal groups and external organizations or industry averages, rather than between groups within the same property.

Techniques for Managing Conflict

Both the level of disagreement and the organizational structure determine whether conflict will help or harm the organization. As the level of conflict increases, it is more likely to be destructive. As an organizational structure becomes more rigid, there is less flexibility and desire to deal with conflict in a beneficial way. Therefore, tension and frustration increase to further hamper the organization's efforts.

There are several techniques which can be used to manage disagreements. Depending on the circumstances, supervisors may wish to generate, reduce, or resolve conflict. Each of these is discussed in this section.

Generating Conflict

As we have noted, conflict sometimes can benefit the organization when it stimulates employees to think creatively about their work or consider alternatives in solving problems and attaining goals. These and related activities can prevent the organization from becoming stagnant. Conflict can be generated by:

1. Bringing in outsiders—hiring new employees, retaining consultants, or having officials from local professional associations visit the property.

2. Changing procedures, particularly those which are "cast in stone."

3. Restructuring the organization, especially with input from key employees.

4. Encouraging competition between internal and external groups or to meet or exceed performance standards.

5. Attempting to select/match supervisors with work groups. For example, if a work group is accustomed to an authoritarian supervisor who represses conflict, replacement with a more participative-style supervisor can foster conflict.

Reducing Conflict

Supervisors commonly think about reducing—not increasing—conflict. Methods to reduce conflict, however, may not deal with the basic issues that caused the problem in the first place. There are two methods that may be useful to supervisors. The first involves an acceptable redefinition of goals. For example, cost controls implemented by the food and beverage department could be matched with guests' quality expectations in order to meet the needs of the marketing department. With this method, goals of both groups become compatible with each other. Another possibility may be uniting conflicting groups/individuals by defining a common external threat, such as a competing organization.

Resolving Conflict

Supervisors should be aware that attempts to dominate or suppress conflict often force the conflict underground rather than resolve it. Suppression or dominance also creates an "I win—you lose" situation in which one party can become disappointed and hostile. Actions that demonstrate suppression or dominance include exhibiting authority, telling one side to give up, and not taking a stand.

Using the art of compromise—finding a middle ground between the two positions taken by the conflicting parties—is a problem-solving technique. Both parties cooperate to generate alternatives and resolve problems that have arisen between them.

Conflict also can be managed by appealing to higher levels in the organization. If the organization is developed properly, any two hostile people and/or groups can find a common superior who can deal with the conflict. With this method, each party considers the amount of power it has and then seeks to get the other party to agree to terms. Various "coming in" and "falling back" positions are necessary as the bargaining process unfolds.

PAGE TWENTY-SIX

Supervision at the Brandywine Room

Stacey had learned much about conflict, especially its benefits, from her college course materials and from speaking with her professor and supervisor. She realized that communication was integral to the conflict management process. The basic procedures to generate, reduce, or resolve conflict, she discovered, essentially involved communication between the conflicting parties. Stacey assembled these concepts into a plan that could resolve disagreements between the Brandywine Room and the laundry supervisor. By a "coincidence," which Stacey had manufactured, she had coffee with the laundry supervisor in the employee dining room.

The laundry was "under attack" in the budget reduction process, Stacey learned. An attempt was being made to reduce the laundry's labor costs and to cut back on linen purchases because of cash flow problems. Stacey now understood why the laundry supervisor was imposing restrictions on when the laundry had to be turned in and when it was to be returned. Quite simply, the department was trying to reduce labor costs; funds were not available to purchase new linens so that soiled items could be "stacked up" and washed during one shift.

Once Stacey understood this problem, which was beyond the control of the laundry supervisor, she and the supervisor worked out an alternative plan. Stacey would not use tablecloths for the breakfast shift. (The Brandywine Room had beautiful wood-grain tabletops that were being covered with tablecloths.) This would eliminate the need for her afternoon shift to have clean tablecloths for the breakfast tables; it would reduce the frequent washing of linens; and it would hold down replacement costs. As these matters were discussed, Stacey realized that she and the laundry supervisor were practicing conflict resolution by compromise and joint problem-solving. When she returned to her office after this productive session, Stacey developed a diagram to use as a visual aid in a talk on resolving disagreements that she was giving at the next supervisors' meeting.

Conflict and the Problem-Solving Process

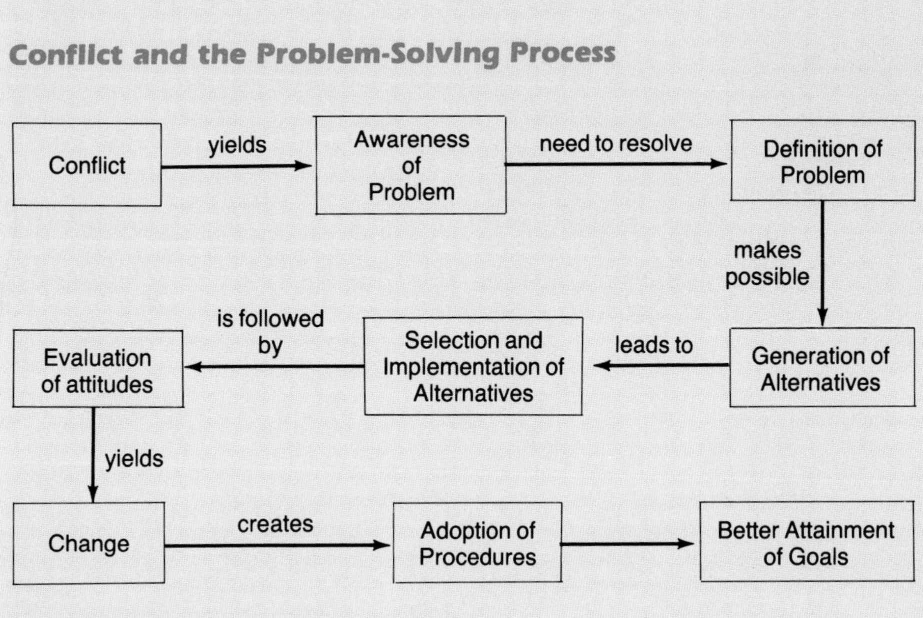

Stacey's problem with the chef was immediate and potentially more damaging. The chef contended that he was responsible for the food, whether it was in the back of the house or in the front of the house. Stacey felt his responsibility ended when the food was placed on the service trays. The dining room staff—including Stacey—was responsible from that point. Until the chef became irritated about stories he heard concerning food presentation, Stacey never had given the matter any thought. The problem had developed only recently. Although Stacey was concerned about authority, responsibility, and her "territory" in the front of the house, she was more concerned about what was "best" for the Brandywine. Surely, bickering about these matters was counterproductive to attaining department and property objectives, she thought.

After talking with the chef, Stacey concluded that the organization was the source of the conflict. Neither the organization chart nor the job descriptions for the chef and dining room supervisor addressed these problems. To resolve the conflict, they agreed to talk to Mr. George, their boss, and abide by his decision.

Realizing that she and the chef were facing an authority situation where one party would win and the other lose, Stacey attempted to refocus mutual efforts on other matters. She asked the chef to recommend wine accompaniments to entrées during the dinner shift. She also requested help in conducting a training session on food order expediting and pickup for food servers. In her own way, Stacey was trying to replace the competition between two groups—front and back of the house—with ways that both groups could work toward achieving organizational goals.

14 Working with Employee Groups

PAGE TWENTY-SEVEN

Supervision at the Brandywine Room

Stacey recalled the "good old days" when she was a food server in the dining room. She had several friends who also worked there and sometimes they ran around together after work. As she remembered it, the individual members of the group had many of the same interests and shared many of the same ideas about the Brandywine, its employees, and the management staff.

Now that she was the dining room manager, it occurred to Stacey that there might be ways to use employee groups to help her in the task of improving work procedures. There were, of course, formal groups comprised of employees who worked the same shifts. She realized, however, that in larger departments, such as housekeeping, a formal group might be comprised of individuals who just worked the same floor or who were supervised by the same manager.

There were many procedures for interacting with formal groups. She was, however, interested in learning more about informal work groups too. Should she, as a supervisor, ignore them since they weren't "legitimate?" Should she seek them out? If so, how? How could informal employee groups help her? As she thought about it, many questions came to mind. Stacey realized that she had to work with employee groups and, since this was the case, she could be a more effective supervisor if she knew how to interact with them.

"When will I ever know everything there is to know about being a supervisor?" thought Stacey. She knew the answer was never, but she also realized she was learning a lot and that, with every "lesson," her ability to manage her employees was improving.

Hospitality industry supervisors must work with groups of employees. Some groups are formal—developed by and directly for the benefit of the organization. Other groups are informal and evolve because of the mutual interests of employees—even if, in so doing, the best interests of the organization are not served. While some procedures for interacting with employee groups are identical to those for working with individual employees, there are many substantial differences.

While it is common to think of a group as a unit comprised of two or more persons, it is important to never lose sight of the fact that a group is, first of all, made up of individuals. As one applies his/her knowledge of how to manage individuals to the task of managing groups, the job becomes difficult at best.

Employee Groups in the Hospitality Operation

Formal Groups

At its broadest level, the hospitality operation itself is comprised of a group of employees. At the highest organizational level, all employees of a property have the same boss—the general manager. However, as work is organized, smaller, formal work groups must be established. Therefore, the property is divided into departments (rooms, food and beverage, engineering, sales, etc.). In many properties, departments are too large and unwieldy for one person to manage effectively; a further subdivision into sections is necessary. For example, a food and beverage department might be divided into food, beverage, and catering. The rooms department might be divided into front office, housekeeping, laundry, etc. Work sections can be further divided into work stations (specific floors of the property for housekeeping or specific areas of the kitchen for food and beverage). Work stations can be divided into work shifts. Such divisions are examples of formal work groups. Each has a formal manager/supervisor who coordinates, directs, and controls the work of the group. Usually, work tasks within a position are related; generally, the further down the organization, the more closely related tasks become.

Informal Groups

Informal groups develop for several reasons. Common interests along with location (proximity to others in the group) are major factors in group formation. Additionally, economic concerns can unify members. Individuals often seek satisfaction of specific personal needs as they interact in groups. For example, an individual's security needs can be met when a group can work together and do things that individual members working alone cannot do. One's social needs for belonging, esteem, status, and/or recognition are other factors which favor group membership. Even the highest level of human need—that of self-realization—can be met when informal groups develop for professional and accomplishment-related reasons.

Groups, whether formal or informal, develop guidelines for acceptable behavior which all members are expected to follow. There are several advantages to membership in a group from an individual's perspective. These include:

1. *Companionship.* Most individuals have a need for relationships with others.

2. *Understanding.* Many people like to have others who will listen to their troubles and problems.

3. *Help in resolving problems.* Groups provide valuable assistance to their members by generating alternatives and by making and evaluating decisions.

4. *Protection of interests.* The saying, "There is safety in numbers," illustrates this point. Outside pressures are better managed when a united front or group defenses can be established.

We can look at the development of groups from the perspectives of the individual employee and the entire group.

The Individual Employee and the Group

Think about when you first started your job. When you were hired, you automatically became a member of several formal groups (the organization itself, perhaps a specific department, and an individual work section or shift). Depending upon the effectiveness of the orientation program, you either were made to feel comfortable (a member of the group) or there was an awkward transitional period during which you did not feel like part of the group.

At the same time feelings of affiliation were developing for the formal group, a related process was evolving for informal groups. As noted earlier, individuals tend to seek out others with common interests. Therefore, while new on the job, you probably observed the job situation and the people around you. Likewise, your new colleagues attempted to learn about you. Initial periods of neutrality toward individuals and groups gradually turned to positive or negative feelings as you encountered specific actions. You liked people who were friendly. You began to dislike people who said or did things that you did not appreciate.

Over time, you began to understand formal and informal restrictions about what you could—and could not—do. For example, you learned about formal rules, policies, and procedures and, at the same time, became more affiliated with those you felt comfortable with. In effect, your attitudes and behavior were being modified to fit your new situation.

Finally, as you began to accept or reject the beliefs and attitudes of specific individuals, you were influenced by the individuals and groups—both formal and informal—with which you came into contact. In fact, if you are now an accepted member of a group, you may be equally concerned about your group's—as well as your own—feelings toward a given situation.

The process by which an individual becomes accepted into a group essentially applies to both formal and informal groups. We all know, for example, about the "company person" who totally supports the formal organization and related work groups. By contrast, we know that some employees favor concerns of the informal group much more than those of the formal organization.

The Group Development Process

The stages by which an individual is accepted into a group can also be used to outline the evolution of the group itself. For example, as the group first forms, its members may initially mistrust each other; an acceptance process is necessary during which mistrust is changed into mutual trust and respect. A second stage occurs as group members begin to communicate frankly with each other. This communication process yields a structure for making effective group decisions. As group members become involved in group activities and begin to cooperate rather than compete, members begin to find satisfaction and become committed to ensuring the success of the group. Lastly, group members will try to maximize the success of the group as common goals are met. Group members become motivated to really help each other.

As each of the formative stages occurs, the group becomes stronger. If problems arise in the early stages of group formation, strength to resolve the problems may not be present. However, when mature groups face the same problems, creative and effective solutions often can be generated. Whether one looks at the hospitality organization as a whole or at specific formal or informal groups within it, the process of gaining acceptance, the mutual help, strength, and support of individual members, and the emphasis on developing mutual goals are all critical to the success of the group.

Exhibit 14.1 indicates some of the factors that seem to be important in determining whether—and to what extent—groups attain their goals. It is interesting to note that several of the factors (group acceptance of goals, comfortable working atmosphere, participative discussions, and decision-making) were noted in our earlier discussion of motivation. This seems reasonable since, in a complex, labor-intensive hospitality operation, individuals do not work alone. Rather, they work as members of a group. Supervisors must utilize techniques that recognize the employee not only as an individual with individual concerns but also as a member of formal and informal work groups. The characteristics suggested in Exhibit 14.1 are applicable to both formal and informal groups.

Types of Formal Groups

The most common type of formal work group in the hospitality operation is a **command group**. This group includes the manager and his/her subordinates. Depending upon the level in the organization, a supervisor can be the manager of his/her employees and, at the same time, a subordinate to his/her own boss. Managers and supervisors are generally members of at least two command groups. (See Exhibit 14.2.)

A second type of formal organizational group is called a **task group**. Groups of this type work together to accomplish essentially nonroutine tasks. A special committee, formed to address a specific situation or problem, is an example of a task group. A work team is a second example

Exhibit 14.1 Characteristics of Successful Groups

1. Common goals are defined and accepted by the group.
2. Members have the resources necessary to attain goals.
3. The group knows how to function, with members helping each other and operating as a team.
4. The atmosphere of the group is comfortable because members do not criticize each other personally.
5. Members feel free to express their ideas and feelings without fear of ridicule. There is healthy disagreement, with no one personally attacking another member's ideas or positions.
6. There seldom is a power struggle. The members strive for a group consensus and not just a simple majority when making decisions. The group leader does not always dominate; group attention focuses on "what must be done" rather than "who controls."

Exhibit 14.2 The Supervisor and Command Groups

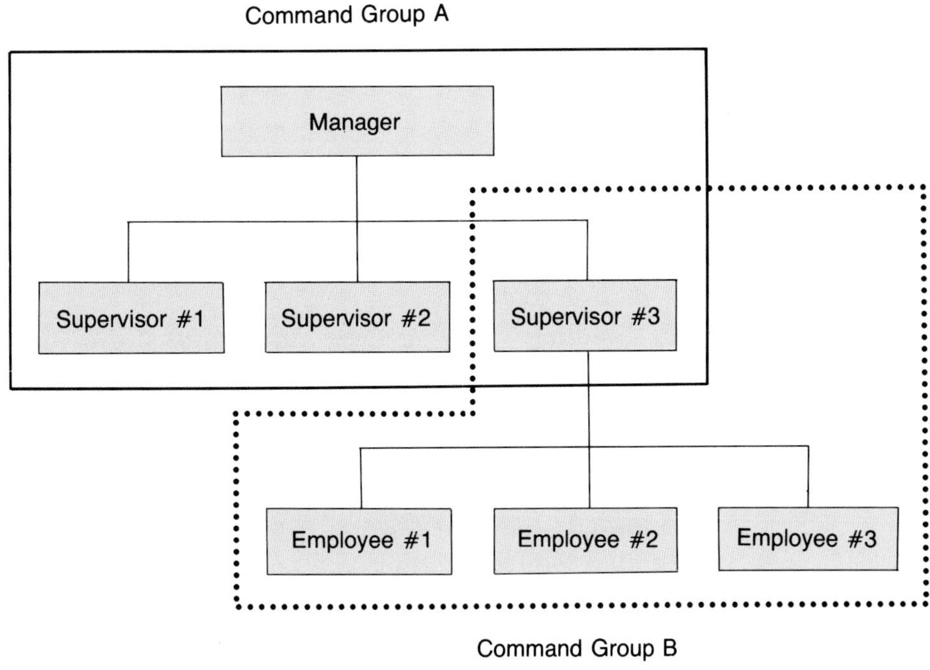

of a task group. Activities of such a group might involve developing a new menu or analyzing a job for job breakdown/training purposes. While a committee might be a long-lived task group (also called a task force or a project team), it is normally formed only to deal with a specific

Exhibit 14.3 Overlap of Formal and Informal Groups

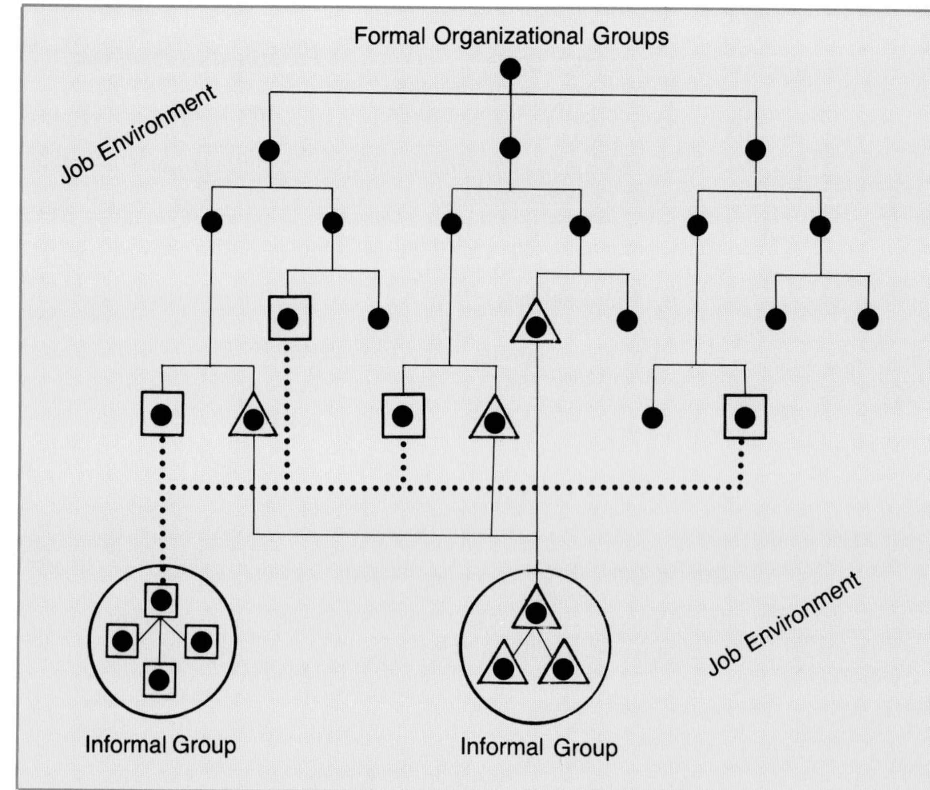

problem—after which it is dissolved. Task groups, then, might be helpful in resolving certain problems facing the supervisor's formal group.

Focus on Informal Groups

Contrary to what some supervisors think, informal groups are not, by definition, "good" or "bad." They emerge whenever employees come together and interact regularly. Informal groups might help or hinder the property's attainment of goals; they might react in favor of or against management actions, depending upon the specific instance.

As noted in Exhibit 14.3, employees can be members of formal and informal groups at the same time. In Exhibit 14.3, one informal group (dotted line) is comprised of members from four different work sections (formal groups). A second informal group (solid line) has members from three separate formal groups. It is also quite common for several members in a very large formal work group to form an informal group within the same work section.

Normally, informal work groups serve several purposes:

1. They enforce the common cultural and social values of the group members.

2. They appeal to members' status, belonging, and esteem needs which might not be met by formal groups.

3. They provide a structure in which members can communicate.

4. They have an impact on the job situation; it may be beneficial or detrimental to the organization.

Possible disadvantages of informal work groups include: (1) as the members' social and cultural values are enhanced, there is increased likelihood of resistance to change; and (2) as members of the informal group solidify feelings and act cooperatively, conflict becomes possible.

Informal groups often communicate with an informal communication system called the grapevine. Helpful information or counterproductive rumors can be spread with equal ease. Left uncontrolled, the grapevine can cause innumerable problems for the supervisor.

Finally, as informal group members conform with each other they may show less initiative and creativity in the resolution of job-related problems.

Identifying Informal Groups

Supervisors must know how to identify informal employee groups. One way to do this formally involves the process of sociometry.[1] Sociometry is a tool for gathering information useful in summarizing informal relationships between group members. Some common-sense techniques are also possible. For example, a supervisor can gather information from conversations with members of the work group and can observe how various employees relate to each other. Do they seem friendly? Do they take breaks together? Do they seem to enjoy conversations? Do they talk about spending time together off the job? Over time, these types of informal observations and information can help a supervisor assess membership in informal work groups within the property.

Assessing and Managing Group Effectiveness

In some instances, a supervisor may have some control over factors influencing the effectiveness of a formal or informal group.

Consider, for example, the number of employees in the formal work group. Normally, there is an optimal number above or below which effectiveness suffers. While the number of employees varies according to the specific job situation, there are many instances in the hospitality industry when too few employees make high levels of output impossible and when too many employees reduce productivity. The effective use of staffing guides (see Chapter 16) can be helpful in determining the number of employees needed in a supervisor's command group.

Further, the desire that members have to remain in the group must be assessed. As the level of this desire increases, there is more likelihood that the group can accomplish its objectives. Generally, the closeness of members of a formal work group is determined by the cohesiveness of informal groups that exist within the formal group. If, for example, the supervisor believes that members of the informal group support organizational goals, he/she should attempt to make informal groups more cohesive. This can be done by enhancing the status of informal group members and/or ensuring that no obstacles to the continuation of informal groups exists.

If, on the other hand, an informal group is seen to be detrimental to attaining organizational goals, efforts to reduce the closeness of individual group members should be attempted. The supervisor might, for example, limit the status, design organizational obstacles to discourage group closeness, etc. The supervisor must, however, be aware that major conflicts can result when efforts to discourage membership in informal groups are unsuccessful. Attitudes of group members toward the organization and the job affect work quality and quantity. If group members direct negative concerns to behavior not in concert with organizational goals, their effectiveness is obviously limited. By contrast, if group members' attitudes reinforce behavior contributing to organizational goals, these goals are more likely to be attained. While attitude change was discussed in Chapter 11, it is important to note that attitudes are extremely difficult to change. Since the attitudes of group members affect group behavior, the supervisor must attempt to change the attitudes, redirect the group, or address the factors causing the attitude in order to be effective.

Members of the work group themselves can have an impact on group effectiveness. For example, to increase productivity, supervisors normally need to seek the support of both formal and informal group leaders. If the supervisor can effectively appeal to the group leaders, their assistance and support can help move the group toward desirable activities.

Working with Group Leaders

Leaders of formal work groups are hired or appointed to lead the group. Leaders of informal groups, however, generally emerge through the interaction of members of the informal group. Factors influencing the emergence of an informal group leader include what is brought to the group situation (status, pay, education, etc.) and the benefits which the individual provides to the group (suggestions, directions, confidence, and reassurance).

Leaders of formal and informal groups essentially provide two services: they direct the group toward attainment of its goals and, at the same time, help fulfill other needs of the group.

The effective supervisor knows how to approach formal and informal group leaders and to solicit their support and/or sanction for planned activities.

All too often, supervisors in the hospitality industry believe that they should not involve informal groups in their plans. However, informal groups can be very effective in attaining their goals; to the extent that these goals are in harmony with those of the organization, the wise supervisor should actively encourage groups—through involvement with their leaders—to work for the organization's benefit.

Techniques for Managing through Employee Participation Programs

Should the supervisor make a decision alone, involve others, or delegate entirely the authority to make decisions to subordinates? Studies have shown that group solutions to problems are often better than the *average* solutions of individuals. However, the *best* individual solutions are frequently better than group decisions.[2] Advantages of group decision-making include the possibility that errors will be discovered through group review, that additional alternatives will be generated to resolve problems, and that resistance to decisions will be lessened since the group has had input.

There are several obvious advantages to the development and implementation of employee participation programs. As employees focus their ideas on problems at hand and on decisions to be made, it is more likely that decisions will be correct. As employees are allowed to participate in decision-making, the result becomes *our* decision not *management's* decision; therefore, the problems relating to resistance to change and defense of status quo are minimized. Other advantages are:

- Improved productivity
- Increased quality of work output
- More alternatives which can be useful in decision-making
- Increased employee motivation/morale levels
- Greater cooperation between the supervisor and employees
- Greater employee commitment to goals
- Reduced employee resistance to change
- Establishment of more effective communication channels

These advantages, of course, relate to the increased ability to attain organizational goals. This objective is better than a commonly practiced effort to manipulate employees into "doing what the manager wants them to do." When a supervisor has a definite plan in mind, it is always better to defend, justify, and sell this idea to employees than it is to pretend that they had a role in developing plans and procedures.

Supervisors must be concerned about how they solicit employee participation. Sometimes, employees know what the supervisor wants to hear; this shapes the type of input they provide. Likewise, when groups are called together for participative input, care must be taken to ensure that all members of the group—not just its spokesperson—are allowed to contribute.

There are at least three common types of group participation programs. The first, and probably the most common activity, involves the formation of task groups or work committees, which we noted earlier. This technique is used frequently at upper management levels but can be used effectively at lower levels of the organization as well. Many properties, for example, have committees with representatives from all organizational levels who provide input on matters of property-wide interest. This same concept can be applied by a supervisor to generate participation in work decisions within a specific department or work section. Consider, for example, a formal committee that might be appointed to develop job lists or job breakdowns for training purposes, ideas for energy management techniques, new recipes, etc. The supervisor who utilizes this method must be certain that the benefits of such a plan are not offset by high costs or time commitments which reduce its usefulness.

Various types of employee suggestion programs provide other examples of formalized participation programs. The suggestion box and letters to the editor in the company newsletter are often used in the hospitality industry.

While formal suggestion programs provide many useful ideas, some effort is required to implement and maintain them. Often they require written communication and some employees may not believe that the suggestion is worth the effort involved. Also, as supervisors view suggestions to be criticisms, their comments and actions—whether or not intentional—can discourage employees from participating in the program.

Employee unions are, of course, a third example of a formal employee participation program. Their role in formalizing areas of employee participation in the management and operating process are well known. The topic of unions is discussed in Chapter 15.

The Employee Participation Process

Supervisors practicing human relations principles involve their employees in problems and decisions which affect them. In effect, participative leaders are democratic leaders. In order for this process to work, the employees must be actively involved in the process. This implies mental and emotional involvement (recall our earlier concept of the "whole employee"), not just physical involvement such as "going through the motions" because the boss requires it. There must be a decided effort to participate; that is, employees must actually believe that their interests and goals will be served if they actively participate in those areas in which they are permitted input. Third, employees must accept responsibility to participate in the decision-making process. As this responsibility is accepted, there are many spin-off advantages to the organization. Teamwork is enhanced and problems stemming from negative conflict are reduced. When supervisors share their authority, their own responsibility is not weakened.

In order for an employee participation program to work, several conditions must exist. These are illustrated in Exhibit 14.4. This exhibit also reviews some of the possible benefits to be gained from an effective employee participation program. Briefly, it indicates that several factors influence the effectiveness of supervisors and employee participation activities. These include:

1. Factors within the employee (his/her interests and abilities .

2. Job situation factors (the availability of adequate time, whether the benefits to employee participation exceed costs, and whether the topic of the participation program falls within job assignments.

Exhibit 14.4 The Supervisor and Employee Participation

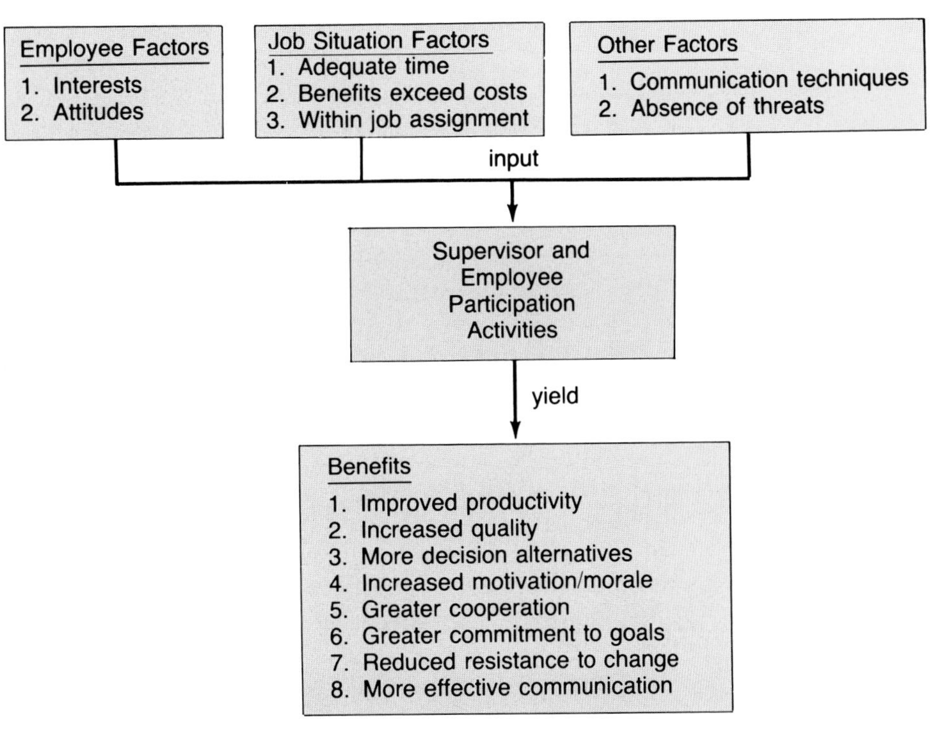

3. Other factors, such as communication techniques and the absence of threats (if supervisors feel threatened by employee participation or employees feel threatened to give desired responses, ineffectiveness will result).

The desire and ability of a supervisor to solicit employee participation is usually a function of his/her leadership style (see Chapter 3). It is true, of course, that the decision to encourage—or discourage—participation is not an "all or nothing" situation. There is a continuum along which participation might be solicited. This concept is illustrated in Exhibit 14.5. For example, let's assume that the employee participation activity involves making a decision. At one extreme the affected employees or group might make the decision unilaterally—without input from the supervisor (recall the laissez-faire leadership style). In this instance the supervisor has delegated one hundred percent of his/her decision-making authority to the employees. Regardless of whether this is done "by design or by default" the impact is the same: the employees—not the supervisor—make the decision.

At the other extreme, the autocratic supervisor might make the decision alone. In this instance, employees (as individuals or groups) are given no opportunity for input into the decision-making process.

Exhibit 14.5 Continuum of Employee Participation

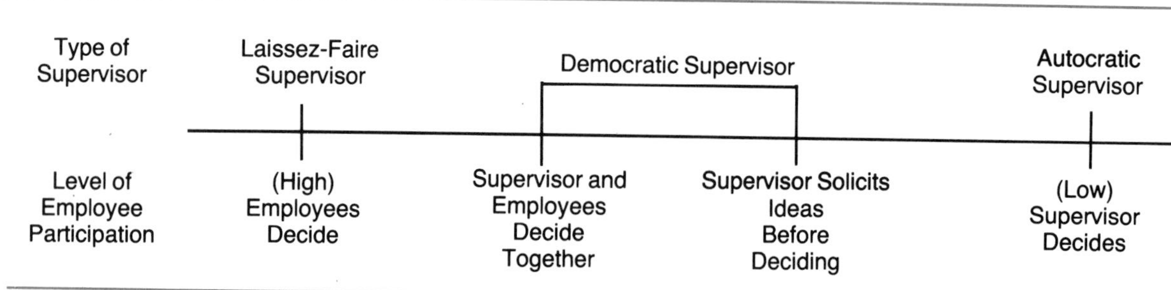

In between these two extremes are participative leadership styles in which the supervisor and employees make a mutual decision or the supervisor seeks the employees' ideas before making a decision.

No one leadership style and/or level of employee participation is always right or always wrong. Just as employees are individuals so are the job situations in which they work. Decisions about the amount of employee participation must be made on a by-situation basis. To the extent possible, the effective supervisor attempts to vary his/her leadership style to allow participation based upon the individual employee and situation.

We must also note that an effective supervisor does not use identical amounts of employee input for each decision to be made. For example, employees might be allowed to give a great deal of input to decisions affecting their work schedules and/or vacation times, a lesser amount of input to decisions affecting job assignments, and even less input to matters dealing with how the supervisor will forecast the volume of required sales/work output.

Barriers to Employee Participation

Employee participation procedures are not a universal solution to problems faced by the supervisor. As shown in Exhibit 14.4 certain conditions must be present within both the employee and the job situation itself in order for employee participation techniques to be useful. There are other barriers to employee participation that must be considered. For example, some employees do not have esteem and ego needs which can be nurtured by participation activities. They may feel very comfortable working in an authoritarian relationship in which total power and discretion is retained by the supervisor. Other employees may not have the intelligence, knowledge, and/or access to information needed to make effective decisions in a participative situation.

Consider also that the organizational climate must be conducive to participation. For example, if only one supervisor in a hospitality operation saw benefits to employee participation, his/her actions would probably be viewed as negative, both by superiors, (who would view the activity as unnecessary delegation) and by employees (who might consider the supervisor to be weak and ineffective). Contrast this with an organizational structure in which employee participation is "a way of doing business." In this instance, the supervisor who did not encourage participation would be viewed as a weak supervisor by superiors and probably as a "tyrant" by employees.

There are different types of problems which simply do not lend themselves to participative employee input. Examples are strategic decisions that affect the entire organization and routine, minor decisions in which time and effort for employee participation is simply not worth it. Likewise, group participation in matters affecting only one or two individuals is not appropriate.

Informal Participation Methods

In most operations it is relatively simple for a concerned and interested supervisor to begin utilizing informal methods of gaining employee participation in the problem-solving and decision-making process. Consider, for example, the situation that arises as a decision must be made. Perhaps there is a recurring problem that must be resolved. As part of the decision-making process the supervisor might think of all possible ways to resolve the problem. This could be followed with a request for ideas from employees affected by the decision. In doing this, the supervisor might talk to:

1. Every employee who is affected.
2. Those employees whom he/she thinks would have special ideas or would be interested in participating in the decision.
3. Influential group leaders.
4. Experienced employees only.
5. Only those employees who do the work effectively.

As a result of talking with any or all of the above groups, a supervisor is likely to generate helpful alternatives. As the supervisor continues with the problem-solving process, some or all of the individual employees noted above could be contacted about ideas regarding the advantages and disadvantages of each of the alternatives. Suggestions for implementation procedures, for evaluating the effectiveness of the decision, and for determining the impact of the decision on other subsystems within the operation could be requested.

Our brief discussion about involving employees in the process of making a decision should illustrate the wide variety of methods which the supervisor has available. We have now noted that, depending upon the leadership style, all, many, or none of the opportunities for employee participation can be used by a supervisor. Likewise, all, many, or none of the affected employees can become involved.

As the supervisor considers whether or not to involve the employees in decision-making, he/she should be aware that disagreement can result—and that it must be managed. The supervisor will need to address conflicting interests and will need additional time for decision-making. Also, it is sometimes difficult to keep even the best-intentioned employees in an objective frame of mind; their own personal biases and concerns often influence the decision-making process.

When a supervisor decides to involve employees, it is important that the task at hand is actually one of decision-making and not persuasion. Effective managers must use persuasive tactics, but this should not be done under the camouflage of employee participation.

NOTES

1. Details of the process are beyond the scope of this book. Interested readers are referred to J.H. Jacobs, "The Application of Sociometry to Industry," *Sociometry*, May 8, 1954, pp. 181-198.

2. James A. Stoner, *Management* (Englewood Cliffs, N.J.: Prentice-Hall, 1978), p. 298.

PAGE TWENTY–EIGHT

Supervision at the Brandywine Room

Stacey had learned much as she read and talked with people about procedures for managing groups. As part of her task of revising the orientation process for new employees, she had studied the hotel's organization chart. It had not been revised for several years and with the help of Ms. Case and her staff in the Personnel Department, it was redrawn to apply to the dining room. The revised organization chart had been inserted in the new employee orientation handbook. After several reviews at staff meetings, Stacey was confident that she—and the employees—knew about the dining room's formal organization and the formal employee groups working within it.

Learning about informal employee groups was an entirely different matter. It was ironic that, while Stacey was concerned about "knowing the employees" and "recognizing individual differences" she had never looked beyond each specific employee to determine how they felt about each other. Now she realized the need to consciously look for relationships between employees in an attempt to define informal employee groups. She realized that some of her employees might belong to informal groups in other departments; the reverse was also possible—activities of her employees might well be influenced by interests of employees who were not even on the dining room staff.

Stacey did not have time to undertake any formalized plan to determine members of informal employee groups. Rather, she just "kept her eyes and ears open." Over time, she was able to collect information. She knew, for example, that several of her staff members rode home together, others were on the same bowling team, several always had lunch together. She also knew that some were dating each other and that interests in country music, partying, and athletics were forces that brought others together.

She began to realize that some employees seemed better respected than others. For example, one drove a new car; some of the younger workers were fascinated by it. Another was on everyone's "best dressed" list. Stacey knew others who were always on the "winning team" and collected trophies every baseball and bowling season.

By sifting through these observations, Stacey was able to develop a "picture" of the informal organization in her department. Now that she knew this, what help could it be? The chance to test her new-found supervisory skills came suddenly. The Personnel Department had sent her a memo indicating that the long-awaited procedures to develop staffing guides had been established. After a series of explanatory meetings with Mr. George, she knew what she had to do: staff members needed to be told about the new plans and procedures. They would immediately be concerned that efforts were underway to "make them work harder" or that jobs would be eliminated; she needed to share accurate information with the staff. Stacey soon developed a fact sheet and distributed it during a meeting with her formal work group leaders. She explained that there would be little, if any, direct impact upon employees. In fact, proper scheduling might help employees; efforts to "match" guests with staff members could result in bigger tips. Next, she met with each work group leader individually and, through a question and answer process, confirmed that there were no individual problems which had not surfaced at the group meeting.

Stacey called a meeting of all her employees and discussed the matter with them. Again, fact sheets were distributed and questions were answered. She directed her group leaders to meet with each employee and to resolve any questions; if matters arose which needed her attention, she requested notification.

She spoke with a number of employees who had indicated some concerns. In almost every instance, she was able to use a reasoning process to resolve the problem that was imagined by the employee.

She managed to have coffee with each informal group leader whom she had been able to identify. At these sessions she explained what the staffing guideline process would involve and asked for the group leaders' reactions and cooperation.

When Stacey knew all the details about the development of the staffing guidelines, she conducted another general staff meeting. Throughout the process of explaining, defending, and justifying the staffing guidelines, she actively sought—and used when possible—the input from informal group leaders.

Stacey was especially interested in using the informal leaders as a "sounding board" to alert her to employee concerns that could be dealt with on a one-to-one basis.

As a result of involving employee groups—both formal and informal—Stacey was confident that the actual process of developing staffing guidelines could be carried out without difficulty.

Part IV: Special Supervisory Concerns

Many hospitality operations have employee unions, while other operations are facing unionization drives. The effective supervisor must know how to work with employee unions. Legal and contractual matters are among the concerns that must be addressed in a relationship between the supervisor and the union representative. Unions are a factor that affect the management of employees. Effective supervisors know what they can and cannot do as they manage employees in unionized operations.

The supervisor is an important component of the overall effort to control a property's labor costs. While performance standards must be set to control costs, they cannot sacrifice quality or quantity requirements. Supervisors must know how to measure productivity by establishing guidelines for scheduling work so that the operating budget and economic goals are met. Overtime must be controlled, and reasons for excessive labor and costs must be explained. Therefore, supervisors must keep up with new ways of holding down labor costs.

Supervisors who are concerned about their personal and professional futures often seek out hospitality organizations that have effective and ongoing management development programs. Procedures used to plan and monitor a career, plus ideas about the future of the hospitality industry, are important to supervisors who care about their jobs and must make decisions about their careers.

These special supervisory concerns are reviewed in this final section of this book. The work is hard and rewarding, but effective supervisors know how to use techniques that help themselves and their organization reach mutual goals.

15 Working with Employee Unions

PAGE TWENTY-NINE

Supervision at the Brandywine Room

The hotel where Stacey Francis worked was not unionized. While Stacey had heard that some employees were discussing unionization earlier, to her knowledge, no employee group had yet attempted to affiliate with and be represented by a union. Sure, the hotel had problems. Many were evident in the Brandywine Room itself. However, on the whole, employees seemed sympathetic to management and what it was trying to accomplish. Stacey had no idea what would happen if employees attempted to unionize.

With the pressure from ongoing problems and a heavy workload, Stacey didn't have a chance to learn about employee unions. She had little "professional advice" to offer a friend at another hotel who called to say that the union was "working on" her property. Stacey immediately became interested in the situation, and made an appointment with her friend to discover "what unions are all about."

Employee unions generally have been most successful in organizing large hospitality properties located in large metropolitan areas. While the lodging and food service industry is labor-intensive, its employees are spread among thousands of operations throughout the country. Traditionally, unions have not organized small, scattered properties because this has not been economically feasible.

Developing a strategy to deal with employee unions from the initial election through negotiations rests with managers at levels higher than supervisors. Since supervisors are in direct contact with unionized employees, it is important that they understand basic information about employee unions and know specific actions which can, and cannot, be taken in working with these employees.

Why Employees Join Unions

Employees who want to join unions usually have several common reasons, including:

Increased Bargaining Power. Individual employees have only a little power/strength in comparison to the hospitality organization. Often, an employee's only bargaining strength is threatening to quit if employment conditions do not improve. Since few employees are irreplaceable, this lack of strength is a clear problem. Unions, then, present an opportunity for employees to band together and make demands of management which could not be made without the strength of the group.

Desire for Self-Expression. Unions allow employees to communicate their concerns, feelings, and complaints to management. Effective unions provide management with a structure for hearing these concerns. Formalized grievance procedures, which are established by unions, allow employees to express these concerns. These procedures become an integral part of the organization's operations.

Minimizing Favoritism. When concerns are addressed in union bargaining agreements, fewer decisions are based on personal relationships between employees and the supervisor. Equal treatment, generally based on seniority, is a common concern of all employee unions.

Social Reasons. Employees are influenced by their colleagues' attitudes and behaviors. They form groups with persons they like and with whom they can associate. If the group favors a union, then the "desire to go along with the crowd" becomes an important reason for unionizing.

Problems with Advancement Opportunities. If employees believe they cannot receive reasonable pay increases, better jobs, and greater status, they often turn to employee unions for assistance in reaching these goals.

Union Shop Provisions. In hospitality operations where a contract has been reached, union shop provisions require all employees to join the union and pay dues. Refusal to join may be cause for discharge.

Reasons for Employee Dislike of Unions

The majority of hospitality employees do not belong to unions, and there may be other reasons for this besides the fact that unions do not actively seek to organize small properties with relatively few employees. Reasons for dislike of unions may center on one or more of the following:

Cultural and Social Factors. Employees may distrust unions because of past experiences, because they want to control their own destinies without union restraints, and because of misconceptions that unions encourage workers to be less productive. Many professionals do not like unions because the status and recognition these professionals seek sometimes excludes the "union alternative."

Individualism. Some employees want to represent their own interests to management. They would rather work things out by themselves without "outside interferences." Esteem and ego needs might prompt these feelings.

Identification with Management. Some employees, especially managers or those aspiring to management positions, identify with top management and other nonunion employees. Therefore, they may develop management views toward unions. Some employees believe that union membership hinders promotional opportunities.

Fear of Punishment. Employees may appear to be anti-union out of fear that they will be punished if they join a union. Even though employees are protected by various laws, these thoughts can surface.

Growth of Unions

Unions for skilled craftsmen formed by the early 1880s in the United States, but the growth of unions in this country did not increase until World War I. During the Great Depression of the early 1930s, however, union membership decreased due to a decline in the work force. The most rapid growth of unions occurred from 1935 to 1955, and was prompted by the 1935 National Labor Relations Act. Growth in national union membership increased from approximately 14 million members in 1950 to more than 23 million in 1978. Expressed as a percentage of the total labor force, the 1950 and 1978 rates represent approximately 22% of the workers.[1] This slow rate of growth can be attributed to many small companies, strong anti-union areas of the country, and a reluctance by salaried and professional employees to join a union. The number of these professional staff members has increased while the force of blue-collar employees in many industries—the "lifeline" of the union—has decreased. (This can be due in part to labor-saving equipment taking over jobs that traditionally have been held by union members.)

The Law and Unionization

Before the 1930s, unions were prosecuted by the courts on the basis that these employee groups interfered with an employer's right to conduct business. In 1936, however, the United States Congress passed legislation to balance the power between labor and management. The National Labor Relations Act guaranteed the rights of unions to exist and allowed workers to join unions without retaliation from the employer. Employers were prohibited from interfering with union operations, discriminating against a worker because of legal union activities, or punishing employees who reported management violations of the union agreement. In addition, employers were required to bargain in good faith with unions.

The Labor Management Relations Act (1947) retracted some of the power given to unions during the 1930s. Under this law, unions were not allowed to coerce workers into joining unions, restrictions were placed on strikes, unions were required to bargain in good faith, and closed shops were prohibited.

Structure of Unions

There are approximately 175 national and international unions in the United States. (Unions are considered to be "international" if they have members in Canada as well as in this country.) By contrast, there are approximately 78,000 local unions in the country.[2]

The local is the basic unit of organization for a union. For example, it may represent all of the carpenters or electricians in a single community. A local union also may represent only members within a specific property, which is the case in the hospitality industry. Local unions generally are run democratically with an election of officers. Members have a vote, and they receive advance notice of upcoming issues and elections.

Only large unions have full-time officers. Most small unions have a president who devotes part of his/her work time to union duties. Shop stewards are elected to represent employees in a specific department within the operation. Normally, the union president has a regular job, is paid by the employer, and uses some time from the job—in addition to his/her personal time—for completing union duties. Local unions carry out contract negotiations, build membership, administer grievances, manage the bargaining agreement, and conduct strikes or other work actions when necessary.

Many unions have intermediate organizations which coordinate activities of local unions. Established on a regional basis, these groups govern the activities of locals within a specific area and provide administrative assistance to local unions.

The national or international union is found at the top of the union's organization chart. Basic policies are established, services are provided, information is collected and disseminated, and strike and retirement funds are administered at this level. Many unions employ staff specialists such as attorneys and public relations personnel, among others, to provide specialized assistance. These specialists develop training programs, attempt to organize nonunion properties, and carry on related key responsibilities of the union organization.

The Impact of Unions on Management

Once a union represents hospitality employees, management's options in dealing with employees are altered in the following ways:

Fewer Options

Less Freedom to Act. Management no longer can make unilateral decisions or deal individually with employees. Management must follow closely all requirements imposed by the union-employer bargaining agreement.

Uniform Treatment of Employees. Regardless of an employee's skill or ability, management must treat equally all employees in like classifications. Seniority—not other factors that "define" good employees—becomes the most important determinant of management actions.

Possible Benefits

Personnel Administration. Unionization can improve policies and procedures when property management develops supervisory training programs that deal with areas of union impact, for example. Effective human relations practices demand good supervisory skills. Therefore, unions can have a positive impact on hospitality operations.

Representation of Employees. In unionized properties, management deals with one representative of employee groups, rather than with individual employees.

Centralized Decision-Making. As properties unionize, top management may recover much of the responsibility for making decisions about labor concerns that had been delegated to the supervisors. Management may feel that activities affecting the entire organization must be centralized and administered by top-level specialists.

The Collective Bargaining Process

Collective bargaining involves relationships between employers and unions not only during negotiations for an agreement but during routine dealings between management and unions. There are laws that affect the collective bargaining process. Collective bargaining encompasses organizing employees, negotiating and administering contracts, interpreting agreement clauses, and resolving agreement disputes.

Most union contracts involve a single property dealing with a single union. A single hospitality operation also may have separate bargaining agreements with a number of different unions. For example, a large hotel may have agreements with 15 or more separate employee unions.

Union agreements today are negotiated for a period extending three or more years. Preparing for contract bargaining is quite difficult and time-consuming for the company and union. The company, for example, must gather information about prevailing wage rates, fringe benefit practices, and current financial position. Analysis of current contract provisions and speculation about union concerns also must be addressed. The union also needs time to gather information, survey its membership, and plan its negotiation strategy. Laws require that management and union representatives meet during negotiations, bargain in good faith, reach decisions, and write down the agreements reached on matters of mutual concern. While there are many topics that might be negotiated, Exhibit 15.1 lists concerns typically noted in many union-management bargaining agreements.

Exhibit 15.1 Common Topics of Concern in Union-Management Bargaining Agreements

1. Union recognition
2. Union security
3. Management security
4. Dues check-off procedures
5. Union representation
6. Duties/responsibilities of stewards
7. Grievance procedures
8. Seniority rights
9. Probationary periods
10. Promotions and job openings
11. Leaves of absence, vacations, and sick leave
12. Discipline and discharge procedures
13. Hours of work, scheduling, and overtime
14. Prohibition of discrimination
15. Safety concerns
16. Meals, uniforms, and dressing rooms
17. Wages and benefits
18. General provisions (discipline, breaks, layoffs, posting of jobs, etc.)
19. Successors
20. Strikes/lockouts
21. Conflict of laws
22. Duration of agreement

Procedures for Resolving Disputes

As disputes develop over the contract and employees file grievances alleging management's refusal to abide by the agreement, several actions can be taken to resolve these differences. When employees strike and refuse to work, they are attempting to pressure management to grant their demands as well as the union's demands. On the other hand, management may shut down a business during a labor dispute in an attempt to get the union and employees to agree to management's terms.

Labor and management disputes generally can be negotiated in ways that are acceptable to both parties. When this is not possible, intermediate actions, which happen before strikes/lockouts occur, often are attempted. Some of these actions include:

Voluntary Arbitration. In this process, both labor and union representatives agree to accept the findings of an outside, disinterested person who is empowered by both parties to make decisions that will be binding on both groups.

Compulsory Arbitration. This is imposed by the government and is a final attempt to bring both sides together. The responsibility for resolving problems rests with the government-appointed arbitrator. Compulsory arbitration is not used in the United States to settle labor disputes in the private sector—including the hospitality industry.

Mediation. Mediation refers to a third party helping management and the union reach an agreement. Mediation differs from arbitration in that advice is given instead of a final, ultimate decision, as in arbitration.

Conflicts between perspectives of management's *rights* and *obligations* are at the heart of unionization problems. Unions and management might best attain their goals by practicing human relations principles that emphasize "making what's good for the organization also good for the employees." This is not always easy to do. If supervisors provide higher levels of management with information about employee needs and views, however, there is a possibility to develop policies and plans that satisfy both groups. Remember, when managers try to give employees what they want from their jobs, there is less need, from the employee's perspective, to join a union.

The Supervisor and the Union Organizing Campaign

The supervisor is an important consideration in an employee's decision as to whether a union is desirable. Also, the supervisor may be the one most affected by a union. This section reviews actions a supervisor can and cannot take during a union organizing drive. A property will need competent legal advice when it faces possible unionization. The following information will not substitute for such advice, but is presented to put leadership principles in the context of the unionization process.

There are certain actions which legally can be taken. All employees should be encouraged to vote. Union advocates could be outvoted if the "apathetic majority" that opposes unions took the time to vote.

Assessing the Union's Strength

Management should assess the union's strength by obtaining estimates from supervisors, assessing employee attitudes, and studying the union's campaign tactics. If the union's positions are extreme, it may be concerned about succeeding. If the union cites broad issues, it may be searching for ways to interest employees. Other procedures include: estimating the number of employees attending union-related meetings (management cannot attend the meetings, but it can obtain estimates from the "grapevine"); estimating the number of home visits by union organizers (this will help assess the union's concern about winning an election; the more home visits, the greater the union's concern); and gauging the intensity with which union authorization cards are being distributed.[3]

Assessing these factors and studying all information about the union (including the successes/failures with other organizing efforts) will help in planning strategies.

Management's Campaign

Management must determine its strengths and weaknesses while planning responses to union issues. The assessment should be made *from the employees' perspective*, which includes: how management is viewed, how well management meets employees' needs, the reputation of the union, feelings of informal employee leaders, and the impact of management and union campaigns on the employees.

Guidelines for Conducting a Campaign

While there are no "magic" techniques that will prevent employees from joining unions, the following techniques can be helpful: assess *exactly* what the issues are, prioritize the issues, determine time limitations for the campaign, assess the size and membership of the employee group that will vote, determine the *best* way(s) to communicate with this group, and assess the employees' attitudes.

Other methods to use in trying to avert unionization of a property are: consider how to get "management's message" to employees; directly relate management's efforts to the union's campaign; respond to union materials by being calm and understanding, while being factual in emphasizing organization benefits; appoint one management official to conduct the campaign; recognize the supervisor's importance in the campaign (he/she is the link between top management and the employees) and keep supervisors informed about all areas of the campaign; and explain management's position to the community.

Management Actions

There are several important management actions that can affect the outcome of a union election campaign. Management should:

1. Review existing employee benefits and emphasize those that equal or exceed industry averages.

2. Relate management's past successes in dealing with employee grievances.

3. Indicate how management has developed and improved benefits and working conditions.

4. Inform employees of all management policies that favor them.

5. Publicize details about the union.

6. Describe union disadvantages.

7. Explain that if the union wins the election, it still must bargain with management. There is no law that requires both sides to agree on the issue. Management obviously cannot pay more than it can afford.

8. Remind employees that all sides lose when there is a strike.

9. Tell employees that they do not need to vote for the union even if they have signed a union authorization card to hold the election, and point out statements made by the union which management feels are untrue. (Tell management's position on each issue.)

Campaign Don'ts

There are management actions that laws and legal opinions forbid during a unionizing campaign.

1. Management cannot promise benefits to employees who vote against the union and cannot make any type of threat to employees who vote for the union.

2. Supervisors cannot attend union organizing meetings or attempt to covertly determine whether any employees are participating.

3. Supervisors cannot grant unscheduled wage increases, special benefits, or concessions to employees during the pre-election period.

4. Employees cannot be refused permission to wear union buttons unless the buttons are extremely large or are considered in poor taste.

5. Union organizers cannot be forbidden from soliciting employee membership during their *nonworking* hours as long as they do not interfere with ongoing work of other employees.

6. Supervisors cannot hold private meetings with employees to discuss unions and/or elections. They also cannot question employees about union activities.

7. Supervisors cannot question employees about how they intend to vote. They also cannot threaten layoffs.

8. Meetings with employees cannot be conducted within 24 hours of the upcoming election.

Working with the Union

Once hospitality employees have unionized, the working relationship between the supervisor and employees is affected. The supervisor must continue treating all employees fairly and consistently, but he/she may find that some of his/her authority has eroded. While a supervisor must comply with all contract provisions, he/she no longer will deal directly with the employees on matters covered by the contract. Instead, the steward, who acts as an intermediary, becomes involved. Therefore, the relationship between the supervisor and the steward is very important.

The Steward and the Supervisor

The supervisor and the steward are in unique positions within a hospitality operation. While the supervisor ranks between the employees and higher management levels, the steward plays two roles at the same time—he/she is an employee and a union representative. In their positions, the supervisor and steward share the same responsibilities to understand, interpret, and enforce the contract, while acting as representatives of the employees. The supervisor at times may have to speak for management to the employees or represent the employees to management. In the same way, the steward acts on behalf of the union to the employees and represents the employees to the union. Individuals in these positions must inform each other about decisions they make, positions they hold, and problems that may develop. The supervisor and steward must protect management and employee rights while maintaining an effective working relationship.

The Grievance Process

If the steward agrees, an employee may file a formal grievance when he/she is not satisfied with the way a supervisor "resolved" a complaint. While the specific grievance process is outlined in the union contract, certain components of the process are typical.

In most grievance procedures, the supervisor meets with the steward and employee in an attempt to resolve the problem. If this is not possible, the supervisor's boss or another management official may meet with the union's grievance committee to try to solve the problem. If they are unsuccessful, top management officials meet with the grievance committee to search for a solution. If necessary, top administrative officials discuss the problem with representatives of the national or international union. If resolution is impossible, the matter goes to mediation or arbitration.

Supervisors and stewards must be aware that informal employee complaints can develop into formal grievances that can take great amounts of time and money to resolve. Grievances can be prevented if supervision principles are applied within restraints imposed by the union contract.

Management Rights

Management rights may be limited to those that are expressly included in the labor contract.[4] A list of basic concerns that management must exercise and protect include the rights to schedule and allocate overtime; to establish, change, and enforce rules, policies, and procedures; to discipline and terminate employees; to develop or change work schedules, as needed; to adjust or change job tasks; to increase workloads of staff members; and to have jobs performed by employees who management deems are qualified.

Other concerns of management involve the rights to assess employee eligibility for merit increases and job promotions, to require tests for employment, to assign bargaining unit work to a supervisor, to set work standards, and to close down departments or the entire property if a strike occurs.

Management rights should belong to and be retained by supervisors of the property; they should be able to exercise these rights in operating the business. Unfortunately, these basic rights can be jeopardized during contract negotiations or day-to-day bargaining.[5] Practices that can diminish these rights include careless wording of contracts and failure to understand the implications of contract wording.

A right may be yielded if only part of it is contained in the contract. (Remember that management rights may be limited to those that are *expressly* outlined in the contract.) Forgetting to specify a necessary provision in the contract during negotiations can result in the exclusion of a basic right. Clear language in the contract is vital in order to avoid this situation.

Basic management rights can be lost by default if they are not used. This can occur during mediation/arbitration because past administrative practices often are considered. Management may forfeit its rights when it fails to explain the contract to supervisors and subordinates, resulting in supervisors not supporting management on contract matters. Lack of preparation for contract negotiation, grievance, mediation, and arbitration sessions jeopardizes management's position.

In dealing with unions, managers must be fair, firm, and practice good faith to ensure that basic management rights are not lost while working to attain the goals of all parties.

NOTES

1. Randall S. Schuler, *Personnel and Human Resource Management* (St. Paul, Minn.: West, 1981), p. 388. See pp. 384-391 for other interesting information about unions.
2. Statistics are from Dale S. Beach, *Personnel: The Management of People at Work*, 4th ed. (New York: Macmillan, 1980), p. 78.
3. This discussion is based on Herbert K. Witzky, *The Labor-Management Relations Handbook for Hotels, Motels, Restaurants and Institutions* (Boston: CBI, 1975), pp. 236-238.
4. Witzky, pp. 126-133.
5. Witzky, pp. 236-238.

PAGE THIRTY

Supervision at the Brandywine Room

After gathering information about unions from her friend, her college professors, Mr. George, and the hotel's Personnel Department, Stacey realized that many activities affecting the relationship between the union and the organization concerned strategies established by top management. Supervisors were in daily contact with, and greatly influenced, employees who may or may not want to join the union.

Stacey also found information that explained how the supervisor operated after employees unionized. She listed the most important points of her research for future reference. Her list follows:

1. A union changes the relationship between the supervisor and the employees. Many direct dealings between the two parties

no longer are possible so the supervisor must work through the union instead of directly with the employees.

2. The supervisor must be familiar with rights guaranteed by the National Labor Relations Act, as amended. If he/she does not know these requirements, the company—not the supervisor or the supervisor's department—will be responsible.

3. The supervisor cannot interfere with, restrain, or coerce employees in exercising their right to participate in union activities.

4. Supervisors should consider any anti-union activity to be a violation of the law.

5. Supervisors cannot threaten employees about unionizing efforts by promising benefits to those who resist unions, withholding benefits from union sympathizers, or showing favoritism toward one union over the other.

6. Supervisors cannot interfere with the formation or management of a union. Employees have the right to elect or reject a union.

7. There are limits on the degree to which a supervisor can participate in employees' union activities. Generally, the lower the organizational level, the greater the amount of union activity which is permitted.

8. Actions cannot be taken against rival unions that are attempting to organize employees. Supervisors cannot show favoritism, link benefits to membership in a union that is sanctioned by the employer, or give financial aid to any union.

9. Unions cannot have unlimited access to company facilities nor can employees be urged to start their own labor organization.

10. Supervisors cannot discriminate against employees because of their union activities. Personnel decisions cannot be based on anti-union strategies.

11. Employees cannot be fired because of union activities. Special benefits cannot be given to employees who do, or do not, participate in the union.

12. Supervisors cannot refuse to hire employees because of pro-union sentiments.

13. Supervisors cannot discharge, demote, or discipline employees solely because of union activities.

14. Supervisors cannot transfer or lay off employees for anti-union reasons nor can they refuse to reinstate employees after strikes if they otherwise are eligible to be rehired.

15. Supervisors cannot subject pro-union employees to unfair working conditions to which other employees are not subjected. Supervisors should talk with their superiors before initiating personnel actions that might be construed as "anti-union."

16. Supervisors cannot discharge or discriminate against employees who file grievances or testify in any union proceedings.

17. Neither supervisors nor their superiors may refuse to bargain collectively with representatives of the employees.

18. Neither supervisors nor their superiors can refuse to provide the union with information it needs to bargain intelligently. They also cannot change any of the terms or conditions of the union contract without union discussion.

19. Management at all levels is forbidden to show hostility toward unions during negotiations. They also cannot be extremely unyielding during the bargaining process.

As a result of her research, Stacey became well aware of many restrictions placed on supervisors when a property is unionized. A union, she realized, had to be dealt with by more than higher management levels. Managers, supervisors, and employees—regardless of their level in the organization—are deeply affected by employee unions. Supervisors must know the contract and understand the contract when higher levels of management become involved in personnel-related decisions. The supervisor must know the union steward, be able to interact professionally and consistently with him/her, and, at all times, must be knowledgeable to protect management's rights that are needed to effectively run the hospitality operation.

16 The Supervisor and Labor Control Systems

PAGE THIRTY-ONE

Supervision at the Brandywine Room

The memo from the director of the Food and Beverage Department came as no surprise. Stacey Francis had been expecting it for several days.

TO: All Food and Beverage Supervisors
FROM: Director, Food and Beverage Department

Upon the request of the hotel's general manager, the Food and Beverage Department has agreed to undertake a pilot study to implement labor staffing guides for each operating unit of this department. All supervisors within the Food and Beverage Department are to attend a preliminary information meeting. We will contact you personally to provide more details and arrange a specific time. Thank you for your cooperation.

Stacey was interested. She had been looking forward to learning more about staffing guides for some time. How should we match productivity with output? How many labor hours should be scheduled? How do we coordinate labor costs and the labor budget with the actual labor hours that can be used every day? How do we know when we are using more labor than we should? These questions had been bothering Stacey for months.

Chapter 1 explained that the supervisor and all management personnel perform a number of activities. The control function was described as a series of subsystems requiring that:

1. Performance standards be established.
2. Operating information be assessed.
3. Comparisons between standard (expected) and actual performance be made.
4. Corrective action be taken.
5. Evaluation be undertaken to determine whether the corrective action was successful in reducing operating problems.

The supervisor must use these control techniques to manage resources. Labor is one resource with which all supervisors must be concerned. How do supervisors make the most effective use of our labor resources? Practice of supervision principles discussed throughout this book is the answer. However, the economic issues of wages and salaries paid to staff members affect the implementation of these basic principles. This chapter will provide a step-by-step approach that supervisors in any hospitality operation can use to control labor costs.

An Overview of the Labor Control Process

While a labor control plan can be effective within one department, commitment from the organization's top management is vital as labor control procedures are developed. The objective of every employee and each department should be to help the hospitality operation attain its goals. To do this effectively, organization-wide policies and procedures must be developed. Many supervisors know that their labor costs are high, and are getting higher. They assume that this is to be expected since the hospitality industry is labor-intensive. Labor costs increase as each wage and salary adjustment is made. Employee turnover also takes its toll in rising costs. In addition, many supervisors try to reduce costs in areas other than labor because they are uncertain of how to effectively manage staff members. As with any problem, the first step toward a solution is to be aware that a problem exists. So, how does a supervisor tell if there is a labor control problem?

Identifying Labor Problems

In many operations, a labor control problem exists when costs are higher compared to competing properties of the same size. Or, expressed as a percentage of sales, labor costs are higher than the national or state averages. Yet neither of these common ways to evaluate labor costs is useful. The question to ask is: "Are *my* labor costs higher than what *my* labor control plan says they should be?" If they are, a problem has been identified. If they are not higher, then labor is under control.

Financial data can help determine if there is a labor cost control problem. The labor costs for the past year or month plus raises in wages and salaries should equal what labor costs should be. This plan, however, assumes that labor costs were under control during the previous financial period. If labor costs have always been higher than necessary, this plan merely perpetuates an ineffective labor control system into successive financial periods.

The property's operating budget, if developed correctly, is the best source of labor plans. The budget is a profit plan that spells out the best estimates of expected income, allowable expenses, and expected profit. It sets an allowable level of labor costs that top management, owners, and investors consider to be adequate. This budgeted labor expense becomes a goal. As operating budgets are developed and monitored, there must be an assurance that budgeted labor and other goals are met. This comparison between actual labor costs and budgeted labor goals is an integral part of the supervisor's "game plan" to control labor.

Reviewing Labor Costs

A labor control problem occurs when actual labor costs exceed budgeted labor costs. What are other signs that a review of labor costs is in order?

1. When operating procedures are changed. Since labor control plans are based on how work is done, more efficient procedures may mean employees can spend less time doing required tasks. For example, the use of a convenience food product in the kitchen may reduce the amount of time required to prepare food products. New equipment for cleaning carpets or revisions in bed-making procedures will change required hours in the housekeeping department.

2. When staffing plans have not been reviewed for a long time. Over time, supervisors and their employees may do things differently. Just as organizational charts and job descriptions become out of date, work procedures used as the basis for establishing time plans may be obsolete.

3. When staffing and scheduling plans have never been carefully considered. In a new operation, there is little time to carefully develop work details. Over time, shortcuts are learned through experience. If required labor needs were determined hastily or if a long time has passed since they were developed, labor control problems may exist.

4. If there is concern that the bottom line of the budget is not what it should be. Supervisors should look first at those categories of costs that can be controlled. Supervisors should examine the largest expenses and labor certainly is among them.

5. If employees can't perform the work in the amount of time allotted. Complaints (such as "we need more help"), overtime, and production bottlenecks are clues that there are labor control problems.

6. Guest complaints can suggest labor control problems. When service is slow, quality standards are not being met.

Staff Planning

Labor control begins long before an employee reports to work. When the supervisor defines the work to be done, labor control starts.

He/she must know exactly what work must be done in his/her operation. Once this is known, a tool called a "job breakdown" (see Chapter 7) is used. Job descriptions that outline the tasks to be performed and the knowledge, skills, and abilities necessary to do the job must be developed. Recruitment, selection, orientation, training, supervising, and employee performance reviews are critical components in labor control programs.

Many hospitality operations hire staff and schedule employees in order to achieve payroll savings and improve productivity. A complete staff planning system includes monitoring the results of staffing and scheduling procedures in order to "fine-tune" the staffing program.

Controlling Labor Costs

If the hospitality property wastes $500 in labor costs every week and if its bottom line profit is ten percent (ten percent of all sales is profit), then the property must generate $5,000 in sales every week to have $500 profit "left over" to pay for the unnecessary labor costs of $500. No hospitality operation can afford to have $5,000—or $500, $50, or $5—in wasted sales.

Supervisors should understand that the budget responds more quickly to labor cost reductions than to income increases. Because of the expense incurred in generating food sales revenue, for example, only a small percentage of income actually drops to the bottom line. By contrast, if labor costs can be reduced by $50 a week, the entire $50 becomes bottom line profit.

Labor costs can—and must—be controlled. This task must be a high priority as supervisors plan their time. More than 30% of all income generated by the typical lodging or food service property is used to meet payroll costs. The need to spend time on factors that most determine profitability is apparent.

Supervisors must allocate the necessary resources to effectively plan and implement a labor control system. Top management must set priorities and admit that all aspects of a supervisor's job are important, but some time and effort must be spent in designing a labor control system.

This commitment of time, effort, and attitude is perhaps the most important element in a labor control system. A labor control program will be successful if management wants it to be. It won't be successful if management does not see the need for it.

Establishing Quality Standards: The First Step

Assume that the supervisor realizes there are problems and wants to control labor costs. Quality standards must be considered in an effort to reduce labor costs. For example, a housekeeper may be able to clean one or more additional rooms; a food server might attend to one more table; a few more check-ins might be permitted before additional front desk staff are scheduled.

However, professional supervisors recognize that these examples and related efforts are not the best ways to reduce labor costs. The wisest and the only effective approach to controlling labor costs is to consider quality standards first. The supervisor must assess what work must be done and how it is to be done. When developing labor staffing plans, it is absolutely critical that supervisors consider their property's quality requirements.

Now consider how quality makes a difference. For instance, Hotel A has a 75-point checklist that housekeepers must follow to service a room. This hotel also does extensive tableside flambe work in the restaurant. The property also prides itself on short, "express" check-in lines with concierge assistance to guests awaiting check-in.

Contrast this operation with Hotel B where only basic clean-up duties must be performed in rooms. Less service is required in the dining room, and long waits for check-in are tolerated.

The point is simple: quality standards must be developed to provide the basis for how the work is to be done. Unfortunately, properties give little thought to this important concern. Rather, the status quo is often the measure of expected quality.

Supervisors, then, must work with department heads and others to establish minimum quality levels. When possible, quality expectations should be recorded so they can be the basis for developing training programs, evaluating employee performance, and revising operating procedures.

An examination of existing quality levels can be revealing. After the management team has decided what has to be done, it can look at what is currently practiced. Many guests have stayed in a hotel or dined in a restaurant and noticed obvious problems. How can the property's supervisor—who spends many hours in the operation—not notice these troubles? Could he/she visit another property and quickly notice its violations of quality standards? The answer may be yes. Supervisors sometimes get too busy to notice, or work habits may force them to ignore certain problems in their departments. Therefore, a supervisor should study his/her property to focus specifically on quality standards such as facility cleanliness, employee work habits, and the products and services.

Define Quality Levels

You now know that labor costs must be controlled, but not at the expense of quality. Supervisors must define minimum quality standards to be incorporated into the work. The question for supervisors is not: "How can I better control labor costs?" Rather it is: "Given the minimum quality levels required, how can labor costs be controlled?" This approach emphasizes the critical role that quality standards must play in establishing a base for controlling labor costs.

A **standard** is defined as the number of work units that an employee can produce during a work period while still meeting quality requirements. Examples of work standards include a specified number of rooms that a maid is expected to clean in one shift, the number of guests one food attendant is to serve in the dining room during a workshift, or the number of dishes that a dishwasher is expected to clean per labor hour. In each instance, quality expectations are defined first and then they are factored into the standard that is established.

All work should have a standard against which actual performance can be measured. Many times a supervisor already knows how long it

Exhibit 16.1 Room Inspection Report Form

ROOM INSPECTION REPORT

Date ____________________ Room No. ____________________

	Points			
Doors & Locks	5	OK____	Out of Order ______	
Door Bumpers	5	OK____	Out of Order ______	Missing ______
Rate & Law Card in Holder	5	OK____	Missing ______	
Light Switch & Entrance Light	5	OK____	Out of Order ______	Other ______
Waste Basket — Brown	5	OK____	Dirty ______	Other ______
Desk Lamp & Bulb	5	OK____	Out of Order ______	Other ______
Dresser — Desk — Chair	10	OK____	Dirty ______	Condition ______
Mirror	10	OK____	Dirty ______	Dusty ______
Matches & Ash Trays	5	OK____	Dirty ______	Missing ______
Stationery, Pen, Telephone Book, Bible	5	OK____	Missing ______	
Television — Radio	10	OK____	Reception ______	Out of Order ______
Tray, Ice Bucket, Opener	5	OK____	Dirty ______	Missing ______
Water Glasses	10	OK____	Dirty ______	Missing ______
Floor Lamp & Bulb	5	OK____	Out of Order ______	Other ______
Draperies	5	OK____	Dirty ______	Unhooked ______
Patio Door (Locked)	5	OK____	Dirty ______	Unlocked ______
Sofa, Table & Chairs	10	OK____	Dirty ______	Condition ______
Pictures	5	OK____	Dirty ______	Straight ______
Night Stand — Remote Control	5	OK____	Dirty ______	Out of Order ______
Bedside Lamps & Bulbs	5	OK____	Dirty ______	Out of Order ______
Telephone, Calldex	5	OK____	Dirty ______	Out of Order ______
Bedding	10	OK____	Dirty ______	Other ______
Bed	5	OK____	Dirty Underneath ______	
Thermostat — Set, Fan On	10	OK____	Other ______	
Walls & Ceiling	10	OK____	Dirty ______	Other ______
Carpet	10	OK____	Dirty ______	Other ______
Carpet	10	OK____	Condition ______	
Table Tents (2), Door Knob Signs (2)	5	OK____	Missing ______	
A/C Filter	5	OK____	Dirty ______	
Comment Card	5	OK____	Missing ______	Stamped ______
HMI Strips on Glass Doors	10	OK____	Missing ______	
Furniture	10	OK____	Dusty ______	
TOTAL POINTS	220			

takes to do a particular job according to pre-established quality standards. In many operations, however, this information is not known. Perhaps a job has not been studied recently or work procedures have changed since the last analysis.

An example of establishing performance standards follows. It focuses on the housekeeping department.

Developing a Performance Standard

When developing a performance standard for the housekeeper, a question to ask is: "How long should it take to clean a room?" The answer to this question partly lies in defining what is a "clean room." The housekeeping director, selected floor supervisors, and other employees can develop a detailed checklist of what must be done to prepare a guestroom for occupancy. An example of required tasks that are listed in the room inspection report is shown in Exhibit 16.1.

Exhibit 16.1 (Continued)

BATHROOM INSPECTION REPORT

	Points			
Lights	5	OK_____	Dusty _____	Out of Order _____
Wash Basin & Drain	10	OK_____	Dirty _____	
Water Faucets	10	OK_____	Dirty _____	Spotted _____
Waste Basket — White	5	OK_____	Dirty _____	Other _____
Facial Tissue	10	OK_____	Missing _____	
Mirror	10	OK_____	Dirty _____	
Bath Tub & Drain	10	OK_____	Dirty _____	
Bath Tub Faucets & Shower Head	10	OK_____	Dirty _____	Spott _____
Bathroom Tile & Grouting	10	OK_____	Dirty _____	
Towel Rack	5	OK_____	Dirty _____	
Bath Towels (DD-4, DS-3, S-2)	10	OK_____	Missing _____	
Face Towels (DD-4, DS-3, S-2)	10	OK_____	Missing _____	
Wash Cloths (DD-4, DS-3, S-2)	10	OK_____	Missing _____	
Sanitary Napkin Bag, HMI Bag	5	OK_____	Missing _____	
Toothbrush	5	OK_____	Missing _____	
Bath Mat, Tub Mat, Rug	10	OK_____	Dirty _____	Missing _____
Soap, Toilet	10	OK_____	Missing _____	
Soap, Bath	10	OK_____	Missing _____	
Commode	5	OK_____	Dirty _____	Other _____
Toilet Paper	5	OK_____	Missing _____	
Toilet Paper Holder, Towel Hook	5	OK_____	Broken _____	
Shower Curtain	5	OK_____	Dirty _____	Unhooked _____
Ventilator	5	OK_____	Dusty _____	
Door Hook	5	OK_____	Other _____	
Bathroom Floor	10	OK_____	Dirty _____	
Shaver Outlet Sign	5	OK_____	Missing _____	
Water Glasses	10	OK_____	Dirty _____	
Coat Hangers (10)	5	OK_____	Missing _____	
Luggage Rack	5	OK_____	Missing _____	
Laundry Bag & List	5	OK_____	Missing _____	
TOTAL POINTS	225			

Source: Don B. Campbell and Ray W. Ribaric, "A Science for the Seventies: Work Management (Part I)," Lodging, *March 1976, p. 16.*

The room inspection report can double as a written checklist of quality standards for a "clean" room. Note that the checklist identifies each element in the room requiring attention. The trainer now knows what tasks an employee must perform and can design appropriate training activities. The housekeeper knows what tasks must be performed in order to meet requirements. In addition, the floor supervisor, or other staff member who routinely inspects rooms, can evaluate the status of the room according to the same standards used by management and housekeepers.

Now that all concerned parties know what work must be done to properly clean a room, the supervisor must determine how long the work should take. The floor supervisor personally can clean several rooms and carefully note the time required. If rooms are different sizes or have different furniture and fixtures, the required cleaning times for these differing rooms must be noted. The individual cleaning times for each room can be averaged to produce the amount of time reasonably required to clean all rooms.

Exhibit 16.2 Time Required to Clean Hotel Rooms Properly

Room Number	Required Time (Minutes)
101	25
212	33
317	30
391	31
416	28
485	40
508	28
525	25
615	32
653	36
Total Required Time	308

308	÷	10	=	30.8
number of minutes		number of rooms cleaned		average minutes per room

Exhibit 16.3 Calculation of Standard Number of Rooms to Be Cleaned per Shift

Length of full-time workshift	8 hours	(480 minutes)
Length of lunch and break periods	− 1 hour	(60 minutes)
Number of work minutes per shift	7 hours	(420 minutes)

420	÷	35	=	12
number of work minutes		average minutes per room		standard number of rooms per shift

Suppose that over five days a floor supervisor cleans ten rooms. The actual time required to clean the rooms properly is shown in Exhibit 16.2. The ten rooms were cleaned in 308 minutes—an average of 30.8 minutes per room.

Some time is required to move the cleaning cart between rooms and to perform miscellaneous duties not directly related to cleaning rooms. Therefore, the supervisor might establish an average of 35 minutes to clean a room. With this information, the standard number of rooms that a housekeeper is expected to clean per shift, while maintaining quality standards, can be calculated. This calculation is illustrated in Exhibit 16.3. Since the average room takes 35 minutes to clean, the housekeeper working an eight-hour shift is expected to clean 12 rooms, according to prescribed quality standards.

Exhibit 16.4 Labor Costs Incurred Because Standards Are Not Met

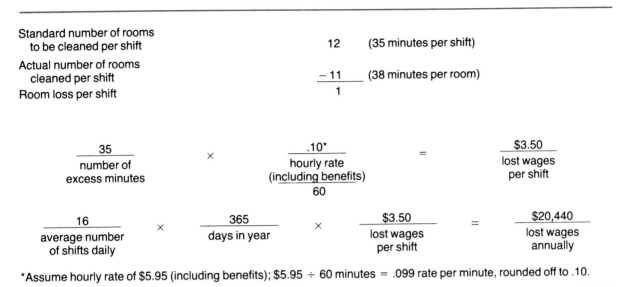

Standard number of rooms to be cleaned per shift	12	(35 minutes per shift)
Actual number of rooms cleaned per shift	− 11	(38 minutes per room)
Room loss per shift	1	

$$\frac{35}{\text{number of excess minutes}} \times \frac{.10^{*}}{\frac{\text{hourly rate (including benefits)}}{60}} = \frac{\$3.50}{\text{lost wages per shift}}$$

$$\frac{16}{\text{average number of shifts daily}} \times \frac{365}{\text{days in year}} \times \frac{\$3.50}{\text{lost wages per shift}} = \frac{\$20{,}440}{\text{lost wages annually}}$$

*Assume hourly rate of $5.95 (including benefits); $5.95 ÷ 60 minutes = .099 rate per minute, rounded off to .10.

Once the supervisor knows the performance standard, he/she can determine whether—and how much—labor can be saved.

Consider the situation in Exhibit 16.4 when additional labor costs are incurred because standards are not met. Assume that the production standard for the housekeeper is 35 minutes per room or 12 rooms per shift. Also assume that the actual number of rooms cleaned per shift is only 11. Does three minutes more to clean one room really make a difference? The answer is a definite yes.

Exhibit 16.4 indicates that the lost wages per shift amount to $3.50. The supervisor must spend $3.50 per shift to employ an extra housekeeper to clean a room which otherwise could be cleaned by a housekeeper already on staff. If there are 16 full-time housekeepers working 365 days a year and if each housekeeper cleans one room less than the expected standard, this costs the property $20,440 a year. Profits would increase by $20,440 annually if each room was cleaned in three minutes less time. The manager knows by actual trial and observation that the 35-minute standard—not the 38-minute actual time—is a fully attainable objective.

This example shows that once performance standards are established, the supervisor has two vital pieces of information:

1. The amount of time that is required to perform jobs to meet quality standards.
2. The amount of labor dollars that are wasted when performance standards are not met.

Developing the Staffing Guide

A **staffing guide** is an outline that matches production units (number of rooms to be cleaned, number of guests to be served) with the number of labor hours needed to provide quality products and services.

The supervisor first has determined performance standards. He/she then must forecast business volume so that the amount of labor required to perform work according to quality levels can be scheduled. The staffing guide puts all this information together.

Fixed and Variable Labor

Before considering procedures to develop staffing guides, the supervisor must understand the difference between fixed and variable labor. **Fixed labor** is that labor required to operate the property regardless of occupancy or anticipated business volume. For example, one front desk clerk must be available whether one, 10, or 20 guests are to be served. Likewise, one cook is necessary even if only one meal is prepared, and one maid is needed if just one room is serviced. Up to some point, which is determined by the specific property, no additional staff is necessary. For example, one front desk clerk may be able to check in and check out 35 guests. One cook may be able to prepare up to 30 meals. One maid may be able to service up to 15 rooms.

Above some specified level, however, additional labor is necessary. This incremental labor is referred to as **variable labor**, which fluctuates according to the volume of business activity. As more guests are registered, more meals are produced, and more rooms are occupied, additional front desk, cook, and housekeeping labor is needed.

The amount of fixed labor is a benchmark or "base load" of the minimum labor needed to operate the property. When staffing guides are developed, this minimum amount of labor must be incorporated into staffing plans.

Sample staffing guides are shown for a housekeeping department (Exhibit 16.5) and a kitchen department (Exhibit 16.6). In both figures, the number of production units—the occupancy rate for the housekeeping department, the number of covers (guests) for the kitchen—is identified for differing levels of business volume. Based on this information, allowable hours for each position in the department can be calculated. Frequently the required number of hours vary for different work shifts.

The concept of economy of scale suggests that efficiency per unit of output increases as business volume increases. For example, twice as many hours do not have to be scheduled for room attendants when the occupancy is 100% as compared to 50%. In Exhibit 16.5, 400 room attendant hours are required for the morning shift at a 51% occupancy rate. Only 724 hours are needed when there is a 100% occupancy rate.

If the property has developed an operating budget, the staffing guide must not yield higher labor costs than the operating budget permits. Conversely, if the staffing guide is used to develop the labor section of the operating budget, occupancy rates and/or the expected number of covers (guests) to be served are determined and then used to meet budgeted labor costs.[1]

Exhibit 16.5 Housekeeping Department Staffing Guide

HOUSEKEEPING DEPARTMENT STAFFING GUIDE

		Supervisors				Room Attendants				Attendant/Floor				Uniform Control Linen	
%	Occ.	A.M.		P.M.		A.M.		P.M.		A.M.		Weekly			
Occ.	Rms.	#	Hrs.	#	Hrs.	#	Hrs.	#	Hrs.	#	Hrs.	#	Hrs.	#	Hrs.
100	1404	12	96	1	8	98	784	3	24	12	96	4	32	7	56
99	1389	12	96	1	8	97	776	3	24	12	96	4	32	7	56
98	1375	12	96	1	8	96	768	3	24	12	96	4	32	7	56
97	1361	12	96	1	8	95	760	3	24	12	96	4	32	7	56
96	1347	12	96	1	8	94	752	3	24	12	96	4	32	7	56
95	1333	12	96	1	8	93	744	3	24	12	96	4	32	7	56
94	1319	11	88	1	8	92	736	3	24	12	96	4	32	7	56
93	1305	11	88	1	8	91	728	3	24	12	96	4	32	7	56
92	1291	11	88	1	8	90	720	3	24	12	96	4	32	7	56
91	1277	11	88	1	8	89	712	3	24	12	96	4	32	7	56
90	1263	11	88	1	8	88	704	3	24	12	96	4	32	7	56
89	1249	11	88	1	8	87	696	3	24	12	96	4	32	7	56
88	1235	11	88	1	8	86	688	3	24	12	96	4	32	7	56
87	1221	11	88	1	8	85	680	3	24	12	96	4	32	7	56
86	1207	10	80	1	8	84	672	3	24	12	96	4	32	7	56
85	1193	10	80	1	8	83	664	3	24	12	96	4	32	7	56
84	1179	10	80	1	8	82	656	3	24	12	96	4	32	7	56
83	1165	10	80	1	8	81	648	3	24	12	96	4	32	7	56
82	1151	10	80	1	8	80	640	3	24	12	96	4	32	7	56
81	1137	10	80	1	8	79	632	3	24	12	96	4	32	7	56
80	1123	10	80	1	8	78	624	2	16	12	96	4	32	6	48
79	1109	10	80	1	8	78	624	2	16	12	96	4	32	6	48
78	1095	10	80	1	8	77	616	2	16	12	96	4	32	6	48
77	1081	9	72	1	8	76	608	2	16	12	96	4	32	6	48
76	1067	9	72	1	8	75	600	2	16	12	96	4	32	6	48

Fixed Labor and the Staffing Guide

Each lodging and food service property has fixed labor, which is the minimum amount of labor needed, regardless of business volume. Fixed labor dictates a minimum staffing level and can be expressed in terms of employee and/or labor hours. A front desk clerk must be available for check-ins, for example, and a cook must be available when the kitchen is open. Therefore, at least one employee must work for the length of time that registration and meals are available.

Each department sets fixed labor requirements. The number of fixed employees significantly affects the labor control program and the level of labor costs. Top managers should approve the amount of fixed labor that is needed and several times a year should review levels of fixed labor. Many factors, such as change in quality levels, operating procedures, and guest expectations, influence the amount of fixed labor.

Exhibit 16.5 (continued) Housekeeping Department Staffing Guide

HOUSEKEEPING DEPARTMENT STAFFING GUIDE															
		Supervisors				Room Attendants				Attendant/Floor				Uniform Control Linen	
%	Occ.	A.M.		P.M.		A.M.		P.M.		A.M.		Weekly			
Occ.	Rms.	#	Hrs.	#	Hrs.	#	Hrs.	#	Hrs.	#	Hrs.	#	Hrs.	#	Hrs.
75	1053	9	72	1	8	74	592	2	16	11	88	2	16	6	48
74	1038	9	72	1	8	73	584.	2	16	11	88	2	16	6	48
73	1024	9	72	1	8	72	576	2	16	11	88	2	16	6	48
72	1010	9	72	1	8	71	568	2	16	11	88	2	16	6	48
71	996	9	72	1	8	70	560	2	16	11	88	2	16	6	48
70	982	9	72	1	8	69	552	2	16	11	88	2	16	5	40
69	968	8	64	1	8	68	544	2	16	11	88	2	16	5	40
68	954	8	64	1	8	67	536	2	16	11	88	2	16	5	40
67	940	8	64	1	8	66	528	2	16	11	88	2	16	5	40
66	926	8	64	1	8	65	520	2	16	11	88	2	16	5	40
65	912	8	64	1	8	64	512	2	16	9	72	2	16	5	40
64	898	8	64	1	8	63	504	2	16	9	72	2	16	5	40
63	884	8	64	1	8	62	496	2	16	9	72	2	16	5	40
62	870	8	64	1	8	61	488	2	16	9	72	2	16	5	40
61	856	8	64	1	8	60	480	2	16	9	72	2	16	5	40
60	842	7	56	—	—	59	472	2	16	9	72	2	16	5	40
59	828	7	56	—	—	58	464	2	16	9	72	2	16	4	32
58	814	7	56	—	—	57	456	2	16	9	72	2	16	4	32
57	800	7	56	—	—	56	448	2	16	9	72	2	16	4	32
56	786	7	56	—	—	55	440	2	16	9	72	2	16	4	32
55	772	7	56	—	—	54	432	2	16	8	64	2	16	4	32
54	758	7	56	—	—	53	424	2	16	8	64	2	16	4	32
53	744	7	56	—	—	52	416	2	16	8	64	2	16	4	32
52	730	6	48	—	—	51	408	2	16	8	64	2	16	4	32
51	716	6	48	—	—	50	400	2	16	8	64	2	16	4	32

These employees should be as productive as possible. For example, on an average slow shift, when fixed labor is most needed, how much of the employees' time is spent in work normally expected of the position? If the amount of idle time increases, consider the following questions:

1. Must we continue to provide the service? Will quality standards permit, for example, adjusting the hours of dining room, concierge, or parking lot service? If these operating changes can be made, labor costs can be reduced.

Exhibit 16.6 Kitchen Staffing Guide

KITCHEN STAFFING GUIDE					
NUMBER OF COVERS FORECASTED	HOURS REQUIRED—PANTRY*		HOURS REQUIRED	HR. REQ. COOKS*	
	LUNCH	DINNER	UTILITY**	LUNCH	DINNER
775			39.0		
750			39.0		
725			38.0		
700			37.0		
675			37.0		
650			36.0		
625			35.0		
600			35.0		
575			33.0		
550			32.0		
525			32.0		
500			31.0		
475			30.0		
450			30.0		
425			29.0		
400		15.0	29.0		18.0
380		15.0	28.0		18.0
360		14.0	28.0		18.0
340		14.0	27.0		18.0
320		13.0	27.0		18.0
300	11.0	13.0	26.0	15.0	18.0
280	11.0	12.0	26.0	15.0	18.0
260	10.0	12.0	25.0	14.0	18.0
250	10.0	11.0	25.0	14.0	18.0
240	10.0	11.0	24.0	14.0	17.0
230	9.0	11.0	24.0	14.0	17.0
220	9.0	10.0	24.0	13.0	17.0
210	9.0	10.0	23.0	13.0	17.0
200	8.0	10.0	23.0	13.0	14.0
190	8.0	9.0	23.0	13.0	14.0
180	8.0	9.0	22.0	12.0	14.0
170	8.0	9.0	22.0	12.0	14.0
160	7.0	8.0	22.0	12.0	14.0
150	7.0	8.0	21.0	12.0	14.0
140	7.0	8.0	21.0	11.0	14.0
130	7.0	8.0	21.0	11.0	14.0
120	6.0	8.0	20.0	11.0	12.0
110	6.0	8.0	20.0	11.0	12.0
100	6.0	8.0	20.0	10.0	12.0
90	6.0	8.0	19.0	10.0	12.0
80	6.0	8.0	19.0	10.0	12.0
70	6.0	8.0	18.0	10.0	8.0
60	6.0	8.0	17.0	10.0	8.0
50	6.0	8.0	17.0	10.0	8.0

Source: Don B. Campbell, and Ray W. Ribaric, "A Science for the Seventies: Work Management (Part I)," Lodging, *March 1976, p. 15.*

*Add Hours Required Due to Banquet Business, if any.
**Above 775 covers, add one utility hour for every 50 covers.

2. Can the tasks performed by fixed staff be adjusted? If front desk clerks do selected recordkeeping tasks or a cook performs preparation duties, perhaps this will reduce the amount of variable waged staff needed later.

3. Can work be combined so that salaried labor can perform some slow-time tasks? For example, an assistant restaurant manager can be stationed at the host stand during the early and late dining periods. Reservation calls and occasional seating duties may not significantly interfere with paperwork tasks that the assistant manager can do in the dining room as well as in the office. Therefore, a fixed labor employee will not be needed at the host stand during these slow times.

Once a staffing guide is developed, the supervisor can schedule labor according to the forecasted volume of business.

Forecasting Business Volume

The central idea of the staff planning program is to match allowable labor with the volume of business that is forecasted. Just as quality and productivity standards must be carefully incorporated into staffing guides, so must supervisors carefully think about the process of estimating business volume, such as occupied rooms, food and beverage sales, and special events.

A **forecast** is simply a summary of information relating to anticipated business volume. A large property may establish a forecast committee comprised of departmental representatives from rooms, food and beverage, housekeeping, and other areas. The committee's primary purpose is to predict room sales—generally a major factor in determining a hotel's staffing needs. In a smaller property, the general manager and key department heads may do the forecasting.

Estimating Room Sales

Exhibit 16.7 shows a ten-day volume forecast for room sales. Note that there is a three-day overlap. The form indicates information about the previous three days as well as the upcoming week. This provides the forecast team with an opportunity to evaluate how successful its predictions are. In addition, trends that could affect future forecasts are easier to spot.

The forecast committee should meet at least weekly to forecast daily room occupancy rates. In many properties, after the number of rooms sold is known, food and beverage sales can be calculated since there is a relationship between these two factors. For example, a certain percentage of room occupants will translate into the number of breakfast covers or the amount of late night bar business. In other properties—especially those doing a large banquet business or generating a large amount of food and beverage sales from the community—the relationship between room sales and food and beverage covers may be less. In any case, there is a direct relationship between room sales and the need for variable

Exhibit 16.7 Ten-Day Volume Forecast Form—Rooms

TEN-DAY VOLUME FORECAST—ROOMS

Date Prepared ______________
Week Ending ______________

Motor-Hotel ______________
(LOCATION)

DATE																						
DAY	THUR.		FRI.		SAT.		SUN.		MON.		TUES.		WED.		THUR.		FRI.		SAT.		Totals	
	— Previous Week																					
ROOMS DEPARTMENT	F	A	F	A	F	A	F	A	F	A	F	A	F	A	F	A	F	A	F	A	F	A
Rooms occupied—Indv.																						
Groups																						
Arrivals—Ind. Resv.																						
Group Resv.																						
Estimated walk-ins																						
Sub-Total																						
Departures—scheduled																						
estimated																						
Sub-Total																						
TOTAL ROOMS OCCUPIED																						
House Count																						
In House																						
Arrivals																						
Walk-ins																						
Sub-Total																						
Departures																						
TOTAL HOUSE COUNT																						

SPECIAL COMMENTS
(i.e. types of groups—V.I.P. etc.)

Source: David L. Balangue, "Payroll Productivity (Part IV: Staff Planning)," Lodging, November 1978, p. 39.

F = Forecast
A = Actual

labor personnel, such as front desk clerks, housekeepers, and bell staff. For this reason, the forecast of room sales is at the heart of the hotel's business volume forecast.

Determining Factors

Supervisors must know the factors that affect business volume for their properties. The following information should be considered:

1. *Prior forecasts and actual results.* The forecasting team must learn from its experience. Why, for example, did the number of forecasted rooms differ from actual rooms sold in a previous week? Can the planning team discover anything that will help in forecasting room sales for the subsequent week?

2. *Number of reservations.* No-show rates and information about lead time for reservations often can help in estimating the number of reserved rooms that actually will be sold.

3. *Group bookings for rooms.* Experience with different groups can help in estimating the number of blocked rooms that actually will be sold.

4. *Booked food and beverage business.* Experience may indicate a spin-off effect. For example, banquet bookings can lead to room sales. If this is true, then this factor must be considered.

5. *Walk-in business.* The history of walk-in business can indicate its effect on room sales.

6. *No-shows and cancellations.* Again, the property's experience must be used to estimate these variables.

7. *Seasonal fluctuations.* Normal business trends obviously must be considered.

8. *Special events and other factors.* Special events in the community and surrounding area can be factors and should be considered. Other factors that vary for each property also will influence estimates.

Cooperation by all management staff is critical in developing the forecast of room sales. This estimate must represent the consensus of all staff. All department heads should accept the forecast and use it as a basis for employee scheduling.

Three-Day Revised Forecast

In the fast-paced hotel business, ten-day forecasts often are too long-range to provide meaningful assistance. For this reason, many properties constantly update forecasts to reflect changing circumstances. Obviously, such events as snowstorms and local emergencies cannot be anticipated. Conditions not known when a forecast was made ten days earlier can dramatically change business volume. Exhibit 16.8 shows a form which can be used to develop an updated forecast.

Members of the forecast team can meet daily to review yesterday's business, assess today's room occupancy, and consider whether changes are necessary in the remaining days of the ten-day volume forecast. If more than a very slight increase in occupancy is forecasted, labor schedules may have to be revised. If occupancy rates are estimated to be lower, supervisors can be alerted to make last-minute schedule changes.

Forecasting Food and Beverage Revenue

Food and beverage supervisors must develop business forecasts in order to schedule their personnel. Forecasts can be expressed in terms of estimated dollar volume and/or the number of covers to be served. The forecast of sales is based upon factors such as room occupancy, sales history, and a subjective evaluation based upon experience.

The form in Exhibit 16.9 can be used to record sales estimates for the food service operation. This form uses the same basic components as

Exhibit 16.8 Sample Form for Three-Day Revised Forecast—Rooms

THREE-DAY REVISED FORECAST — ROOMS

	Yesterday	Today	Tomorrow
Day			
Date			
Guest Count			
Room Arrivals			
Room Departures			
Room Count			
Room Vacancies			
% of Occupancy			
Forecasted % of Occupancy			
Condition			

does Exhibit 16.7. Information about the previous three days allows current business trends to influence judgments made for the future week. Again, data in this forecast may need revision as the week evolves.

Exhibit 16.9 deals only with food sales since many properties determine beverage sales by applying a percentage factor to forecasted food sales. An analysis of past food and beverage sales for each outlet yields the level of this percentage factor. An example of how to calculate this estimate is illustrated in Exhibit 16.10.

How successful supervisors are in developing an accurate business forecast depends, in large measure, on the historical information they use. Wise personnel use all information that is available on sales history.

Just as the forecasting system for room sales must be updated by assessing differences between forecasts and actual sales, differences between actual and forecasted food covers must also be examined. Supervisors should assess reasons for differences and fine-tune the system to increase the accuracy of future sales forecasts.

After business volume has been estimated, staff can be scheduled. Note that the supervisor first determines required labor based upon minimum quality and productivity standards. He/she then makes adjustments due to varying volumes of business. A system to forecast business volume also must be developed. The next logical step is to match the required labor with the forecast of sales.

Exhibit 16.9 Ten-Day Volume Forecast Form—Food

TEN-DAY VOLUME FORECAST—FOOD

Motor-Hotel ____________________
(Location)

Date Prepared ____________________
Week Ending ____________________

DATE DAY	THUR.		FRI.		SAT.		SUN.		MON.		TUES.		WED.		THUR.		FRI.		SAT.		Totals	
	Previous Week																					
FOOD DEPARTMENT	F	A	F	A	F	A	F	A	F	A	F	A	F	A	F	A	F	A	F	A	F	A
Dining Room																						
Breakfast																						
Lunch																						
Dinner																						
Total D.R. Covers																						
Coffee Shop																						
Breakfast																						
Lunch																						
Total C.S. Covers																						
Banquet																						
Breakfast																						
Lunch																						
Dinner																						
Total Banquet Covers																						
Room Service																						
Total R.S. Covers																						
TOTAL FOOD COVERS																						

SPECIAL COMMENTS
(i.e. types of groups—V.I.P. etc.)

Source: David L. Balangue, "Payroll Productivity (Part IV: Staff Planning)," Lodging, November 1978, p. 39.

F = Forecast
A = Actual

How to Schedule Staff

An effective scheduling procedure is the key to making the staff planning process work. The schedule writer knows the amount of allowable labor time from the staffing guide and the volume of business anticipated from the business forecast. If scheduled labor does not exceed allowable labor, the staffing plan will work. For example, assume the staffing guide permits 60 hours of employee time when 120 rooms are

Exhibit 16.10 Estimating Food Covers and Beverage Revenue

Assume the total occupancy rate (see Exhibit 16.7) is estimated at 225 guests for the day. Factors such as events in the hotel, conventions in the city, and related statistical history must also be factored into the forecasts. Knowing this, the food and beverage manager can estimate food covers and beverage sales. (There is only one food outlet in the property.)

Estimates of Covers to be Served

Breakfast: 20% of house guests plus 65 walk-in customers

255	×	20%	=	51	+	65	=	116
number of house guests		percent		breakfast to house guests		walk-in customers		estimated breakfast covers

Lunch:

105	×	$4.55	=	$477.75
number of lunches		check average		lunch sales

Dinner:

160	×	$8.55	=	$1,368.00
number of dinners		check average		dinner sales

Beverage Revenue

Based on experience, beverage sales are approximately 22% of lunch and dinner sales. No relationship between breakfast sales and beverage income has been discovered.

$477.75	+	$1,368.00	=	$1,845.75	×	22%	=	$406.06
lunch sales		dinner sales		total sales		beverage income percent		estimated beverage

In this property, labor for the day being analyzed will be based upon breakfast, lunch, and dinner covers of 116, 105, and 160 meals respectively. The allowable labor in the staffing guide for the beverage section is based upon beverage revenue of $406.06.

cleaned. The work schedules planned for housekeeping personnel normally should total no more than 60 hours.

Remember the point made earlier about fixed labor. Whether one, three, or five rooms must be cleaned, a housekeeper must be available to clean these rooms. After business volume increases, then the concept of variable labor, which is central to labor cost control, comes into play.

Whenever possible, scheduling should meet volume demand day-by-day and hour-by-hour. An optimal schedule often requires split and short shifts. These practices may not always be possible because of union restraints, labor availability, or other factors. However, the basic principle of trying to match labor hours with work should be followed when possible.

We already noted that staffing guides should be developed on the basis of labor hours—not employees. When the staffing guide is developed in this manner, the schedule maker has a greater flexibility in designing plans to control labor costs. If the staffing guide says that 45 hours of front desk labor or 35 hours of food server help are required, for example, these hours can be spread out to match the level of anticipated business volume. No matter how the labor hours are scheduled, labor will be controlled if the actual business volume is similar to the forecast and the number of standard labor hours are not exceeded.

If more than the allowable number of hours is scheduled, employees will not work efficiently. Labor costs will be higher and efficiency will be lower than permitted by the staffing guide. Conversely, if fewer than the allowable number of hours are scheduled, the quantity of work may increase, but quality will suffer.

Schedule Worksheet

A schedule planner can use a schedule worksheet (Exhibit 16.11) to figure out when employees are needed. In the example shown, business volume permits only 18 labor hours for the assistant cook position. Three employees are scheduled to do the work and are available during peak business volume. While the starting and ending times of the workshifts differ, the total number of scheduled work hours equals the standard--18 labor hours.

This form is not needed to schedule employees for every workshift. In many operations business volume stabilizes and it flows according to definite patterns. Once the schedule planner gets the program down to a routine, the form is not necessary. However, as special problems are anticipated or planned, a schedule worksheet is a helpful tool for labor control.

Techniques for Developing Schedules

Generally all staff members should not begin and end workshifts at the same time. Schedules should be staggered to meet work needs. Since work flow may not be constant, personnel can be scheduled accordingly.

If there are not enough administrative tasks for full-time employees to do, some jobs, such as "head bartender" or "head dishwasher," can involve management and nonmanagement tasks. This approach establishes a way to determine jobs for fixed labor. Salary and wages can be set on the basis of reasonable pay for all the work performed so that the property and the employee can benefit from combining management and nonmanagement tasks. Using part-time staff, temporary employees, and flexible schedules also helps to schedule labor effectively in specific situations.

Personal preferences of employees and requests for special considerations should be honored when possible. For example, employees may have transportation problems or unusual family obligations. At the same time, managers should remember employee scheduling policies, such as rotating the arrival times of staff members or specific clean-up or close-up tasks at the end of the shift.

The supervisor must remain alert to more effective ways to schedule labor. Yet, the primary concern always is not to exceed allowable labor hours reported in the staffing guide. A review of the scheduling is in order to ensure that proper quality of services is provided while the staffing guide is followed.

Exhibit 16.11 Schedule Worksheet Sample

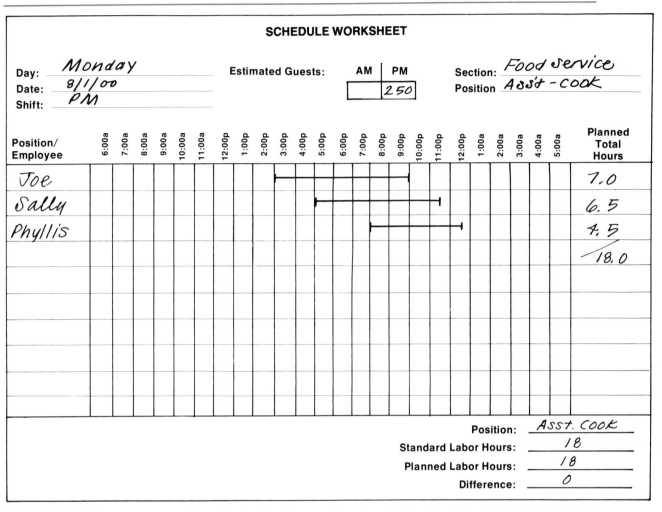

SCHEDULE WORKSHEET

Day: Monday
Date: 8/1/00
Shift: PM

Estimated Guests: AM: | PM: 250

Section: Food Service
Position: Asst-Cook

Position/ Employee	6:00a	7:00a	8:00a	9:00a	10:00a	11:00a	12:00p	1:00p	2:00p	3:00p	4:00p	5:00p	6:00p	7:00p	8:00p	9:00p	10:00p	11:00p	12:00a	1:00a	2:00a	3:00a	4:00a	5:00a	Planned Total Hours
Joe																									7.0
Sally																									6.5
Phyllis																									4.5
																									18.0

Position: Asst. Cook
Standard Labor Hours: 18
Planned Labor Hours: 18
Difference: 0

Source: Jack D. Ninemeier, Planning and Control for Food and Beverage Operations, *(East Lansing, Mich.: Educational Institute of the American Hotel & Motel Association, 1982), p. 186.*

Timetable for Developing Schedules

Employee schedules normally are made out on a weekly basis. The actual time period covered by the schedule should equal the days covered by the business forecast. If the next week's business forecast is available on Wednesday, the labor schedule for the following week can be developed at that time. In the sample employee schedule (Exhibit 16.12) for the cook position within the food and beverage department, the number of daily work hours for each employee in that position is listed. The schedule writer must refer to the staffing guide to confirm that the total number of hours to be worked each day does not exceed the specified standard for allowable labor hours.

After the employee schedule is written, there are several alternatives for distribution. In some properties, especially smaller ones, the schedules may be posted immediately for employee review. In larger

Exhibit 16.12 Sample Employee Schedule

EMPLOYEE SCHEDULE

Week of: 7/14/00

Shift: PM
Section: Food
Position: Cook

Supervisor: Julie

Employee	7/14 Monday	7/15 Tuesday	7/16 Wednesday	7/17 Thursday	7/18 Friday	7/19 Saturday	7/20 Sunday
Joe	12:00-7:00	–	12:00-7:00	1:00-7:30	–	12:00-7:00	–
Ann	–	12:00-7:00	1:00-7:30	12:00-7:00	–	–	12:00-7:00
Jean	3:00-8:00	1:00-5:00	3:00-8:00	–	–	1:00-7:30	1:00-7:30
Sue	–	3:00-8:30	12:30-8:30	12:30-7:30	12:00-7:00	–	–
Mary	12:30-6:30	12:30-6:00	–	–	3:00-7:00	3:00-8:00	3:00-8:00
Stacey	3:00-7:00	3:00-7:00	3:00-7:30	3:00-7:30	–	–	12:30-8:30
Phyllis	1:00-5:00	1:00-5:00	–	–	3:00-8:00	12:30-8:30	3:00-7:00
June	1:00-7:00	–	–	1:00-7:00	1:00-8:30	3:00-7:00	–
Salley	–	–	3:00-8:00	1:00-7:00	3:00-7:30	–	1:00-6:00
Karen	1:00-7:00	1:00-7:00	–	–	1:00-5:00	1:00-6:00	2:00-7:00
Betty	–	–	3:00-7:00	3:00-8:00	3:00-7:00	2:00-7:00	–

Source: Jack D. Ninemeier, Planning and Control for Food and Beverage Operations, *(East Lansing, Mich.: Educational Institute of the American Hotel & Motel Association, 1982), p. 188.*

properties, the department manager may need to approve the tentative schedule.

Other properties prefer to incorporate a top management sign-off system in which the schedule planner forwards a proposed schedule to a level higher than department head before it is made available to the employees.

As a compromise between no management and routine management approval, top managers may have to approve the schedule when labor hours in addition to those permitted by the staffing guide will be needed.

Overtime Control

A primary goal of a labor staffing program is to minimize the amount of overtime incurred. There are two types of overtime, neither of which benefits the property.

1. Hours worked over the statutory minimum for which additional compensation must be paid. (State and federal laws require time-and-one-half rates for nonexempt positions. Union restraints and other restrictions may impose further overtime requirements.)

2. Hours in excess of those permitted by the staffing guide.

Overtime of either type must be controlled and both must normally be minimized.

There are situations in which overtime will be incurred. During especially busy periods, key personnel may have to remain on duty for longer than normal periods. At other times, staff members must fill in for other employees for reasons beyond the property's control. When business is greater than forecasted, equipment breaks down, or new employees must be trained, more labor hours may be necessary than those specified by the staffing guide.

The point is that overtime must be controlled, which means that planning is necessary. Overtime that is not planned indicates a serious problem. Unplanned overtime means there is a flaw in the procedure used to schedule labor hours. The schedule writer should try to avoid scheduling overtime. When overtime is scheduled, however, an overtime request and authorization form can be used before costs are incurred to note and defend the need for the extra overtime. When such requests become common, a problem exists. All concerned parties—the department head, schedule writer, and top management representative—should determine ways to eliminate the need for frequent overtime requests. Changes in the organization's staffing/scheduling procedures may be necessary.

Scheduling Options

Traditional approaches to labor control (such as salaried labor must work full-time, or part-time personnel cannot receive a salary) should not restrict the options of the schedule planner. Creative scheduling possibilities that are appropriate in specific situations include:

Part-Time Staff. Remember to coordinate labor hours with work volume. If most check-ins and check-outs occur at specific times, or the number of meals to be served fluctuates, then these changes in business volumes must be considered when employee hours are planned. During the most labor-intensive period, for example, part-time staff members can work in front desk and dining room positions. In most properties, part-time staff members do not receive the same fringe benefits package as do full-time employees. Therefore, labor costs can be saved two ways. Labor hours are scheduled only when work is required and associated labor costs are reduced if benefits are fewer.

Temporary Staff. Temporary employees are hired for only a short time. In contrast, the positions of permanent employees do not have a fixed end. Temporary employees are very useful when a crunch of business is expected. This alternative can resolve short-term problems.

Split Shifts. Must employees work a traditional straight shift? Some employees may prefer split shifts, part-time shifts, staggered schedules, and other variations. Matching labor hours with sales volume forecasts becomes easier to the extent that managers can use these "variable cost" personnel.

Assessing Actual Labor Hours

Assume that the best labor planning procedures and a staffing guide that incorporates productivity standards while matching labor hours with varying business volume are in effect. This information is used to schedule labor hours. Top management has signed off on the planned number of labor hours. What's next?

The next step in the labor control process is to assess the actual number of labor hours worked. To do this, the same classification system used to develop standards must be followed. For example, if the staffing guide expresses allowable labor on the basis of positions within each shift, actual labor costs must be collected in the same manner. On the other hand, if the staffing guide expresses required labor on the basis of position only—and ignores differences among shifts—then actual labor costs must be assessed this way too.

Exhibit 16.13 can be used to collect information about daily labor hours and associated costs. Information required for this report can be abstracted daily from a manual or time clock record of hours worked for each employee. Labor costs can be calculated with this information. In small properties, the bookkeeper or office staff member may perform this task.

Information about actual labor hours can be assembled and compared weekly with standard labor hours. The weekly section labor hour report (Exhibit 16.14) is designed for this purpose. The actual labor hours worked each day during the week are recorded (column 9). The actual labor hours can be compared with the standard labor hours (column 10) as taken from the employee work schedule. In the example illustrated in Exhibit 16.14 there were 216.5 labor hours planned for the dining room staff. The actual labor hours worked totaled 224.5.

For every position—desk clerk, housekeeper, cook, etc. —the actual number of hours worked must be known. This information is necessary for payroll because the number of labor hours worked is used to calculate wages for nonsalaried positions. Additionally, a manager must know the number of labor hours worked in order to evaluate the effectiveness of the labor control system. The actual number of labor hours is recorded either by a manual payroll system or use of a time clock.

Systems for Recording Labor Hours

Manual Payroll System. Small properties, or departments within large properties, may choose to keep records of time worked with a manual payroll system. While this system can be very workable and cost effective, caution should be taken to ensure that no shortcuts evolve over time or during rush periods. With a manual system, supervisors must verify (by initial) the actual times that employees begin and stop work. This re-

Exhibit 16.13 Daily Labor Report Form

DAILY LABOR REPORT

Date ______________ Position ______________

Day ______________ Shift ______________

EMPLOYEE NAME	PAY RATE	NUMBER OF EMP.	TOTAL HOURS	EARNINGS			
				REG.	O.T.	TOTAL	
TOTAL							

quirement, however, generates a frequent shortcoming. What happens when supervisors are very busy or not immediately available when an employee begins or ends work?

Time Clock System. Automated time clocks are easily cost-justified even for many small properties. Time clock equipment can range from a simple device that just stamps time cards entered into the machine to very

Exhibit 16.14 Weekly Section Labor Hour Report

WEEKLY SECTION LABOR HOUR REPORT

Week of: 7/14/00 **Section:** Food Service **Supervisor:** Sandra
Shift: PM

Position/ Employee	Actual Labor Hours Worked 7/14 Mon	7/15 Tues	7/16 Wed	7/17 Thurs	7/18 Fri	7/19 Sat	7/20 Sun	Total Labor Hours Actual	Standard
(1)	(2)	(3)	(4)	(5)	(6)	(7)	(8)	(9)	(10)
DINING ROOM									
Jennifer	7	-	7	6.5	7	6	-	33.5	31.0
Brenda	-	7	6.5	7	6.5	6.5	5	38.5	38.5
Sally	-	5	8	7	8	10	-	38.0	36.0
Patty	8	6	6	4.5	-	-	6	30.5	31.0
Anna	4	4	6.5	-	4.5	-	5	24.0	22.0
Thelma	6	5	5	5	5	-	-	26.0	24.0
Elsie	6	-	-	6	6	8	8	34.0	34.0
								224.5	216.5
COOK									
Peggy	4	4	4	4	4	-	-	20.0	20.0
Kathy	4	4	4	-	-	4	4	20.0	20.0
Tilly	4	-	-	4	4	4	4	20.0	18.0
Gert	-	4	4	4	4	4	-	20.0	20.0
Sam	4	4	-	-	-	-	4	12.0	12.0
								92.0	90.0
DISH WASHING									
Terry	-	-	6	6	6	-	-	18.0	18.0
Andrew	6	6	-	-	8	5	5	30.0	30.0
Robert	8	8	8	8	-	-	6	38.0	38.0
Carl	5	-	5	5	5	6	-	26.0	26.0
								112.0	112.0
Total (all personnel)								428.5	418.5
Difference								+10.00	

Remarks:
7/19 – Sally stayed 2 hours - special cleaning
7/18 · Jennifer, Sally and Elsie given extra hours to learn tableside flaming
7/20 – Tilly stayed 2 hours - clean storeroom shelves

Source: *Jack D. Ninemeier,* Planning and Control for Food and Beverage Operations *(East Lansing, Mich.: Educational Institute of the American Hotel & Motel Association, 1982), p. 190.*

sophisticated, computerized devices that automatically calculate labor records and reports. Time clocks provide documentation and verification of actual hours worked and are more precise than manual timekeeping systems.

In larger properties, a dual time clock system may be required. With this plan, employees punch a time clock as they enter and leave the property through the designated employee entrance. Within their departments, employees punch a second time clock when beginning and ending work. There are at least two advantages to this plan. The time employees spend in the property but not working can be monitored. When employees work in several departments, direct labor costs can be charged more readily to the correct cost center.

There also should be verification that no "ghosts" are on the payroll. In some operations, a nonexistent employee may be receiving paychecks. Perhaps the person has left the operation or has never worked in the property. Dishonest staff members, perhaps a payroll clerk working in collusion with a supervisor, might be able to withdraw these monies from the property through payroll fraud.

Another concern is that employees receive the proper pay rates. Pay rates should be checked against personnel files. All pay rates should be authorized by management and be part of the employee's personnel records. More than one person should be responsible for calculating hours worked, as well as making out and distributing payroll checks.

Attaining Labor Goals

The staffing guide recaps the number of allowable labor hours for each position according to varying business volumes and establishes labor performance standards. Daily and weekly labor reports show the actual hours worked by employees in each position. Standard and actual hours must be reviewed to discover deviations between performance standards and actual results. Generally, some deviation may be tolerated. If a labor performance standard for a housekeeping position is 210 hours a week (based upon the forecast of room occupancy for that time period), a variance of one or two percent (approximately 2.15 and 4.25 hours respectively) may be permitted. The amount of variance that can be tolerated before corrective action is taken depends on:

- The extent to which the supervisor permits standards to be exceeded. If management believes that the standards are reasonable, especially if some tolerance already is built into them, allowable deviations are likely to be small.

- Whether there are larger control problems in other areas. Corrective actions should focus on areas where variances are greater and reflect the largest amount of lost profits.

- Whether variances can be explained. It is one thing when labor hours are excessive because a new employee is being trained.

It is another matter when hours are consistently excessive and the supervisor does not know the reason.

If a form similar to that in Exhibit 16.14 recaps standards and actual labor hours for management review, the form can provide an explanation for the variance. If reasons for variances are acceptable, there probably is little or no need for corrective action. On the other hand, if actual hours exceed standard hours and there is no defensible reason for the difference, a problem may exist.

Whether variances are explainable or unexplainable, a plan to resolve the problem must be developed: Is the performance standard expressed in the staffing guide incorrect? If so, it should be adjusted. Is a piece of equipment broken? If so, when will it be fixed? Is a new employee being trained? If so, how long will it take? Can scheduled hours be reduced as the trainee becomes more proficient? These and similar concerns should be addressed to arrive at a mutually acceptable plan that will reduce variances between standard and actual labor hours.

Potential Savings

The difference between labor standards and actual results of the labor control program represent potential savings to the property. When weekly labor hours suggested by the staffing guide are exceeded, wage costs for the additional hours represent lost profit. Each dollar spent for labor above the required maximum takes one dollar of profit away from the bottom line.

Potential savings can be calculated by comparing standard labor hours and actual hours. For example, in Exhibit 16.14 note that 224.5 actual labor hours were used during the week in the dining room. This is eight more hours than the 216.5 hours permitted. The excess number of hours multiplied by the average hourly rate (including fringe benefits) for the position yields the approximate amount of lost profit (potential savings). To arrive at the exact amount, the number of additional hours worked by each dining room employee can be multiplied by the employee's hourly rate (including fringe benefits).

As the variance between standard and actual labor hours increases, the amount of potential savings becomes larger. As this amount of lost profit grows, the need for corrective action becomes stronger. The comparison step incorporated in the labor control program enables the manager to see the results of the labor control efforts and to assess if and when corrective action is needed.

Corrective Action Procedures

A comparison between actual and standard labor hours may identify the need for specific corrective action procedures. Discussions about observed problems among management, the immediate supervisor, affected staff, and others often will identify possible alternatives for resolving problems that are causing the labor variances. These options must be analyzed to assess where the problem is occurring and which alternative is likely to resolve the problem.

Concerns when selecting the corrective action plan include its probability of success. Whether and how much the variance can be reduced must be assessed for each alternative. Estimates of cost become important. The cost to implement each alternative must be carefully calculated. Knowledge of past actions that have and have not resolved similar problems can be helpful.

The alternative chosen must be feasible and capable of being implemented. While this may seem obvious, some managers waste time wishing things were different instead of accepting the situation and working within its restraints. The best plan to resolve a labor control problem is often a compromise between two or more possible solutions. In addition, an alternative might be tested. One employee or one shift may use revised procedures to test the proposed solution for possible success. Supervisors often study similar hospitality operations, review hospitality literature, and converse with management staff who have similar responsibilities as they attempt to identify ways to reduce labor problems.

After a corrective action program is defined, managers should be aware of several important points in implementation. Employees affected by corrective action procedures often resist changes. They may want to defend the status quo, saying, "We have always done it this way." As these employee concerns arise, managers may resolve them by explaining and defending the need for changes and, when possible, telling employees how the changes will make the workplace better for them.

Employees must be trained in new procedures. Too often, managers are in a hurry. They demonstrate new procedures only one time to employees and then forget about additional training, reinforcing, and coaching. They also may fail to provide all tools and equipment required to perform the work.

Concerns when evaluating corrective action include the need to (a) assess changes over several analysis periods, (b) revise the staffing guide if corrective action plans significantly tighten up the labor control program, (c) postpone evaluations until staff members learn what they are supposed to do, and (d) continue the evaluation process over several fiscal periods. Changes often may produce positive results temporarily, but problems may occur. The evaluation process must be continuous. Labor control—beginning with the review of differences between standard and actual results, followed by corrective action, and concluding with evaluation—must be a constant concern.

Summary

This chapter has discussed the need for basic procedures to effectively control labor costs. The process must begin with a commitment from top management. Design of systems that incorporate minimum quality standards is of special concern as labor control plans are developed. Exhibit 16.15 recaps each of the steps in the labor control program outlined in this chapter. Use of the staffing guide and development of business forecasting systems are important activities that can guide

Exhibit 16.15 Review of the Labor Control Process

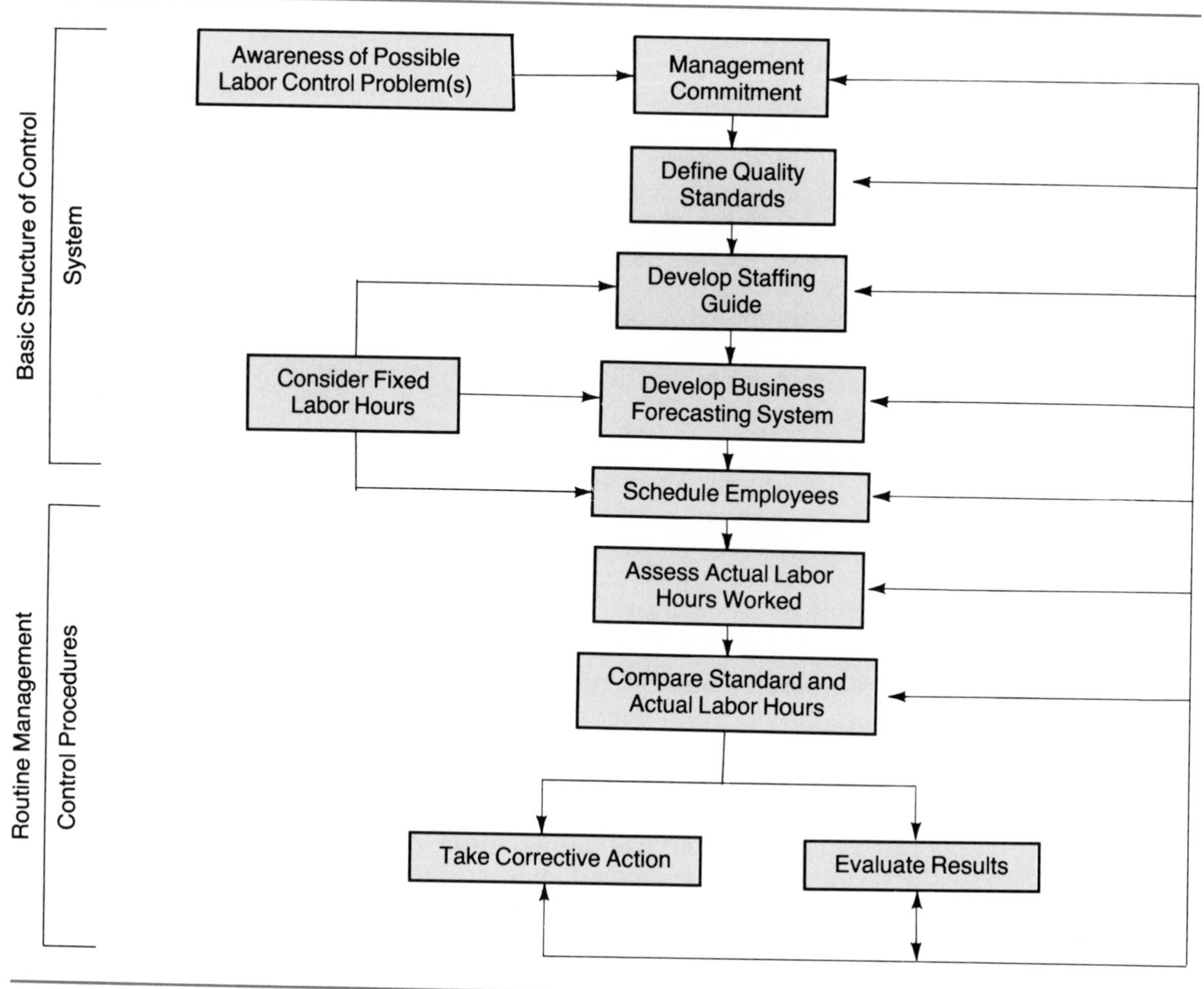

the actual employee rescheduling task. The process of assessing actual labor hours worked and comparing corrective action and evaluation phases are critical components of the labor control system. You should begin to see how each step in the process is interrelated. For example, when results of the control system are evaluated, this can affect each step in the labor planning control process.

NOTES

1. This concept is explored more completely in Jack D. Ninemeier, *Planning and Control for Food and Beverage Operations* (East Lansing, Mich.: Educational Institute of the American Hotel & Motel Association, 1982).

PAGE THIRTY-TWO

Supervision at the Brandywine Room

Stacey was enthusiastic after attending the supervisory meeting that addressed the upcoming labor staffing plan. In principle, the concept made sense to her. Stacey was aware that departments such as hers with a large number of employees were among those areas where significant labor savings could result. She learned in a college class that using control as a management activity did work. This involved developing performance standards, assessing actual performance data, and subsequently taking corrective action if necessary. If these concepts could be incorporated into plans to control labor cost, Stacey was sure that the hotel was "on target."

She also was impressed with the great impact the supervisor had on the success of the labor staffing program. The staffing process involved cooperation between all management levels, Stacey realized. Without such a plan, there is no way to ensure that plans to control labor will be implemented.

As manager of the dining room, Stacey was interested in developing a performance standard for a food server.

She learned at the supervisory meeting that a position performance analysis form can be used to establish a productivity standard for a food server. Development of such a form required that the supervisor, working along with the host and selected other front- of-house personnel, define expected quality levels of service provided to guests in the dining room at lunch. For example, tasks to be performed by buspersons and food server staff should be defined. The sequence of activities (greeting the guest, approaching the table, providing beverage, salad, entrée, dessert orders, etc.) should be outlined and aspects of quality requirements be established. An observation period should be scheduled during which employees are closely supervised and instructed to follow all policies and procedures. A trial period should be set to identify and observe a "better than average" food server in order to analyze job performance.

Stacey was told that she would be responsible for answering such concerns as:

- Is the server providing the required quality of service?
- Does the server seem rushed or overworked?
- Could the server do more work and maintain the required quality standard?
- How many guests are served during the shift?
- How many additional or fewer guests should be served in order to meet performance standards?

After reviewing, evaluating, and analyzing food servers during several shifts, Stacey now could determine a labor performance standard for that position. She understood that a position performance analysis form should be completed for each position (food server, host, busperson) in each shift since menus and service styles may differ by meal period and require different tasks.

POSITION PERFORMANCE ANALYSIS

Position: Service

Name of Employee: Joyce

Shift: AM — Lunch

	4/14	4/15	4/16	4/17	4/18
No. Guests Served	38	59	25	45	50
No. Hours Worked	4	4	4	4	3.5
No. Guests/Labor Hour	9.5	15	6.2	11.2	14.3
Review Comments	Even work flow; no problems	Was really rushed; could not provide adequate service	Too much "standing around"; very inefficient	No problems; handled everything well	Worked fast whole shift; better with less guests

General Comments

Joyce is "better than average" waitress; with all the tasks that service personnel must do in our restaurant, approximately 10 guests per labor hour can be served by one waiter/waitress. When the number of guests goes up, service quality decreases; Joyce really had to rush; some guests waited longer than they desired. When guests/labor hour drop, Joyce is not busy; there is a lot of unproductive time.

Suggested Meals/Labor hour: 10
(this position)

Performance Review by: Stacey Francis
Manager

Source: Jack D. Ninemeier, Planning and Control for Food and Beverage Operations *(East Lansing, Mich.: Educational Institute of the American Hotel & Motel Association, 1982), p. 180.*

The director of the Food and Beverage Department developed a sample performance analysis form for Stacey. In the form, a food server has been observed over five lunch shifts. For each shift, the number of guests served and the number of hours worked is recorded and the number of guests per labor hour is calculated. On April 14, 38 guests were served during a four-hour work period. This yields 9.5 guests per labor hour (38 guests divided by 4 hours equals 9.5 guests per hour). The supervisor, in this case Stacey, would record review comments relating to the efficiency of work and any observed problems.

All supervisors, including Stacey, learned that a similar position performance analysis could be conducted for other positions. Eventually, a performance standard for all positions within the property could be developed. Stacey now knew that after quality standards are defined and incorporated into performance standards, it would be possible to develop an effective staff planning program to help control labor costs.

17 Management Development in the Hospitality Industry

PAGE THIRTY-THREE

Supervision at the Brandywine Room

Stacey Francis had been supervising the Brandywine Room for about 18 months, and, based upon the evaluations from her boss, Mr. George, and her own personal feelings about her work, she was doing a good job. She had learned a lot, and had responded effectively to many special and routine problems that arose. In general, through her interactions with Mr. George and others "up the organization chart," she was beginning to understand how things worked in upper management levels. She was still taking classes at the university and hoped to get a bachelor's degree some day. She knew the hospitality industry could provide very interesting and rewarding job opportunities.

As she talked to some of her fellow supervisors, she was pleased to learn that some of them were also thinking about their futures and wanted to learn more about how to plan their careers objectively. How do things like this happen, she thought? Does a person have to be lucky to have a successful career, or are there ways that one can think about:

1. Where am I now?
2. What are my short- and long-range goals?
3. How do I attain my goals?

Stacey was so intrigued by these very important personal and professional questions that she decided to learn about the process of career management and professional development.

Supervisors in the hospitality industry must have the knowledge, skills, and common sense to consistently make good decisions about the many recurring and special problems that confront them. There is no question that these activities constitute a full-time job. However, supervisors concerned about their own professional and personal development must take time out from their ongoing responsibilities to seriously consider "where they are going." Many people think that careers are shaped by a series of events which constitute good luck or bad luck. They do not realize that, just as a road map can lead us from one destination to another over a planned route, so can a predetermined career management effort help us "get from where we are to where we want to go."

Career planning is an activity that people often leave "until they get around to it." As discussed throughout this book, there is a need for the supervisor—whether acting as a professional making business decisions or as an individual making personal decisions—to set priorities and to do the most important things first. Plans about your future and how to achieve them are very important. Set aside time today—not tomorrow—to consider career goals and alternatives to reach them.

There are many important considerations supervisors should review as they consider their professional futures. Two concepts must be understood.

Management Development. Management development involves training and professional growth whereby supervisors learn to apply knowledge, skills, and attitudes to more effectively manage hospitality operations. The organization will benefit immeasurably if it provides opportunities for supervisors to learn how to do their jobs better. At the same time, supervisors benefit since their effectiveness is rewarded by advancements in their career.

Career Management. Career management is undertaken between the property and the individual to identify and match an individual's needs, abilities, and goals with the organization's demands and rewards. This is an effort that rewards the supervisor and the organization. Management development is one element in a general career management program. There are times when the drive to attain goals may force an individual to leave a specific organization and go to another. The employee and the organization, therefore, must consider exactly how the relationship between the supervisor and the organization can benefit both parties. There is no reason why this relationship of mutual benefit cannot continue indefinitely. Techniques to accomplish this will be reviewed in this chapter. However, a supervisor may need to reexamine career goals or review other job opportunities. This chapter will detail the techniques that can be used in this process.

A Close Look at Career Management

The hospitality operation should be concerned about developing its jobs to be compatible with the employees who perform them. Organizations should create means that allow employees to attain goals that are important to both the operation and the individual. These elements are at the heart of career planning. Properties must be aware of what is best not only for themselves but for the employee as staffing and personnel decisions are made. Employees' abilities and needs must match the job to be done. Employees' concerns about their future with the organization also must be considered. Therefore, the employee and the organization must be involved, as much as possible, in career planning. Each employee must continually consider his/her strengths and weaknesses, needs and interests, and then attempt to meet these concerns on the job. Organizations, at the same time, must offer opportunities for employees to grow on the job. This can be done by creating career development programs.

Organizations institute career development programs in response to their concerns about helping employees grow and attain personal and professional goals while on the job. Programs can range from the company's posture of promoting from within to planned training and development experiences that help the employee gain job-related skills and knowledge needed to climb the organizational ladder.

The Supervisor as a Professional

Supervisors should recognize that they are professionals, and hold in common with other professions advanced, specialized, and formal education and training. Supervisors must have the ability to perform their jobs as expected while exercising a great deal of discretion and judgment. They need skills and experience to solve problems, and they need a sense of ethics and responsibility to the organization, employees, and themselves. Supervisors should identify with others in similar jobs and have ongoing relationships with professional organizations.

As a professional, the supervisor develops goals and plans to attain them. The supervisor also needs to continually evaluate progress and professional goals. As a career evolves, changes will be necessary. The professional recognizes and responds to changes, which he/she considers as opportunities and not obstacles.

Management Development Programs: The Organization's Perspective

The organization and supervisor must be concerned about employees and how to respond to their concerns. Consideration about management training and development must begin at the top of the organization. These officials must recognize the need for management development programs that affect employees at all levels of the organization. Top-level managers must learn and practice skills to create and implement management development programs. They also must instill, through their words and actions, the need for and procedures to implement these activities at all organizational levels.

Procedures for organizing and implementing an ongoing management development program include the following:

Step 1 **Analyze Organization Needs.** Business growth must be forecasted first, then the organizational structure must be studied to determine whether any changes are needed to better deliver the products and services. Current and accurate job descriptions and specifications for all management positions are important factors. This data must address not only the necessary knowledge and skills to perform the job today but also in the future.

Step 2 **Assess Managers' Abilities.** An "inventory" of existing management talent must be taken to determine if the organization currently employs individuals who can, with training and management development, perform all the tasks identified in the job descriptions. This process can help to determine those employees who will be able to perform tasks forecasted for the future. This analysis also will help define the knowledge these employees must gain and the experiences that will be needed to respond effectively in the new positions.

Step 3 **Tailor Development Programs.** Based on this analysis, development programs that are designed to meet the needs of the individual employee should be developed and implemented.

Step 4 **Use a Variety of Management Development Programs.** Structured training programs developed by the organization, organizational encouragement (financial assistance for educational programs), attendance at seminars, and professional association meetings are some inducements for professional development. Employee development programs geared specifically to the hospitality industry are offered through the Educational Institute of the American Hotel & Motel Association (AH&MA). A nonprofit arm of AH&MA, the Institute develops courses, seminars, and certification programs and sponsors professional development chapters for the professional and personal development of persons in the hospitality industry and those wishing to enter the field. Hospitality organizations seeking to implement management development programs may want to consider the opportunities available through the Educational Institute.

Job skills also can be learned and improved through planned work experiences. These are not the routine on-the-job training programs where new employees "tag along" with experienced staff members. Common problems with these programs, and ways to correct them, were reviewed in Chapter 7. In the context of management development programs, however, work experience programs must be more structured than typical training programs. While the hospitality industry lends itself to manager development opportunities, these programs will be only as effective as the pre-planning efforts given them. Examples of management development programs that incorporate job experiences include:

Types of Programs

Use of Understudies. An understudy is an employee who eventually will assume the position for which he/she is being trained. For example, the rooms department manager might select a promising supervisor and teach him/her the job by involving the supervisor in the nonroutine problems and issues that confront the current manager. The supervisor then might assume the duties of the higher level official when he/she is absent from the job. Roles of "assistant department head" and "administrative assistant" are examples of titles given to understudies as they learn new jobs.

Job Rotation. Transferring promising employees to other jobs is another example of how they can develop professionally through on-the-job experiences. With this method, the employee should be used for more than "vacation relief" or "emergency" purposes. Job rotation must be a planned program in which job knowledge and skills are learned through coordinated efforts as the employee "moves on" to learn important job tasks in other positions.

Job Enlargement. Job enlargement involves redesigning existing jobs to encompass new tasks. While often used to combat boredom, job enlargement techniques should be used to provide management trainees the opportunity to learn new job skills. With job enlargement, an employee changes jobs as he/she acquires competencies to effectively perform specific job tasks.

Coaching. Coaching, as an element in training, already has been discussed (see Chapter 7). With coaching, management trainees learn about shortcomings, discuss with the supervisor how problems can be resolved, and are given a formal opportunity for evaluation of subsequent performance.

Learner-Controlled Instruction (LCI). This relatively new approach to training (see Chapter 7), combines formalized training with learning gained through experience. In effect, LCI charts a list of job-related competencies that must be mastered. The management trainee, progressing at his/her own pace, acquires skills and knowledge with the help of experienced staff members. The LCI approach to training can be applied to management development programs. As the assessment of the specific manager is undertaken by the organization, the property's needs can be translated into tasks and structured into LCI programs that can be addressed by individual management trainees.

The Outlook for Job Opportunities

Large Properties

The hospitality industry of the future will likely be dominated by large multi-unit lodging and food service properties. Growth plans for many of these organizations are very ambitious. There will be a need for finding and retaining talented managers for these expanding organizations. Personnel recruiters for these properties frequently cite the tremendous opportunities for advancement and growth as a result of these expansion plans. Therefore, the organization and its employees will benefit from the consideration of an individual's advancement opportunities within the organization. The use of management development programs, such as those just outlined, will be a definite benefit. Implementation of personnel management, communication, and human relations principles noted in this book will be of great importance.

Students aspiring to management positions in the hospitality industry should consider opportunities presented by multi-unit companies. Employees and supervisors currently employed by these organizations should think about advancement possibilities within their organization before they consider alternative positions outside the organization.

Smaller Properties

Employees at all levels within small, single-unit properties should implement career management plans and be aware of opportunities with large companies if their career goals do not mesh with the needs of their current employers. However, this is not to de-emphasize the importance of small properties in the hospitality industry. The hospitality industry grew because thousands of people saw an opportunity to establish their own businesses. Yet, as the small neighborhood grocery store has given way to large regional supermarket organizations, the individual aspiring to management positions in the hospitality industry will see fewer opportunities in small operations simply because, relative to the "giants," there will be fewer of them. There always will be a place for the single-unit hospitality organization that effectively meets the needs of its market. However, there will not be enough of these operations to meet the employment needs of the many people entering the ranks of the hospitality industry.

Procedures for Career Planning

This chapter so far has focused on ways the organization can plan and implement management development programs for employees aspiring to advance within the organization. This must be a cooperative effort between the employee and the organization. Yet, we must know exactly how an individual makes career decisions. While very common, leaving your career to "chance" is not wise. Failure to make decisions because you believe that you cannot influence your career path is imprudent. Career planning decisions must begin with the objectives and the development of a plan.

Exhibit 17.1 outlines the important steps in making decisions about a career.

Step 1

Ask the Question: "What do I want to do?" To find an answer, consider your aptitudes—the abilities, talents, and competencies that you possess. Assessment of your interests also is important. You are more likely to do things that interest you. Consideration of your likes, dislikes, strengths, and weaknesses provides insights into what you like to do and can do well. Exhibit 17.2 is a checklist of personal inventory questions that may help you to better understand yourself so these important questions can be answered. There are many career guides available that can help you explore career goals.

Thinking about "how you got where you are now" also is helpful. If you are currently working in the hospitality industry, how did you get your first job? What are the factors that led you to consider professional opportunities in the industry? If you are not in the hospitality industry now, why are you considering it as a career? Why is it more attractive than other industries?

Step 2

Discover Opportunities. Once you have a general idea about what you want to do, think of ways you can do the type of work you enjoy. Try

Exhibit 17.1 The Career Management Process

Step 1. What Do I Want to Do?
1. What do you like to do?
2. What can you do well?

Step 2. Discover opportunities
1. Analyze personality
2. Consider important positions

Step 3. Select Career Goals
1. Consider long/short range
2. Review alternatives in light of goals

Step 4. Choose Your Plan
1. Assess potential
2. Analyze advantages, disadvantages

Step 5. Select the Organization
1. Sell yourself
2. Make job decision

Step 6. Perform Well on First Job
1. Don't get "comfortable"
2. Learn as much as possible

Step 7. Monitor Progress
1. Maintain "options"
2. Continually reassess career options

Step 8. Plan New Experiences
1. Examine possibilities within the organization
2. Leave the organization if—and when—necessary

to obtain as much information as possible by talking with your peers at work and at school. Consult your supervisors, teachers, counselors, and personnel representatives in your company, among others. Students in schools visited by company recruiters should discuss industry-wide employment alternatives as well as the recruiter's specific company. Read trade publications. They tell you what is happening in the hospitality industry, and they provide employment listings. Participate in career days. Talk with fellow employees in other departments, your boss, and anyone else who can give you information. The point is that, to make a wise career decision, you must gather as much information as possible. Not only will your knowledge increase, but your attitudes will be affected by the information you learn. Therefore, it is to your advantage to make the information search as comprehensive as possible.

Step 3 **Select Career Goals.** After you have an idea about what you want to do and have learned about opportunities that are available, you should select career goals. But, several misunderstandings should be clarified before taking this step.

Making a career decision is not an exact science. There is no way to quantify all the concerns you have and "plug them into a formula" that gives the "right" answer. The self-analysis and information exploration processes just described will help reduce the possibility of errors occurring in your reasoning. However, the possibility of mistakes remains.

There is no way you can possibly make final career decisions. As suggested in Exhibit 17.1, the process of managing your career and mak-

Exhibit 17.2 Checklist of Personal Inventory Questions

1. Do I know my strengths? Yes ____ No ____
2. Do I know my weaknesses? Yes ____ No ____
3. Am I involved in a program to improve my deficiencies? Yes ____ No ____
4. Am I in good physical and mental health? Yes ____ No ____
5. Do I follow a planned program to enhance my health and well-being? Yes ____ No ____
6. Am I willing to relocate? Yes ____ No ____
7. Will I work long hours Yes ____ No ____
8. Will I work nights, weekends, and holidays? Yes ____ No ____
9. Do I like to work with people? Yes ____ No ____
10. Am I willing to start at or near the bottom of an organization and work my way up? Yes ____ No ____
11. Do I like responsibility? Yes ____ No ____
12. Can I handle responsibility? Yes ____ No ____
13. Am I dependable? Yes ____ No ____
14. Can I make mature decisions? Yes ____ No ____
15. Can I follow orders? Yes ____ No ____
16. Can I work as a member of a team? Yes ____ No ____
17. Do I like close supervision? Yes ____ No ____
18. Do I like working with details? Yes ____ No ____
19. Am I comfortable working in a job that has many routines? Yes ____ No ____
20. Can I manage other people? Yes ____ No ____
21. Do I like to follow through on my work from beginning to end? Yes ____ No ____
22. Do I like to make decisions and solve problems? Yes ____ No ____
23. Do I like to work with people rather than with things? Yes ____ No ____
24. Do I get along well with people? Yes ____ No ____
25. Can I work well under pressure? Yes ____ No ____
26. Can I do hard work? Yes ____ No ____
27. Do I like to seek creative ways to do things when there are no set procedures? Yes ____ No ____
28. Do principles in the "art and science" of management interest me? Yes ____ No ____
29. Would I like to be a professional manager? Yes ____ No ____
30. Do I like to study people? Yes ____ No ____
31. Do I learn from my past mistakes? Yes ____ No ____
32. Do I believe that the guest is always right? Yes ____ No ____
33. Do I recognize that there is always a better way? Yes ____ No ____
34. Do I think it is fun to learn? Yes ____ No ____
35. Am I a creative and inventive person when it comes to making decisions? Yes ____ No ____

ing career decisions is ongoing. People change and so do their interests and opportunities.

There are no "magic tests" that give perfect insight to career management decisions. Tests for aptitude, interests, skills, and knowledge can be helpful. Yet, they will not provide the answer to a career choice. You cannot define all the abilities that will guarantee success on a future job. Therefore, you should be flexible as career management decisions are made.

Prolonging career management decisions over extensive time periods is not wise. Certainly, you may need time to make these important decisions. However, "thinking about it for a year or two" generally comes from procrastination more than from an earnest attempt to make a better decision.

When selecting career goals, you must honestly attempt to match the findings of Steps 1 and 2 with a realistic appraisal of what you should try to accomplish. At the same time, you need to be realistic. Remember, there are only so many hotels in the United States where you could be employed. To set a career goal of "being the general manager of a 1,000-room hotel" is not a realistic goal for many people. As an alternative, develop a strategy that indicates:

- Where I am now.
- Where I want to be in one year, five years, and ten years.
- What intermediate steps can make such a goal possible. However, remember to be flexible and change career goals as your career evolves.

When attempting to select career goals, a "balance sheet" approach might be used. With this plan, you study the advantages and disadvantages of attaining each goal. For example, one goal might require that you either continue your education, relocate to another part of the country, or accept a lower paying job. These factors should be weighed against how the alternative seems to fit into your career plan. Remember that your interests, abilities, aptitudes, and related concerns should be addressed as career goals are established.

Step 4 **Choose Your Plan.** After your career goals are determined, you should decide what plan you will use to obtain these goals. Perhaps you now are in the "right" organization. You might, in effect, be on the first rung of the career ladder that will take you toward your goal. Or, you may realize that your current job does not have the growth potential that you need. Alternatively, you may be in school and considering vocational opportunities after graduation. In any event, the process for making this first career decision (staying, moving on, entering an organization) is basically the same. You must consider your short- and long-range career goals and decide how your career can be advanced. Your assessment of the situation will depend on the information you have gathered and how you analyze the advantages and disadvantages of attaining a goal for each alternative.

Remember the discussion about the manager as decision-maker presented in Chapter 1. The same process used to make management decisions also can be used to make career decisions. Once the problem is defined (which position in the long run will be most beneficial in attaining my goals?), the process of generating, selecting, and implementing alternatives is similar.

Step 5 **Select the Organization.** As a result of the analysis process, you must implement an action plan. To do this, select the organization that you believe will best help you attain your goals. First, you need to discover what the organization wants in employees for a particular position. Then, you must convince recruiters that you possess these qualities. An effective resumé and command of job interview skills also are helpful. Knowledge about the company and about yourself are important prerequisites for obtaining the job of your choice.

The availability and type of management development programs offered by the company are important factors when making a job selection decision. A company with management development programs is willing to invest resources in preparing employees to perform effectively on the job. The company wants to help you become a better employee and has an interest in keeping you. An understanding of the company's attitudes on this point and a detailed investigation of the way the management development process works in the organization are very important.

After interviewing with and studying as many organizations as possible, a job decision must be made. From your perspective, this decision must be the one that seems the most likely to "keep you on the track" of obtaining your career management goals.

Step 6 **Perform.** Once hired, you must perform well on the job. Learn as much as possible. Constantly evaluate how your new experiences and job information can benefit you and the company. Don't become comfortable with doing your work routinely; contribute ideas whenever possible; ask your supervisor how you can improve; study and learn job-related information on your own.

As you perform well, you are likely to be recognized and advancement opportunities are likely to occur. If you have selected an organization with an active management development program, you and the organization are likely to benefit when you are recognized as a candidate for the activities that this program involves.

The importance that professional development activities can play in your professional development should not be overlooked. As noted in Exhibit 17.1 (Step 6), you should learn as much as possible. This is an important principle in the career management process.

Step 7 **Monitor Your Progress.** In today's fast-changing hospitality industry, personal obsolescence is a constant concern. Be on guard against the possibility that you become incapable of performing work to the standards or expectations of your supervisor. Active involvement in professional, educational, and training programs, as well as management development activities offered by the organization, serves as a safeguard against becoming an ineffective resource for your organization.

At the same time, be sure that you are on your way to attaining your career goals. Frequently reflect on where you are and whether you want to continue with or change your career goals. When you are not moving forward in your career, don't rationalize that you "really don't want to." Examine the current situation and, if you are not comfortable with it, continue the process of finding and evaluating alternatives that are compatible with your career goals. Monitoring your career performance and making decisions accordingly are important steps in the career management process.

Step 8 **Plan New Experiences.** As you observe your progress, you will want to plan new experiences. As noted earlier, first examine those possibilities for career development that exist in your current organization. If an analysis suggests that other alternatives have potential benefits, they should be considered. Frank discussion with your supervisor should yield alternatives that will be useful to you. You must be professional in your relationship with current or new supervisors.

Special Concerns in Career Management Decisions

Remember these special concerns as you undertake a career management program:

1. Some jobs do not offer significant challenges but they might be necessary steps to the top. Especially in entry positions, it is more important to learn the organization's procedures than to think that you can provide immediate help. You first must learn how things are done in the organization before attempting to implement changes.

2. Recognize that experiences on your first jobs may not be similar to those on subsequent jobs. Often you have to defer attainment of ego, status, and self-actualization needs during your first job experiences.

3. Remember that it is unlikely that all of the supervision principles discussed in this book will be practiced. At times, your supervisor will do things that seem incorrect. As a result, your training, motivation, and performance review experiences may be less effective than desired. Work is not always done "by the book."

4. Do not set unrealistically high goals. At the same time, do not fail to attain realistic goals by making excuses that you really like your current job and want to keep on doing what you are doing. Attempt to find challenges in the job that you do. For example, challenge yourself to do the job as well as it can possibly be done. Think about ways to make the job better. (Telling your supervisor about the suggestions can be beneficial.)

You should understand that the organization may be uncertain about its goals and the best methods to attain them. Consider the role that you might play in helping to resolve these problems.

Perhaps the most important concern to be addressed when your career management decisions are being made is that plans and strategies should be developed. This is more effective than the traditional view that you cannot influence your future. The hospitality industry is changing. The person who can meet the needs of this changing industry will likely be very successful and will be prepared to meet any reasonable goals.

The Supervisor and the Future of the Hospitality Industry

There is no question that the hospitality industry is changing. The wants and needs of the consumer are changing, and they dictate what the commercial end of the industry must do during changing times. Not-for-profit institutional food services also are changing. These services are recognizing economic incentives that require effective management as well as the use of basic management principles. Therefore, practice of basic principles of supervision, which are important in any industry, will be utilized increasingly in the hospitality industry.

Entry-level employees, those whom supervisors must manage, will likely come to their jobs with more concerns in the future. Growth in the industry will create unfilled positions. This will make organizations compete with each other for personnel to fill these positions. As this occurs, there will be an increasing need to meet employees' needs on the jobs in order to retain them. As a result, there will be interest in the quality of work life. Supervisors will need to practice the principles of human relations, motivation, and supervision.

Energy management concerns will occupy a larger amount of the supervisor's time. Problems with energy resources probably will worsen. Limited energy resources will be a critical problem that the supervisor will have to manage as part of his/her work.

Technology will recognize and deal with many of today's problems. Additional and better types of equipment, products, systems, and facilities will be available. Therefore, the kind of technical knowledge needed by an effective supervisor will increase.

The supervisor of tomorrow will need to know and practice effective people-related skills while at the same time learning how to manage new technologies. If a supervisor's job is difficult today, it will be even more difficult in the future. The principles of supervision must form the foundation on which new skills, some of which may not even be known today, can be built as supervisors manage tomorrow's hospitality operations.

It is hoped that you will become excited about the future of the hospitality industry and will want to become—or remain—a part of it. Do not be intimidated by the knowledge, skills, and abilities that are needed to perform the important job of supervising people. Rather, be challenged by the opportunities and meet these challenges by learning and practicing the principles of supervision. Many of them are reviewed in this book; others will be learned on the job. The supervisor who is open to "better ways of doing things" will be able to perform more effectively and will be rewarded for it.

PAGE THIRTY-FOUR

Supervision at the Brandywine Room

Stacey Francis welcomed the chance to learn some basics about planning and managing her career. Based upon her experience and knowledge of the hospitality industry, Stacey was convinced that she had made the correct choice when she decided to go to college, major in hotel and restaurant management, and obtain a part-time job in the industry. Luck had been on her side; she had found a good job. What should she now do to "map out" a career path?

After studying the procedures for making career management decisions, Stacey realized that she should assess what she liked to do. She liked her present position because things were always different. There was no routine of doing the same work all the time. She liked working with people—both employees and guests—though interacting with many people at times was a real challenge. Stacey knew she would not like a "desk job." She liked to be on her feet, make fast decisions, and test her knowledge with the results of her decisions.

Stacey talked with her supervisor, Mr. George, and he explained that promotion opportunities for dining room managers frequently led to assistant manager positions. In the past few years, he explained, the company that owned the hotel had purchased several properties, and there was a continuing need for good food and beverage managers to work in all the properties that the company had acquired.

Stacey realized that there were many opportunities with her present company. Even in her supervisory position, she had been able to participate in several management development programs. Stacey was active in the professional development chapter, attended monthly supervisory meetings, and had enrolled in a correspondence course at the hotel's expense. Mr. George explained several other opportunities for formal management development and continuing education activities that the hotel sponsored.

As a result of these factors, Stacey decided to seek an assistant restaurant manager position as soon as there was an opening. She developed a tentative schedule that called for her to occupy one of these positions within 18 months. By that time, if no positions had opened up, if she had been passed over for a promotion, or if for any other reason the goal was unattainable or undesirable, Stacey would rethink her current position and goals. Since her present company offered so many opportunities, she saw no reason to seek employment elsewhere.

Stacey knew that she was performing well on her first management position in the hotel. She vowed to learn all she could and not to "begin to feel comfortable or fall into a rut." Stacey would still set her priorities on resolving problems and involving her manager so he would understand her interests and abilities.

Stacey had developed a good professional relationship with her immediate boss, Mr. George, and with the personnel director, Ms. Case. They would be fair in dealing with her should openings occur, Stacey felt. She would at least know of these opportunities and be judged fairly for her abilities to perform them.

Stacey knew that she could perform her job even better in the future. She was confident of her skills and had a positive attitude because she knew that she was making a contribution to the hotel's objectives. Stacey knew that she could only attain her goals if the property was successful.

Because of this, Stacey felt an obligation to her present employer. The property had, first of all, hired her when she needed a job. Her previous boss had been very understanding as concessions were made to accommodate her needs. Her present supervisor was a good teacher, and she had established an excellent relationship with people in many departments. Because of this, Stacey undertook the professional responsibility and obligation to recognize the operation's concerns as her own personal goals were established. She realized that she needed to continuously consider her needs and those of the organization as decisions were made. She thought it reasonable to "take the first step" whenever differences between the property and her own personal needs were concerned. Stacey was confident that responsible and professional people who were working together to achieve a common goal could resolve problems and move forward. She realized that she was a professional decision-maker and problem-solver. If she could resolve the problems of the organization, she certainly could manage her own resources and efforts as she attempted to attain personal and professional goals.

The Educational Institute Board of Trustees

The Educational Institute of the American Hotel & Motel Association is fortunate to have both industry and academic leaders, as well as allied members, on its Board of Trustees. Individually and collectively, the following persons play leading roles in supporting the Institute and determining the direction of its programs.

Stevenson W. Fletcher, III, CHA
Department Head
Hotel, Restaurant & Travel Administration
University of Massachusetts
Amherst, Massachusetts

Creighton Holden, CHA
Chairman
Carriage House Inns, Inc.
Columbia, South Carolina

Douglass Fontaine, CHA
President & General Manager
La Font Inn
Pascagoula, Mississippi

Robert P. Hyde
Executive Vice President
The Western Union Telegraph Co.
Upper Saddle River, New Jersey

Paul R. Handlery, CHA
President
Handlery Hotels, Inc.
San Francisco, California

Arnold F. Karr, CHA
Executive Vice President
Greater Chicago Hotel & Motel Association
Chicago, Illinois

Kai W. Herbranson, CHA
Senior Vice President & Area Manager
North America Division
The Sheraton Centre Hotel
Toronto, Ontario, Canada

J. William Keithan, Jr., CHA
Hospitality Industry Consultant
2226 Eastmount Way, West
Seattle, Washington

Tom F. Herring, Sr., CHA
President
La Posada Motor Hotels
Laredo, Texas

James D. Landon, CHA
Hospitality Industry Consultant
Dallas, Texas

Anthony G. Marshall, CHA, Dean
School of Hospitality Management
Florida International University
Tamiami Campus
Miami, Florida

Harold J. Serpe, CHA
President
Midway Hospitality Corporation
Brookfield, Wisconsin

Porter P. Parris, CHA
Hospitality Industry Consultant
Houston, Texas

Peter E. Van Kleek, CHA
Director—Hospitality
and Development
Johnson & Wales College
Providence, Rhode Island

Anthony M. Rey, CHA
Senior Vice President,
Community Relations
Resorts International, Inc.
Atlantic City, New Jersey

Robert V. Walker, CHA
Chairman of the Board
The Kahler Corporation
Rochester, Minnesota

Kenneth Scripsma
Coordinator, Hotel Management
Program
Orange Coast College
Costa Mesa, California

Ferdinand Wieland, CHA
General Manager
Hotel du Pont
Wilmington, Delaware

Index